D1451870

ROMANITAS

ESSAYS ON ROMAN ARCHAEOLOGY
IN HONOUR OF SHEPPARD FRERE
ON THE OCCASION OF
HIS NINETIETH BIRTHDAY

ROMANITAS

ESSAYS ON ROMAN ARCHAEOLOGY IN HONOUR OF SHEPPARD FRERE ON THE OCCASION OF HIS NINETIETH BIRTHDAY

Edited by

R. J. A. Wilson

Oxbow Books
23rd August 2006

Published by
Oxbow Books, Park End Place, Oxford OX1 1HN

© Oxbow Books and the individual authors, 2006

ISBN-10 1-84217-248-4
ISBN-13 978-184217-248-3

A CIP record for this book is available from the British Library

This book is available direct from

Oxbow Books, Park End Place, Oxford OX1 1HN
(Phone: 01865-241249; Fax: 01865-794449)

and

The David Brown Book Company
PO Box 511, Oakville, CT 06779, USA
(Phone: 860-945-9329; Fax: 860-945-9468)

or from our website

www.oxbowbooks.com

*Cover: Roman mosaic panel from Butchery Lane, Canterbury,
excavated by Sheppard Frere in 1946; c. AD 200,* in situ

*Printed in Great Britain at
The Short Run Press,
Exeter*

CONTENTS

Sheppard Sunderland Frere, CBE, MA (Cantab., Oxon.), D.Litt. (Oxon.), Litt.D. (Cantab.),
D.Litt. (h.c.) *(Leeds), D.Litt.* (h.c.) *(Kent), FBA*

SHEPPARD SUNDERLAND FRERE
AN APPRECIATION

When Sheppard Frere retired from the Chair of the Archaeology of the Roman Empire at Oxford in 1983, he was presented with a Festschrift written by a group of his friends and colleagues, published as *Rome and her northern provinces* (1983). John Wacher, one of its editors, ended his appreciation of the honorand by expressing the wish that he and Janet enjoyed a long and happy retirement. That wish has been amply granted; not only that, but Sheppard has continued to write and publish during his so-called retirement at a prodigious rate. The list of his publications since 1983 in the pages that follow is an eloquent demonstration of that. This has been no *otium* of the traditional kind: no less than twenty books, an astonishing statistic, have flowed from his pen (some in collaboration with others) over the past two dozen years, including two further editions of his magisterial survey, *Britannia: a history of Roman Britain* (the latest, the fourth, in 1999). Truly *mirabile dictu* was his achievement in bringing the whole of *Roman Inscriptions of Britain Volume II* to fruition in eight separate fascicules in six short years, after many years of delay at the hands of others: this was carried out with the help of one of the contributors to this volume, Roger Tomlin, in an extraordinary surge of academic activity in the late 1980s and early 1990s. And few scholars when in their eighties can have published no less than seven papers in as many years in the leading journal in his or her field – in this case *Britannia*, the journal of which, thirty-six years ago, he was the founding editor. There is indeed much to be grateful for. Sheppard Frere has been for many years not only the doyen of Romano-British archaeology, but also the very worthy inheritor of the distinguished mantle handed down from Francis Haverfield, R. G. Collingwood and Ian Richmond. That we know and understand so much about the Roman province of Britain, perhaps archaeologically more than any other province in the Roman world, owes not a little to the contributions of this quartet of great scholars.

But it is not only on the printed page that the influence of Sheppard Frere has been felt. Like many great teachers he has supervised over the years numerous doctoral theses (many of which have subsequently been turned into books); and he has launched many of the students who wrote them into successful archaeological or academic careers of their own, advising them and often helping them in numerous practical ways. The personal reminiscences of the contributors to this volume at the start of each chapter give just a hint of the multifaceted contributions that he has made to the lives of others. Above all he has shown encouragement to countless archaeologists up and down Britain where he felt encouragement was due; at the same time he has never been afraid to speak his mind whenever and

Visiting the Roman bath-house at Bothwellhaugh (North Lanarkshire) under excavation in 1975: (left to right) Roger Goodburn, Marion Wilson, Sheppard Frere and Bernard Scott (a local Councillor)

wherever he encountered shoddy standards or bureaucratic idiocy. His role as a visitor to excavation sites and advisor to excavation directors is legendary; a hitherto unpublished photograph of his visit to Lawrence Keppie's excavation of a Roman military bath-house at Bothwellhaugh south of Glasgow in 1975 is included here as an illustration of this invaluable, selfless aspect of his personality and of his tireless activities.

Sheppard's ninetieth birthday seemed too important a milestone not to acknowledge publicly in some appropriate and lasting way; so a group of his past students and close friends were invited at comparatively short notice to say 'happy birthday' to him in a way that we thought Sheppard himself would like best – a collection of papers on Roman archaeology in his honour. Several more of his students were invited to contribute and would have liked to do so, but felt unable because of other pressing commitments. The resulting volume is a modest token of our affection for Sheppard, of our gratitude for what he has done for us personally, and of our admiration for his massive contribution to Roman archaeology. Above all we wish him and Janet many more healthy and happy years of retirement, confident that his hunger for archaeological news and views will continue unabated in the years that lie ahead.

RJAW

A BIBLIOGRAPHY OF THE PUBLISHED WORKS OF SHEPPARD SUNDERLAND FRERE

compiled by Roger Goodburn and Sally Stow

Editorial note: *a bibliography of published works down to 1982 appeared in the earlier Festschrift presented to Sheppard Frere,* Rome and her northern Provinces *(1983), and we are grateful for the work of John Hopkins, who compiled it, which laid the foundations for the list that appears below. Several items published between 1939 and 1982 which did not appear in the 1983 publication have been added here, together with a listing of the copious publications from 1983 onwards which Sheppard has published in his highly productive 'retirement'.*

1939
'Three flint implements from Shrimpling', *Norfolk Archaeology* 27, 29–30

1940
'A survey of archaeology near Lancing', *Sussex Archaeological Collections* 81, 140–72
'A food vessel from Needham, Norfolk', *Antiquaries Journal* 20, 272–4

1941
'Roman pottery from Lancing in the Bristol Museum', *Sussex Notes and Queries* 8, 190–1
'A Claudian site at Needham, Norfolk', *Antiquaries Journal* 21, 40–55
'A medieval pottery at Ashtead', *Surrey Archaeological Collections* 47, 58–66
'An Early Bronze Age burial at Epsom College', *Surrey Archaeological Collections* 47, 92–5
'A Late Bronze Age hoard from Banstead', *Surrey Archaeological Collections* 47, 95

1942
'An Iron Age site near Epsom', *Antiquaries Journal* 22, 123–8

1943
'Axe-hammer from Loddon, Norfolk', *Antiquaries Journal* 23, 154–5
'A Roman coin from Ewell', *Surrey Archaeological Collections* 48, 154
'A Roman ditch at Ewell County School', *Surrey Archaeological Collections* 48, 45–60
'A Romano-British site at Woodmansterne', *Surrey Archaeological Collections* 48, 152–4
'Beaker sherd from Chanctonbury', *Sussex Notes and Queries* 9, 156

1944
'An Iron Age site at West Clandon, Surrey, and some aspects of the Iron Age and Romano-British culture in the Wealden area', *Archaeological Journal*, 101, 50–67

1945

'Romano-British finds at Littleton', *Transactions of the London and Middlesex Archaeological Society*, n.s. 9, 203–4

(with R. R. Clarke) 'The Romano-British village at Needham, Norfolk', *Norfolk Archaeology* 28, 187–216

'The date of the 'Caesar's Camp' pottery', in A. W. G. Lowther, "Caesar's Camp', Wimbledon, Surrey: the excavations of 1937', *Archaeological Journal* 102, 19–20

1946

'Polished axes from Guildford and Leith Hill, and South Norwood', *Surrey Archaeological Collections* 49, 90–2

'Polished axe from Bury Hill, Dorking', *Surrey Archaeological Collections* 49, 92–3

(with W. Hooper) 'Late Bronze Age celt from Betchworth', *Surrey Archaeological Collections* 49, 102

'Bronze objects from Farnham', *Surrey Archaeological Collections* 49, 103

(with A. H. A. Hogg) 'An Iron Age and Roman site on Mickleham Downs', *Surrey Archaeological Collections* 49, 104–6

'A brooch from the Roman villa, Walton Heath', *Surrey Archaeological Collections* 49, 108

'Roman pottery from Betchworth', *Surrey Archaeological Collections* 49, 110–11

'Two Roman coins from Ewell', *Surrey Archaeological Collections* 49, 111

'A Roman coin from Shamley Green, Wonersh', *Surrey Archaeological Collections* 49, 112

'Romano-British pottery from Sanderstead', *Surrey Archaeological Collections* 49, 112–13

'A Saxon burial on Farthing Down, Coulsdon', *Surrey Archaeological Collections* 49, 114

1947

Roman Canterbury: the city of Durovernum [Roman Canterbury 1], Maidstone, pp. 24

(with J. P. T. Burchell) 'The occupation of Sandown Park, Esher, during the Stone Age, the Early Iron Age and the Anglo-Saxon period', *Antiquaries Journal* 27, 24–46

(with E. C. Curwen) 'A Romano-British occupation site at Portfield gravel pit, Chichester', *Sussex Archaeological Collections* 86, 137–40

1948

(with A. Williams) 'Canterbury excavations, Christmas, 1945 and Easter, 1946', *Archaeologia Cantiana* 61, 1–45

1949

(with A. Williams) *An account of the excavations in Butchery Lane* [Roman Canterbury 4], Maidstone, pp. 47

'The excavation of a Late Roman bath-house at Chatley Farm, Cobham', *Surrey Archaeological Collections* 50, 73–98

'Canterbury excavations 1944–8 ', *Antiquity* 23, 153–60

'Canterbury excavations: preliminary reports April, 1948 to April, 1949', *Archaeological News Letter* 2, 79–80

1950

'The Iron Age pottery from Harting Down huts 1 and 2', in P. A. M. Keefe, 'Harting Hill hut shelters', *Sussex Archaeological Collections* 89, 187–91

1952
'Roman pottery from Oxshott', *Surrey Archaeological Collections* 52, 82–3
'Deciphering the palimpsest of Canterbury', *Illustrated London News*, 27th December

1953
'Canterbury excavations, Easter, 1953', *Archaeologia Cantiana* 66, 163–4
Review of A. Fox, *Roman Exeter (Isca Dumnoniorum): excavations in the war-damaged areas, 1945–7* (1952), in *Antiquaries Journal* 33, 232–3

1954
'Canterbury excavations, summer, 1946: the Rose Lane sites', *Archaeologia Cantiana* 68, 101–43
'Canterbury excavations', *Spinks' Numismatic Circular* 62, 290 and 490

1955
An account of the excavations at the Rose Lane sites, Summer 1946 [Roman Canterbury 7], Maidstone, pp. 43
'Verulamium. The excavations at Bluehouse Hill, 1955', *Archaeological News Letter* 6, 8–10
'Subterranean chamber at Waddon', *Antiquaries Journal* 35, 90
Review of I. A. Richmond, *Roman Britain* (1955), in *Archaeological Journal* 112, 137–8
Review of F. T. Baker, *Roman Lincoln 1945–54: ten seasons' excavations in Lincoln* (1955), in *Antiquaries Journal* 35, 252

1956
'Excavations at Verulamium, 1955: first interim report', *Antiquaries Journal* 36, 1–10
'Verulamium', in 'Roman Britain in 1955, I: sites explored', *Journal of Roman Studies* 46, 134–6
'Canterbury', in 'Roman Britain in 1955, I: sites explored', *Journal of Roman Studies* 46, 144–6
'Canterbury excavation', *Spinks' Numismatic Circular* 64, 16
Review of R. E. M. Wheeler, *A short guide to Roman York* (1956), and G. Webster, *The Roman army* (1956), in *Archaeological Journal* 113, 165

1957
Roman Canterbury: the city of Durovernum, 2nd revised edition, Canterbury (n.d.; 1957?), pp. 27
'Excavations at Verulamium 1956: second interim report', *Antiquaries Journal* 37, 1–15
'Bignor Roman villa, 1956', *Sussex Notes and Queries* 14, 228–9
'Late Roman objects from Chalton, Hants.', *Antiquaries Journal* 37, 218–20
'Canterbury excavations', *Spinks' Numismatic Circular* 65, 299

1958
'Excavations at Verulamium 1957: third interim report', *Antiquaries Journal* 38, 1–14
(with O. Brogan) 'The Camp du Charlat, Corrèze', *Antiquaries Journal* 38, 218–22
'Lifting mosaics', *Antiquity* 32, 116–19
Review of G. C. Boon, *Roman Silchester: the archaeology of a Romano-British town* (1957), in *Antiquaries Journal* 38, 113

1959
'Excavations at Verulamium 1958: fourth interim report', *Antiquaries Journal* 39, 1–18

'Verulamium', in 'Roman Britain in 1958, I: sites explored', *Journal of Roman Studies* 49,
      120–3
'The Iron Age in southern Britain', *Antiquity* 33, 183–8
'Roman Canterbury', *South East Naturalist and Antiquary* 54, 17–21
Review of H. H. Scullard, *From the Gracchi to Nero: a history of Rome from 133 B.C. to A.D. 68*
      (1959), in *Antiquaries Journal* 39, 301
Review of M. A. Cotton and P. W. Gathercole, *Excavations at Clausentum, Southampton, 1951–
      1954* (1958), in *Antiquaries Journal* 39, 114 and *Journal of the British Archaeological Association*
      22, 79
Review of W. J. Wedlake, *Excavations at Camerton, Somerset: an account of thirty years'
      excavations covering the period from Neolithic to Saxon times, 1926–56* (1958), in *Antiquaries
      Journal* 39, 303
Review of A. L. F. Rivet, *Town and country in Roman Britain* (1958), in *Surrey Archaeological
      Collections* 56, 163, *Antiquity* 33, 67–8 and *Past & Present* 16, 1–9

1960
'Excavations at Verulamium 1959: fifth interim report', *Antiquaries Journal* 40, 1–24
'Verulamium excavations 1959', *Watford and south-west Hertfordshire Archaeological Society
      Bulletin* 15, 3–4 and 7
(with I. Smith) 'Excavations at High Rocks, Tunbridge Wells, 1954–1956. Appendix B. The
      pottery', *Sussex Archaeological Collections* 98, 207–11
Review of A. A. M. van der Heyden, and H. H. Scullard (eds), *Atlas of the Classical World*
      (1959), in *Antiquaries Journal* 40, 80
Review of R. Goodchild, *Cyrene and Apollonia, a historical guide* (1959), in *Antiquaries Journal*
      40, 82
Review of G. J. Copley, *An archaeology of South East England: a study in continuity* (1958), in
      Surrey Archaeological Collections 57, 104–05

1961
(Editor) *Problems of the Iron Age in southern Britain. Papers given at a C.B.A. conference held at
      the Institute of Archaeology, December 12 to 14, 1958* (Occasional Paper No. 11), London,
      pp. xii + 308
'Some problems of the Later Iron Age' in ibid., 84–92
'Excavations at Verulamium, 1960: sixth interim report', *Antiquaries Journal* 41, 72–85
'Some Romano-British sculptures from Ancaster and Wilsford, Lincolnshire', *Antiquaries
      Journal* 41, 229–31
'Civitas – a myth?', *Antiquity* 35, 29–36
'Late Bronze Age pot from Farnham', *Surrey Archaeological Collections* 58, 112
(with M. A. Cotton) 'Enceintes de l'âge du fer au pays des Lémovices', *Gallia* 19, 31–54
Review of Lincoln Archives Committee (ed.), *Lincolnshire Architectural and Archaeological
      Society. Reports and Papers, Volume 8, for 1959 and 1960*, in *Antiquaries Journal* 41, 104–05
Review of B. R. Hartley, *Notes on the Roman pottery industry in the Nene Valley* (1960), in
      Antiquaries Journal 41, 105

1962
Roman Canterbury: the city of Durovernum, 3rd edition, Canterbury, pp. 29
'Excavations at Verulamium, 1961. Seventh and final interim report', *Antiquaries Journal* 42,
      148–59
Review of Royal Commission on Ancient and Historical Monuments in Wales and

Monmouthshire, *An inventory of the ancient monuments in Caernarvonshire, Vol. II (Central)* (1960), in *Antiquaries Journal* 42, 104–5

Review of P. Corder (ed.), *The Roman town and villa at Great Casterton, Rutland: third report for the years 1954–1958* (1961), in *Antiquaries Journal* 42, 261–2

Review of E. M. Clifford, *Bagendon, a Belgic oppidum: excavations 1954–56* (1961), in *Journal of Roman Studies* 52, 272–3

Review of E. Birley, *Research on Hadrian's Wall* (1961), in *Journal of Roman Studies* 52, 274

Review of Royal Commission on Historical Monuments (ed.), *The city of York: I. Eboracum, Roman York* (1962), in *Archaeological Journal* 118, 256–7

1963

'Excavations at Dorchester-on-Thames, 1962', *Archaeological Journal* 119, 114–49

'A Romano-British relief from Keisby, Lincs.', *Antiquaries Journal* 43, 292

Review of D. Baatz, *Lopodunum – Ladenburg a. N. Die Grabungen im Frühjahr 1960* (1962), in *Germania* 41, 153–5

Review of D. R. Dudley and G. Webster, *The rebellion of Boudicca* (1962), in *Antiquaries Journal* 43, 311–12

Review of E. M. Clifford, *Bagendon, a Belgic oppidum: excavations 1954–6* (1961), in *Numismatic Chronicle* ser. 3, 7, 253–4

Review of D. F. Allen, *Sylloge of coins of the British Isles: the coins of the Coritani* (1963), in *Numismatic Circular* 71, 77 and *Journal of Roman Studies* 53, 213–4

Review of *Ordnance Survey map of southern Britain in the Iron Age* (1962), in *Journal of Roman Studies* 53, 239–40

Review of D. A. White, *Litus Saxonicum: the British Saxon Shore in scholarship and history* (1961), in *Medieval Archaeology* 6–7, 350–2

Review of D. R. Dudley and G. Webster, *The rebellion of Boudicca* (1962), in *Past & Present* 24, 102–3

1964

(with K. K. Kenyon) *The Roman Theatre of Verulamium (and adjacent buildings): official guide*, Derby, n.d. [1964?], pp. 16

'Verulamium, three Roman cities', *Antiquity* 38, 103–12

'Ivinghoe', *Records of Buckinghamshire* 17, 315

'Verulamium – then and now', *Bulletin of the Institute of Archaeology, University of London* 4, 61–82

Review of P.-M. Duval, *Paris antique, des origines au troisème siècle* (1961), in *Journal of Roman Studies* 54, 230–1

Review of A. Grenier, *Manuel d'archéologie gallo-romaine. III. L'architecture: (i) L'urbanisme, les monuments, (ii) Ludi et circenses* (1958), in *Journal of Roman Studies* 54, 259–60

Review of *Victoria History of the County of Essex. III. Roman Essex* (1963), in *Antiquaries Journal* 44, 256–7

1965

'Ian Archibald Richmond, 1902–65', *Journal of Roman Studies* 55, xiii–xiv

Comment on M. G. Jarrett, 'Town defences of Roman Britain', in *Antiquity* 39, 137–8

Review of W. Bonsor, *A Romano-British bibliography 55 B.C. – A.D. 44* (1964), in *Archaeological Journal*, 122, 246

Review of W. Gardner and H. N. Savory, *Dinorben: a hill-fort occupied in Early Iron Age and Roman times* (1964), in *Journal of Roman Studies* 55, 296

Review of E. B. Thomas, *Römische Villen in Pannonien* (1964), in *Antiquity* 39, 315–16

1966
'The end of towns in Roman Britain', in J. S. Wacher (ed.), *The Civitas Capitals of Roman Britain* (1966), 87–100

(with B. R. Hartley) 'Fouilles de Lezoux (Puy-de-Dôme) en 1963', *Cahiers de civilisation médiévale* 9, 557–63

Review of G. Webster and D. R. Dudley, *The Roman conquest of Britain* (1965), in *Antiquaries Journal* 46, 348–9

Review of R. G. Collingwood and R. P. Wright, *The Roman inscriptions of Britain. I: inscriptions on stone* (1965), in *Archaeological Journal* 123, 230–1

Review of M. J. T. Lewis, *Temples in Roman Britain* (1966), in *Antiquaries Journal* 46, 352

Review of A. S. Robertson, *The Roman fort at Castledykes* (1964), in *Journal of Roman Studies* 56, 269–70

Review of B. W. Cunliffe, *Winchester excavations 1949–1960. I* (1964), in *Antiquaries Journal* 46, 354

Review of R. Merrifield, *The Roman city of London* (1965), in *Antiquity* 40, 158–9

Review of P. Salway, *The frontier people of Roman Britain* (1965), in *Geographical Journal* 132.4 (December 1966), 521–2

1967
Britannia: a history of Roman Britain, London, pp. xvi + 432

1968
'Richmond, Wheeler and Hod Hill', *Antiquity* 42, 292–3

(with M. A. Cotton) 'Excavations in the Iron Age hill-fort at High Rocks, near Tunbridge Wells, 1957–1961. Appendix B: the pottery', *Sussex Archaeological Collections* 106, 187–93

(with M. A. Cotton) 'Ivinghoe Beacon excavations, 1963–5', *Records of Buckinghamshire* 18, 187–203

1969
Review of I. A. Richmond, *Hod Hill. II: excavations carried out between 1951 and 1958 for the Trustees of the British Museum* (1968), in *Antiquaries Journal* 49, 154–5

Review of R. M. Ogilvie and I. A. Richmond (eds), *Cornelii Taciti: De Vita Agricolae* (1967), in *Antiquaries Journal* 49, 155

Review of A. L. F. Rivet, *The Iron Age in northern Britain* (1966), in *Antiquaries Journal* 49, 153

1970
'The Roman theatre at Canterbury', *Britannia* 1, 83–113

'Mould for bronze statuette from Gestingthorpe', *Britannia* 1, 266–7

'A Romano-British votive relief from Witham', *Britannia* 1, 267

Contributions to the *Oxford Classical Dictionary*, second edition, 28, 89, 144, 202, 209–10, 217, 258, 291, 292, 367, 468, 535, 539, 610–11, 782, 874, 909, 911, 925, 1078, 1094, 1113, 1114–15, 1128, 1134, 1135

Review of V. E. Nash-Williams, *The Roman frontier in Wales*, 2nd edition revised by M. G. Jarrett (1969), in *Antiquaries Journal* 50, 381–2

Review of A. L. F. Rivet (ed.), *The Roman villa in Britain* (1969), in *Antiquity* 44, 149–50

Review of The Ordnance Survey, *The Antonine Wall: 2½ inch map* (1969), in *Antiquity* 44, 82–3

Review of P. Salway (ed.), *Roman archaeology and art: essays and studies by Sir Ian Richmond* (1969), in *Britannia* 1, 323–4

Review of J. Liversidge, *Britain in the Roman Empire* (1968), in *English Historical Review* 85, no. 335, 346–8

1971

'The urbanization of Roman Britain', in *Britannia Romana* [Accademia Nazionale dei Lincei, Quaderno 150], 3–26

'The forum and baths at Caistor by Norwich', *Britannia* 2, 1–26

1972

Verulamium excavations: Volume I [Society of Antiquaries of London Research Report 28], London, pp. xvi + 384

'The Caistor intaglio', *Britannia* 3, 295–6

Review of B. W. Cunliffe, *Excavations at Fishbourne 1961–1969. Vol. I: The site; Vol. II: The finds* (1971), in *Antiquity* 46, 76–8

1973

'Longthorpe Roman fortress', *Durobrivae* 2, 20–1

Review of W. Schleiermacher, *Cambodunum-Kempten: eine Römerstadt im Allgäu* (1972), in *Britannia* 4, 354–5

Review of D. Hill and M. Jesson (eds), *The Iron Age and its hill-forts: papers presented to Sir Mortimer Wheeler on the occasion of his eightieth year* (1971), in *Britannia* 4, 341–2

1974

Britannia: a history of Roman Britain, 2nd revised edition, London, pp. 487

'The Roman fortress at Longthorpe, England', *Actes du IXᵉ Congrès International d'Études sur les Frontières Romaines*, Mamaia, 351–4

(with J. K. St Joseph) 'The Roman fortress at Longthorpe', *Britannia* 5, 1–129

'Ancient Britain', *Encyclopaedia Britannica* (15th edition), 193–8

Editor of the translation of A. Mócsy, *Pannonia and Upper Moesia*, London, pp. xxii + 453

Review of G. Gamer and A. Rüsch [from a manuscript of the late Friedrich Wagner], *Corpus Signorum Imperii Romani. Deutschland, I, 1: Raetia (Bayern südlich des Limes) und Noricum (Chiemseegebiet)* (1973), in *Britannia* 5, 493–4

Review of D. Baatz, *Kastell Hesselbach und andere Forschungen am Odenwaldlimes* [Limes-forschungen 12] (1973), in *Britannia* 5, 494–6

1975

Principles of publication in rescue archaeology: report by a working party of the Ancient Monuments Board for England, Committee for Rescue Archaeology, Department of the Environment, London, pp. 16

'The origin of small towns', in W. Rodwell and T. Rowley (eds), *The small towns of Roman Britain: papers presented to a conference, Oxford, 1975* [BAR British Series 15], Oxford, 4–7

'The Silchester church. The excavation by Sir Ian Richmond in 1961', *Archaeologia* 105, 277–302

'Verulamium and the towns of Britannia', in H. Temporini and W. Haase (eds), *Aufstieg und Niedergang der römischen Welt*, II, 3, 290–327

'The cities of Roman Britain 1960–74', in E. Frézouls and W. Muller-Wiener (eds), *Le programme d'études urbaines du groupe de recherche d'histoire romaine à Strasbourg* [Lettre d'information III], Strasbourg, 7–55

Preface, in P. Crummy, *Not only a matter of time: a survey outlining the archaeology of the Colchester district and methods of counteracting the erosion of its archaeology*, Colchester

Review of M. Todd, *The Coritani* (1973) and B. Cunliffe, *The Regni* (1973), in *Antiquaries Journal* 55, 145–6

Review of G. Webster, *The Cornovii* (1975) in *Times Literary Supplement*, 31st January 1975, 101

Review of R. Dunnett, *The Trinovantes* (1975), in *Times Literary Supplement*, 12th September 1975, 1017

1976

Review of G. M. Leather, *Roman Lancaster: some excavation reports and some observations* (privately produced, no date), in *Britannia* 7, 402–3

Review of B. W. Cunliffe, *Excavations at Portchester Castle. Volume I: Roman* (1975), in *Antiquity* 51, 163–4

Review of M. Giacchero, *Edictum Diocletiani et collegarum de pretiis rerum venalium* (1974), in *English Historical Review* 91, no. 360, 619–20

1977

'The fort at Strageath and the Roman occupation of Scotland', in *Studien zu den Militärgrenzen Roms*, II, Cologne, 7–12

'Roman Britain in 1976. I. Sites explored, *Britannia* 8, 355–425

'Verulamium and Canterbury: continuity and discontinuity', in *Thèmes de recherches sur les villes antiques d'Occident*, Paris, 185–94

Review of J. Percival, *The Roman villa: an historical introduction* (1976), in *Times Literary Supplement*, 8th April 1977, 440

1979

'Town planning in the western provinces', in *Festschrift zum 75 jährigen Bestehen der Römisch-Germanischen Kommission, Beiheft zum Bericht der Römisch-Germanischen Kommission* 58, Mainz, 87–103

'Verulamium: urban development and the local region', in B. C. Burnham and H. B. Johnson (eds), *Invasion and response: the case of Roman Britain* [BAR British Series 73], Oxford, 273–80

'The Roman fort at Strageath', in D. J. Breeze (ed.), *Roman Scotland: some recent excavations*, Edinburgh, 37–41

'Priorities for rescue archaeology', *Kent Archaeological Review* 56 (Summer 1979), 122

Review of Royal Commission on Ancient and Historical Monuments of Scotland, *Lanarkshire: prehistoric and Roman monuments* (1978), in *Britannia* 10, 395–6

1980

'Hyginus and the First Cohort', *Britannia* 11, 51–60

'Wheres and whyfores': review of A. L. F. Rivet and C. Smith, *The place-names of Roman Britain* (1979), in *Times Literary Supplement*, 11th January 1980, 42

Review of A. L. F. Rivet and C. Smith, *The place-names of Roman Britain* (1979), in *Britannia* 11, 419–23

Review of The Ordnance Survey, *Map of Roman Britain* (1978), in *Britannia* 11, 442–3

1981

'The Flavian frontier in Scotland', in J. Kenworthy (ed.), *Agricola's campaigns in Scotland*

[Scottish Archaeological Forum 12], Edinburgh, 89–97

'Verulamium in the third century', in A. King and M. Henig (eds), *The Roman West in the third century: contributions from archaeology and history* [BAR International Series S109 (ii)], Oxford, 383–92

Foreword, in B. Philp, *The excavation of the Roman forts of the Classis Britannica at Dover, 1970–77,* Dover, x

Review of M. Todd, *Roman Britain, 55 B.C. – A.D. 400* (1981) and A. Birley, *The Fasti of Roman Britain* (1981), in *The Times Literary Supplement,* 6th November 1981, 1304

1982

(with P. Bennett and S. Stow) *The archaeology of Canterbury, Volume I: Excavations at Canterbury Castle* [Kent Archaeological Society, for the Canterbury Archaeological Trust], Maidstone, pp. 236

(with P. Bennett and S. Stow) *The archaeology of Canterbury, Volume II: Excavations on the Roman and medieval defences of Canterbury* [Kent Archaeological Society, for the Canterbury Archaeological Trust], Maidstone, pp. 180

'The Bignor villa', *Britannia* 13, 135–95

Foreword, in J. S. Wacher and A. D. McWhirr, *Cirencester, Excavations, Volume I: The early military occupation,* Cirencester, 15–16

Review of E. B. MacDougall and W. F. Jashemski, *Ancient Roman gardens* (1981), in *Garden History* 10, no. 2 (Autumn 1982), 168–9

1983

Verulamium excavations, Volume II [Society of Antiquaries of London Research Report 41], London, pp. xvi + 346

(with J. K. S. St Joseph) *Roman Britain from the air,* Cambridge, pp. xviii + 232

(with S. Stow) *The archaeology of Canterbury, Volume VII: Excavations in the St. George's Street and Burgate Street areas* [Kent Archaeological Society for the Canterbury Archaeological Trust], Maidstone, pp. 368

'Roman Britain in 1982. I. Sites explored', *Britannia* 14, 279–335

1984

Verulamium excavations, Volume III [Oxford University Committee for Archaeology, Monograph 1], Oxford, pp. viii + 298

'The early development of the cities of Roman Britain', *Revue Archéologique de Picardie* 3–4, 11–17

'The cities of Britain in the crises of the third century', *Revue Archéologique de Picardie* 3–4, 239–44

'British urban defences in earthwork', *Britannia* 15, 63–74

'Canterbury: the post-war excavations', *Archaeologia Cantiana* 100, 29–46

'Roman Britain in 1983. I. Sites explored', *Britannia* 15, 265–332

'Excavations at Dorchester on Thames, 1963', *Archaeological Journal* 141, 91–174

Review of J. Maloney and B. Hobley (eds), *Roman urban defences in the West* (1983), in *Antiquaries Journal* 64, 464–5

Review of P. Leach, *Ilchester I: excavations 1974–5* (1982), in *Britannia* 15, 373

1985

'Civic pride: a factor in Roman town planning', in F. Grew and B. Hobley (eds), *Roman urban topography in Britain and the western Empire. Proceedings of the third conference on urban* archaeology organized jointly by the Council for British Archaeology and the Department of Urban Archaeology of the Museum of London [CBA Research Report 59], London, 34–6

'Roman Britain in 1984. I. Sites explored', *Britannia* 16, 251–316

'Drumlanrig fort', *The Scotsman*, 22nd July

1986

'*RIB* 1322', *Britannia* 17, 329

'Roman Britain in 1985. I. Sites explored', *Britannia* 17, 363–427

'The use of Iron Age hillforts by the Roman army in Britain', in C. Unz (ed.), *Studien zu den Militärgrenzen Roms III: 13. internationaler Limeskongress, Aalen 1983*, Stuttgart, 42–6

Foreword, in M. Millett and D. Graham, *Excavations on the Romano-British small town at Neatham, Hampshire, 1969–1979*, Winchester, xv–xvi

Review of S. Johnson, *Late Roman fortifications* (1983), in *English Historical Review* 101, no. 398, 208–9

1987

Britannia: a history of Roman Britain, 3rd revised edition, London, pp. xvi + 423

(with A. L. F. Rivet and N. H. H. Sitwell) *Tabula Imperii Romani: Britannia Septentrionalis*, London, pp. xvi + 94

(with P. Bennett, J. Rady and S. Stow) *The archaeology of Canterbury, Volume VIII: Canterbury excavations: intra- and extra-mural sites, 1949–55 and 1980–84* [Kent Archaeological Society for the Canterbury Archaeological Trust], Maidstone, pp. 363

'Brandon Camp, Herefordshire', *Britannia* 18, 49–92

'Roman Britain in 1986. I. Sites explored', *Britannia* 18, 301–59

Review of J. Hinchcliffe and C. Sparey Green, *Excavations at Brancaster 1974 and 1977* (1985), in *Britannia* 18, 394

Review of R. Miket and C. Burgess, *Between and beyond the Walls: essays on the prehistory and history of North Britain* (1984), in *English Historical Review* 102, no. 405, 1002

Review of G. W. Meates, *The Roman villa at Lullingstone, Kent. The wall paintings and finds* (1987), in *Archaeologia Cantiana* 104, 410–12

1988

(with F. Lepper) *Trajan's Column: a new edition of the Cichorius plates. Introduction, commentary and notes*, Gloucester, pp. xviii + 339

'Verulamium: social and artistic development', in B. Ford (ed.), *The Cambridge Guide to the Arts in Britain, 1: Prehistoric, Roman and early medieval* [republished 1992 as *The Cambridge Cultural History of Britain. Volume 1. Early Britain*], Cambridge, 67–73

'Roman Britain since Haverfield and Richmond' [a lecture delivered in All Souls College on 23rd October 1987], *History and Archaeology Review* 3, 31–6

'Roman Britain in 1987. I. Sites explored', *Britannia* 19, 415–84

Review of D. N. Riley, *Air photography and archaeology* (1987), in *Britannia* 19, 530–1

1989

(with J. J. Wilkes) *Strageath: excavations within the Roman fort 1973–86* [*Britannia* Monograph 9], London, pp. xviii + 276

'The three forts at Strageath and their garrisons', *Acta archaeologica Academiae Scientiarum Hungaricae* 41, 283–98

'Roman Britain in 1988. I. Sites explored', *Britannia* 20, 257–326

1990
Edited (with M. Roxan and R. S. O. Tomlin) *The Roman inscriptions of Britain, Volume II. Instrumentum domesticum. Fascicule 1: the military diplomata; metal ingots; tesserae; dies; labels; and lead sealings (RIB 2401–2411)*, Gloucester, pp. xiv + 126
'Roman Britain in 1989. I. Sites explored', *Britannia* 21, 303–64

1991
Edited (with R. S. O. Tomlin) *The Roman inscriptions of Britain, Volume II. Instrumentum domesticum. Fascicule 2: weights, gold vessel, silver vessels, bronze vessels, lead vessels, pewter vessels, shale vessels, glass vessels, spoons (RIB 2412–2420)*, Stroud, pp. xiv + 146
Edited (with R. S. O. Tomlin) *The Roman inscriptions of Britain, Volume II. Instrumentum domesticum. Fascicule 3: brooches, rings, gems, bracelets, helmets, shields, weapons, iron tools, baldric fittings, votives in gold, silver, and bronze, lead pipes, roundels, sheets and other lead objects, stone roundels, pottery and bone roundels, other objects of bone (RIB 2421–2441)*, Stroud, pp. xiv + 176
'Roman Britain in 1990. I. Sites explored', *Britannia* 22, 221–92
Review of D. Perring, *Roman London* (1991), in *Antiquaries Journal* 71, 288
Review of G. S. Maxwell, *A battle lost: Romans and Caledonians at Mons Graupius* (1990), in *Britannia* 22, 340
Review of G. S. Maxwell, *The Romans in Scotland* (1989), in *Britannia* 22, 340–1

1992
Edited (with R. S. O. Tomlin) *The Roman inscriptions of Britain, Volume II. Instrumentum domesticum. Fascicule 4: wooden barrels, stilus-tablets, miscellaneous objects of wood, leather objects, oculists' stamps, wallplaster, mosaics, handmills, stone tablets, stone balls, stone pebbles, small stone votives, miscellaneous objects of stone, jet figurine, clay figurines, miscellaneous clay objects, antefixes, tile-stamps of Legion II Augusta, of Legion VI Victrix, of Legion IX Hispana, of Legion XX Valeria Victrix, tile-stamps of the auxiliaries (RIB 2442–2480)*, Stroud, pp. xiv + 207
'Roman Britain in 1991. I. Sites explored', *Britannia* 23, 255–308
Foreword, in N. H. Field, *Dorset and the Second Legion. New light on a Roman campaign*, Tiverton, 1–2
Review of B. Jones and D. Mattingly, *An atlas of Roman Britain* (1990), in *Britannia* 23, 366–7
Review of G. de la Bédoyère, *The buildings of Roman Britain* (1991), in *Times Literary Supplement*, 10th January 1992, 18

1993
Edited (with R. S. O. Tomlin) *The Roman inscriptions of Britain, Volume II. Instrumentum domesticum. Fascicule 5: tile-stamps of the Classis Britannica; imperial, procuratorial and civic tile-stamps; stamps of private tilers; inscriptions on relief-patterned tiles and graffiti on tiles (RIB 2481–2491)*, Stroud, pp. xiv + 162

1994
Edited (with R. S. O. Tomlin) *The Roman inscriptions of Britain, Volume II. Instrumentum domesticum. Fascicule 6: dipinti and graffiti on amphorae, dipinti and graffiti on mortaria, inscriptions in white barbotine, dipinti on coarse pottery, samian barbotine or moulded inscriptions (RIB 2492–2500)*, Stroud, pp. xiv + 102
Review of S. J. Greep (ed.), *Roman towns: the Wheeler inheritance: a review of 50 years' research* (1993), in *Archaeological Journal* 151, 455–6

1995

Edited (with R. S. O. Tomlin) *The Roman inscriptions of Britain, Volume II. Instrumentum domesticum. Fascicule 7: graffiti on samian ware* (terra sigillata*) (RIB 2501)*, Stroud, pp. xii + 152

Edited (with R. S. O. Tomlin) *The Roman inscriptions of Britain, Volume II. Instrumentum domesticum. Fascicule 8: graffiti on coarse pottery cut before and after firing; stamp on coarse pottery. Addenda and corrigenda to Fascicules 1–8* (RIB 2502–2505), Stroud, pp. xiv + 165

The Roman inscriptions of Britain, Volume II. Instrumentum domesticum. Combined epigraphic indexes and concordance with major printed sources, Stroud, pp. x + 93

(with K. Blockley, M. Blockley, P. Blockley and S. Stow) *The archaeology of Canterbury, Volume V: Excavations in the Marlowe Car Park and surrounding areas*, 2 volumes, Canterbury, pp. 1343

'Kenneth St Joseph (1912–1994): Vice-President 1975–1994', *Britannia* 26, ix–xi

1998

'B. R. H[artley].', in J. Bird (ed.), *Form and fabric: studies in Rome's material past in honour of B. R. Hartley* [Oxbow Monograph 80], Oxford, xvii

1999

Britannia: a history of Roman Britain, 4th revised edition, London, pp. xxiv + 431

2000

'A *limitatio* of Icenian territory?', *Britannia* 31, 350–5

'M. Maenius Agrippa, the *expeditio Britannica* and Maryport', *Britannia* 31, 23–8

2001

'The Ravenna Cosmography and north Britain between the Walls', *Britannia* 32, 286–92

(with M. Fulford) 'The Roman invasion of A.D. 43', *Britannia* 32, 45–55

2002

(with M. Fulford) 'The *collegium peregrinorum* at Silchester', *Britannia* 33, 167–75

2003

'Roman archaeology at the Institute: the early years', in *Archaeology International, Institute of Archaeology UCL*, Issue 6 (2002/3), 10–13

2004

'The Roman fort at Colwyn Castle, Powys (Radnorshire)', *Britannia* 35, 115–20

2005

'The south gate and defences of *Venta Icenorum*: Professor Atkinson's excavations, 1930 and 1934', *Britannia* 36, 311–27

'Kay Hartley: an appreciation', *Journal of Roman Pottery Studies* 12, 11–12

NOTES ON THE CONTRIBUTORS

Geoffrey B. Dannell was educated at Christ's College, Finchley, and the London School of Economics, where he took a Bachelor of Science degree in Economics in 1959. He has been a Fellow of Institute of Chartered Accountants in England and Wales since 1963, and a Fellow of the Society of Antiquaries of London since 1974. He started digging as schoolboy in the Verulamium car park in 1954, and two years later joined Sheppard Frere on his classic Verulamium excavation campaigns, where he acted as a site supervisor; later he served in the same capacity for John Wacher at Catterick. Between 1963 and 1975 he directed an important series of excavations on pottery sites in the Nene Valley with Brian Hartley and John Peter Wild. He has a formidable international reputation as a specialist in samian ware, an interest which was first encouraged by Norman Cook and Brian Hartley, and is currently President of *Pegasus*, the European research network focusing on the key samian production site of La Graufesenque near Millau; he is also Treasurer of the Nene Valley Archaeological Trust, and a Trustee of the Rei Cretariae Romanae Fautores. His publications include *Longthorpe II: the military works-depot. An episode in landscape history* [*Britannia* Monograph 8, with J. P. Wild] (1987), and numerous specialised contributions on samian ware to both site reports and academic journals.

Professor Michael Fulford read Archaeology and Latin at Southampton University, where he also completed his doctorate. After serving as Professor Barry Cunliffe's Research Assistant (1971–4), he was appointed to a Lectureship at the University of Reading, where he was later promoted to a Readership and (in 1988) to a personal Professorship; in 1993 he was appointed to the first established Chair in Archaeology at the University. He has also served as Dean of the Faculty of Letters and Social Sciences at Reading and, between 1998 and 2004, as Pro-Vice-Chancellor. A Fellow of the Society of Antiquaries of London and of the British Academy, he has also edited the journal *Britannia* (1994–99), holds a Leverhulme Major Research Fellowship (2003–7) and is currently President of the Society for the Promotion of Roman Studies. He has written extensively on many aspects of Roman, and especially Romano-British, archaeology, with a special emphasis on urbanism, landscape archaeology, and the economy, but he is perhaps best known for his excavations at Silchester, on-going for over thirty years, which have been published in a series of distinguished volumes: *Silchester: excavations on the defences* (1984); *Silchester amphitheatre: the excavations of 1979–85* (1989); *Late Iron Age and Roman Silchester: excavations on the Forum-Basilica* (2000); and *Life and labour in late Roman Silchester: excavations in Insula IX since 1997* (2006). His many other books include *New Forest Roman pottery: manufacture and distribution* (1975), and collaborative volumes on the pottery from *Excavations at Carthage: the British mission* (1984 and 1994); on *Excavations at Sabratha 1948–1951: the finds* (1989 and 1994); on *Developing landscapes of Lowland Britain: the archaeology of the British gravels* (1992); on *England's coastal heritage* (1997); and on *Iron Age and Romano-British settlements and landscapes of Salisbury Plain* (2006).

Roger Goodburn studied chemistry in the University of Sheffield before moving to the Institute of Archaeology in London to take the Diploma in Archaeology under Sheppard Frere and Roy Hodson. In 1969 he transferred to the University of Oxford, and there served as Sheppard Frere's Research Assistant for ten years, where they worked together on numerous projects. He worked on the Celtic Coin Index which Sheppard Frere established in

Oxford, and for four years (1976–79) he compiled the yearly round-up of fresh discoveries in Roman Britain for the journal *Britannia*. He grew up in the village of Winterton, Lincolnshire, and his early interest in archaeology was aroused by the excavations of Ian Stead between 1958 and 1967 on the Roman villa there. After their conclusion he started his own project at Winterton, concentrating on the outbuildings and field systems of the villa, an aspect of villa archaeology that in Britain has been too often neglected. A Fellow of the Society of Antiquaries of London, he has also directed excavations at several other sites in Britain, including the Roman villa at Chedworth. He is currently a part-time Tutor at the Oxford University Department of Continuing Education, where he has taught courses and summer schools in archaeology for many years. His publications include *Chedworth Roman villa* (1972; latest edition 1996), a co-edited book on *Aspects of the* Notitia Dignitatum (1976), and the co-authored *Roman Inscriptions of Britain I: epigraphic indexes* (1983).

Professor Lawrence Keppie studied classics, ancient history and archaeology at the University of Glasgow, at Balliol College, Oxford, and at the British School at Rome, where he was Rome Scholar in Classical Studies in 1971–72. He has also been Hugh Last Fellow at the British School at Rome (1996). His entire academic career was spent on the staff of the Hunterian Museum, University of Glasgow, where he was appointed to a personal chair in Roman History and Archaeology in 1999. The editor of the journal *Britannia* between 2000 and 2004, he took early retirement in 2003 to concentrate on writing and research. His many books include *Colonisation and veteran settlement in Italy, 47–14 BC* (1983), *The making of the Roman army* (1984), *Understanding Roman inscriptions* (1991), *Roman inscribed and sculptured stones in the Hunterian Museum* (1998), and *Scotland's Roman remains*, now in its fourth edition (1986, 1990, 1998, 2004). His collected papers on the Roman army were published as *Legions and veterans* in 2000. He has recently completed a history of the Hunterian Museum, which celebrates its bicentenary in 2007, and is currently engaged on an antiquarian study of the Antonine Wall. Professor Keppie is a Fellow of the Society of Antiquaries of London, of the Society of Antiquaries of Scotland, and of the Royal Society of Edinburgh.

Professor Michael Mackensen studied archaeology at Munich, Freiburg and Oxford, including a doctorate in 1977 from Munich (where he also completed his *Habilitation*), before spending thirteen years as Senior Research Assistant at the Kommission zur archäologischen Erforschung des spätrömischen Raetien at the Bavarian Academy of Sciences in Munich (1982–94). Since 1994 he has been Professor of the Archaeology of the Roman Provinces at the University of Munich. He has directed many excavations and surveys, in Germany (at Kellmünz and Burghöfe in Bavaria, for example), in Syria (Resafa), in Tunisia (Chemtou) and in Egypt (Deir el-Bachit), where he is currently working on the late Roman fort at Nag el-Hagar. The author of numerous papers in academic journals, he has also published books on *Das römische Gräberfeld auf der Keckwiese in Kempten* (1978); *Eine befestigte spätantike Anlage vor den Stadtmauern von Resafa. Resafa I* (1984); *Frühkaiserzeitliche Kleinkastelle bei Nersingen und Burlafingen an der oberen Donau* (1987); *Die spätantiken Sigillata- und Lampentöpfereien von El Mahrine (Nordtunesien)* (1993); *Das spätrömische Grenzkastell Caelius Mons–Kellmünz* (1995), and *Militärlager oder Marmorwerkstätten. Neue Untersuchungen im Ostbereich des Arbeits- und Steinbruchlagers von Simitthus/Chemtou. Simitthus III* (2005).

Professor William Manning read chemistry and geology at the University of Nottingham before taking a postgraduate diploma in Archaeology and then his doctorate in Roman Archaeology at the Institute of Archaeology in London. After serving as an Archaeological Assistant at Reading Museum (1960–63) and as a Research Assistant at the British Museum (1963–4), he was appointed in 1964 to a lectureship at what is now the University of Cardiff, where he became successively Senior Lecturer, Reader, and, from 1983, Professor of Roman Archaeology; he has been Professor Emeritus since his retirement in 2000. He was elected a Fellow of the Society of Antiquaries of London in 1967 and a Corresponding Member of the Deutsches Archäologisches Institut in 1976. A Festschrift by his colleagues and former research students, entitled *Artefacts and archaeology*, was published in his honour in 2002. His books include *A catalogue of Romano-British ironwork in the Museum of Antiquities, Newcastle upon Tyne* (1976), *Catalogue of the Romano-British iron tools, fittings and weapons in the British Museum* (1985), *Roman Wales* (2001), and, together with several collaborators, the seven volumes of the *Report on the excavations at Usk 1965–1976*, which were published by the University of Wales Press between 1979 and 1995.

Dr C. Sebastian Sommer read chemistry at the University of Mainz before turning to Roman archaeology, which he studied at Munich and Freiburg before going to Oxford to do his Masters degree, later completing a doctorate at Munich. Between 1984 and 2001 he worked in the Baden-Württemberg archaeological service (Landesdenkmalamt), where he directed many important excavations, especially at Ladenburg (Lopodunum) and Rottweil (Arae Flaviae). His excavations of the Roman villa at Oberndorf-Bochingen, where parts of two buildings to roof-height were found collapsed in perfect condition under the ploughsoil, have also attracted international attention. Since 2002 he has been Chief Inspector (Landeskonservator) of Archaeology for the Landesamt für Denkmalpflege in Bavaria. A Corresponding Member of the German Archaeological Institute (since 1995) and a Fellow of the Society of Antiquaries of London (2006), he is the author and co-author of numerous publications, including *Römische Keramik aus der Töpfersiedlung von Schwabmünchen* (1983), *The military vici in Roman Britain* (1984), *Kastellvicus und Kastell. Untersuchungen zum Zugmantel im Taunus und zu den Kastellvici in Obergermanien und Rätien* (1988) and *LOPODVNVM I – Die römischen Befunde der Ausgrabungen an der Kellerei in Ladenburg 1981– 1985 und 1990* (1994). Since 2002 he has also edited *Das archäologische Jahr in Bayern*, the yearly round-up of excavations in Bavaria.

Sally Stow studied Classics at St Andrews University, and while there excavated with the Scottish Field School of Archaeology, first at Cardean, and then at Strageath under the direction of Sheppard Frere. She then transferred to the University of Oxford, where she took the two-year Postgraduate Diploma in Classical Archaeology, again under Sheppard Frere's supervision. Later she worked with him on the publication of his post-war Canterbury excavations. She is currently active in the promotion of archaeology at adult education level. She is the co-author (with Sheppard Frere and others) of five volumes in the 'Archaeology of Canterbury' series: *Volume I: Excavations at Canterbury Castle* (1982); *Volume II: Excavations on the Roman and medieval defences of Canterbury* (1982); *Volume VII: Excavations in the St. George's Street and Burgate Street areas* (1983), *Volume VIII: intra- and extra-mural sites, 1949– 55 and 1980–84* (1987) and *Volume V: Excavations in the Marlowe Car Park and surrounding areas* (1995).

Dr Roger Tomlin read Greats at Oriel College, Oxford, where he was tutored by Peter Brunt in Roman history. Transferring to Merton College, he began a doctoral thesis on the late-Roman emperor Valentinian I, which was supervised by Peter Brown and encouraged by Ronald Syme, whose centenary he marked by editing the essays published in *History and Fiction* (2005). He was introduced to the late Roman army by Eric Birley one summer in Durham, and dug for Sheppard Frere and Brian Hartley at Bowes, where he also met the editor of this volume. After three semesters at Cornell University as a visiting assistant professor, he completed his thesis while teaching at the University of Kent at Canterbury.

From there he went to the University of Durham, where he lectured on Roman history and succeeded Richard Wright as an editor of *Roman Inscriptions of Britain*, also being elected to the Society of Antiquaries. In 1977 he returned to Oxford as Lecturer in Late Roman History and a Fellow of Wolfson College, but retained an interest in the epigraphy of Roman Britain, which has resulted in publications on the late Roman army and on Roman epigraphy, notably *Tabellae Sulis* (1988), an edition of the 'curse tablets' found at Bath, and the eight fascicules of *Roman Inscriptions of Britain II* (1990–95), in which he collaborated with the honorand of this volume. At the moment he is finishing *Roman Inscriptions of Britain III*, which deals with stone inscriptions discovered since 1954. He also likes English antiques and oriental rugs, the English countryside, reading and writing, drinking wine, painting and travelling. He owns a house and a car, and has just bought a dish-washer, but not yet a television.

Professor Roger Wilson (Editor) read Literae Humaniores (Classics) at Wadham College, Oxford, where he also completed his doctorate. In 1974 he took up a lectureship at the University of Dublin, where he later became Louis Claude Purser Associate Professor of Classical Archaeology and a Fellow of Trinity College. He then moved to the University of Nottingham as Professor of Archaeology (1994–2005), until being appointed in January 2006 to the Professorship of the Archaeology of the Roman Empire at the University of British Columbia, where he is head of the Department of Classical, Near Eastern and Religious Studies. He has also been Alexander von Humboldt Fellow at the University of Bonn (1987–9), Togo Salmon Visiting Professor of Classics at McMaster University (1998), Balsdon Senior Research Fellow at the British School at Rome (2001/2), and Ian Sanders Memorial Lecturer at the University of Sheffield (2002). A Fellow of the Society of Antiquaries of London, he has directed excavations in Britain and Sicily, and written widely on the Roman archaeology of Italy, north Africa, Germany and Britain, but with a special emphasis on Sicily. His books include a *Guide to the Roman Remains in Britain*, now in its fourth edition (1975, 1980, 1988, 2002), *Piazza Armerina* (1983), *Sicily under the Roman Empire* (1990), and, as editor and contributor, *Roman Maryport and its setting* (1997), *Roman Germany: studies in cultural interaction* (1999), and *Romans on the Solway* (2004). He is currently completing a book on Roman art and architecture and another on his Sicilian excavations at Castagna and Campanaio.

Dr Christopher Young, after studying history at the University of Oxford for his first degree, also took his doctorate there, on Roman potteries of the Oxford region. A Fellow of the Society of Antiquaries of London, and a Corresponding Member of the German Archaeological Institute, he has worked for almost all his career first in the Inspectorate of Ancient Monuments of the Department of the Environment, and then at its successor, English Heritage. He has been responsible for the planning and funding of rescue archaeology in southern England, and later was English Heritage's first Regional Director for the North of England. In 1995, he became Director for the Hadrian's Wall World Heritage Site, responsible for the completion and implementation of the Management Plan for the Wall. In 1999, he became English Heritage's first Head of World Heritage and International Policy, where he advises on the development of Management Plans and new nominations for World Heritage Sites in England, and develops polices for their protection and enhancement. He has also worked for UNESCO in Laos and Mongolia and on other World Heritage matters. He has excavated Roman kiln sites around Oxford, and also at Carisbrooke Castle, and his publications include *The Roman Pottery Industry of the Oxford Region* (1977), *Excavations at Carisbrooke Castle, 1921–1996* (2000), and numerous articles on a wide variety of topics.

ADDRESSES OF THE CONTRIBUTORS

Geoffrey B. Dannell, BSc (Lond.), FCA, FSA
28 and 30 Main Street, Woodnewton, Peterborough, Cambridgeshire PE8 5EB
geoffrey.dannell@btinternet.com

Professor M. G. Fulford, BA (Soton), PhD (Soton), FBA, FSA
Department of Archaeology, University of Reading, Whiteknights, Reading RG6 6AH
m.g.fulford@reading.ac.uk

Roger Goodburn, BSc (Sheffield), Dip.Arch. (Lond.), FSA
48 Lashford Lane, Dry Sandford, Abingdon OX13 6DZ

Professor Lawrence J. F. Keppie, MA (Glasgow), MPhil. (Oxon.), DPhil. (Oxon.), FSA, FSA
(Scot.), FRSE
Hunterian Museum, University of Glasgow, Glasgow G12 8QQ
l.keppie@museum.gla.ac.uk

Professor Dr. Michael Mackensen, MA (Munich), Dr. Phil. (Munich), Dr. Phil. Habil. (Munich)
Institut für Vor- und Frühgeschichte und Provinzialrömische Archäologie
Ludwig-Maximilians-Universität, Geschwister-Scholl-Platz 1, D-80539 Munich
M.Mackensen@vfpa.fak12.uni-muenchen.de

Professor William Manning, BSc (Nottingham), PhD (Lond.), FSA
108 Plymouth Road, Penarth, Vale of Glamorgan CF64 5DN
william.manning@ntlworld.com

Dr C. Sebastian Sommer, MPhil. (Oxon.), Dr. Phil. (Munich), FSA
Bayerisches Landesamt für Denkmalpflege (Abteilung B), Hofgraben 4, D-80359 Munich
sebastian.sommer@blfd.bayern.de

Sally Stow, MA (St. Andrews), Dip.Class.Arch. (Oxon.)
48 Lashford Lane, Dry Sandford, Abingdon OX13 6DZ

Dr Roger S. O. Tomlin, MA (Oxon.), DPhil. (Oxon.), FSA
Wolfson College, Oxford OX2 6UD
roger.tomlin@history.ox.ac.uk

Professor Roger J. A. Wilson, MA (Oxon., Dub.), DPhil. (Oxon), FSA
Department of Classical, Near Eastern and Religious Studies
University of British Columbia, 1866 Main Mall, Vancouver V6T 1Z1
roger.wilson@ubc.ca

Dr Christopher J. Young, MA (Oxon.), DPhil. (Oxon.), FSA
Head of World Heritage and International Policy
English Heritage, 1 Waterhouse Square, 138–142 Holborn, London EC1N 2ST
Christopher.Young@english-heritage.org.uk

LIST OF ILLUSTRATIONS

Photographic credits

Front cover: by courtesy of Canterbury Museums; back cover and photograph on page vi: by courtesy of Bartle Frere; photograph on page viii: Strathclyde Regional Council, by courtesy of Hunterian Museum, University of Glasgow; Figs 1.1 and 1.2: photographs by R. J. A. Wilson; Figs 2.1, 2.3, 2.7: by courtesy of Museum of London; Figs 5.1 and 5.4: photographs K17-AI, 182, 7th July 1975, and K17-AI 145, 1st July 1975, both copyright reserved, by courtesy of Cambridge University Collection of Air Photographs; Figs 7.1, 7.3: by courtesy of the Hunterian Museum, University of Glasgow; Figs 7.2, 7.4: by courtesy of Glasgow University Library; Fig. 7.5: by courtesy of Edinburgh University Library, Dk.1.2.A74, nos 1–6; Fig. 7.6: by courtesy of Edinburgh University Library, Dk.1.2.A74, nos 7–9.

Maps, plans, geophysical plots and line-drawing credits

Figs 1.3, 1.4: after S. J. Greep (ed.), *Roman towns: the Wheeler inheritance* (1993), 84, fig. 5, and 86, fig. 7, by courtesy of Verulamium Museum; Fig. 1.5: after J. Wacher, *The towns of Roman Britain* (1995), 292, fig. 131, by courtesy of Winchester Museums Service Archaeology Unit; Fig. 1.6: after A. Down, *Roman Chichester* (1988), 15, fig. 15, by courtesy of Phillimore, Chichester; Figs 1.7, 1.12: drawn by Peter Hart-Allison, and reproduced by kind permission of the Museum of London Archaeology Service; Fig. 1.8: after E. Howe, *Roman defences and medieval industry: excavations at Baltic House, City of London* (2002), 7, fig. 5, by courtesy of the Museum of London Archaeology Service; Fig. 1.9: after P. Barker *et al.*, *The baths basilica, Wroxeter: excavations 1966–90* (1997), 3, fig. 3, by courtesy of English Heritage; Fig. 1.10: after G. Webster, *The legionary fortress at Wroxeter: excavations by Graham Webster 1955–85* (2002), 8, fig. 1.7, by courtesy of English Heritage; Fig. 1.11: after *Historia* 52 (2003), 342, Abb. 2; Figs 2.2, 2.4: drawn by Roger Tomlin; Figs 2.5, 2.6: drawn by Richard Grasby; Fig. 2.8: courtesy of the Museum of London; Fig. 3.1: map drawn by Margaret Mathews; *RIB* inscriptions reproduced by kind permission of the Trustees of the Haverfield Bequest; Figs 4.3–4.7 and 4.9: drawn by Marion O'Neill; Figs 5.2, 5.6: after D. Hopewell, *Britannia* 36 (2005), 244 and 230, figs 8 and 2, by kind permission of the Society for the Promotion of Roman Studies; Fig. 5.3: after R. J. A. Wilson and I. D. Caruana (eds), *Romans on the Solway* (2004), fig. 5.6, by kind permission of the Trustees of the Senhouse Roman Museum; Fig. 5.5: after J. A. Biggins and D. J. A. Taylor, *Britannia* 35 (2004), 163, fig. 3, by kind permission of the Society for the Promotion of Roman Studies; Fig. 5.7: after L. J. F. Keppie, *The Antonine Wall* (2001), fig. 27, by courtesy of the Society of Antiquaries of Scotland; Fig. 5.8: after H. Kaiser and C. S. Sommer, *Lopodunum I* (1994), fig. 263a, b and n, and fig. 264h; Fig. 5.9: after P. J. Casey and B. Hoffmann, *Britannia* 29 (1998), 115, fig. 2, by kind permission of the Society for the Promotion of Roman Studies; Fig. 9.1: after M. Bonifay, *Études sur la céramique romaine tardive d'Afrique* (2004), 455, fig. 256; Fig. 9.2: after M. ed-D. Mustafa and H. Jaritz, *Annales du Service des Antiquités de l'Égypte* 70 (1985), 22, fig. 1; Fig. 9.3: after U. A. Wareth and P. Zignani, *Bulletin de l'Institut Français d'Archéologie Orientale* 92 (1992), pl. 22; Figs 9.4, 9.5: drawn by Florian Schimmer.

LIST OF ABBREVIATIONS

ACKNOWLEDGEMENTS

The Editor would like to thank all the contributors for their efficiency in sending in their chapters on time and for turning around the proofs at very short notice; to David Brown, for kindly agreeing to publish the volume and for his hard work on the layout; to the Cambridge University Air Photograph Library, for generously agreeing to waive copyright fees for two aerial photographs which appear here (Figs 5.1 and 5.4), in recognition of Kenneth St Joseph's and Sheppard Frere's long and fruitful academic partnership; to Leslie Dunwoodie and Chiz Harward of MoLAS, for most generously allowing the publication of Fig. 1.12 here for the first time, in advance of their own publication; and to the holders of copyright as listed on p. xxviii, for permission to reproduce illustrations here.

Chapter 1

URBAN DEFENCES AND CIVIC STATUS
IN EARLY ROMAN BRITAIN

R. J. A. Wilson

I first met Sheppard Frere in 1969, when as an undergraduate I attended his lectures at Oxford on Roman Britain (I still have the lecture notes I took then). Later I participated in his excavations at Bowes and Longthorpe, and then became his research student when I embarked on a doctorate on Roman Sicily. He was, rightly, always a great stickler for the correct use of the English language (and he writes like an angel himself): in the first draft of my first chapter he scribbled in the margin 'ghastly neologism!' against my (grammatically incorrect) modern usage of the word 'hopefully', then just gaining currency. I have never used it since! Like all great teachers he dispensed wisdom in an unobtrusive way – words of advice he gave me then, the truth of which I have learned to appreciate more and more over the years, were often offered without his realising the significance of their impact on his students. What follows is an affectionate birthday tribute to a great scholar. It is symptomatic of his enormous contribution to Roman, and especially Romano-British, archaeology that the idea for my writing this chapter stems from a discovery that he himself made just over fifty years ago – the '1955 ditch' at Verulamium.

Introduction

At the heart of the notion of 'civilization' in the Greek and Roman worlds lay the physical entity of the city, and under Rome, in the newly-conquered lands in the north-west provinces (including Britain), the foundation of towns was a central part of imperial policy. Indeed those new urban foundations, in Gaul, Spain and Britain, many of which continue to be flourishing and vibrant communities to this day, together with the road system which linked and supplied them, are arguably the two greatest legacies in western Europe which Rome has handed down to the modern world. Legally these urban centres belonged to a series of different categories which are too familiar to rehearse in detail again here: they include *coloniae, municipia, civitates peregrinae* and *vici*.[1] There has been a tendency in recent years, in considering the British examples, to move away from this traditional framework for discussion, because it is thought to be unproductive and unhelpful in charting the evolution of Romano-British urbanism;[2] but just because epigraphic evidence throws virtually no light on this problem for Britain does not mean that Britain was any different from the rest of the Roman West in having a clear legal framework in which its urban network operated. That framework is best understood in north Africa, where an abundance of inscriptions documents with unusual clarity the differing ranks of individual communities at different times.[3] There one can trace in detail the change in status of many individual settlements with ambitions to rise in the urban hierarchy, from being an unchartered community, through that of *municipium*, and finally to the coveted rank of *colonia*. Of course standards are relative to each province individually, and not to the Roman world as a whole. One might, for example, have thought that Dougga, in building a fine Capitolium and a theatre in the 160s,[4] had done enough to warrant at least municipal status, but it became a *municipium* only in 205, and a *colonia* still later in the third century, certainly by 261.[5] Dougga, for all its prominence today as an exceptionally well-preserved Romano-African town, was not high in the pecking order of Roman urban centres in the African landscape. Towns had to work hard for their change in status, but they clearly thought that the civic pride and tax breaks that came with promotion were prizes worth having; and although it is hazardous to generalize from province to province, there is no real reason to doubt that urban communities in Britain had any lesser aspirations in this regard.

In Britain it is well known that there were three *coloniae* founded in the first century, Colchester, Lincoln and Gloucester, where *veterani* were settled, ex-soldiers from the legions who were therefore already Roman citizens.[6] In the second century, when this means of land settlement for legionary veterans died out, the practice of raising existing communities to colonial status (so-called 'honorary' *coloniae*) became more common. The only known example in Britain is that at York, attested as such on an inscription in Bordeaux dated to AD 237.[7] Only one certain *municipium* is known, Verulamium, or rather, to be more exact, it is so described by Tacitus in his *Annals*.[8] All this is very familiar ground to students of Roman Britain. The intriguing question is to speculate how many other places in Britain received municipal or colonial rank in the first and second centuries AD, because it is highly unlikely that the list given above is complete.

A word at the outset about the use of the word *municipium*. A *municipium* is usually taken in the Latin West to mean a town which had received the *ius Latii*, that is, a grant which enabled the chief magistrates of a city (and their families) to have Roman citizenship automatically on laying down their duties after their term of office. This is the so-called 'minor' Latin right: the *maius* version, by which all decurions (city councillors) received citizenship, is only attested in north Africa and is unlikely to have operated in Britain.[9] It is assumed that this was an urban rank which had to be applied for, in the same way that grants of colonial status were awarded by the Emperor on the recommendation of provincial governors; but Millar has pointed out that there is no unequivocal evidence of such a process happening in the Roman world – rather *municipium* may have been no more than a neutral title, like our 'municipality'.[10] On the other hand, Tacitus, for example, when describing Verulamium as a *municipium*, does seem to be using the term in a meaningful way, to indicate that it had a certain status which distinguished it from other communities.[11] Whatever the precise meaning of the term *municipium*, the existence of the *ius Latii* is secure; but as Galsterer-Kröll has rightly pointed out, in Gaul at least it is certain that communities could receive the *ius Latii* without necessarily changing their names to include the word *municipium* in their titles.[12] Clearly there is no straightforward formula which applied across the western Empire, and we should therefore be cautious in our use of the term *municipium*. In what follows I have employed it in inverted commas, to indicate a community which is likely to have received the *ius Latii*, whether or not it also took the title of *municipium.*

The purpose of this chapter is to ask whether, in the almost complete absence of epigraphic evidence, there is another clue which might be used to promote the idea that other communities in Britain received chartered status, either as *coloniae* or as '*municipia*'. Is the presence of an early defensive circuit in some Romano-British towns a helpful pointer to the civic status of that community? Before trying to answer that question, a summary of the evidence presently available is called for. I am concerned here to review only those places which had defences, whether of earth-and-timber or of stone, in the 140 or so years between the conquest in AD 43 and *c.* AD 180. The matter of the wholesale provision at the end of the second century of earth defences around Romano-British towns does not concern me here: the honorand of this volume has argued forcefully and definitively that it was an exceptional phenomenon without parallel in the Roman Empire, which can only be explained in terms of exceptional defensive needs – either those associated with the stripping of the British garrison by its governor Clodius Albinus in his bid for the imperial purple in AD 196/7, an act already predictable in 193, or with the unsettled times immediately preceding this, during the reign of Commodus.[13]

Defences of stone: the coloniae

1. Colchester

The Roman city walls of Colchester are among the more complete surviving Roman walled circuits in Britain, and they still survive impressively, especially on the western side (Fig. 1.1). They were long believed to belong to the mid-Roman period, in line with most other urban stone defences in Britain;[14] but excavations by the Colchester Archaeological Trust, at Lion Walk[15] and more especially at Culver Street,[16] have shown conclusively that the stone wall was originally a freestanding structure; the dating evidence sealed beneath shows that it was constructed sometime between AD 65 and 85. The earth bank behind the walls came later, apparently not before AD 150/200.[17] The foundation of *colonia Claudia Victricensis* dates to AD 49;[18] so in less than 35 years after the foundation, and possibly less than 20 years afterwards, Colchester already possessed a fine girdle of city walls in stone, the earliest in Britain.

There is nothing particularly surprising in this. The walls were built above all for reasons of civic pride, to show the world that Colchester was a *colonia*, a status

Fig. 1.1 Colchester, Roman walls on the west side, south of the Balkerne Gate, looking north

which marked it out as different from that of other urban communities in Britain at the time. In this it was being no different from many other *coloniae* which showed off their status elsewhere in the Roman West at an early date in exactly the same way: one thinks of places like Orange, Fréjus, Arles or Nimes in Gaul, or Mérida in Spain.[19] Of course some *coloniae*, especially those on or near the frontiers, such as Xanten and Cologne in Lower Germany,[20] clearly fortified themselves early on with the needs of military defence in mind, as well as that of civic pride (we know from dendrochronology, for example, that the stone defences of Xanten were being erected in AD 105/6, only seven years after the foundation): but an alleged military function for walled circuits in the early Empire can and has been overplayed. Philip Crummy, for example, in a recent discussion of the Colchester walls and their dating,[21] stressed that in his view the walled circuit at Colchester was erected in the aftermath of the Boudican rebellion entirely for military reasons: a mistake had been made in not defending the fledgling city before Boudica and her followers did their worst, and this mistake needed immediate rectification.[22] But at Colchester in the third quarter of the first century, I would suggest, with armies campaigning far away in the north, and urbanization getting under way in the southern part of the province, defensive considerations (notwithstanding the setback of the Boudican revolt) is unlikely to have played any part in the city councillors' deliberations, when they asked the emperor via the provincial governor for permission to erect their walls.

2. Lincoln

Lincoln is a different case: there the area occupied by the early *colonia* coincided with the preceding legionary fortress with its turf and timber defences, and the circuit of those defences was retained for the earliest city: the Flavian timberwork was removed and the earth bank faced with a narrow stone wall, *c.* 1.2 m wide. The date can be fixed no closer than the later first or the early second century AD, but the work is unlikely to have been still in progress much after the death of Trajan in 117.[23] Since the *colonia* was probably founded in the years soon after the withdrawal of *Legio II Adiutrix* in 86, the stone wall can almost certainly be seen as an action of the early colonists rather than as a refurbishment of the legionary defences by the military. If so, its presence is also a mark of Lincoln's colonial status, although its early date, possibly within a few years of the foundation of the *colonia*, and certainly less than 30 years, was no doubt dictated more by the state of the turf and timber ramparts (which if not refurbished since the 70s would have been in need of replacement by *c.* AD 100)[24] than by the urgency with which the colonists wished to express pride in their civic status in this traditional manner. The contrast with Exeter, another early town which developed out of a legionary fortress, but without chartered status, is striking: there the legionary defences were not maintained, and they gradually fell into disrepair, being eventually levelled as the town in time expanded over them.[25]

3. Gloucester

At Gloucester exactly the same occurred as at Lincoln: the site of the legionary fortress, built in the 60s on a fresh site to replace that at nearby Kingsholm, was taken over by the early colonists for their new town, and the same circuit-line of defences was also adopted. Refurbishment occurred in the late 80s or early 90s (coin evidence indicates that it cannot have taken place before AD 87/8), which included the insertion of a dry-stone wall in front of the earthen bank of the defensive circuit.[26] Whether that was a military operation carried out while still a legionary fortress, or the first actions of the newly-founded *colonia*, is a matter for debate: the foundation date of the *colonia* appears to fall in Nerva's reign (AD 96/8), since *Nerviana* is among its titles,[27] but, as Mark Hassall has pointed out, this might have been a refoundation of an original Domitianic grant of chartered status, the change of title occurring after Domitian's *damnatio memoriae*.[28] For our purposes, however, it does not matter whether *colonia Nerviana Glevensis* already had city walls of stone *ab initio* (courtesy of the army), or set about early in its life acquiring them.

4. York

Little can be said of the walls surrounding the Roman *colonia* at York. Its circuit has been assumed to lie (in part) under the medieval walls, but what remains of the Roman structure has only been seen for certain at three points, the last in 1939; none was uncovered in controlled excavation.[29] Its date has not been established; nor do we know if it was accompanied by an earth bank behind, and if so whether

Fig. 1.2 London, fragment of Roman city wall, inner face, seen from the south-west, now preserved in an underground car-park; excavated in 1957 on London Wall near its junction with Basinghall Street

that bank was contemporary with the stone wall or whether it represents an earlier or (as at Colchester) a later phase.

All the above is well known; but the fact is worth stressing that first Colchester and then Lincoln and Gloucester possessed circuits of stone walls far earlier than any other British urban community, and their very presence was indubitably intended as a clear signal of their separate and elevated chartered rank as *coloniae*. The walls were status symbols, totems of civic pride; they were decidedly not intended as military fortifications, nor were they built and maintained out of defensive fear.

Defences of stone elsewhere before the end of the second century: the case of London

The rest of the stone defences of Romano-British towns, with one exception, date not earlier than the third century,[30] and do not concern us here. The one exception is London, where a substantial walled circuit of stone was constructed on the landward side of Londinium, probably sometime in the closing years of the second century (Fig. 1.7, p. 14). This was a huge undertaking: a wall 2,956 m long, requiring an estimated 30,000 cu m of stone and flint and over a million facing stones, was built to a width (at base) of 2.6 m, with a V-shaped ditch outside.[31] Even the inside face, although it was covered by a rampart, was carefully built with proper facing stones (Fig. 1.2), the width being reduced the higher the wall went by a series of offsets. The finding of a coin, quite worn, of Commodus of AD 183/4 sealed beneath the thickening added to the west wall of the Cripplegate fort, contemporary with the building of the rest of the wall, provides an approximate *terminus ante quem non*, at least for that particular part of the building programme;[32] and another crucial chronological pointer is occupation rubbish inside one of the internal towers bonded with the wall, which included a forger's coin hoard (and his moulds), with the earliest of the forged coins dating to AD 215.[33] It looks therefore as if the wall was built sometime after 185 and was already in use by about 215, although how long it took to build is unknown (if there was no urgency and not unlimited funds, the construction project might have dragged on for a long time). It is, for example, possible that a start had been made in some sectors before 185: a single coin from a single find-spot is obviously not sufficient evidence to date the whole project. A possible context to explain the building of London's stone defences will be discussed below (pp. 30–1).

Earth-and-timber defences in the first century

1. Verulamium

It was Sheppard Frere's excavations 51 years ago at Verulamium which identified an intriguing defensive ditch well inside the line of the known, visible urban defences (the '1955 ditch': see Fig. 1.3). It was a substantial obstacle, about 5.80 m wide and 3.58 m deep where best preserved; nothing was left of an accompanying rampart.[34] It was typical of the excavator's foresight and his determination to gain fuller information about the new discovery that he called in what was then a tool in its infancy – the proton magnetometer – to find the course of the rest of the circuit.[35] These early defences, enclosing an area of 119 acres (48 ha), proved difficult to date. Sheppard Frere considered the possibility that they were erected in a hurry in 61, after the Boudican attack, but he preferred a Claudian date, in the decade AD 50/60, on the grounds that a military defence immediately after the attack made little sense, and because Tacitus says that Boudica's followers avoided only forts and military posts, not defended towns.[36] Frere also pointed out that the fact that two stone monumental arches marked the position of the line of these early defences across Watling Street where it passed through the town, long after the '1955' ditch had been filled in as the town expanded over it, suggests that the line of the latter was thought worthy of commemoration as a proud reminder of the past history of the city's urban development – presumably its promotion to the rank of '*municipium*' – rather than to recall a panic defence erected for an imagined military purpose in the immediate aftermath of the trauma of AD 60/1.[37] The date of the granting of a municipal charter is taken to be Claudian, because Tacitus calls

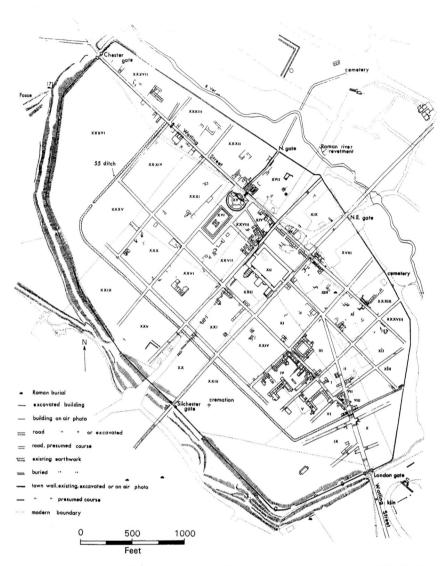

Fig. 1.3 Verulamium, overall plan; the line of the early defences is marked '55 ditch' along its north-west side

Verulamium a *municipium* when describing the events associated with Boudica's uprising, and so this status must be earlier than AD 60, and the grant of a municipal charter is more plausibly Claudian in date than Neronian.[38]

Such a position is perfectly logical, and takes of course Tacitus' statement at face value. It would mean that Verulamium had been selected as a show-place Claudian town in the early years of the conquest, perhaps along with other places in Britain, a policy which finds a parallel in another newly-acquired province in Claudius'

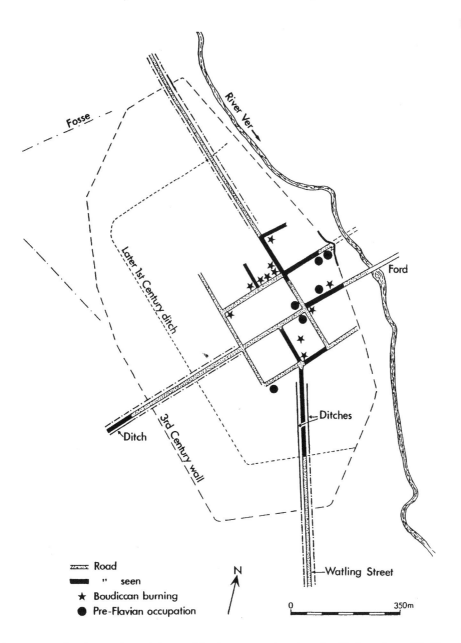

Fig. 1.4 Verulamium, plan of the pre-Flavian town showing the ditches along Watling Street

reign, Noricum, where five settlements were founded with the title *municipium Claudium*.[39] There is, however, a possible alternative chronology. If Tacitus was writing loosely and anachronistically, his reference to Verulamium as a *municipium* may refer to its status when he was composing his work *c.* AD 115, and not *sensu stricto* at the time of the Boudican rebellion.[40] If that is the case, the date of Verulamium's promotion to municipal status could belong any time during the first century AD, and if the defences are themselves an indication of this altered civic status (as many believe[41]), then they too might be later than the Claudian period. Niblett has pointed out that there is no pre-Flavian occupation known south of *Insula* XI, three *insulae* inside the course of the southern side of the early defences.[42] That in itself is not an insurmountable objection to a Claudian chronology, because the defences may have been erected along a pre-ordained line marked out at the time of the foundation, with the intention that the town would in time grow to fill the space allocated for it. More tellingly, however, Niblett has also noted that when side ditches were dug in the mid-first century along the southern sector of Watling Street (Fig. 1.4), they were substantial features 3 m wide and 10 m away from the street, more appropriate to Roman roads in the countryside than in a town: she suggests, therefore, that that part of Watling Street was envisaged at the time as lying outside the urban nucleus – something which does not make sense if the early defences were already in place enclosing the relevant stretch of Watling Street.[43] The ditches lining the road were filled in during the Flavian period, so they would not have interfered with the first-century earth defences at the point where their lines cross, *if* those defences were themselves of (later) Flavian date. An alternative possibility, therefore, to the Claudian chronology is that Verulamium was promoted to the rank of '*municipium*' (with a grant of the *ius Latii*) during the Flavian period, surely under Vespasian, and that the completion in stone in the late 70s of a huge and imposing forum and basilica complex (it covers some 5 acres [2.2. ha]), at the time (as far as we know) the largest and most advanced example of its type in the province,[44] may have been intended as an affirmation of its new status. If the earth defences were also an affirmation of that new status, they too may belong to the 70s. The third-century stone arches on Watling Street, as Sheppard Frere noted,[45] were intended to be a reminder of the line of that early circuit, an interesting 'heritage' feature (to use modern terminology) in the later Roman town, and clearly one of which the inhabitants of Verulamium, as noted above, were sufficiently proud to think worthy of commemoration. That notion best fits with an interpretation of the defences as themselves being a token of civic pride, in celebration of Verulamium's elevation to municipal status – not as elegant as the stone defences of a *colonia*, and requiring more maintenance and repair, but a status symbol nonetheless.

2. Winchester

The archaeology of early Roman Winchester is rather curious. The Iron Age enclosure known as Oram's Arbour, perhaps of late second- or early first-century-BC date, seems not to have been occupied after *c.* 50 BC, but its earthworks were sufficiently prominent to have influenced the course of the Roman defences on the west side of the town (Fig. 1.5).[46] An early rampart of Roman date has been found at two points buried within and below the later defensive bank (the latter ascribed

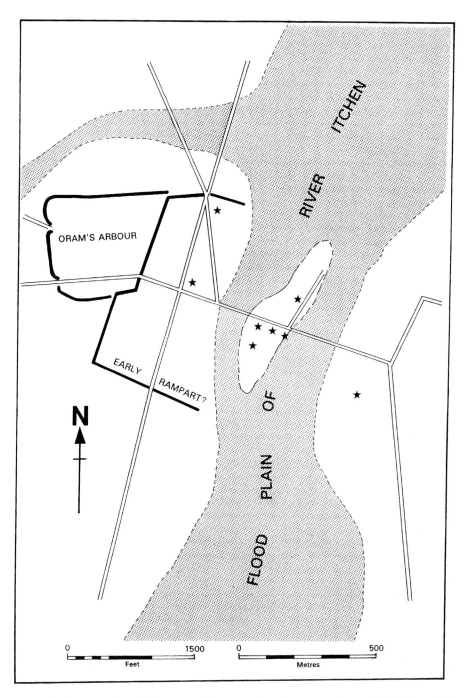

Fig. 1.5 Winchester, plan of the assumed course of early ramparts, c. AD 75, in relationship to both the original course of the River Itchen and the Iron Age earthwork (Oram's Arbour), abandoned c. 50 BC

to the end of the second century) on the west side of the town, and the plan has also been recovered of a timber south gate, comprising three sets of pairs of posts, set within the ends of the early rampart. An *as* of Nero (AD 54–68) was found in one of its postholes, which led the excavator, Martin Biddle, to propose a Flavian date, *c.* AD 75, for the early defensive circuit, although other evidence has been adduced to suggest it might be a little later, possibly *c.* AD 90/100.[47] The course of the eastern side of these defences is unknown, and they may never have been completed on the low-lying ground closest to the original course of the river; but in an extraordinary act of manipulating the landscape, the river Itchen was diverted into a new stream bed further east, enabling the former bed to be drained and filled in, and provide safe ground for the Roman town to expand eastwards. That may not have occurred until *c.* AD 100,[48] but the latest evidence shows that elements of the street grid in the eastern half of the town may have already begun to be laid out during the Flavian period rather than as late as 100. In that case the diversion of the river may also have been part of the Flavian building programme; but it is certain that an early bank does not underlie the east defences of the later Roman town.[49]

3. *Silchester*

Silchester was an Iron Age settlement before the Roman invasion of AD 43, but whether or not it was defended then has in the past been a matter of dispute. Both the 'Outer' and the 'Inner' earthworks have been claimed as being of Roman (first-century) date, the inner built shortly after AD 43, and the outer to defend the early Flavian town.[50] The latter earthwork, even though dating evidence is scarce, is now generally accepted as being of Iron Age date,[51] and the inner earthwork almost certainly is too. Boon on the basis of material recovered in a section through it suggested a *terminus post quem* of *c.* AD 25, but still proposed an early Roman date, i.e. after AD 43.[52] Re-examination of the material in the light of more recent pottery research suggests that a date in the late first century BC or very early first century AD is likely for this earthwork.[53] This Inner Earthwork is also therefore more likely to be of late Iron Age date rather than early Roman; at any rate it is certain that the earliest stone building of the Roman town, the bath-house, lies over its course, implying that by the time of the latter's construction the rampart had already been demolished. The bath-house is often dated to the Neronian period on the basis of a tile-stamp, and although the building could be as a late as the early Flavian period,[54] its oblique alignment to the main Flavian street-grid (as has often been observed) suggests that it belongs very early in the laying out of the town, when a different orientation of the street system was contemplated.

If both Outer and Inner Earthwork are indeed accepted as being of Iron Age date, as seems certain, the only candidate for early Roman defences at Silchester is a short section of a substantial ditch: this was partially uncovered near the later East Gate, running north-west–south-east and roughly parallel to the later north-east wall, but some 65 m inside it.[55] Pottery from the primary silts of this apparently defensive feature dates to *c.* AD 75, so the ditch was probably dug in the early Flavian period; it had become completely filled by *c.* AD 150. Since a length of only

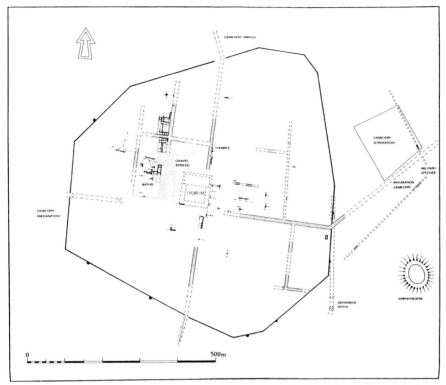

Fig. 1.6 Chichester, overall plan, showing the position of the early military ditches north of the amphitheatre, and the defensive ditch (found at The Cattlemarket) outside the south-east corner of the later walled circuit. The Chapel Street site mentioned in the text lies north-west of the Roman forum, and is represented here by the plan of the later Roman town-houses which overlie the timber structures of Claudian and Neronian date.

5 m was uncovered, and then only the southern lip of the ditch, the nature and extent of this possible defence for the early Roman town at Silchester remain uncertain until more of it has been located elsewhere.

4. Chichester

Whether the early Roman town at Chichester was surrounded by defences or not is far from clear.[56] Chichester is assumed to have been the principal urban nucleus of the client king Cogidubnus or Togidubnus (of whom more below: pp. 20–3), yet the earliest phase here, of Claudian and Neronian date, is interpreted as military, on the basis of 'military-style' buildings of that date located in the heart of the modern town, west of Chapel Street, and of quantities of military equipment found in various parts of the town (Fig. 1.6).[57] This is spread over an area of 5.5 ha, suggestive perhaps of the possibility that a vexillation fortress was sited here;[58] but

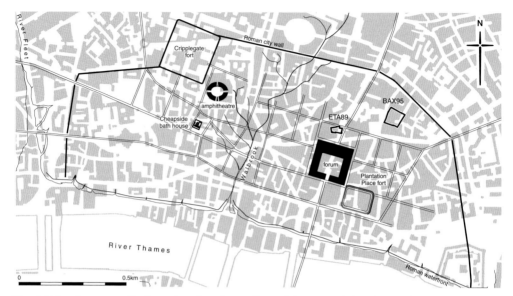

Fig. 1.7 London, overall plan, showing the outline of the stone defensive wall of the late second century, and the location of the Baltic House (BAX95), 7 Bishopsgate (ETA89) and Plantation Place excavation sites. The forum shown here in outline is the Hadrianic one; its Flavian predecessor was largely contained within its courtyard. Aldgate is the Roman gate nearest the southern tip of the North-point, and the military ditch here, mentioned in the text, was found inside the line of the walls parallel to and on the north side of the street running between the gate and the V-shaped road junction 130 m further west. The site at Northumberland Alley, also mentioned in the text, lies 60 m south-east of this fork in the Roman street. Aldersgate is the first gate west of the Cripplegate fort.

no appropriate defences have ever been located, as the comparatively insubstantial nature of the ditches found to the east of the modern town, in the area of the St Pancras cemetery, were thought by Alec Down, their excavator, to have belonged to a short-lived temporary camp.[59] Another ditch on the east side of the town, in The Cattlemarket just east of the line of the later defences,[60] was more substantial, over 7 m wide and 2.5 m deep, but dating evidence was scarce. The excavator, keeping his options open, suggested that it was possibly recut from an earlier Iron Age ditch (if its line perpetuates that of the Iron Age dykes further north, as seems possible), and that this was done by the military soon after the conquest to provide a protection for their base; this in turn, he proposed, might have been maintained by Togidubnus as part of the defences of the early Roman town.[61] The ditch was, however, apparently backfilled in the 60s, and so these early 'defences' were not a lasting feature of the town as they were at Winchester and Verulamium; in fact it may not have been a Roman feature at all. A short stretch of ditch outside the later west defences might also be either Iron Age or Roman. Without further evidence the extent and function of these ditches (and their presumed associated banks) are impossible to establish: none can at present be claimed confidently as defending the early Roman town.

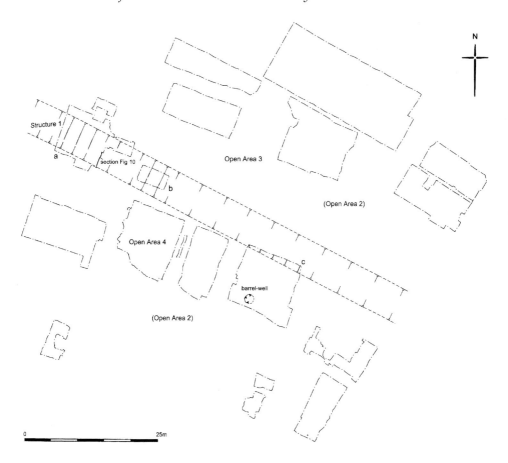

Fig. 1.8 London, Baltic House, plan of the first-century defensive ditch

5. London

At London the situation is more complex. We have already seen how Londinium, apart from the known *coloniae*, is exceptional in having stone defences before or at the end of the second century (Fig. 1.7). Was this defensive circuit preceded by other, earlier defences of turf and timber on a different alignment, enclosing a smaller area, which were superseded as the city grew to reach its maximum extent, as defined by the line taken by the late second-century walls? One site is of special interest in this context. In an excavation at Baltic House, in the north-east sector of the Roman city, published in 2002, a major V-shaped ditch, with 'angle-breaker' cleaning-slot along the bottom, was traced through three sectors over a length of 50 m across the site (Fig. 1.8).[62] Significantly, perhaps, the ditch runs parallel to the later stone defences on their north-east side, but about 100 m inside it. Although severely truncated by later activity, the ditch at Baltic House was 4.2 m wide and at least 1.65 m deep; it is estimated that originally it was up to 6 m wide and perhaps as much as 2.45 m deep. The material in its primary silts belonged to the period AD 70/100, so the ditch was probably dug in the early Flavian period rather than before. In the second century, probably around AD 120/30, it was deliberately backfilled; the quantities of dirty brick-earth found in the backfill may derive from the demolished rampart.

No military artefacts were recovered from the site, and it seems at least a possibility that the ditch formed part of an early earthwork defence around the burgeoning civilian settlement during the early Flavian period.[63] Such an interpretation would be more convincing if further stretches of a similar defensive ditch on an appropriate alignment were known. Further to the east, running parallel with Aldgate and Fenchurch Street, two separate stretches of what were taken to be military ditches (one had a sword pommel in the bottom) have been identified,[64] but these are on an alignment (west-south-west to east-north-east) approximately at right-angles to the line later taken by the late second-century stone defences, as well as to the ditch uncovered at Baltic House; it seems, therefore, impossible that they formed part of the same continuous feature with the latter. In any case the Aldgate/Fenchurch Street ditch, which if continuous stretched for at least 100 m, was dug in the 40s or early 50s AD and had a very short life, being deliberately backfilled before any primary silt had accumulated in the bottom. It is possible that this belonged to some short-lived military post set at the outskirts of the newly-founded town, although this is far from certain. However another 'military' ditch, in Northumberland Alley just to the south of Fenchurch Street, might conceivably be part of the early urban defences, if one envisages these as defining an area smaller than, but following roughly the same orientation (north-west/south-east) as, the later town wall of stone: like the Baltic House stretch of ditch, it lies at a similar distance (in this case *c.* 120 m) inside the later stone defences. The excavators, however, saw the Northumberland Alley ditch as military and part of the same 'fort' as the Aldgate/Fenchurch Street ditch, even though the two sets of ditches are not at strict right-angles to one another, and that at Northumberland Alley took longer to be backfilled: pottery evidence placed the backfilling of the latter in the Neronian period (AD 60/80).[65] If that chronology is right, it can have nothing to do with the Baltic House defences, which probably date, as we have seen, to the early Flavian period.

This by no means exhausts the list of early defensive ditches which have been found in London: at two other sites, 7 Bishopsgate and Plantation Place (Fig. 1.7), double-ditch systems have been discovered which are likely to be of military origin, and they will be discussed further below (pp. 25–8). One other feature, however, which is relevant to London's urban defences may also be noted here. John Wacher has drawn attention to a published section of the Roman city wall, at Duke's Place immediately north of Aldgate, which shows a wide, shallow U-shaped ditch preceding the construction of the stone defences: it survived on the berm of the later defences, between the late second-century stone wall and its contemporary V-ditch.[66] Wacher thought that this earlier feature 'excites suspicions' that London had a defensive circuit, erected after AD 120, along the line later taken by the stone defences, even though no trace of a defensive bank associated with it has ever been found.[67] The excavator, John Maloney, however, stressed that the pre-wall feature at Duke's Place was too small to have been defensive, and he interpreted it as a boundary ditch, as indeed is implied by its U-shaped profile;[68] the same feature had been located on other stretches of the London defences, at nearby Crosswall and elsewhere.[69] What is clearly the same feature has now also been found on the line of the walled circuit much further west, the stretch heading from the south-west corner of the Cripplegate Roman fort in the direction of Aldersgate. Here an excavation in 1997/8 uncovered a 38-m length of shallow U-shaped ditch up to 6.60 m wide and about 1.50 m deep, on the same alignment as, and underlying, the later stone defences.[70] The pottery assemblage in the primary fill of the ditch indicated, according to the excavator, that it was dug about AD 100, but since it appears to respect the ditch system of the Cripplegate fort, and so is contemporary with or later than the fort, a slightly later date is more likely: the Cripplegate fort is now thought to date *c.* AD 120.[71] If so, the shallow ditch may be roughly contemporary with that found at Duke's Place. The excavator at Aldersgate, in line with Wacher's interpretation, thought that the ditch might indicate that London had earlier earthwork defences on the line later taken by the city wall; but the ditch is too wide and too shallow to be anything other than a boundary ditch, defining a demarcation line. It is particularly interesting that the Aldersgate ditch indicates that the western sector of the Roman city, usually thought to lie outside the urban area (not least because of early cemeteries in the area) until the late second century,[72] was envisaged as being included within the city as early as the Hadrianic period, if, that is, the boundary line underlay the later city wall for its entire circuit on this western side. A possible context for this shallow ditch will be suggested below (p. 31).

Earth-and-timber defences in the second century earlier than **c. AD 180**

1. Verulamium

It has long been known that Verulamium had an intermediate phase of earthen defences between those of the first century (the '1955 ditch') and the third-century circuit with its stone walls. The 'Fosse' earthwork, as the intermediate defensive bank is known (it is only partly visible on Fig. 1.3, p. 8), enclosed a portion of land in the western corner of the town with an unusual re-entrant angle, ignored by the third-century defences. Only the west and part of the south sides of this earthwork are known, and so the area of the town it enclosed is uncertain. It may be that it was never finished,[73] but if so it is curious that there are signs of a strengthening and widening of the earthwork at one point, inexplicable if the project to erect these defences had been aborted without being completed. Sherds from within the bank near its original grass-line date to the late first century, and the 'most reasonable view is that the Fosse was being built in the second quarter of the second century at a time when the 1955 ditch was being extensively back filled and built over'.[74] Furthermore by the middle of the second century, Verulamium had built large and imposing gateways of stone at the two points where travellers along

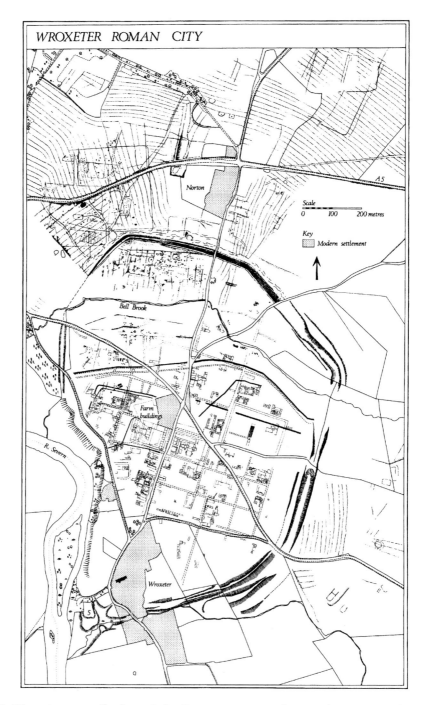

Fig. 1.9 Wroxeter, overall plan of the Roman town, as known from excavation, aerial photography and geophysical survey

Watling Street entered the town, whether from north or south. Each gate, 3.5 m across, had double carriageways for traffic, a pedestrian arch on either side, and imposing, projecting semicircular towers flanking the whole. These were pure propaganda monuments, designed to impress upon the visitor the notion that he/she had arrived at a place of importance.

2. Cirencester

A similar sequence may have occurred at Cirencester. An early defensive bank of *c.* AD 100/120 has been postulated by Holbrook on the basis of observations of short stretches on the north-east and south-west sides of the later defences, mostly overlain by and incorporated into that later circuit;[75] but these two sections of early bank have also been explained in other ways, unrelated to each other – the one in a possible military context, the other as an upcast bank from ditch-digging.[76] Be that as it may, the main circuit of defences, which at 240 acres (96 ha) enclosed a bigger area than anywhere else in Britain apart from London, came earlier than the vast majority of such earthen defences elsewhere: the pottery suggests a *terminus post quem* of *c.* AD 140, so the provision of these defences is probably early Antonine (*c.* AD 140/160).[77] Interestingly, the two principal gates of the town, the Bath Gate and the Verulamium Gate, had projecting semicircular towers as at Verulamium, although on a less imposing scale, and the temptation is to date them to the same period as the earth defences; unequivocal dating evidence was not, however, forthcoming from the excavation of either gate.[78]

3. Wroxeter

The dating of the defences at Wroxeter is much less clear. The overall site plan (Fig. 1.9) shows three separate lines of fortification: the straight line to the right of the modern farm buildings marking the northern defences of the mid-first-century legionary fortress, together with the double ditches of what was probably a military annexe immediately to the west of the modern farm buildings; another, gently curving, ditch running east–west across the town, between the fortress and the Bell Brook; and the main line of urban defences which are clear on the north, east and south of the Roman town. Current orthodoxy proposes that the second of these, that between the Bell Brook and the legionary fortress, is also military, mainly on the basis of a section dug across it by Kathleen Kenyon in 1936/7, when it was dated to the first century.[79] Graham Webster, therefore, proposed that it was designed to defend the *canabae* of the legionary fortress (Fig. 1.10).[80] Several objections can be raised to this. First, the dating proposed by Kenyon cannot be accepted without question, especially in view of the advances in our understanding of Romano-British pottery in the intervening seventy years. Secondly, it might be questioned whether there was enough room for *canabae* to develop adequately within the area so defended, especially when the principal focus of activity to the north of the fortress is likely to have been along the principal north–south road, of which barely 150 m would have been available for settlement. Thirdly, it might be questioned whether a short-lived military feature will have left such a mark on the later development of the Romano-British town, including a curving road just inside it; the latter remained a feature of the developed town-plan even after the defence itself had been levelled and forgotten.[81] An alternative proposal is to see this defensive bank and ditch as having nothing to do with the military phase (the rest of the defences of this phase were buried deep below the urban structures and left no surface trace when the Roman town was built over them), but rather to interpret it as an part of an early defensive circuit belonging to the civilian town.[82] In the absence of fresh work, its date can only be surmised (second or third quarter of the second century?). As the town expanded to its full extent, that bank was levelled and a new line of defences was erected to the north of the Bell Brook, enlarging the town by a further 89 acres (36 ha). The main circuit of defences is described as being of mid-second-century date in the latest publications,[83] but as late-second-century by others:[84] absence of modern work makes precision impossible. If the ditch and assumed bank south of the Bell Brook were indeed civilian and not military, and part of an urban defensive circuit, presumably it continued round the east and south sides of the town to be incorporated in the later defences; but this has yet to be confirmed by excavation. Clearly further work is needed.

The role of client kings

Before an attempt is made to make sense of the data above, and set early urban defences in context, a word must be added about the role of the client kings at the beginning of the urbanisation process, and especially about the activities of Tiberius Claudius Togidubnus (or Cogidubnus)[85] – not least because it has been suggested that three of the possible early defensive circuits, those of Silchester, Chichester and Winchester, were built by him as client king. This is not the place to re-examine in detail his career, on which much has already been written,[86] nor can any hypotheses be conclusive when we do not know when he died; but a few points may be made which are relevant to the discussion of early defences in Romano-British towns.

Tacitus' statement that '[C]ogidibnus remained most loyal down to a time I myself can remember', implies that his pro-Roman sympathies were long-lasting, from his emergence shortly after AD 43, down into the later first century.[87] Since Tacitus was born c. AD 56, we might take this to mean that Togidubnus was still alive c. 75; but the phrase is too ambiguous and vague for us to be sure. Certainly if the main Fishbourne palace was indeed designed by and for the latter, as seems very probable, and if Cunliffe's dates are correct for its construction, then Togidubnus is likely to have been still alive in the 70s.[88] The case for making him owner of the Fishbourne palace has, incidentally, been greatly strengthened since the 1990s by the finding, in its immediate environs, of a gold ring, itself a rare find in first-century Britain, inscribed 'Ti(berius) Cl(audius) Catuarus'.[89] The fact that Catuarus is a Celtic name, and that the first two names indicate that he too had received citizenship from Claudius (or Nero), whether directly or through a

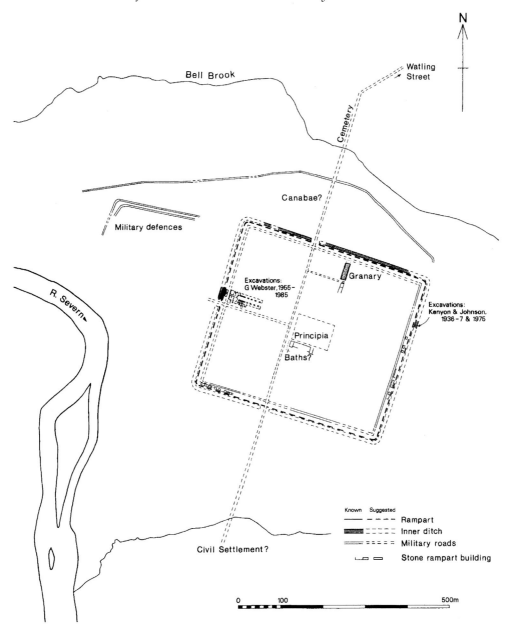

N

Bell Brook

Watling
Street

Cemetery

Canabae?

Military defences

Excavations:
G Webster, 1955 –
1985

Granary

Excavations:
Kenyon & Johnson,
1936 – 7 & 1975

R. Severn

Principia

Baths?

Known   Suggested

——— – – – – Rampart
▬▬▬ ═ ═ ═ ═ Inner ditch
═══ ═ ═ ═ ═ Military roads
└─□ ▭ ▭ Stone rampart building

Civil Settlement?

0   100   500m

Fig. 1.10 Wroxeter, outline plan of the legionary fortress, showing also the double ditches of what may have been a military annexe to the west, and the hypothetical military defences around the canabae *to the north*

kinsman, seems too great a coincidence to have been accidental in the light of its findspot; and although we cannot prove that Catuarus was indeed related to Tiberius Claudius Togidubnus, it does seem very likely.

Cunliffe originally thought that the changes detectable in the palace around AD 100 were an indication that Togidubnus had recently died (if so, presumably well into his eighties);[90] but even if he had died much earlier and his client-kingdom had already been broken up and absorbed into the Roman province, there is no reason why his son and heir should not have continued to live in the palace (assuming he had one: was it Catuarus?) – the transition in ownership from father to son need have left no archaeological trace.[91] What of Togidubnus' activities elsewhere? There is general agreement that his kingdom, as presumably settled with Rome when the arrangement was agreed, embraced a large part of central southern England, including the later *civitas* capitals of Chichester, Silchester and Winchester. At Chichester it is thought that a short-lived military phase was followed by civilian activity in the late Claudian and Neronian periods, presumably the first steps in laying out the town under Togidubnus' guidance.[92] The famous dedication inscription mentioning his name from a temple of Neptune and Minerva is a prominent example of early *Romanitas*, since it is likely to come from a classical-style temple; but whether it is Neronian or Flavian is disputed.[93] At Silchester, at the site of the later stone forum, the earliest building of Roman date, which is surely to be interpreted as part of the first timber forum, belongs to the late 40s or early 50s, and may well be his work;[94] while the first amphitheatre, a potent symbol of pro-Roman sympathies, has been dated to between the late 50s and the early 70s, a precociously early example.[95] All this plausibly is Togidubnus' work; whether the second timber forum, of Flavian date (*c.* AD 85), is also his is more debatable.[96] At Winchester we have a rather different picture. The place does not seem to have been occupied as an Iron Age centre of power at the time of the Roman invasion, and evidence for Claudian and Neronian activity there is scarce.[97] This may be due to the paucity of modern excavation, when there have been so few opportunities to uncover early Roman levels in the historic centre of Winchester; but while pre-Flavian activity there is thought to have been at a very low level, occupation in Flavian times was intensive, marked by elements of the street-grid, the erection of early defences, and possibly the beginning of building work on the forum. If Togidubnus had died *c.* AD 75/80, he may have had no part in all this: indeed, although the area may have been included in his kingdom, Winchester may not have been one of his 'capitals' at all. It has also been suggested that Togidubnus' name may have occurred on an inscription from Bath, where the first phase of the great temple/bathing complex has been dated to *c.* AD 70 'or a little earlier' (and a Neronian or early Flavian date for the temple has been argued independently on the basis of architectural details); the fragment itself is undated, and in any case the identity of the person named is unverifiable, but it remains an intriguing possibility.[98]

Where does this leave the so-called early defences at Chichester, Silchester and Winchester? Were they built by Togidubnus? Wacher, anxious to find a military context to explain their erection, thinks that they can be associated with the events of 69/70 and the uncertainties attending the civil wars on the Continent in that year; but this is unnecessary.[99] If Togidubnus commanded the respect of his people, no such defence would be needed, and in any case a tactical or strategic function for such defences at this time is hard to fathom. In fact, as we have seen, early defences at Silchester and Chichester are problematic, now that the Inner and Outer earthwork at the former are thought to belong to the Iron Age rather than later (p. 12): we are left with the lip of one short stretch of ditch at Silchester, apparently dug around AD 70 (p. 12), and a short, undated stretch of ditch at Chichester, which may or may not be urban in character, and which in any case had been backfilled by the Flavian period (p. 14). Only at Winchester are early urban defences certain. If really datable as early as *c.* AD 75, Togidubnus was probably alive then and could have ordered their construction; but if he died *c.* AD 75/80 and they were erected after *c.* AD 80 (as has been suggested) rather than a few years earlier, they might belong to the period when the new *civitas* of the 'Belgae' was being created (artificially, for Roman administrative convenience) out of the carve-up of Togidubnus' client kingdom.[100] We will return to Winchester again in the discussion of the overall context of these defences below (p. 30).

We know nothing of the possible urbanising tendencies of Prasutagus, or Esuprasto as we should now probably more correctly call him;[101] and although a short-lived client-kingdom centred on Verulamium has been hypothesized, on the basis of the remarkable Folly Lane burial of *c.* AD 55,[102] and is perhaps supported by the apparent absence, or near absence, of military posts in the whole of the surrounding region,[103] this is far from certain.

The role of the army

In 1972 Sheppard Frere concluded, in his discussion of the pre-Boudican timber shops and houses which he excavated at Verulamium, that both their method of construction and their stark rectangular plans were so innovatory and so unlike anything encountered in Britain before the Roman conquest,[104] that their construction must be due to the military: 'we cannot doubt that military architects or craftsmen were lent or sent to aid the construction of the new city.'[105] This very plausible view was challenged by Millett in 1990, who was keen to demonstrate his alternative standpoint that the impetus for the establishment of towns in Britain came from the native élite's desire to enjoy a Roman life-style, and that the building work was therefore very firmly in their hands and under their control.[106] He drew support for this view from Blagg's conclusion, based on the few fragments of architectural details to have survived from early Roman Britain, that military and civilian building-styles seem to belong to different traditions.[107] In places such as London, where there was no local élite to act as the driving force (since it was not a *civitas* capital), Millett believed that the impetus for urban growth still came entirely from civilians, in this case from foreign traders.[108] In recent years two important new discoveries, one in Germany and one in Britain, have thrown fresh and very bright light on the whole question of the extent and nature of the Roman army's role in urban foundation in the West – especially in provinces where, like Britain, there was no pre-existing tradition of nucleated urban settlement on the Mediterranean model.

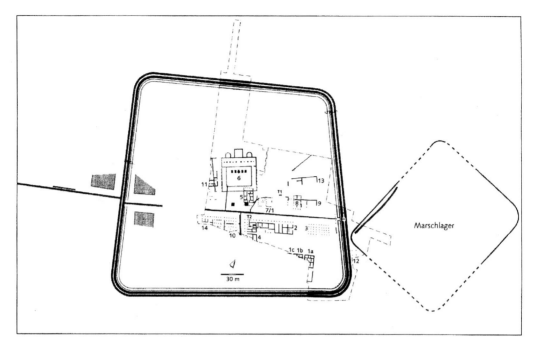

Fig. 1.11 Waldgirmes, plan of the Augustan town, before AD 9, with temporary camp ('Marschlager') to east

During the 1990s excavations commenced at an Augustan site at Waldgirmes north of Frankfurt (Fig. 1.11), and for several years it was assumed that this was another fort connected with Augustus' campaigns east of the Rhine, an occupation cut short in dramatic fashion when three legions under P. Quinctilius Varus were annihilated in the Teutoburg forest in AD 9.[109] Both the nature of the earth-and-timber fortifications, and the regular layout of the timber buildings within, looked not substantially different from those of Augustan forts which had been excavated elsewhere east of the Rhine, at Haltern, Oberaden, Anreppen and elsewhere.[110] But there was a puzzle: there were significant quantities at Waldgirmes of native, Germanic pottery types (which are non-existent in the other Augustan forts) – not what one would expect of a military base occupied by the Roman army with its efficient mechanisms of supply. Then, at the centre of the site, where the excavators expected to uncover a timber military *principia* of Augustan type, they found to their surprise the stone footings of a forum, the earliest building to make use of stone in Germany.[111] Dio, writing in the early third century AD, had stated how everything was so peaceful in this new tract of Roman territory that 'cities were being founded; the barbarians were adapting themselves to Roman civilization, establishing centres for trade, and coming together in peaceful assemblies';[112] but nobody had taken the statement seriously. Now it is clear that at least one town *was* being founded, and that it was being built for the native inhabitants by the army:

the regular layout, the plans of the buildings and the type of defences at Waldgirmes all betoken military involvement, and there is even a temporary camp alongside the settlement to the east where the soldiers clearly bivouacked while they were constructing the fledgling town.[113] Although this example is in Germany and not in Britain, and of Augustan rather than Julio-Claudian date, there is no reason why just such a scenario was not a commonplace also in Britain, where the local population, whether élite or otherwise, did not have the technical know-how to construct buildings in the Roman manner; and if that was true of timber buildings, it becomes even more manifest when applied to stone buildings, especially sophisticated stone structures like bath-houses, which needed heating engineers and hydraulic experts to make sure that such buildings were properly constructed and could function.[114] In the early years of Roman Britain that expertise is likely to have been supplied by the army.

The second relevant discovery comes from London. Between 1999 and 2003, an excavation at Plantation Place just to the south-east of the Roman forum discovered what is clearly the north-east corner of a Roman fort (Fig. 1.12).[115] It was defended by double ditches, between 1.3 m and 1.9 m deep, and behind it was a rampart approximately 7 m wide, which astonishingly at one point survived up to 0.73 m high. The external face was made up of turf blocks reinforced by timber uprights set in a base plate, and the core was a mixture of turf blocks, brick-earth and reused mud-bricks, many of them burnt. The core was strengthened by timber strapping, of which up to three layers survived; the timbers had been extensively charred before re-use in the rampart. Set into the back of the northern rampart was a small rectangular building (8 m by 6 m) with hearths, plausibly interpreted as a cookhouse; a cellar (5 m by 3 m, and 1 m deep) lay at the north-east angle of the rampart, probably under a corner tower of which evidence for large posts and base-plates were recovered. Inside the rampart was a poorly-laid *intervallum* road, lined on the south side with buildings severely truncated by later activity, but of which a small granary, recognizable by its longitudinal internal sleeper walls, and a latrine pit at the north-east corner, were identified. The military character of the site is abundantly clear – the double-ditch system, the timber strapping of the rampart, identified buildings (granary, latrine, cookhouse) of typically military type, and the numerous military objects found, one of the largest assemblages of military small finds from Roman London. The fort overlay two phases of timber buildings which had been destroyed in a single conflagration, clearly that caused by the Boudican rebels in AD 60/1. The fact that the fort rampart had made use of charred timbers and burnt mud-brick, presumably derived from the debris left after this attack, indicates that this fort was built in the immediate aftermath of the Boudican assault. There is little secure dating evidence to indicate how long the fort remained in use, but the excavators think that it may have been in operation for as little as a year or two, and certainly not beyond AD 70, although it was kept in 'mothballs' for some time afterwards; but by AD 85, when it was already in disrepair, the fort was completely levelled in preparation for the urban re-development of this part of the city. It lay on the fringes of the known pre-Boudican settlement, and interestingly its northern ditches cut through the major east–west road known from both the pre- and post-AD 60 urban plan. The fort's size can only be guessed at present; observation derived from earlier excavations on nearby sites suggests that it might have covered about two-and-a-half acres (*c.* 1 ha).

It used to be thought that London took time to recover from the Boudican destruction,[116] but the evidence of massive quay-building, datable to AD 63/4, at Regis House on the then bank of the Thames, immediately upstream from the Roman bridge,[117] and the equally recent discovery of bucket-chain water-lifting devices, one of which comes from a well dated dendrochronologically to AD 63 but which had gone out of use by AD 70,[118] make it clear that rebuilding of Londinium was not long delayed after AD 60/1. Indeed the find-spot of the water-lifting mechanisms, so close to the long-known Cheapside baths, might indicate that the Cheapside baths are themselves of Neronian date rather than Flavian as usually claimed; another example of a bucket chain was in fact found in the excavation of the latter building in 1955 but was not recognized for what it was at the time. Other prompt post-Boudican activity is indicated by timbers on a nearby site in Cheapside, excavated in 1990, which were felled in AD 62, and a timber soakaway at 1, Poultry, made from a tree cut down in the winter of AD 61/2.[119] At the Regis House quayside of AD 63/4, the discovery of scale armour (*lorica squamata*) and parts of a leather tent (and tent pegs) strongly suggested to the excavators that military labour had been employed in its construction, a conclusion further strengthened by a branded mark on one of the quayside beams possibly recording an auxiliary unit of Thracians.[120] The conclusion must surely be that the Plantation Place fort was built not to provide a military stranglehold on a potentially rebellious urban population,[121] but rather as a sign of Rome's determination that it meant business, and that urban reconstruction as soon as possible after 61 was its official policy: the army was called in as a practical step to help rebuild the shattered city.

We have come rather a long way from civilian urban defences, but the journey is a salutary one, since distinguishing military from non-military ditches and accompanying ramparts (if they survive) is no easy task. There is no physical difference between the two: a Roman 'defensive' ditch, whether built by the army around a fort or built by an urban community out of pride rather than military necessity, is generally V-shaped; both sometimes have a cleaning-out slot, the so-called 'ankle-breaker', in the bottom.[122] The early urban defences we have been considering, however, including those at Colchester, Winchester, Verulamium (in both first- and mid-second-century phases) and Cirencester, have only a single ditch (and that is normal also in the late-second-century urban circuits as well, at least in the initial phase[123]), whereas military forts (but not temporary camps) can have either one or two (or more) ditches.[124] So whereas two ditches or more is likely in the early Empire to indicate a military post, a single-ditched enclosure can be either civilian or military. That is why, for example, at Caistor St Edmund, the triple ditches identified from the air to the south and east of the walled perimeter of the later town must be military in character, belonging to an army base which preceded the urban foundation, and not part of an early phase of urban defences as was long assumed.[125]

The Plantation Place fort is unlikely to have been the only military structure in

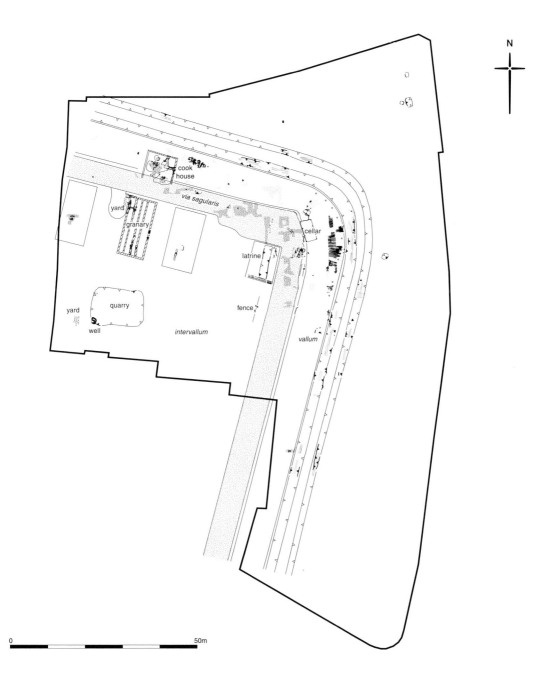

N

cook
house

via sagularis

yard

granary

cellar

latrine

quarry

yard

well   intervallum

fence

vallum

0   50m

Fig. 1.12 London, Plantation Place, plan of the north-east corner of a Roman fort established in the aftermath of the Boudican destruction

London. The likelihood of a Claudian post to guard the bridgehead remains strong; and other ditches discussed above near Aldgate might have had a military function (p. 16).[126] Another site of interest is 7 Bishopsgate (ETA89 on Fig. 1.7, p. 14), where excavation in 1995–6 located a pair of parallel V-ditches 2 m apart over a distance of 50 m; each was originally about 1.4 m deep and 2.5 m wide.[127] The site lay near the centre of an area of localised high ground on Cornhill, and both that location and the presence of double ditches suggest that the features formed part of another short-lived fort; but quite when in the first century it was built is unclear. The ditches had a very short life, and after backfill *c.* AD 70, a road was laid out immediately to the north. That would suggest they might belong to the 60s. If so, there may have been more than one fort in London in the aftermath of Boudica's revolt; alternatively the likely military post on Cornhill predates that event. The ditches there have nothing to do with the wider and later one at Baltic House discussed above, which, if extended on the same alignment, would have passed to the north of 7 Bishopsgate; the single ditch at Baltic House, as suggested above, may have been civilian rather than military, and formed part of the urban defences around London in the later first century AD (pp. 15–16).

If the army did indeed play a major part in building urban infrastructure in Britain in the first century AD, that might also go a long way towards explaining the plentiful amounts of military small finds found in first-century contexts at many of them. In the 1960s and 1970s, when the first evidence was found for major fortresses lying beneath towns like Gloucester, Exeter and Lincoln, it became fashionable to imagine forts below nearly all Romano-British towns, even if structural evidence was wanting. That many towns in Britain had a military origin, in the sense that forts were established on the site first, and a town only developed after the military phase was over, is undeniable;[128] but not everywhere where a lost piece of military equipment has been found need have had a fort – the presence of soldiers deployed on urban foundation programmes is an alternative explanation.

This is especially likely to be the case at those towns which were being established in areas which lay within client kingdoms. From Rome's perspective, one of the advantages of establishing a pro-Roman client kingdom was that it freed up troops to deal with the hostile parts of the new province; unless, therefore, a client king needed military assistance, as happened with the Iceni in AD 47, or with Cartimandua of the Brigantes on more than one occasion, soldiers are unlikely to have been deployed within the boundaries of a client kingdom on a military basis.[129] Take Togidubnus' kingdom, for example. Michael Fulford entertained in the early 1990s the possibility that a military fortress existed beneath Silchester, interpreting the earliest timber building there, under the later stone forum, as part of a military *principia,* and seeing the plentiful military finds from Silchester as further proof of military occupation.[130] But that early timber building has now more plausibly been identified as part of the first timber forum/basilica of the new town,[131] and one explanation for the military equipment is that it was lost by soldiers who were deputed there to help Togidubnus build his new town for him. At Winchester, also part of Togidubnus' kingdom but where Claudian or Neronian activity is scarce, what was thought in the 1970s to be part of a possible small fort is now discounted as being sited in a most improbable low-lying position;[132] Winchester may not have had a fort at all. And at Chichester, likely on the basis of the Fishbourne palace, the Neptune and Minerva inscription, and the name of the later *civitas* centred there ('*Regini*' or '*Regnenses*', i.e. 'people of the [client] kingdom')[133] to have been Togidubnus' main base of operations, has the military phase been correctly interpreted? Could what are taken to have been military buildings in the 40s under Chichester[134] have been precocious urban activity within the client kingdom (as at Silchester), encouraged by the Roman government and carried out by the army, and could the military ditches to the east of the 'town' belong to the camp where the soldiers were bivouacked, comparable to the situation at Waldgirmes forty years earlier? Equally, if there really was no fort at Verulamium in the Claudian period, as is now the orthodox view,[135] possibly because here too there was a short-lived client-kingdom until *c.* AD 55,[136] is the early military equipment found in the town explicable by the presence of soldiers who were deployed to lay out the rectangular timber buildings of the early town – buildings which struck Sheppard Frere as having been built with the help of the army?

Urban defences and civic status

In the first century AD, and for most of the second century, it was the exception, not the rule, for the towns of Britain to be defended. Present evidence suggests that there were town walls of stone at Colchester, Lincoln, Gloucester and, shortly before the end of the second century, also at London. Earth ramparts and timber breastworks, which would have needed constant maintenance, were present at Verulamium, Winchester and probably London, and less certainly at Silchester, during the first century, and at Verulamium (a new circuit) and Cirencester by the mid-second century; the last two also had imposing gates of stone probably provided at the same period. Wroxeter may also have had earth defences by the mid-second century. All the rest, as far as we know, are likely to have lacked such defences. How do we explain the distinction, both between those which had defences at this period and those which did not, and between those with stone defences on the one hand and earth ramparts on the other?

The stone walls we have already explained (pp. 3–4 and 6): Colchester first, and then Lincoln and Gloucester, acquired and maintained stone walls because they were proudly displaying their status as *coloniae*, which marked them out as special in the urban landscape of first-century Britain. Earth defences were clearly less prestigious, but the coincidence of their presence at Verulamium and the chance record in Tacitus that this very town was a '*municipium*', strongly suggest that earth defences were themselves symbolic in Britain of chartered status, whether of a grant of *ius Latii* or of the title *municipium*. Their alleged presence at Silchester, Chichester and Winchester has been explained as being due to the fact that all three lay within Togidubnus' kingdom; but the re-assignment of both the Inner and Outer Earthworks to the Iron Age leaves Silchester with only one short stretch of putative ditch as a possible early urban defence, not enough from which to draw firm conclusions.[137] The evidence at Chichester is also exiguous; and the defences of Winchester, as we have seen, may well post-date Togidubnus' death and the break-up of his kingdom. If that is so, Winchester might have been a rather different case: not promotion for an existing town as a reward for commendable effort towards urban development, as elsewhere, but a brand-new town, designated a 'municipium' ex novo, which was created in the Flavian period when the new civitas of the Belgae was being formed: major engineering works were carried out on the river Itchen to make space for a sizable town (which in time grew to be the fifth largest in Roman Britain), and as a mark of its elevated status as a 'municipium', urban defences of earth were erected.[138] At Verulamium, if the grant of municipal status was in fact Flavian and not Claudian, as I have argued above (pp. 8–10), it too may have been elevated at the same time, probably during Vespasian's reign. It was Vespasian who made a wholesale grant of the ius Latii to the towns of Spain in AD 73/4:[139] in Britain, a much newer province and consequently much more underdeveloped, his grants of municipal status will have been more restrained. If Togidubnus did not die until c. AD 80 rather than earlier, the grant at Winchester will have come from Titus or Domitian, not Vespasian, because the status would only have been awarded to towns included within the Roman provincia. Whether Chichester can be included in this list of Flavian grants of ius Latii as municipia is much more doubtful, not least because, as we have seen (pp. 13–14), unequivocal evidence for early urban defences has not been found.[140]

London may also have been promoted around the same time. The status of London has been much discussed: the view of Francis Haverfield, that it was a conventus civium Romanorum, has had its adherents over the years, and has most recently been forcefully re-stated by Wilkes;[141] but such associations were normally found in communities where the 'Roman' element in the population needed separate identification (and juridical status) from the rest. That is why they were particularly frequent in the late Republican period, and why they continued in the Empire in the Greek East, where groups of Roman citizens demanded a separate identity from the self-governing Greek poleis in which they found themselves;[142] but in the context of late first-century London, a cosmopolitan town without a need to distinguish a 'Roman' element in the community from anyone else, it seems more questionable. There is no reason in theory why London should have been different from anywhere else with aspirations to urban advancement, in having to go through the usual stages of promotion, first to that of 'municipium', and subsequently to the rank of colonia. Is there, however, any archaeological evidence to support such promotions?

If earth defences were a mark of 'municipium' status in Britain, could the Baltic House ditch, inside the line later taken by the city wall yet roughly parallel with it, be part of just such a defensive circuit? If it was, London's promotion to municipal status may also have been Vespasianic, judging from the date at which the Baltic House ditch was dug, viz. in the early Flavian period. By Hadrianic times, however, the ditch at Baltic House had been filled in, and the excavators were puzzled to explain why, when London did not appear thereafter to have any further defences until the later second century.[143] Roger Tomlin, in Chapter Two below (pp. 49–64), tentatively suggests on the basis of fragmentary epigraphic evidence that Londinium may have been promoted to the rank of *colonia* by Hadrian. On archaeological grounds alone, I would argue that colonial rank had certainly been achieved by the 180s, since I do not think that the stone walls of London are explicable in any other way – as with the walls of Colchester, Lincoln and Gloucester, the stone defences of London must surely have been intended to betoken proudly that the city had already become a *colonia*. The attempt to explain these walls as a product of the late second-century 'crisis',[144] built in stone when the rest of the British towns received earthworks, is ludicrous – not only does the careful workmanship as well as the sheer scale of the enceinte suggest that this was not a hurried project executed in just four years, but the deliberate decision also to leave the riverfront undefended makes a military function for the walls (defending the city against expected barbarian attack) untenable. If colonial promotion was indeed granted by Hadrian, and the walls were not begun until the 180s, the gap of 50 years while the city got its act together is not inconceivable, especially if the project had dragged on for years and that parts had in fact been begun before the 180s.

There is also one piece of fascinating archaeological evidence which might lend support to the argument from epigraphy for the Hadrianic date of London's promotion to colonial rank; it also can explain the excavators' puzzlement as to why the Baltic House defensive ditch was filled in (and its accompanying defensive bank probably pushed into it) as early as the 120s. At several places along the line of the later stone wall, and partly underlying it, a broad, shallow ditch, described as a boundary ditch, has been detected (pp. 16–17). In two sections of it at least, it can with good reason be dated to the Hadrianic period.[145] Surely this ditch is the demarcation line dug by the inhabitants of London at the time of the city's promotion to the rank of *colonia*, indicating where the line of their new, proud defences were to be built; at the same time the old defences were flattened, and the city expanded, in time, over their course. The fact that Londoners did not get around to building the new enceinte for perhaps another 50 years is immaterial – Trier, promoted to the rank of *colonia* by the mid-first century at least, had to wait well over a century for its girdle of walls.[146] So the tentative conclusion from the archaeological evidence is that Londinium was made a *municipium* in the first century, probably under the Flavians, and promoted to *colonia* in the first half of the second century, probably under Hadrian. If that is right, the magnificent new forum, one of the most imposing Roman buildings north of the Alps, started before promotion, was (when finally completed) a triumphant vindication that colonial status was within Londinium's grasp;[147] the status symbol of stone walls, not surprisingly perhaps, was a project not completed until some decades later.

No other cities can be suggested as candidates for colonial status in the second century, as York may not have received its promotion until the early third century; but we might expect this town also to have been granted municipal rank before it was advanced to that of *colonia* – whether surrounded at the time by an earth rampart preceding the later stone phase, or on a different circuit, is unknown.[148] Elsewhere, if earth defences are symbolic of promotion to the rank of '*municipium*', as here suggested, it is interesting that Verulamium, already so promoted, built a further circuit of earth defences in the Antonine period, and Cirencester, second-largest of Romano-British towns in terms of defended area, also with Antonine defences, may have likewise been promoted to the rank of *'municipium'*,[149] perhaps under Hadrian or Antoninus Pius. Large stone gates with projecting semicircular towers at both Verulamium and Cirencester, surely also status symbols, likewise distinguish these places from what was happening elsewhere in Britain at the same time – a further argument for thinking they had elevated urban status as *'municipia'*. Wroxeter may have had the same rank. The defences there are ill-dated; but the suspicion that there was an earlier defensive circuit preceding the final one strengthens the notion that this place, too, might have been promoted to the status of *'municipium'* by the mid-second century. That promotion, if real, is unlikely to have been as early as AD 129/30, when Wroxeter's forum and basilica were completed, if we are to take the famous forum inscription at face value: for there the town styles itself as *civitas Cornoviorum*,[150] not as *municipium Aelium Cornoviorum* or similar.[151]

   Much of the above is, of course, highly speculative. The basic premise that an earthwork defence was itself a symbol of civic status is hypothetical; nor is it a hypothesis that finds parallels in contemporary Continental practice, where no fixed pattern emerges in the protection of *municipia*,[152] and where urban ramparts of earth, as far as we know, are rare at any period.[153] If the above suggestions are right, Britain was clearly following its own rules, at least where *'municipia'* were concerned; but if the different defensive treatment of individual towns was due to differing civic status, it may help to explain some of the anomalies which have made Romano-British defences such a contentious topic over the years. To that debate the honorand of this volume has made an outstanding contribution; indeed without his discovery of the '1955 ditch' at Verulamium, this essay would, quite simply, never have been written at all.

Acknowledgements

I am very grateful to Professor Lawrence Keppie and Dr John Peter Wild for reading this chapter in typescript and for their characteristically constructive suggestions for its improvement. As already noted on page xxix, Chiz Harward and Leslie Dunwoodie most generously gave permission to publish here Fig. 1.12 in advance of their own publication, and warmest thanks are due to them too.

Notes

1. In a British context, cf. the discussion of Wacher 1995, 15–32, but the distinction there made between 'Roman'-status *municipia* and Latin ones (18) is no longer valid, as the Tabula Siarensis from Spain now makes it certain that *municipia civium Romanorum* only existed in Italy, not in the provinces: see Gonzalez 1984 and 1987.
2. E.g. Laurence 2001, 88 ('this emphasis on the development of a legalistic hierarchy confines the debate and does not represent the nomenclature used'); Creighton 2006, 75–6.
3. Cf. especially Teutsch 1962; Gascou 1972; and Gascou 1982a and b.

4. Capitolium, AD 166/9: *CIL* VIII.1471; 15513–14; Khanoussi and Maurin 2000, 87–90, nos 31–2. Theatre, AD 168/9: *CIL* VIII.26528; 26606 = *ILS* 9364; Khanoussi and Maurin 2000, 90–2, no. 33.

5. Cf. Gascou 1982a, 210–11 (*municipium Septimium Aurelium liberum*: *CIL* VIII.26539); 1982b, 274–5 (*respublica coloniae Liciniae Septimiae Aureliae Alexandrianae Thuggae*: *CIL* VIII.1487 = *ILS* 541). For a selection of key inscriptions still at Dougga, see now very accessibly Khanoussi and Maurin 2000.

6. See now most conveniently Hurst 1999a, for an up-to-date assessment.

7. Courteault 1921; for a photograph Wacher 1995, 178, fig. 80; Ottaway 2004, 84, fig. 43.

8. Tacitus, *Annales* XIV.33: *eadem clades municipio Verulamio fuit.*

9. For this distinction, Sherwin-White 1973, 255; Millar 1992, 405–06.

10. Millar 1992, 398–400 and 403–07.

11. See note 8; the passage comes immediately after that noting London as not being a *colonia.*

12. Galsterer-Kröll 1973.

13. Cf. Frere 1984, especially 68–72; 1999, 243–4.

14. R. E. M. Wheeler, in Hull 1958, 62–3, dated them 'not earlier than the Antonine period', and probably of late second-century date.

15. Crummy 1984, 14–16; and see next note.

16. Crummy 1992, 14–18; cf. also the important, detailed review of the evidence in Crummy 1999, 95–8; and Crummy 2003.

17. Crummy 1997, 86; 1999, 98 ('the argument that wall and bank were built as one is unsustainable'); 2003, 50–2 (noting that the dating of a Silvinus stamp on a piece of samian found in a construction level for the wall, which could be as early as AD 65, is 'more likely to be early to mid-Flavian' [52]). The latter would make the date for the wall closer to AD 70/85 than Neronian.

18. Tacitus, *Annales* XIV.31.5: *in coloniam Camulodunum*; the exact titulature is recorded on *ILS* 2740 (Rome): Wacher 1995, 126, fig. 51; Crummy 1997, 53.

19. Cf. Esmonde Cleary 2003, 72–4, with references, and discussion on 77–9: cf. 78: 'the association [*sc.* of town walls] with superior [civic] status is indisputable'. For Mérida's walls, Richmond 1930 has still not been superseded.

20. Cf. Precht 1983; Hellenkemper 1983 (but the Claudian date for the walls at Cologne is now being questioned: cf. Wilson and Creighton 1999, 19–20).

21. Crummy 1999, 95–100.

22. Cf. Crummy 1999, 99–100: 'the absence of defences at Colchester in 60 betrays an ill-founded confidence and complacency on the part of the Roman administration. The cost of this arrogance must have brought about a radical change of policy.' That Colchester was undefended in AD 60 is known both from archaeological evidence and from Tacitus' statement (*Annales* XIV.32), *neque fossam aut vallum praeduxerunt*: 'they had constructed neither ditch nor rampart'. As will become clear from this chapter (cf. especially pp. 29–32 below), I fundamentally disagree with Crummy's contention (1999, 99) that 'in time, early defensive ditches will be recognized in many other places, to the extent that it will become apparent that this was the normal state of affairs after 60/61'.

23. Jones 1980, especially 51–2.

24. So Jones 1980, 51. Experience at Vindolanda, where a simulated Turf Wall milecastle rampart and timber gate were built in the 1970s, and indeed the defences at the Lunt fort near Coventry, have shown that major refurbishment of earth and timber defences is needed after a maximum interval of thirty years.

25. Henderson 1984, 17–21; 1988, 115–18.
26. Hurst 1986; 1988, especially 54–6; and 1999b, especially 114–15.
27. *CIL* VI.3346.
28. M. Hassall in Hassall and Hurst 1999, 181–5; for an opposing view, H. R. Hurst, ibid. 186–9. Lincoln, probably also founded during Domitian's reign, might have experienced exactly the same thing: but no inscriptions survive which give *Lindum*'s full official titles.
29. RCHME 1962, 49 with figs 38–9; Ottaway 1999, 145; 2004, 90, with fig. 4 on 92.
30. Wacher 1998; Frere 1999, 244–6.
31. Maloney 1983, 96–104 is the most detailed recent discussion, with full reference to earlier bibliography; for the estimates of materials, Marsden 1980, 126–7.
32. Grimes 1968, 50–1.
33. Marsden 1970, 2–6; 1980, 126.
34. Frere 1983, 44–9. The intriguing possibility has been suggested to me that the Verulamium ditch was only meant to be a ditch to mark the *pomerium* and was not accompanied by a bank. Demarcation ditches in Roman times, however, seem to have been flat-bottomed (as with the Vallum of Hadrian's Wall) or shallow and U-shaped (as in London: see pp. 16–17 below); I know of no parallel with a V-shaped ('military') ditch without accompanying rampart (the latter in any case provides a useful way of disposing of the spoil).
35. Aitken 1960.
36. Frere 1983, 47.
37. Frere 1983, 17–19 and 75–82 for one of the arches, there dated to *c.* 275/80. The first-century defences were neglected from towards the end of the Hadrianic period or a little later (*c.* 135/45), when the ditch began to silt up, and the rampart was demolished into the ditch soon after (AD 150/70): Frere 1983, 45.
38. Tacitus, *Annales* XIV.33. A 'probably Claudian' date for these early defences represents Sheppard Frere's latest thinking on the subject: Frere 1999, 241. If there really was a client kingdom until *c.* AD 55 centred on Verulamium, as has been suggested (see pp. 23 and 29), the notion of a *municipium* in the Claudian period is ruled out, since the settlement would have lain outside the *provincia*.
39. Alföldy 1974, 81–2, 87–93; Fischer 2002, 66–9, 78–83, 85–7.
40. Rivet 1964, 65; see also the discussion by Wacher 1995, 18, 221–2 and 226–7.
41. Cf. Frere 1985, 36: 'The early boundary at Verulamium was itself a symbol of rank . . . until the crises of the late 2nd and of the 3rd centuries urban defences were a mark of rank except in frontier regions, where special dispensation was no doubt given.' For the suggestion that the early defences were connected with Verulamium's chartered status as a *municipium*, cf. Frere 1964, 65 and 80; and in general Frere 1999, 241: 'such provision [*sc.* of defences] seems (with a few easily understood exceptions) to have been a privilege of chartered cities during the first two centuries'.
42. Niblett 1993, 85; 2001, 72.
43. Niblett 1993, 86; 2001, 69–71.
44. Cf. Frere 1985, 35: 'at the time of erection it was certainly the largest building in Roman Britain'. Cf. Frere 1983, 59–72 for a full discussion of this complex.
45. Frere 1983, 17–19.
46. Current knowledge of early Roman Winchester is summarized by Qualmann 1993, Wacher 1995, 291–5, and Beaumont James 1997, 27–32.
47. Biddle 1975b, 110; for the later date, Hartley 1983, 87 and 92. Frere 1984, 66, reports (pers. comm.) that Martin Biddle's *terminus post quem* for the walls was '*c.* AD 80'.

48. E.g. evidence from The Brooks, in the north-east sector of the enlarged Roman town, suggests that the major period of laying out the town dates from the Flavian period with roads lined with timber box-drains: Zant 1993, 50–2.
49. Wacher 1995, 291–3.
50. Boon 1969.
51. Wacher 1995, 274.
52. Boon 1969, 13–14.
53. Fulford 1984, 233; Fulford and Timby 2000, 308 and 546–7; contrast Wacher 1995, 273–4, who following Boon 1969 still wants to allow for the possibility that it was built after AD 43.
54. Cf. note 114 below.
55. Fulford 1984, 37–41 and 83.
56. Wacher 1995, 261 assumes that it was, on insufficient evidence; cf. 265, more cautiously. For a helpful, up-to-date survey of what is known about early ditches at Chichester, cf. Magilton 2003, 159–61.
57. Down 1988, 10–12; cf. also note 134 below.
58. Cf. the sensibly cautious discussion of Manning 2002, 30; cf. also Manley and Rudkin 2005, 143–4. It is noteworthy that Chichester is not reckoned to be either a possible fortress or a supply base on the map of Julio-Claudian military sites presented in Frere 1999, 58.
59. Down and Rule 1971, 67; Down 1981, 84; Down 1988, 14; as recorded these ditches were between 4.5 m and 5.2 m wide and about 2 m deep, but Magilton 2003, 159–60 doubts whether both ditches were part of the same feature.
60. The later Roman defences of Chichester have now been shown to belong to the third century, and probably the late third century (as at Canterbury), and both stone wall and defensive bank were contemporary: J. R. Magilton in Down and Magilton 1993, 108–9; Magilton 2003, 162–6.
61. Down 1988, 14; Down 1989, 59–61. The ditch is considered to be of Iron Age date in Manley and Rudkin 2005, 143 with fig. 271, and in Magilton 2003, 161 (who also discusses the ditch outside the west defences: see below).
62. Howe 2002, 6–16.
63. So Howe 2002, 9.
64. Chapman and Johnson 1973, 1–7 and 71–3; Rivière and Thomas 1987, 13–17.
65. Rivière and Thomas 1987, 15.
66. Maloney 1983, 97 with 100, fig. 95.
67. Wacher 1995, 97.
68. Maloney 1983, 97.
69. Crosswall: unpublished (cf. Maloney 1983, 87). Other probable sightings of this ditch have occurred at 1 Crutched Friars (Merrifield 1965, 291, no. 336), 85 London Wall (Sankey and Stevenson 1991, 117–18) and opposite 57 London Wall (unpublished, but cf. Butler 2001, 46).
70. Butler 2001, 45–7.
71. Howe and Lakin 2004, 25–41 and 53–9.
72. The western boundary of the first- and early second-century city is usually drawn as a straight line in a north-north-east to south-south-west direction, from the south-west corner of the Cripplegate fort to the Thames; cf. (for example) Maloney 1983, 96, fig. 92; Watson 1998, 12–14, fig. 2; Watson 2003, 8, fig. 6 ('city boundary prior to construction of [city] wall').
73. Cf. Frere 1983, 35–6.

74. Niblett 2001, 84

75. Holbrook 1998, 94–6.

76. Brown and McWhirr 1967, 190–1; Wacher and McWhirr 1982, 54–5.

77. Holbrook 1998, 96.

78. ibid. 44; J. S. Wacher, in ibid. 45–6.

79. Kenyon 1938, 176–8.

80. Webster 2002, 8, fig. 1.7 (= Fig. 1.10 here).

81. As well seen in, e.g., the plan in White and Barker 1998, 77, fig. 39.

82. So, for example, Frere and St Joseph 1983, 165. Wacher, however, thinks that this ditch was not part of a defence but that it 'may be no more than an early water course, or perhaps attempts to canalise the flow' of the Bell Brook (1995, 369). Nevertheless his plan of Wroxeter (364, fig. 165) clearly marks this line as 'early town defences'.

83. E.g. White and Barker 1998, 77.

84. E.g. Wacher 1995, 371.

85. The reading Cogidubnus is in most Tacitean manuscripts, but the reading of one, with an initial T for the king's name, is now preferred: Murgia 1977, 339; Tomlin 1997; Birley 2005, 467; and now Coates 2005.

86. For a brief summary of the salient facts, Birley 2005, 466–8, with references. The recent account of Russell 2006, 33–43, is untrustworthy: he equates Togidubnus with the Togidumnus who opposed the Claudian invasion (and whom most believed was killed in it), and also thinks that one of Togidubnus' relatives was Sallustius Lucullus, governor of Britain under Domitian (Suetonius, *Dom.* 10.2-3, not *RIB* 2334*, which is certainly [*pace* Russell] a *falsum*); this is based on Russell's assumption (45–54) that the 'Lucullus son of Amminius' on *RIB* 90 was the same man, and that Amminius was the same as the Adminius who fled to Rome in AD 40! So he makes Sallustius Lucullus, *inter alia* senator and governor of Britain, a Briton; in fact he comes from Italian stock (Birley 2005, 95–9).

87. Tacitus, *Agricola* 14: *is ad nostram usque memoriam fidissimus mansit*. Tacitus may have served in Britain as military tribune *c.* 77/8 (Birley 2005, 281), in which case he could say this from personal experience.

88. So Bogaers 1979, 254, questioning the conclusion of Barrett 1979 that [T]ogidubnus died in the mid-60s under Nero. Birley 2005, 468 thinks that he probably died in the late 70s, after the construction of Fishbourne but not long after.

89. Tomlin 1997.

90. Cunliffe 1971a, 153; 1971b, 169.

91. Cunliffe has now revised this view (1998, 109), and thinks Togidubnus may have died around AD 80.

92. Down 1988, 21–7; Russell 2006, 68–74.

93. *RIB* 91: cf. Barrett 1979, 239–42; Bogaers 1979, 254.

94. Fulford and Timby 2000, 37–44 and 565–9. I find unconvincing Creighton's recent suggestion (2006, 67–8) that this might belong before AD 43.

95. Fulford 1989, 13–27 and 179–83.

96. Fulford and Timby 2000, 44–58 and 569–73. For a full discussion of this phase of Silchester's development, cf. Fulford 2003.

97. Cf. Zant 1993, 5 and 50–2. Biddle 1975a, 111, speaks of a 'massive intensification of activity' in the Flavian period, including the defences and the first full phase of urbanization.

98. Inscription: Cunliffe and Davenport 1988, 132, no. Mi2 with pl. LXV; proposed link with Togidubnus: Henig 1999. Archaeological dating of the baths/temple: Cunliffe and

Davenport 1988, 65. Neronian or early Flavian date for the temple (which would allow for the possibility of Togidubnus as patron): Blagg 1979.

99. Wacher 1995, 261 and 293, suggesting the creation of a pro-Vespasianic stronghold in Togidubnus' kingdom. Frere 1999, 241, also suggests that early defences at Silchester, Winchester and Chichester are explicable because they lay inside [T]ogidubnus' kingdom 'where normal rules did not apply'.

100. See notes 47, 97 and 138.

101. This form of the name derives from a silver coin found in Norfolk in 1999: see Chadburn 2006.

102. Cf. below, note 136.

103. Cf. the distribution map of Julio-Claudian forts in Frere 1999, 58: if we remove a fort from Verulamium (see note 135), the only one within the surrounding area is at Little Brickhill 25 miles to the north-west, where aerial photography suggests a two-phase fort (Branigan 1985, 35–7).

104. There have of course been more recent discoveries of Iron Age rectangular buildings in Britain, notably at Skeleton Green (Partridge 1981, 37–40), but they remain extremely rare.

105. Frere 1972, 11.

106. Millett 1990, 69–74.

107. Blagg 1980.

108. Millett 1990, 88–91.

109. On Waldgirmes, see most recently Becker and Rasbach 2003, Becker 2003 and von Schnurbein 2003, with full earlier bibliography.

110. Cf. Kühlborn 1995 for a convenient summary

111. Becker and Köhler 2001.

112. Dio LVI.18.2.

113. For a completely different interpretation of this site, which I think implausible, cf. Creighton 2006, 91. He thinks that the town was created by a local aristocratic élite: 'perhaps the inspiration for the form of the town came from some of the founders who may have spent time as Roman auxiliaries . . . Their model of nucleation was coming from the dense settlements of Roman troops called forts . . .'. In my view the similarity of the layout of the town at Waldgirmes to a Roman fort is, quite simply, because it was built by the army (Creighton does not mention the presence of an adjacent temporary camp).

114. This would surely have included early examples like the pre- (or immediately post-) Boudican baths at Verulamium (Niblett 2001, 65), the baths at Silchester, and the Huggin Hill baths in London of *c.* 75/80 (cf. N. C. W. Bateman, in Watson 1998, 48: 'the sophistication and precision of the design indicates a military surveyor' – a conclusion unnecessarily, I think, challenged by Creighton 2006, 96). The Silchester building is often dated to the Neronian period (which it may well be: see above p. 12, and most recently Fulford and Timby 2000, 568) on the basis of a tile-stamp bearing Nero's name, but the tile comes only from the cess-pit of the baths' latrine, and was not from a structural context (*RIB* II.2482.2). Nevertheless the discovery at Silchester of Neronian stamps made in a tilery in imperial ownership (probably nearby) during Nero's reign – further examples have been found in the basilica excavations as well (*RIB* II.2482.3–5; Fulford and Timby 2000, 118 with fig. 95) – again points to official government assistance in urban development at this time, presumably when it was still part of Togidubnus' client-kingdom and therefore not technically within the Roman province of Britannia (contrast Frere 1999, 283 with n. 1, who suggests that the tile-stamps

indicate that Silchester formed part of the imperial *patrimonium* at the time, after its confiscation from, or the elimination of, a *princeps* of the Atrebates; and Fulford and Timby 2000, 568, who think that the tiles cannot be taken as evidence of support for [C]ogidubnus, because Nero's track record points to a preferred policy of confiscating client kingdoms rather than assisting projects within them).

115. The material in this paragraph is based on unpublished information kindly supplied by Chiz Harward and Leslie Dunwoodie of MoLAS, whom I thank most warmly for discussing this excavation with me, and generously allowing me to mention it here in advance of their own publication: see Dunwoodie, Harward and Pitt, forthcoming. For an early interim report, Brigham 2001 (interpreting the defences as urban); and there are brief notes on the excavation in *Britannia* 32 (2001), 365–6; 33 (2002), 336; and 34 (2003), 342.

116. E.g. Marsden 1980, 36; Perring and Roskams 1991, 119 ('The crisis of confidence which followed the rebellion and the consequent restriction in the flow of capital into the province meant that even prime commercial sites . . .were not built on for a decade.').

117. Brigham, Watson and Tyers 1996, 35–6.

118. *Britannia* 33 (2002), 327–31; full report in Blair *et al.* 2006.

119. Cheapside: Milne 1995, 48. No. 1 Poultry: Dunwoodie 2004, 29–30.

120. *Britannia* 27 (1996), 449.

121. Too much emphasis should not, I think, be placed on the fact that its northern ditches cut an east–west street (of what further west is certainly a major artery), which some might think is a deliberate element of military suppression and aggression (cf. Suetonius Paullinus' reputation for this in the aftermath of AD 61 until his recall: Tacitus, *Annales* XIV.38–9), but there may have been good reasons for siting the fort where it was, and a road can always deviate if necessary.

122. But of course the sharpness of the 'V' depended also on the nature of the subsoil through which the ditch was being cut. Cf. in general Johnson 1983, 45–52 (*fossae fastigatae*: the *fossa Punica* does not concern us here); for camp ditches, see also Welfare and Swan 1995, 17–18. For a possible explanation of the close relationship between urban and military defences, see note 138 below.

123. There are some apparent exceptions, but they may be late Roman additions: e.g. Wroxeter appears to have had double ditches, at least in part (Wacher 1995, 371), at what period is uncertain; and a triple ditch system has been claimed at Dorchester, but the original circuit had one 'or possibly two' ditches (ibid. 328). The outer ditch at Caerwent is often assumed to date from the fourth century (ibid. 384), but recent re-evaluation of earlier sections has left open the possibility that the outer ditch 'could have been dug at the same time as the wall or even when the rampart was constructed' (Manning 2003, 175). At Silchester Fulford has suggested that there was a double-ditch system, on the basis of results from early excavations (Fulford 1984, 65); if there was a second ditch (at the south gate apparently 20 m from the wall), it may have been a late Roman addition. The double ditches of a small site like Neatham in the late second century point to its probable function as an official *mansio* (Millett and Graham 1986, 157–9; Burnham and Wacher 1990, 269; cf. also note 125 below). The presence of only a single ditch around defended towns, even *coloniae* on the front line of the *limes*, such as Cologne and Xanten (Horn 1987, Abb. 396 and 541), seems to be true of Continental urban defences also in the first and second centuries (Xanten has a second ditch only to strengthen the corners: Precht 1983, 34, fig. 26).

124. Johnson 1983, 48; Welfare and Swan 1995, 17 and passim.

125. Wacher 1995, 250–1; Frere 2005, 319–21. For the earlier view, cf. (e.g.) Frere and St

Joseph 1983, 158. By the same token, I take the small, square, fortified 'station' underlying the later town at Chelmsford as being quasi-military in nature, or at least 'official' and non-urban: erected *c.* AD 80 and levelled in Hadrian's time, this fortification had a triple ditch-system on its south side, and not much within the defences beyond a large *mansio* of timber and adjacent stone baths, the whole being rebuilt in stone (and the baths enlarged) in the second century. This must initially have been an official *mansio* of the *cursus publicus* and therefore run by government; it was not part of a fledgling town, even though one did indeed later develop there (in the second century) around the stone *mansio*: cf. Drury 1988; Wacher 1995, 209–11.

126. Grimes 1968, 183–4 mentions a ditch at St. Bride's Church, Fleet Street, to the west of the City, which he thought military, but its 'broad irregular-U profile' makes its military character far from certain.

127. Sankey 2002, 2–4.

128. For the major towns, cf. most usefully Webster 1988, and for the phenomenon in an Empire-wide context, Keppie 2000a. For military equipment in the towns, mostly discussing later material (and with a different explanation to that offered here), cf. Bishop 1991.

129. Frere 1999, 63 and 84.

130. Fulford 1993, 19–28.

131. Cf. Fulford and Timby 2000, 565–9: for the military finds, G. C. Boon, in ibid., 583–5. For further discussion of this building, Fulford 2003, 99.

132. For the fort proposal, Biddle 1975a, 110 with 107, fig. 2, top; 1975c, 296–7, figs. 10, 11 and 21; but cf. Zant 1993, 50: 'it seems unlikely that a Roman military base would have been erected in such a tactically unsound location'; cf. ibid. 5: 'as yet no conclusive proof of Claudian military activity has been found'.

133. On the name, cf. the discussion of Rivet and Smith 1979, 445–6.

134. Cf. Down 1988, 9, fig. 5, for the distribution pattern of military equipment finds at Chichester; ibid. 10, fig. 7 for 'military-style' timber buildings. Cf. also Down 1978, 139–40 and 290–301, the latter for a catalogue of military pieces found at Chichester. Cf. also the comments of Fulford 2003, 97, noting the irregularities of the buildings, more suggestive of a stores base than a planned fortress; but contrast Magilton 2003, 162, who questions whether these remains are military: he is 'not yet convinced that early Chichester succeeded a military base on the same site'.

135. On the unlikelihood of the existence of a fort, and on the re-interpretation of the 'timber tower' as part of a causeway, see Niblett 1999, 409–11 and, in brief, Niblett 2001, 56–7. Cf. also ibid. 57–8 on the considerable quantities of Roman military equipment in the town, which she explains either as objects of ritual deposition or as owned by native Britons who had chosen to serve in the Roman army: but there is rather a lot to explain it all away in this way.

136. For the apparently pro-Roman attitude of the local élite, and the possibility that the occupant of the Folly Lane burial was a local *princeps* who, briefly, had client-king status, see Niblett 1999, 412 (and in brief Niblett 2001, 60). The case is perhaps strengthened by the apparent absence of forts in the Verulamium district: see note 103 above.

137. Cf. also the scepticism of Esmonde Cleary 2003, 80.

138. Contrast ibid., 80: 'the late first-century earthwork at Winchester remains more of a mystery . . . for the moment the early defences of Winchester will have to be noted but not explained.' That towns could be created fast when there was a political motive and government-driven initiative (and the likely practical help of the army) is shown by

recent evidence from Germany, e.g. at Ladenburg (Wilson 2006, 206–7 with references). It is also possible, if the army played a major role in the early laying-out of towns, at Winchester as elsewhere (as argued above: pp. 23–29), that the close similarity between urban earthworks in the first century and contemporary fort ramparts is explicable in terms of their both being built by the army.

139. Pliny, *NH* III.30: *universae Hispaniae Vespasianus imperator . . . Latium tribuit*: 'the emperor Vespasian gave the Latin right to the whole of Spain'. On this, cf. Sherwin-White 1973, 252 and 360–1, but especially Richardson 1996, 190–210.

140. At none of these places is a Vespasianic grant of *ius Latii* provable. The case at Verulamium rests on the date of the forum inscription (AD 79) and the suggested Flavian date of the first-century defences; but if the forum was completed before the award was made, rather than in celebration of it, promotion to the rank of *municipium* might have been conferred by Titus or Domitian. The case at Winchester rests largely on the date of the defences (*c.* AD 75 or *c.* AD 90?), and the likelihood that a new *civitas* was being created *ex novo* after Togidubnus' death (p. 23); in any case, although earth defences took no time at all to construct by comparison with stone walls, there might still have been delays between the promotion to '*municipium*' and their erection. At Chichester, where first-century urban defences are far from certain, the case is weaker, although this too was being formally incorporated into the Roman province as a new *civitas* after Togidubnus' death; if urban development had advanced far under his guidance, with a classical-style temple to Neptune and Minerva (*RIB* I, 91) and possibly a bath-house (so Down 1988, 42), it might have been a candidate for promotion under Vespasian or one of his sons. Once again a lot hinges on the date of Togidubnus' death (and whether or not it ever had first-century urban defences). The presence of a *collegium fabrorum* there (*RIB* 91) is sometimes cited as confirmation of its status as a *municipium* (e.g. Wilkes 1996, 29), since such organisations were only allowed in places with a municipal charter; but *RIB* 91 was erected when Chichester was still part of a client-kingdom nominally independent of Rome, and 'Roman' labels were not applicable. If early defences did exist at Chichester, they are most likely to be found (on the analogy of Verulamium and probably London) inside the line of the later urban circuit. I have not included Silchester in this list, partly because the precise significance of the fragmentary first-century ditch there is uncertain, and also because, after a precocious start in the 40s, 50s and 60s, Silchester failed to live up to its early promise, and had no stone forum/basilica until Hadrianic times (Fulford and Timby 2000, 573–6): the town may not have been considered worthy of promotion to municipal rank in the first century. The argument that the *collegium peregrinorum* there (*RIB* 69–71) can be taken as evidence of Silchester's municipal rank is rightly by dismissed by Frere and Fulford 2002, 171 with note 12.

141. Haverfield 1911; Wilkes 1996, who suggests (30) that the *conventus* status might have been brought to an end by Hadrian during his visit in AD 122, by a conferral of municipal status as *municipium Aelium*.

142. On *conventus civium Romanorum*, see Sherwin-White 1973, 225–7 and 344–50 (but the notion of *municipia civium Romanorum* there discussed is now discounted by more recent discoveries: all provincial *municipia* are likely to have possessed only Latin status: cf. note 1 above, and Gonzalez 1984 and 1987).

143. Howe 2002, 14: 'the construction of the [Cripplegate] fort [*c.* AD 120] coincides with the apparent disuse of the BAX95 [Baltic Exchange] boundary ditch to the east but still does not explain why the ditch was deliberately backfilled before the construction of the [city] wall'.

144. E.g. Maloney 1983, 104: 'the task [of building the city wall] could have been comfortably completed between the years AD 193 and 197'. Contrast Wacher 1998, 48 and 49, who suggests that the walls would have taken eight years to build *if* 400 skilled or semi-skilled labourers were available annually (which he doubts). Esmonde Cleary (2003, 83) also thinks that the walls imply colonial status for London.

145. The section at Duke's Place is '*c.* 120' (Maloney 1983, 97), and that at Aldersgate was 'probably associated with the Cripplegate fort [*c.* AD 120] as it seems to have respected the rounded SW corner of the fort' (Butler 2001, 45).

146. The city wall, including the Porta Nigra, has been dated on secure archaeological grounds to the last third of the second century (Kuhnen 2001, 143–53, with the earlier literature cited on 249). The date of colonial status is unsure: the earliest inscriptions mentioning the city as *colonia Augusta Treverorum* are of Claudio-Neronian date (Wightman 1985, 58 with literature cited on 342, notes 19 and 21).

147. On archaeological evidence, the basilica was begun as early as *c.* AD 100, but not finished, after long delays, until *c.* 130 (Brigham 1990; Milne 1992, 16–25; supplementary details in Dunwoodie 2004); so if colonial promotion indeed occurred under Hadrian, the forum/basilica complex cannot have been conceived and built to celebrate a promotion already gained, but rather as an ambitious project to proclaim the worthiness of Londinium's candidature to be promoted a *colonia*.

148. On York, see Roger Tomlin's comments below, p. 51 with notes 22–3 on p. 61: Aurelius Victor's use of the word *municipium* to denote the place (Eboracum) where Septimius died is not decisive; indeed it may have been Severus' presence there which had caused promotion to colonial rank to happen, in which case it was already a *colonia* before Septimius died. Cf. also Ottaway 1999, 146, who thinks promotion may have occurred a little later, when York became capital of *Britannia Inferior* not later than 216, after the division of the original province into two.

149. As suggested also by Frere 1984, 68.

150. *RIB* 288; but cf. Galsterer-Kröll 1973, pointing out that in Gaul even places styled *civitas* or *oppidum* can be shown to possess the *ius Latii*.

151. Morris' view (1982, 70–1) that Leicester was also a '*municipium*' because an auxiliary soldier gives his *origo* as Ratae rather than Coritanus can be discounted: cf. Frere 1999, 197.

152. E.g. of the eight *municipia* in Noricum, only one (Aguntum) is known to have had defences, and there only a 600-Roman-feet stretch of wall was built (Alföldy 1974, 92 with fig. 8). In Germania Superior, the *municipium* of Rottweil (Aquae Flaviae) was undefended throughout its life, even though some *vici* there received stone defences *c.* 200 (S. Gairhos in Schmidt, Kempa and Wais 2005, 195–7, cf. 156 [Rottweil]); contrast Germania Inferior, where the *municipium* of Voorburg was defended with stone walls, probably in the late second century (Esmonde Cleary 2003, 78, with reference). In Spain some *municipia* were given stone walls (e.g. *municipium Claudium Baelonense* in Baetica, apparently Augustan: Sillières 1997, 73–82, at 81), but most were not; in Africa similarly there is no consistency of policy (Daniels 1983).

153. An earth rampart is known to have preceded the stone defences at Tongeren (Tongres) in Gallia Belgica (Wightman 1985, 88, the former ascribed to the time of the Batavian revolt in 69/70), as did the *oppidum Batavorum* at Nijmegen, for which the same date and purpose have been ascribed (van Enckevort and Thijssen 2003, 63). The town of Reims (Durocortorum) also had an earthwork circuit, of uncertain date (Wightman 1985, 78, fig. 7); Esmonde Cleary (2003, 76) thinks it might belong to a preceding Iron Age *oppidum*, so out of line is it with practice elsewhere in Gaul. The vast majority of

the Gaulish towns, apart from *coloniae*, however, remained undefended until the late Empire: the distribution map of known defences by comparison with Britain (Esmonde Cleary 2003, 74, fig. 8.1) is striking (cf. Février 1980, 245: 'la plus grande part de la Gaule demeure vierge'). Faimingen (Phoebiana) in Raetia has an earth rampart with stone gates in the second century, replaced by a stone wall with fresh gates on a new line just outside the old (Czysz *et al.* 1995, 210, Abb. 35), but this may have had special status as a sanctuary site for the worship of Apollo Grannus. The undated earth rampart around Lepcis Magna, enclosing a vast 1,050 acres (425 ha), unique in Africa, has been linked to an emergency defence at the time of unrest in the area in the late first century (Daniels 1983, 11); Frere 1984, 65, suggests it may have been a *civitas libera*.

References

Adams, C. and Laurence, R. (eds) 2001: *Travel and geography in the Roman Empire*, London and New York

Aitken, M. 1960: 'Verulamium 1959: the magnetic survey', in Frere 1960, 21–4

Alföldy, G. 1974: *Noricum*, London

Barrett, A. A. 1979: 'The career of Tiberius Claudius Cogidubnus', *Britannia* 10, 227–42

Beaumont James, T. 1997: *English Heritage Book of Winchester*, London

Becker, A. 2003: 'Lahnau-Waldgirmes: eine augusteische Stadtgründung in Hessen', *Historia* 52, 337–50

Becker, A. and Köhler, H.-J. 2001: 'Das Forum von Lahnau-Waldgirmes', in Hansen and Pingels 2001, 171–7

Becker, A. and Rasbach, G. 2003: 'Die spätaugusteische Stadtgründung in Lahnau-Waldgirmes', *Germania* 81, 147–99

Biddle, M. 1975a: 'The study of Winchester: archaeology and history in a British town, 1961–83', *Proceedings of the British Academy* 69, 93–135

Biddle, M. 1975b: 'Excavations at Winchester 1971. Tenth and final interim report: part I', *Antiquaries Journal* 55, 96–126

Biddle, M. 1975c: 'Excavations at Winchester 1971. Tenth and final interim report: part II', *Antiquaries Journal* 55, 295–337

Bird, J. (ed.) 1998: *Form and fabric: studies in Rome's material past in honour of B. R. Hartley* [Oxbow Monograph 80], Oxford

Bird, J., Hassall, M. and Sheldon H. (eds) 1996: *Interpreting Roman London: papers in memory of Hugh Chapman* [Oxbow Monograph 58], Oxford

Bishop, M. C. 1991: 'Soldiers and military equipment in the towns of Roman Britain', in Maxfield and Dobson 1991, 21–7

Birley, A. R. 2005: *The Roman government of Britain*, Oxford

Blagg, T. F.C. 1979: 'The date of the temple at Bath', *Britannia* 10, 101–07

Blagg, T. F.C. 1980: 'Roman civil and military architecture in the province of Britain: aspects of patronage, influence and craft organization', *World Archaeology* 12, 27–42

Blair, I., Spain, R., Swift, D., Taylor, T. and Goodburn, D. 2006: 'Wells and bucket-chains: unforeseen elements of water supply in early Roman London', *Britannia* 37, 1–52

Bogaers, J. E. 1979: 'King Cogidubnus: another reading of *RIB* 91', *Britannia* 10, 243–54

Boon, G. C. 1969: 'Belgic and Roman Silchester: the excavations of 1954–8 with an excursus on the early history of Calleva', *Archaeologia* 102, 1–82

Branigan, K. 1985: *The Catuvellauni*, Gloucester

Brewer, R. (ed.) 2002: *The Second Augustan Legion and the Roman military machine*, Cardiff

Brigham, T. 1990: 'A reassessment of the second basilica in London, AD 100–400: excavations at Leadenhall Court, 1984–86', *Britannia* 21, 53–97

Brigham, T. 2001: 'Excavations at Plantation Place, London', *ARA: Bulletin of the Association of Roman Archaeology* 10 (February 2001), 8–10

Brigham, T., Watson, B. and Tyers, I. 1996: 'Current archaeological work at Regis House in the City of London (part 1)', *London Archaeologist* 8.2, 31–8

Brown, P. D. C. and McWhirr, A. D. 1967: 'Cirencester 1966', *Antiquaries Journal* 47, 185–97

Burnham, B. C. and Wacher, J. 1990: *The 'small towns' of Roman Britain*, London

Butler, J. 2001: 'The city defences at Aldersgate', *Transactions of the London and Middlesex Archaeological Society* 52, 41–111

Chadburn, A. 2006: 'The currency of kings', *British Archaeology*, March/April 2006, 27–9

Chapman, H. and Johnson, T. 1973: 'Excavations at Aldgate and Bush Lane House in the City of London, 1972', *Transactions of the London and Middlesex Archaeological Society* 24, 1–73

Coates, R. 2005: 'Cogidubnus revisited', *Antiquaries Journal* 85, 359–66

Courteault, P. 1921: 'An inscription recently found at Bordeaux', *JRS* 11 (1921), 101–07

Creighton, J. 2006: *Britannia: the creation of a Roman province*, London

Creighton, J. and Wilson, R. J. A. (eds) 1999: *Roman Germany: studies in cultural interaction* [*JRA* Supplementary Series 32], Portsmouth, Rhode Island

Crummy, P. 1984: *Colchester Archaeological Report 3: excavations at Lion Walk, Balkerne Lane and Middlesborough, Colchester, Essex*, Colchester

Crummy, P. 1992: *Colchester Archaeological Report 6: excavations at Culver Street, the Gilberd School and other sites in Colchester, 1971–1985*, Colchester

Crummy, P. 1997: *City of Victory. The story of Colchester – Britain's first Roman town*, Colchester

Crummy, P. 1999: 'Colchester: making towns out of fortresses and the first urban fortifications in Britain', in Hurst 1999a, 89–100

Crummy, P. 2003: 'Colchester's Roman town wall', in Wilson 2003, 44–52

Cunliffe, B. 1971a: *Excavations at Fishbourne 1961–9. Volume 1: the site* [Society of Antiquaries Research Report 26], London

Cunliffe, B. 1971b: *Fishbourne: a Roman palace and its garden*, London

Cunliffe, B. 1998: *Fishbourne Roman palace*, Stroud

Cunliffe, B. and Davenport, P. 1988: *The temple of Sulis Minerva at Bath. Volume 1: the site*, Oxford

Czysz, W., Dietz, K., Fischer, T. and Kellner, H.-J. 1995: *Die Römer in Bayern*, Stuttgart

Daniels, C. 1983: 'Town defences in Roman Africa: a tentative historical survey', in Maloney and Hobley 1983, 5–19

Down, A. 1978: *Chichester Excavations III*, Chichester

Down, A. 1981: *Chichester Excavations V*, Chichester

Down, A. 1988: *Roman Chichester*, Chichester

Down, A. 1989: *Chichester Excavations VI*, Chichester

Down, A. and Magilton, J. 1993: *Chichester Excavations VIII*, Chichester

Down, A. and Rule, M. 1971: *Chichester Excavations I*, Chichester

Drury, P. J. 1988: *The mansio and other sites in the south-eastern sector of Caesaromagus* [CBA Research Report 66], London

Dunwoodie, L. 2004: *Pre-Boudican and later activity on the site of the forum: excavations at 168 Fenchurch Street, City of London* [MoLAS Archaeology Studies Series 13], London

Dunwoodie, L., Harward, C. and Pitt, K. forthcoming: *Roman fortifications and urban development on Cornhill: excavations at Plantation Place, City of London* [MoLAS Monograph], London

Esmonde Cleary, S. 2003: 'Civil defences in the West under the High Empire', in Wilson 2003, 73–85

Février, P.-A. 1980: *Histoire de la France urbaine I: la ville antique*, Paris

Fischer, T. 2002: *Noricum* [Orbis Provinciarum], Mainz am Rhein

Frere, S. S. 1960: 'Excavations at Verulamium 1959: fifth interim report', *Antiquaries Journal* 40, 1–24

Frere, S. S. 1964: 'Verulamium – then and now', *Bulletin of the Institute of Archaeology, University of London* 4, 61–82

Frere, S. S. 1972: *Verulamium excavations, Volume I* [Society of Antiquaries of London Research Report 28], London

Frere, S. S. 1983: *Verulamium excavations, Volume II* [Society of Antiquaries of London Research Report 41], London

Frere, S. S. 1984: 'British urban defences in earthwork', *Britannia* 15, 63–74

Frere, S. S. 1985: 'Civic pride: a factor in Roman town planning', in Grew and Hobley 1985, 34–6

Frere, S. S. 1999: *Britannia: a history of Roman Britain*, fourth edition, London

Frere, S. S. 2005: 'The south gate and defences of *Venta Icenorum*: Professor Atkinson's excavations, 1930 and 1934', *Britannia* 36, 311–27

Frere, S. S. and Fulford, M. 2002: 'The *collegium peregrinorum* at Silchester', *Britannia* 33, 167–75

Frere, S. S. and St. Joseph, J. K. S. 1983: *Roman Britain from the air*, Cambridge

Fulford, M. 1984: *Silchester defences 1974–80* [*Britannia* Monographs 5], London

Fulford, M. 1989: *Silchester amphitheatre: the excavations of 1979–85* [*Britannia* Monographs 8], London

Fulford, M. 1993: 'Silchester: the early development of a *civitas* capital', in Greep 1993, 16–33

Fulford, M. 2003: 'Julio-Claudian and early Flavian *Calleva*', in Wilson 2003, 95–104

Fulford, M. and Timby, J. 2000: *Late Iron Age and Roman Silchester: excavations on the site of the forum-basilica 1977, 1980–86* [*Britannia* Monograph 15], London

Galsterer-Kröll, B. 1973: 'Zum *ius Latii* in den keltischen Provinzen des Imperium Romanum', *Chiron* 3, 277–306

Gascou, J. 1972: *La politique municipale de l'Empire romain en Afrique proconsulaire de Trajan à Septime-Sévère*, Rome

Gascou, J. 1982a: 'La politique municipale de Rome en Afrique du Nord I: de la mort d'Auguste au début du IIIᵉ siècle', *Aufstieg und Niedergang der römischen Welt* II.10.2, 136–229

Gascou, J. 1982b: 'La politique municipale de Rome en Afrique du Nord II: après la mort de Septime-Sévère', *Aufstieg und Niedergang der römischen Welt* II.10.2, 230–320

Gonzalez, J. 1984: 'Tabula Siarensis, Fortunales Siarenses et municipia civium Romanorum', *Zeitschrift für Papyrologie und Epigraphik* 55, 55–100

Gonzalez, J. 1987: 'El *ius Latii* y la lex Irnitana', *Athenaeum* 65, 317–33

Greep, S. J. (ed.) 1993: *Roman towns: the Wheeler inheritance. A review of 50 years' research* [CBA Research report 93], York

Grew, F. and Hobley, B. (eds) 1985: *Roman urban topography in Britain and the western Empire. Proceedings of the third conference on urban archaeology organized jointly by the Council for British Archaeology and the Department of Urban Archaeology of the Museum of London* [CBA Research Report 59], London

Grimes, W. F. 1968: *The excavation of Roman and mediaeval London*, London

Hansen, S. and Pingels, V. (eds) 2001: *Archäologie in Hessen. Neue Funde und Befunde. Festschrift für Fritz-Rudolf-Herrmann zum 65. Geburtstag* [Studia Honoraria 17], Rahden

Hartley, B. R. 1983: 'The enclosure of Romano-British towns in the second century A.D.', in Hartley and Wacher 1983, 84–93

Hartley, B. and Wacher, J. (eds) 1983: *Rome and her northern provinces. Papers presented to Sheppard Frere in honour of his retirement from the Chair of the Archaeology of the Roman Empire, University of Oxford, 1983*, Gloucester

Hassall, M. and Hurst, H. R. 1999: 'Soldier and civilian: a debate on the bank of the Severn', in Hurst 1999a, 181–89

Haverfield, F. 1911: 'Roman London', *JRS* 1, 141–72

Hellenkemper, H. 1983: 'The Roman defences of Cologne – Colonia Claudia Ara Agrippinensium', in Maloney and Hobley 1983, 21–8

Henderson, C. 1984: 'The Roman walls of Exeter', *Devon Archaeology* 2, 13–25

Henderson, C. 1988: 'Exeter (*Isca Dumnoniorum*)', in Webster 1988, 91–119

Henig, M. 2000: 'From Classical Greece to Roman Britain. Some hellenic themes in provincial art and glyptics', in Tsetskhladze, Snodgrass and Prag 2000, 172–85

Holbrook, N. (ed.) 1998: *Cirencester: the main Roman town defences, public buildings and shops* [Cirencester Excavations V], Cirencester

Horn, H. G. (ed.) 1987: *Die Römer in Nordrhein-Westfalen*, Stuttgart

Howe, E. 2002: *Roman defences and medieval industry: excavations at Baltic House, City of London* [MoLAS Monograph 7], London

Howe, E. and Lakin, D. 2004: *Roman and medieval Cripplegate. Archaeological excavations 1992–8* [MoLAS Monograph 21], London

Hull, M. R. 1958: *Roman Colchester* [Reports of the Research Committee of the Society of Antiquaries of London 20], London

Hurst, H. R. 1986: *Gloucester, the Roman and later defences* [Gloucester Archaeological reports 2], Gloucester

Hurst, H. 1988: 'Gloucester (*Glevum*)', in Webster 1988, 48–73

Hurst, H. R. (ed.) 1999a: *The coloniae of Roman Britain: new studies and a review* [JRA Supplementary Series 36], Portsmouth, Rhode Island

Hurst, H. R. 1999b: 'Topography and identity in *Glevum colonia*', in Hurst 1999a, 113–35

Johnson, A. 1983: *Roman forts of the 1st and 2nd centuries AD in Britain and the German provinces*, London

Jones, M. J. 1980: *The defences of the upper Roman enclosure* [The Archaeology of Lincoln 7.1], London

Kenyon, K. M. 1938: 'Excavations at Viroconium 1936–7', *Archaeologia* 88, 175–228

Keppie, L. J. F. 2000a: 'From legionary fortress to military colony: veterans on the Roman frontier', in Keppie 2000b, 301–16

Keppie, L. J. F. 2000b: *Legions and veterans: Roman army papers 1971–2000*, Stuttgart

Khanoussi, M. and Maurin, L. (eds) 2000: *Dougga, fragments d'histoire. Choix d'inscriptions latines éditées, traduites et commentées (Ier–IVe siècles)* [Ausonius Mémoires 3], Bordeaux and Tunis

Kühlborn, J.-S. (ed.) 1995: *Germaniam pacavi – Germanien habe ich befriedet. Archäologische Stätten augusteischer Okkupation*, Münster

Kuhnen, H.-P. (ed.) 2001: *Das römische Trier* [Führer zu archäologischen Denkmälern in Deutschland 40], Stuttgart

Laurence, R. 2001: 'The creation of geography: an interpretation of Roman Britain', in Adams and Laurence 2001, 67–94

Magilton, J. 2003: 'The defences of Roman Chichester', in Wilson 2003, 156–67

Maloney, J. 1983: 'Recent work on London's defences', in Maloney and Hobley 1983, 96–117

Maloney, J. and Hobley, B. (eds) 1983: *Roman urban defences in the west* [CBA Research Report 51], London

Manley, J. and Rudkin, D. 2005: *Facing the palace: excavations in front of the Roman palace at Fishbourne (Sussex, UK), 1995–99* [*Sussex Archaeological Collections* 141 for 2003], Lewes

Manning, W. 2002: 'Early Roman campaigns in the south-west of Britain', in Brewer 2002, 27–44

Manning, W. 2003: 'The defences of Caerwent', in Wilson 2003, 168–83

Marsden, P. 1970: 'Archaeological finds in the City of London, 1966–9', *Transactions of the London and Middlesex Archaeological Society* 22.3, 1–9

Marsden, P. 1980: *Roman London*, London

Maxfield, V. A. and Dobson, M. J. (eds) 1991: *Roman frontier studies 1989. Proceedings of the XVth International Congress of Roman frontier studies*, Exeter

Merrifield, R. 1965: *The Roman city of London*, London

Millar, F. G. B. 1992: *The Emperor in the Roman world*, second edition, London

Millett, M. 1990: *The Romanization of Britain. An essay in archaeological interpretation*, Cambridge

Millett, M. and Graham, D. 1986: *Excavations on the Romano-British small town at Neatham, Hampshire* [Hampshire Field Club Monograph 3], Winchester

Milne, G. (ed.) 1992: *From Roman Basilica to medieval market: archaeology in action in the City of London*, London

Milne, G. 1995: *English Heritage Book of Roman London*, London

Morris, J. 1982: *Londinium: London in the Roman Empire*, London

Murgia, C. E. 1977: 'The minor works Tacitus: a study in textual criticism', *Classical Philology* 72, 323–43

Niblett, R. 1993: 'Verulamium since the Wheelers', in Greep 1993, 78–92

Niblett, R. 1999: *The excavation of a ceremonial site at Folly Lane, Verulamium* [*Britannia* Monograph 14], London

Niblett, R. 2001: *Verulamium: the Roman city of St Albans*, Stroud

Ottaway, P. 1999: 'York: the study of a late Roman *colonia*', in Hurst 1999a, 137–50

Ottaway, P. 2004: *Roman York*, Stroud

Partridge, C. 1981: *Skeleton Green: a late Iron Age and Romano-British site* [*Britannia* Monograph 2], London

Perring, D. and Roskams, S. 1991: *The archaeology of Roman London, volume 2: early development of Roman London west of the Walbrook* [CBA Research Report 70], London

Precht, G. 1983: 'The town walls and defensive systems of Xanten – Colonia Ulpia Traiana', in Maloney and Hobley 1983, 29–39

Qualmann, K. E. 1993: 'Roman Winchester', in Greep 1993, 66–77

Richardson, J. S. 1996: *The Romans in Spain*, Oxford

Richmond, I. A. 1930: 'The first years of Emerita Augusta', *Archaeological Journal* 87, 98–116

Rivet, A. L. F. 1964: *Town and country in Roman Britain*, London

Rivet, A. L. F. and Smith, C. 1979: *The place-names of Roman Britain*, London

Rivière, S. and Thomas, A. B. 1987: 'Excavations at 94–97 Fenchurch Street and 9 Northumberland Alley', *Archaeology Today* 8.9 (October 1987), 13–17

RCHME 1962: *An inventory of the historical monuments in the City of York. Volume 1. Ebvracvm, Roman York*, London

Russell, M. 2006: *Roman Sussex*, Stroud

Sankey, D. 2002: 'Roman, medieval and later development at 7 Bishopsgate, London EC2:

from a 1st-century cellared building to the seventeenth properties of the Merchant Taylor's Company', *Transactions of the London and Middlesex Archaeological Society* 53, 1–24

Sankey, D. and Stevenson, A. 1991: 'Recent work on London's defences', in Maxfield and Dobson 1991, 117–24

Schmidt, S., Kempa, M. and Wais, A. (eds) 2005: *Imperium Romanum: Roms Provinzen an Neckar, Rhein und Donau*, Stuttgart

Sherwin-White, A. N. 1973: *The Roman citizenship*, second edition, Oxford

Sillières, P. 1997: *Baelo Claudia: una ciudad romana de la Bética*, Madrid

Teutsch, L. 1962: *Das römische Städtewesen in Nordafrika*, Berlin

Tomlin, R. S. O. 1997: 'Reading a 1st-century gold signet ring from Fishbourne', *Sussex Archaeological Collections* 135, 127–30

Tsetskhladze, G. R., Snodgrass, A. M. and Prag, A. J. N. W. (eds) 2000: *Periplous. Papers on classical art and archaeology presented to Sir John Boardman*, London

Van Enckevort, H. and Thijssen, J. 2003: 'Nijmegen – a Roman town in the frontier zone of *Germania Inferior*', in Wilson 2003, 59–72

Von Schnurbein, S. 2003: 'Augustus in *Germania* and his new "town" at Waldgirmes east of the Rhine', *JRA* 16, 93–107

Wacher, J. S. 1995: *The towns of Roman Britain*, second edition, London

Wacher, J. S. 1998: 'The dating of towns walls in Roman Britain', in Bird 1998, 41–50

Wacher, J. S. and McWhirr, A. D. 1982: *Early Roman occupation at Cirencester* [Cirencester Excavations I], Cirencester

Watson, B. (ed.) 1998: *Roman London: recent archaeological work* [JRA Supplementary Series 24], Portsmouth, Rhode Island

Watson, S. 2003: *An excavation in the western cemetery of Roman London. Atlantic House, City of London* [MoLAS Archaeological Studies Series 7], London

Webster, G. (ed.) 1988: *Fortress into city: the consolidation of Britain, first century AD*, London

Webster, G. 2002: *The legionary fortress at Wroxeter: excavations by Graham Webster 1955–85* (edited by J. Chadderton) [Archaeological Report 19], London

Welfare, H. and Swan, V. 1995: *Roman camps in England: the field archaeology*, London

White, R. and Barker, P. 1998: *Wroxeter: life and death of a Roman city*, Stroud

Wightman, E. M. 1985: *Gallia Belgica*, London

Wilkes, J. J. 1996: 'The status of Londinium', in Bird, Hassall and Sheldon 1996, 27–31

Wilson, P. (ed.) 2003: *The archaeology of Roman towns: studies in honour of John S. Wacher*, Oxford

Wilson, R. J. A. 2006: 'What's new in Roman Baden-Württemberg?', *JRS* 96, 198–212

Wilson, R. J. A. and Creighton, J. 1999: 'Introduction: recent research on Roman Germany', in Creighton and Wilson 1999, 9–34

Zant, J. M. 1993: *The Brooks, Winchester, 1987–88: the Roman structural remains* [Winchester Museums Service, Archaeology Report 2], Winchester

Chapter 2

WAS ROMAN LONDON EVER A *COLONIA*? THE WRITTEN EVIDENCE

R. S. O. Tomlin

Some years ago, when he was about my age, Sheppard Frere invited me to join Richard Wright and Mark Hassall in editing The Roman Inscriptions of Britain. *In doing so, he changed the course of my academic life. Years later, I seconded his unflagging energy in editing the second volume (RIB II), and now I am delighted to be joining friends and colleagues in celebrating his ninetieth birthday. In Roman Britain, Claudia Crysis and Aurelius Timotheus are his only equals, and Julius Valens must look to his laurels.*[1]

Introduction

My own more leisured approach to editing the third volume (*RIB* III) has led me in many directions, one of which is to wonder whether Roman London ever became a *colonia*. I use this term, not in the Tacitean sense of a chartered settlement of veterans in conquered territory, to help against rebellion and to encourage respect for the law, but of a grant of titular status by Hadrian or one of his successors.[2] This question has been asked before, but I am tempted by a piece of Purbeck 'marble' in the Museum of London to push the epigraphic evidence just a little further.[3] But first I should recapitulate what we know already.[4]

I begin as usual with Tacitus' observation that London in AD 61 was full of traders and provisions, but not distinguished by the title of *colonia*. His terminology is specific, since he has just been speaking of depopulated Italian *coloniae*, and he next calls Verulamium a *municipium*; and if we press his language, he implies that London did not have the title of *colonia* at the time of writing either, since he would have written *nondum* ('not yet') instead of *non*.[5] This argument from silence is not decisive: Tacitus may not have known or cared what its formal status was in *c*. AD 120, but we might at least expect him to have known what it was some twenty years earlier, when he was writing the *Agricola*.

The evidence of two later authors is inconclusive, however, since their terminology is not specific. The first is the anonymous panegyric of AD 297/8 which says that the army of Constantius Caesar reached the 'town' of London, *oppidum Londiniense*, but this does not indicate its formal status. It was contemporary usage, and no more than rhetorical variation here; in the very same sentence London is also called *civitas* and *urbs*.[6] *Civitas* was the usual late-Roman term for an urban area, a 'city', and the western bishops who attend the Council of Arles (AD 314) all come from what is called a *civitas*, whatever its formal status.[7] My second author is the historian Ammianus Marcellinus, writing in the 390s, who also refers to London as an ancient 'town', *vetus oppidum*. This too is only rhetorical variation.[8]

Tacitus does not specify the formal status of London in AD 61 or later, but Haverfield was surely right in suggesting that it was a *conventus civium Romanorum*. This has been well argued by John Wilkes.[9] A new inscription has since shown that resident Gallic businessmen referred to themselves informally as *Londinienses*.[10] Nonetheless, most readers of Tacitus would agree that London had also become the provincial 'capital', if we use inverted commas to qualify the built-up area in which the provincial procurator and his staff were based, and where the governor and his staff lived when he was not on tour or directing military operations.[11] This can be deduced from London's position at the focus of the Roman road-system: centuries later, when Constantius Caesar, Count Lupicinus and Count Theodosius were regaining control of Britain at different times, they all made for London.[12] It is also implied by the anomalous Cripplegate fort, where Mark Hassall locates the governor's bodyguard (*singulares*), and by a mass of epigraphic evidence from London: the superb tombstone of Julius Classicianus, whom Tacitus names as procurator of the province, an unused writing-tablet issued by subordinate British procurators and the building-tiles they stamped, an altar dedicated by an imperial freedman, the tombstones of legionaries who were surely seconded to the governor's staff, as the *speculatores* among them undoubtedly were.[13] The legionaries listed on the great inscription of which pieces were found at the Winchester Palace site in Southwark are as likely to be Antonine 'staff officers' as a vexillation of fighting troops or engineers.[14] At all events, they were a unique legionary presence at the heart of the civil province. The 'first known British civil servant', in Tony Birley's phrase, was the *provincialis* Anencletus who served the provincial council; it was London where he buried his wife.[15] At Vindolanda, which provided the governor with 46 *singulares*, a letter was discarded which had been sent to his groom 'at London', where also a centurion was on detached service.[16] Two quite recent discoveries can be added to the list: writing-tablets found in London which record a judicial inquiry into the ownership of woodland *in civitate Cantiacorum*, and the sale of a girl from Gaul to an imperial slave. They imply the presence of land-records, legal authority (the *legatus iuridicus*, if not the governor), and the procurator's staff.[17]

The status of London as the provincial 'capital' has also been sought in the archaeological record, notably the construction of the Flavian forum and its replacement by a much larger complex in the reign of Hadrian. Sheppard Frere, for example, has suggested that they mark the incorporation of London as a *municipium* and then its promotion to the rank of *colonia*.[18] Ralph Merrifield even claimed that 'all provincial capitals were *coloniae*, and London could not be an exception', but this goes too far.[19] The evidence has now been meticulously assembled by Rudolf Haensch, who shows that existing *coloniae* were not necessarily preferred as provincial 'capitals', that promotion of a 'capital' to *colonia* depended on other factors, such as loyalty in civil war, and that some of them only achieved this status in the late-second or third centuries.[20] Thus the *municipium* of Carnuntum, the 'capital' of Pannonia where Septimius Severus was proclaimed in AD 193, only became a *colonia* as a result; likewise Aquincum, which later became the 'capital' of Pannonia Inferior when the province was divided. But in Roman Germany, the 'capital' of Germania Inferior was the old Claudian *colonia* Agrippinensis (Cologne), whereas Mogontiacum, the 'capital' of Germania Superior, remained the civil settlement associated with the legionary fortress at Mainz, technically no more than a *vicus*.[21]

Is Pannonia then, or Germany, the model for Britain? York is first attested as a *colonia* in AD 237, when the province had been divided and it was the 'capital' of Britannia Inferior. Its promotion is likely to mark the presence of Septimius Severus and his entourage during the British expedition (208–11).[22] We do not know whether it was previously a *municipium*.[23] At first sight we would expect that London, as the regular 'capital' of the undivided province, already enjoyed equal or higher status. Even after the division, it was still the 'capital' of Britannia Superior, a consular province with two legions, whereas Britannia Inferior was praetorian with only one. But by comparing Mainz with Cologne, we can see that there was no general rule.

All this evidence is familiar and has been well-studied; it is an attractive inference, but no more, that the capital importance of London was recognized by its incorporation as a *municipium* or titular *colonia*. The occasion may even be guessed: Hadrian's visit to Britain in 122, when he 'made many reforms', just as he marked his visit to Spain a few months later by granting colonial status to his native city of Italica. When he recommended this promotion to the Senate in Rome, he referred austerely to 'ancient *municipia*' which petitioned for what they mistakenly thought was the superior title of *colonia*.[24] London by comparison with Italica and Utica (his examples) was decidedly *arriviste*, and he need have had no qualms in yielding to its petition that he mark his imperial *adventus* by raising it to colonial status. This inference is attractive, as I have said, and I would like to strengthen it by introducing another inscription. John Mann has remarked on the crippling lack of epigraphic evidence for the status of London: 'an inscription-detector would be a great help'.[25] I quite agree, but my item is not new: it has only been overlooked, by me as well as others. I do not claim it is decisive, since my interpretation is only one of several possible, but even if the others cannot be eliminated, they do seem less likely.

The 1989 inscription

This item is a small fragment of monumental inscription found in 1989 during excavation of the Dominant House site in the City of London, at the western end of the Huggin Hill baths. Its context is not actually Roman, but residual, and is probably the late-Saxon building dug into the western end of the *caldarium*. So the fragment may well derive from the Roman baths, but possibly from another public building nearby, which would not affect my argument. But first I should describe it in more detail than was possible when it was reported.[26]

It is a piece broken from a thin panel of Purbeck 'marble', a fragment only 250

Fig. 2.1 London, Huggin Hill, fragment (250 mm wide) of an inscription on Purbeck 'marble' (Britannia 23 [1992], 309, no. 1)

by 210 mm, smaller than an A4 page (Figs 2.1 and 2.2). It carries just six letters, only two of them complete. The extreme right-hand edge is original, that is to say it preserves *c.* 35 mm of the squared edge of the lost panel. 52 mm to the left of this edge, there is part of the scratched vertical setting-out line which defined the right-hand margin of the inscribed area. This edge is 25 mm thick, and the underside is square to it, but the upper face tapers in thickness to 21 mm at the setting-out line, after which it remains constant. In other words, the original panel was slightly dished; its border was evidently blocked-out, but never carved to a profile. Scratched at right-angles to this vertical line are two horizontal setting-out lines for the first row of letters, 69 mm apart; and then a gap of 42 mm until a third setting-out line, which is obviously the survivor of a second such pair for the second row of letters. The ratio of letter-height to gap is 5:3; of margin to gap, 5:4; of margin to letter-height, 4:3. Evidently the panel was marked out with precision before the letters were constructed and carved.

cms

Fig. 2.2 London, Huggin Hill fragment (250 mm wide) of an inscription on Purbeck 'marble' (Britannia 23 [1992], 309, no. 1)

These letters are appropriate to the painstaking preparation, being well-drawn and skilfully incised despite the hard, brittle stone.[27] They are of excellent quality and characterised by exaggerated upper serifs, but it would be difficult to date such a small sample on style alone, although they do not look much earlier than Trajan (98–117), nor later than Antoninus Pius (138–61). The use of Purbeck 'marble' suggests a date well within the first half of the second century.[28]

The reading is straightforward, but I should emphasise (since it was not stated in the first report) that we have the last three letters of two lines:

R. S. O. Tomlin

[...]
[...]MAX▸
[...]NIA
[...]

One more letter in the second line, and I would hope this paper were redundant, but MAX in the line above can certainly be identified: it is *maximus* abbreviated; the case not specified. Since it can only be part of the imperial titulature, the title *pontifex maximus*, it is probably in the dative, a dedication *to* the emperor.[29] An ablative absolute (dating by the emperor) is possible, but a nominative (the emperor as agent) is impossible if [...]NIA is also in the nominative case. If the emperor is either Trajan, Hadrian or Antoninus Pius, PONT MAX will be followed by TRIB POT (perhaps reduced to TR P) with iteration-numeral, and then by COS with iteration-numeral, quite likely III.[30] The titles, if Trajan's, will probably include IMP with iteration-numeral; IMP II is possible, but less likely, for Hadrian and Antoninus Pius. There may also be P P for *pater patriae*, a title assumed by Trajan and Antoninus Pius soon after their accession, but by Hadrian only in 128.

So lines 1–2 would have read something like this:

[. . .   PONT] MAX
[TRIB POT *000* COS III P P . . .]NIA

I spell this out, to emphasise the second line and its concluding letters NIA. They are surely the end of a word. By extending the vertical setting-out line downwards, we can see that there was no room for another letter after A; but also that it was not crammed into the space available, another sign that the inscription was carefully set out, and even that the lettering was centred. The style is more like *RIB* 330 (Caerleon) than *RIB* 288 (Wroxeter), both of which are contemporary inscriptions of the highest quality. It is unlikely that NIA belongs to a word divided between two lines. If it were, then a cognomen like [CALPVR]NIA[NVS] would seem to be the only possibility; but this would be a clumsy division out of keeping with the apparent style, and would also require the man's *nomen gentilicium* and *praenomen* to the left of it, in a line which is already packed with imperial titulature.

The width of this line 2 is problematic. Has anything been lost here, apart from imperial titles and the word [. . .]NIA? Is any restoration more compelling than that of the single word [. . .]NIA? A negative answer is the most economical, but of course it cannot be certain. The more words, however, that are posited between the titles and [...]NIA, the wider the inscription becomes: difficult in itself, and especially in Purbeck 'marble'.

This can only be argued in general terms. In default of a surviving stone-cutter from Roman London, I consulted Richard Grasby, a professional cutter of inscriptions who has lately been studying Roman method.[31] Suppose that line 2 were 21 letters, 14 for the missing titles, 7 for the word ending [. . .]NIA; it would be less if the word were [OM]NIA and TRIB POT were abbreviated to TR P, but more if the numeral were more than two digits. As an interesting exercise, Richard applied the controlling grid he has observed at Caerleon (*RIB* 330) and elsewhere, one letter occupying each square, the letter I and medial points being placed on grid lines and given a single unit value, one-twelfth of the line-height. He based the letter-widths in units on those of *RIB* 330 and the Wroxeter inscription (*RIB* 288), with some width-reductions implied by the square M and the narrow X. The 21 letters would be 165 units, 949 mm. To these he added 28 spaces (2 units each on average), 56 units, 322 mm; and two margins and borders at 3 inches each, 144 mm. Total: 1,415 mm, 57 inches. It is worth comparing this figure with the eight inscribed panels of Purbeck 'marble' whose maximum measurement, whether width or height, is known or calculable:

RIB 15: less than 450 mm (estimated)
RIB 91: now 1,125 mm, but originally *c.* 1,575 mm
RIB 113: 1,140 mm
RIB 188: 890 mm
RIB 193: 460 mm
RIB 202: 370 mm
JRS 46 (1956), 146, no. 3: at least 4,300 mm in four panels (estimated)
Britannia 10 (1979), 339, no. 1: 850 mm (estimated)

The Huggin Hill inscription, a notional 1,415 mm wide, but only 21 mm thick, is just feasible in Purbeck 'marble', but there would be very great danger of its breaking either when being masoned, tooled and carved, or when handled and fixed. So it probably consisted of two panels butted together, worked *in situ* after they had been bedded into the wall or back-filled with poured concrete. A tiny fragment of Purbeck 'marble', only 50 mm by 43 mm, was found in 1969 at the other (eastern) end of the Huggin Hill baths; the different thickness (30 mm) and the sans-serif lettering show that it belongs to another inscription (Figs 2.3 and 2.4). It carries part of two letters, one of which is too close to a sawn edge for this to be the edge of the whole inscription.[32] The only Purbeck 'marble' inscription we know for certain to have been incised on multiple panels, the Agricolan text from the forum at Verulamium, consists of much thicker panels, 75 mm at the border edge,

cms

*Fig. 2.3 and 2.4 London, Huggin Hill, fragment (50 mm wide) of a second inscription on Purbeck 'marble' (*Britannia* 8 [1977], 426, no. 1)*

tapering to 63 mm, three times as thick as the Huggin Hill [. . .]MAX | [. . .]NIA fragment. This is an index of the strength required, even to span *c.* 1,100 mm.[33] So Huggin Hill probably consisted of two panels; and at only 21 mm thick, they are unlikely to have been much wider than 750 mm. But we cannot calculate from the material alone what the inscription's width might have been. We must return to the text.

The restoration of [...]NIA remains crucial. The word must be either neuter plural (whether nominative or accusative), or feminine singular (whether nominative or ablative); and unless it is the adjective *omnia*, it must be a noun or proper name. I have already mentioned [OM]NIA, but this will not do. It is hardly found in imperial dedications, and after the emperor's name and titles it would be impossibly abrupt, unless it were preceded by 'all' the objects it qualified; thus a dedication to Caracalla marks the total restoration of an African temple with its sanctuary and portico: *templum [cum] sanctu et porticu . . . omnia a solo resti[tuit]*.[34] There cannot have been enough space in line 2.[35] But in this civilian context, and at this date, a reference to *moenia* ('city walls') is also unlikely.

If then a neuter plural can be excluded, what about an ablative singular? *De sua pecunia* (or similar) suggests itself, but this phrase is usually found abbreviated at the end of a building-inscription. Even if it were inscribed in full, it would not follow hard upon the imperial titles: emperors do not build things 'with their own money', and in any case, the building would have to be specified first. The phrase is typical of private citizens, and there is a possible parallel in a dedication to the deified Marcus as the father of Commodus with his titles, which are followed directly by reference to the dedicators, an association of rich freedmen responsible for imperial cult, *Augustales pecunia sua posuerunt*.[36] But an inscription of this sort would be quite unusual, and the spacing would again be difficult; in any case, *Augustales* would only be found in a *municipium* or *colonia*.[37] Nor can we see [...]NIA as the dedicator's place of origin, as in *L(ucius) Iul(ius) T(iti) f(ilius) Galer(ia tribu) Leuganus Clunia*.[38] Considerations of space apart, a name of this formal amplitude would be found on a tombstone, not an imperial dedication.

So we are compelled to a feminine noun or proper name, in the nominative case; evidently the dedicator, whether corporate body or woman. If it be a proper name, it can only be the *nomen gentilicium* of a woman. There are endless possibilities, for example *Iunia* or *Sempronia*, but the person dedicating a public building in a provincial 'capital' to the Emperor is almost bound to be the governor, an officer or official, or a civic magistrate – certainly not a woman. Dedications by women to the Emperor are hard to find.[39] Female benefactors are very unusual, even in Italy.[40]

If a woman is out of the question, then, we are reduced to a corporate body, and I can only think of [BRITAN]NIA or [COLO]NIA. For *[Britan]nia* there is a parallel from London itself, a lost dedication to the divinity of an early emperor: *num(ini) C(aesaris) [Aug(usti)]* | *prov[incia]* | *Brita[nnia]*.[41] It is not a dedication made by a province to an emperor with his full name and titles, but an example of this can be found at Mérida (Emerita Augusta), the 'capital' of Lusitania, a dedication by the province to Titus Caesar in 77 or 78: *T(ito) Caesari Aug(usti) f(ilio)* | *Vespasiano pontif(ici)* | *imp(eratori) XII trib(unicia) pote(state) VII* | *co(n)s(uli) VI* | *provincia Lusitania* (etc.).[42] But something of the kind at Huggin Hill would again make line 2 rather long. Besides, we might expect *provincia Britannia* to have been centred for emphasis, like *provincia Lusitania* in the Lusitanian inscription.

By this long process of elimination, therefore, we arrive at [COLO]NIA, but not for want of something better. It may be a bold restoration, in view of what follows from it, and it is not certain, but it is better than any of the others, since it can follow the imperial titles directly; it requires nothing to its left, and is thus the simplest and most economical restoration. Unlike the others, it is not a special case: there are many inscriptions dedicated to emperors by *coloniae*. Here, for example, is a dedication to Hadrian by Beneventum in 125/6:

imp(eratori) Caesari | divi Traiani Parthici fil(io) divi | Nervae nepot(i) Traiano | Hadriano Augusto | pont(ifici) max(imo) tribunicia pot(estate) X co(n)s(uli) III p(atri) p(atriae) | colonia Iulia Concordia Beneventum optimo et liberalissimo principi.[43]

In my reconstruction of the Huggin Hill inscription, the word *[colo]nia* would be followed by the title and city-name, just as Italica had become *colonia Aelia Augusta Italica*. London owed its promotion to the Emperor, so its title would have contained the adjective *Augusta*, and probably a dynastic name as well, for example *Aelia* for Hadrian. Its new name would have concluded with *Londinium*, or informally with *Londiniensis* or *Londiniensium*. With this in mind, I asked Richard Grasby to undertake a commission from the new *colonia*, in which he modelled its title on that of Italica, and the imperial names and titles on those at Beneventum.[44] His layout (*ordinatio*) is seen in Fig. 2.5. The inscription he cut could not be incorporated in the honorand's presentation-copy of this volume like a giant microfiche, as I would have liked, but on page 58 at least is Richard's drawing (Fig. 2.6) of the three key-words.[46]

Fig. 2.5 *The Huggin Hill inscription (see Fig. 2.2): conjectured layout (*ordinatio*)*

Fig. 2.6 The Huggin Hill inscription (see Fig. 2.2): key-words as cut

Figs 2.5 and 2.6 are not conclusive – the fragment is much too small for that – but they do show that imperial names and titles can be grouped into four lines ending in [COLO]NIA without strain, without any forcing or special pleading, and also within the constraint of a third line ending in MAX. This reconstruction is simple and plausible, but after LONDINIVM it goes beyond all conjecture. The five-line inscription looks very good as it is, but perhaps it concluded with the names of the two annual magistrates (*duoviri*) and the governor. The same excavation produced a residual fragment (130 mm wide) of Purbeck 'marble' from yet a third inscription (Figs 2.7 and 2.8).[47] This reads: [...]VG[...], presumably [... A]VG [...]. There is a space below of at least 50 mm, so this is likely to be the bottom line, with the well-cut [A]VG being part of the governor's titulature, [LEG A]VG [PR PR].[48]

If then we conjecture *colonia Aelia Augusta Londinium* or similar, we might conclude by glancing at another old problem, that of *Londinium Augusta*, 'Augusta which the ancients called London'.[49] Ammianus' words imply that the name 'Augusta' replaced 'London', at least in official usage, the impression also given by the entry in the *Notitia Dignitatum* for 'the treasuries of Augusta', and by the first coins of Magnus Maximus with their mint-marks AVG, AVGOB, and AVGPS.[50] Ammianus does not date this change of name, which has been variously attributed to Constantius when *Augustus* (AD 305/6) or to Count Theodosius (AD 368/9).[51] By implication it was later than 360.[52] But all this takes no account of the Ravenna Cosmography, which by listing *Londinium Augusti* (*sic*) must have read both names on its map of Britain. This map has been inferred but not dated, but it is significant that *Londinium Augusti* is the only detail thought to be as late as the fourth century.[53] Otherwise the map would be dated much earlier: the Cosmographer names three outpost forts of Hadrian's Wall which Constantine probably abandoned in 312; he glosses Colchester, Lincoln and Gloucester as *coloniae*, but not York, a *colonia* before 237; he names at least one fort of the Antonine Wall, which Marcus Aurelius surely

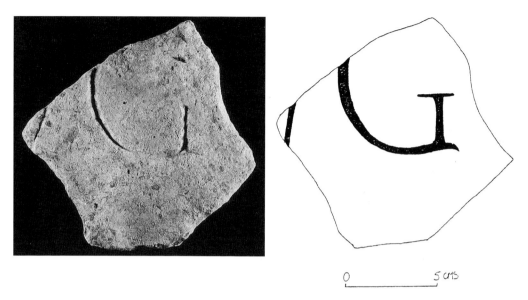

Figs 2.7 and 2.8 London, Huggin Hill, fragment (130 mm wide) of a third inscription on Purbeck 'marble' (Britannia 23 [1992], 309, no. 2)

abandoned soon after his accession (161).[54] These items all suggest a map no later than the second century; a single 'correction' more than a century later, and blundered at that, is inherently improbable. Anyway, *Londinium Augusta* is a difficult combination. Why is the neuter place-name qualified by a feminine adjective? Why not simply *Augusta Londiniensium*? The Cosmographer must have been inured to strange place-names, but even he was uneasy, to judge by his conscious or unconscious emendation of his reading to something grammatical but banal, 'London of the Emperor'. The difficulty disappears if we suppose that the ungrammatical adjective *Augusta* qualified, not *Londinium*, but the crucial word *colonia* in ellipse. *Augusta* was not a new name for London, but a grandiose and ultimately unsuccessful assertion of just one element in its formal titulature.[55]

Notes

1. *RIB* 263 (Lincoln); *JRS* 50 (1960), 236, no. 5 (Chester); *RIB* 363 (Caerleon).
2. Tacitus, *Annales* XII.32: *colonia Camulodunum valida veteranorum manu deducitur in agros captivos, subsidium adversus rebellis et imbuendis sociis ad officia legum.*
3. Despite Millett 1999, 196, who urges an imaginative use of the other material evidence to study the *coloniae* of Roman Britain: 'we have probably pushed the existing epigraphic evidence as far as it can go'.
4. Rivet and Smith 1979, 396–7. Archaeological evidence is considered by Roger Wilson in this volume above (Chapter One), pp. 6–7, 15–17 and especially 30–31.
5. *Annales* XIV.33 (cf. 27, the Italian *coloniae*): *Londinium . . . cognomento quidem coloniae non insigne, sed copia negotiatorum et commeatuum maxime celebre.* The passage was

probably written soon after the accession of Hadrian (Syme 1958, ch. 35).

6. *Pan. Lat.* viii (v), 17.1. The contemporary letter of Constantius to Autun addresses it as a 'town', *Augustodunensium oppido*, but promptly calls it a 'city', *in supra dicta civitate* (*Pan. Lat.* ix (iv), 14.1 and 4). Eumenius, the panegyrist who quotes this letter, once calls Autun a *colonia* (5.1), which it never was, but otherwise refers to it indifferently as *urbs* or *civitas*.

7. Turner 1939. Thus the bishop of Trier (a *colonia*) comes *de civitate Treverorum*; the bishop of London, *de civitate Londenensi* (with MSS variants). The bishop of Lincoln comes exceptionally *de civitate Colonia Londenensium* (*sic*), because *'colonia'* was already part of the place-name, as it still is.

8. Amm. Marc. XXVII.8.7. He refers to Lugdunum, the greatest *colonia* in the three Gauls, as an *oppidum* (XVI.11.4). In cataloguing the cities of Gaul (XV.11), he refers to them indifferently as *municipia, oppida, urbes* and *civitates*, simply for variation. The *coloniae* Cologne (XV.11.7) and Trier (XV.6.4), for example, are *civitates*.

9. Wilkes 1996. Thus also Salway 1981, 582; Millett 1996, 34, after Morris 1982, 92. Selkirk (1995) has suggested that it was an 'imperial *vicus*', a grandiose property speculation, but this may be a *jeu d'esprit*.

10. *Britannia* 34 (2003), 364, no. 5.

11. Frere 1999, 189; Hassall 1996; Mann 1998.

12. *Pan. Lat.* viii (v) 17.1, greeted by LON(DINIVM) on the Arras medallion; Amm. Marc. XX.1.3, XXVII.8.7. There was a customary port of entry for the proconsul of Asia (*Digest* I.16.4, 5), but we do not know whether this principle applied to all provinces. Lupicinus and Theodosius landed at Richborough, not London.

13. Hassall 1973. The epigraphic evidence for government personnel in Britain is collected by Haensch 1997, 457–60, with annotation. Inscriptions cited here are *RIB* 12 (Classicianus); *RIB* II.4, 2443.2 (a stamped but 'uninscribed' tablet); II.5, 2485 with Betts 1995 (procuratorial tiles); *RIB* 11 (*Leg. VI Vict.*); 13 (*Leg. XX VV*); 15 (legionary centurion); 17 + add. (centurion of *Leg. II Aug.*); 18 (*Leg. XX VV*); 19 + add. (*speculatores* from *Leg. II Aug.*).

14. *Britannia* 16 (1985), 317, no. 1. A third-century date has been inferred from the high proportion of *Aur(elii)*, at least 6 (and perhaps 8) out of 23, but the excellent lettering is much earlier. Compare *CIL* III.7449, which lists 75 members of a legionary vexillation in AD 155, where *Aurelius* is already the most common *nomen* with 17 instances, as against *Iulius* 10, *Valerius* 10, *Aelius* and *Flavius* 7 each.

15. *RIB* 21, with Birley 1988, 145.

16. *Tab. Vindol.* 154.5 and 9 (the strength report); 310, with the address *Londini Veldedeio equisioni co(n)s(ularis)*. The fragment of a letter from Carlisle (*Tab. Luguval.* 28), which mentions *cohortales*, apparently connects them with 'London'.

17. Tomlin 1996 = *Britannia* 25 (1994), 302, no. 34; Tomlin 2003.

18. Frere 1999, 197; thus also Wacher 1995, 18 and 91; Merrifield 1983, 71.

19. Merrifield 1983, 71.

20. Haensch 1997, 372–4.

21. The local authorities in the third century were still the *c(ives) R(omani) Mog(. . .)* (*ILS* 7078, 7079), so its status was that of the *canabae* at Carnuntum and Aquincum before they were promoted to *municipia* by Hadrian. Richmond (1946, 74) saw Mainz as an early *municipium* which became a *colonia* in the late third century, but the inscription which he cites (*CIL* XIII.6727) is only a dedication to Diocletian and his colleagues by the *civitas Mog[ontiacensis]*, which is not specific.

22. *JRS* 11 (1921), 101–07, the altar of a *sevir Aug(ustalis) col(oniarum) Ebor(aci) et Lind(i)*.

Compare *Britannia* 1 (1970), 308, no. 14 (York), the third-century but undated sarcophagus of the father-in-law of a local *dec(urio)*. For the vexed question of how and when Britain was divided, see Birley 2005, 333–6. Severus died at York in February 211, and his presence there (*Eboraci*) is explicit in the rescripts of 12th September [209] (*AE* 1986, 628) and 5th May 210 (*Cod. Just.* III.32.1).

23. Aurelius Victor, *Liber de Caesaribus* 20.27, says that Severus died *in Britanniae municipio cui Eboraci nomen*. Richmond (1962, xxxviii, n. 3) notes this reference without committing himself; Mann and Jarrett (1966, 63) cautiously accept it, since Victor calls Lanuvium a *municipium* (15.2), which is technically correct. But he soon refers to it as an *oppidum* (16.1), and his usage, like that of his younger contemporary Ammianus Marcellinus (see above, n. 8), is not specific; he uses *oppidum* freely for *coloniae*, for example Leptis (20.19), Thysdrus (26.2), Tarracona (33.3), Cirta (40.28).

24. Hist. Aug., *Hadrian*, 11.2: *Britanniam petiit, in qua multa correxit*; Aulus Gellius, *Noctes Atticae* XVI.13.4.

25. Mann 1998, 337–8.

26. *Britannia* 23 (1992), 309, no. 1 (*AE* 1992, 1119), now in the Museum of London, where I am grateful to Jenny Hall for allowing me to examine it in 2000. For a plan of the site, see *Britannia* 21 (1990), 343, fig. 21. I am grateful to the excavator, Pete Rowsome, for details of the context.

27. I am grateful to Richard Grasby here (pers. comm.) for his observations based on experience of incising Purbeck 'marble': 'The letters have been cut with some difficulty. Sides of the 'V' cut waver around hard spots in the stone. Fragmented, inaccurate carving of the left sides of the oblique strokes X and A speaks of great difficulty in steering the chisel through the stone. Conchoidal fractures are visible on the top edges of all letters.' The exaggerated upper serifs are a skilful attempt to limit and conceal the damage here.

28. Frere and Fulford 2002, 173, suggest that 'at the end of the first century Purbeck may have ceased to be used as a source of material for monumental inscriptions, whether for geological reasons or because of a change in fashion, although continuing to be exploited for private commissions'. But a fragment from Chichester (*Britannia* 7 [1976], 379, no. 4), although very slight, can be ascribed to a monumental inscription of Hadrian, described as the son of Trajan and grandson of Nerva.

29. PARTH MAX of Marcus Aurelius and Lucius Verus, or the similar territorial titles of Septimius Severus and Caracalla, are unlikely in view of the lettering and the use of Purbeck 'marble'.

30. Trajan became COS III in 100, IIII in 101, V in 103, and VI in 112. Hadrian did not advance beyond COS III in 119. Antoninus Pius became COS III in 140, and COS IIII in 145.

31. For the design and layout of inscriptions, and the construction, proportions and carving of *scriptura monumentalis*, see Grasby 2002. For the *ordinatio* of Classicianus' London tombstone (*RIB* 12), Grasby and Tomlin 2002.

32. *Britannia* 8 (1977), 426, no. 1. There is no sign that it was cut up for re-use, which seems less likely.

33. *JRS* 46 (1956), 146, no. 3. Unfortunately the thickness of the wider single-slab Togidubnus inscription from Chichester (*RIB* 91) is not published, but it cannot have been less than that of the Verulamium slabs.

34. *ILAlg* 6094.

35. This objection applies to the only other instance in the Heidelberg and Frankfurt epigraphic data-bases, which I have gratefully used here and elsewhere. *IRT* 362 is a

dedication to Hadrian by the people of Lepcis, *Lepcitani publice per omnia conservatori suo*.

36. *ILS* 378.
37. The only British instances of *Augustales* belong to the *coloniae* of York and Lincoln (*JRS* 11 [1921], 101, and *RIB* 678).
38. *ILS* 2477, a legionary veteran.
39. I have not searched exhaustively, but I suspect they would be special cases, like *ILS* 323 (to the empress Sabina by the agency of the *duoviri*), *ILS* 392 (to Commodus, but really a cult-dedication), *CIL* X.7276 (to Caracalla, by a senator's widow on her under-age son's behalf).
40. Duncan-Jones 1974, 143, notes that of 83 donors of charitable distributions whose status is known, only six are women.
41. *RIB* 5; compare *CIL* XIV.2508, honouring the provincial patron Gaius Iulius Asper, *provincia Britannia patrono*.
42. *ILS* 261 (Emerita): 'To Titus Caesar Vespasianus, son of the August Emperor, *pontifex*, acclaimed *imperator* 12 times, in the 7th year of tribunician power [from July 77 to July 78], consul 6 times, from the province of Lusitania'.
43. *AE* 1969/70.167: 'To the Emperor Caesar Hadrian Augustus, son of the deified Trajan *Parthicus*, grandson of the deified Nerva, *pontifex maximus*, in the 10th year of tribunician power, consul 3 times, father of his country, from the *colonia Iulia Concordia* of Beneventum, to the best and most generous of princes'.
44. Beneventum anticipates Hadrian's assumption of the title *pater patriae* by combining TRIB POT X with P P, but TRIB POT VIIII, for example, without P P would come to much the same.
45. The spacing between words and letters derives from the residue of units within the square occupied by each letter in the notional grid, 1 unit for C, 2 for T, 6 for E, and so on. These are aggregated, and then distributed quite generously as the fragment implies; the exact figures are given in Fig. 2.5.
46. They have the same proportions and spacing as in the fragment, the same wide serifs, the same 1:12 ratio between stem-width and height.
47. It is much thinner than the other two (only 14 mm), and the letters are somewhat higher (*c.* 90 mm).
48. *Britannia* 23 (1992), 309, no. 2.
49. Amm. Marc. XXVIII.3.1: *Augusta . . . quam veteres appellavere Lundinium*; a variation on XXVII.8.7: *Lundinium, vetus oppidum quod Augustam posteritas appellavit*.
50. *Not. Dig.* Occ. 11.37: *praepositus thesaurorum Augustensium; RIC* IX, 1–2. These accession-coins are very rare, and it is inferred (but almost certain) that they were struck in London. The *Notitia* entry must also be identified with London by inference from Ammianus; its explicit location 'in Britain' is due to the rubric (lines 36 and 37) added by the modern editor.
51. Frere 1999, 204, but Constantine still used the mint-marks PLN, MLN and PLON. Merrifield 1983, 214, forces Ammianus' two allusions (quoted in n. 49 above) to mean that London was still called 'London' when Theodosius arrived, but 'Augusta' when he left. They are only rhetorical variations of the same gloss, and despite XX.1.3 (see next note), they do not imply the change was recent: he uses *posteritas* in the same way to gloss Perinthus' change of name a century ago (XXVII.4.12).
52. Since Lupicinus is said to have made for *Lundinium* without qualification (XX.1.3). Otherwise the visit of Constans in AD 342/3 might also be suggested.
53. Rivet and Smith 1979, 192, but unjustifiably conjecturing that *Augusta* had been added

to *Londinium* by mistake instead of replacing it.

54. Rivet and Smith 1979, s.v. *Fanum Cocidi, Bremenium, Habitancum, Camulodunum, Lindum, Glevum, Eburacum, Velunia* (with p. 211).

55. Wacher 1995, 18. Fuentes 1989 and 1991 argues by analogy with the Cosmography's *Isca Augusta* for Caerleon that London became *Augusta* because Legion II *Augusta* was based there in the third and fourth centuries, but there is no evidence that it was ever there, and good reason to locate elements of it at Richborough (*Not. Dig.* Occ. 28.19 with 9) and later in the Gallic mobile reserve (ibid. 5.241 and 7.84).

References

Ancient Authors

Ammianus Marcellinus
Aulus Gellius, *Noctes Atticae*
Aurelius Victor, *Liber de Caesaribus*
Codex Justinianus
Digest
Eumenius
Historia Augusta
Notitia Dignitatum occidentalis
Panegyrici Latini
Ravenna Cosmography
Tacitus, *Annales*

Modern Works

Betts, I. M. 1995: 'Procuratorial tile stamps from London', *Britannia* 26, 207–29

Bird, J., Hassall, M. and Sheldon, H. (eds) 1996: *Interpreting Roman London: papers in memory of Hugh Chapman*, Oxford

Birley, A. 1988: *The people of Roman Britain*, revised edition, London

Birley, A. R. 2005: *The Roman government of Britain*, Oxford

Frere, S. 1999: *Britannia: a history of Roman Britain*, fourth edition, London

Frere, S. S. and Fulford, M. 2002: 'The *collegium peregrinorum* at Silchester', *Britannia* 33, 167–75

Fuentes, N. 1989: 'Augusta which the old timers call Londinium', *London Archaeologist* 6.5, 120–5

Fuentes, N. 1991: 'London/*Augusta* – a rejoinder', *London Archaeologist* 6.12, 333–8

Goodburn, R. and Bartholomew, P. (eds) 1976: *Aspects of the* Notitia Dignitatum, Oxford

Grasby, R. D. 2002: 'Latin inscriptions: studies in measurement and making', *PBSR* 70, 151–76

Grasby, R. D. and Tomlin, R. S. O. 2002: 'The sepulchral monument of the procurator C. Julius Classicianus', *Britannia* 33, 43–75

Haensch, R. 1997: *Capita provinciarum: Statthaltersitze und Provinzialverwaltung in der römischen Kaiserzeit*, Mainz am Rhein

Hassall, M. 1973: 'Roman soldiers in Roman London', in Strong 1973, 231–7

Hassall, M. W. C. 1976: 'Britain in the *Notitia*', in Goodburn and Bartholomew 1976, 103–17

Hassall, M. 1996: 'London as a provincial capital', in Bird, Hassall and Sheldon 1996, 19–26

Hurst, H. (ed.) 1999: *The coloniae of Roman Britain: new studies and a review* [*JRA* Supplementary Series 36], Portsmouth, Rhode Island

Mann, J. C. 1961: 'The administration of Roman Britain', *Antiquity* 35, 316–20, reprinted in Mann 1996, 141–5

Mann, J. C. and Jarrett, M. G. 1966: 'The division of Britain', *JRS* 56, 61–4, reprinted in Mann 1996, 137–40

Mann, J. C. 1996: *Britain and the Roman Empire*, Aldershot

Mann, J. C. 1998: 'London as a provincial capital', *Britannia* 29, 336–9

Merrifield, R. 1983: *London: City of the Romans* (London)

Millett, M. 1996: 'Characterizing Roman London', in Bird, Hassall and Sheldon 1996, 33–7

Millett, M. 1999: '*Coloniae* and Romano-British studies', in Hurst 1999, 191–6

Morris, J. 1982: *Londinium: London in the Roman Empire* (London)

Richmond, I. A. 1946: 'The four *coloniae* of Roman Britain', *Archaeological Journal* 103, 57–84

Richmond, I. A. 1962: *An inventory of the historical monuments in the City of York, I: Eburacum: Roman York*, London

Rivet, A. L. F. and Smith, C. 1979: *The place-names of Roman Britain*, London

Salway, P. 1981: *Roman Britain*, Oxford

Selkirk, A. 1995: 'What was the status of Roman London?', *London Archaeologist* 7.12, 328–31

Strong, D. (ed.) 1973: *Archaeological theory and practice: essays presented to Professor W. F. Grimes*, London

Syme, R. 1958: *Tacitus*, Oxford

Tomlin, R. S. O. 1996: 'A five-acre wood in Roman Kent', in Bird, Hassall and Sheldon 1996, 209–15

Tomlin, R. S. O. 2003: ''The Girl in Question': a new text from Roman London', *Britannia* 34, 41–51

Turner, C. H. 1939: *Ecclesiae Occidentalis Monumenta Iuris Antiquissimi* I (ed. Schwartz), 396–415

Wacher, J. 1995: *The towns of Roman Britain*, second edition, London

Wilkes, J. 1996: 'The status of Londinium', in Bird, Hassall and Sheldon 1996, 27–31

Chapter 3

CORVÉES AND *CIVITATES*

Michael Fulford

This modest contribution to the celebration of your ninetieth birthday, Sheppard, attempts, by exploiting sources from the northern frontier which refer to provincial organisation, to bridge military and civilian in Britannia, *two areas where you have made a massive contribution to our knowledge and understanding of Roman Britain.*

Five building stones recovered from Hadrian's Wall appear to refer to contributions to this massive building project from three southern *civitates*, the Catuvellauni, the Dumnonii and the Durotriges of Lendiniae (Fig. 3.1). A sixth stone may refer to the Brigantes, or else an otherwise unknown tribe. Some years ago the late C. E. Stevens suggested that they all derived from repair-work of the Wall, following the barbarian incursions of AD 367. He linked these stones and one other one, referring to an individual, to Gildas' description of the building of a Wall from sea to sea *sumptu publico privatoque*, following a devastation of the province. For Stevens that construction related to the restoration of Britain after AD 367, and the building stones for him were clear evidence of construction at both public and private expense.[1] Relating to the south-west part of Britain are four stones, the first two referring to the Dumnonii:

> *RIB* 1843: *civitas Dum(no)ni(orum)*: 'The tribe of the Dumnonii (built this).'

> *RIB* 1844: *civitas Dumnoni(orum)*: 'The tribe of the Dumnonii (built this).'

Both stones were found relatively close to each other: the first was discovered in 1760 near the fort of Carvoran, the latter before 1828 on the Wall a little to the east of Thirlwall Castle.

Further to the east two stones were found referring to the Durotriges:

> *RIB* 1672: *c(ivitas) Dur(o)tr(i)g(um) (L)endin(i)e(n)sis*: 'The canton of the Durotriges of Lendiniae (built this).'

> *RIB* 1673: *ci(vitas) Durotrag(um) Lendinie(n)si[s]*: 'The canton of the Durotrages of Lendiniae (built this).'

Although, as *RIB* records, the provenance of the latter is vague ('found before 1873 somewhere west of Housesteads'), it is relatively close to that of the other Durotriges stone, which was 'found in 1882 at the foot of the crags north of the Wall at Cawfields'. *RIB* 1673 was cut on the back of a small, hitherto uninscribed, altar.

The fifth stone, introducing a personal name, was found to the west of the other four in, or before, 1717 at Howgill, about a mile east of Castlesteads:

> *RIB* 1962: *civitate Catuuellaunorum Toss[o]dio:* 'From the tribe of the Catuvellauni Tossodio (built this).'

The sixth stone, now lost, was reported to Hutchinson before 1794 as having been found at Bleatarn, to the west of Castlesteads:

> *RIB* 2022: *capud pe[d(aturae)] civitat(is) Brig<ig>*: 'The beginning of the length in feet built by the Brigantian canton.'

Interestingly, although the identification of the *civitas* with the Brigantes is not certain, this stone can be linked by the word *pedatura* with another organisation the base of which was in the south of Britain. The *classis Britannica* is recorded on two undated building stones, one (*RIB* 1945) of which was 'found on Hadrian's Wall, probably near Birdoswald,' the other (*RIB* 1944) 'seen in 1604 in the vault at Tredermaine (now Triermain) Castle':

> *RIB* 1944: *ped(atura) cl(assis) Brit(annicae)*: 'The length in feet built by the British fleet.'

> *RIB* 1945: *ped(atura) cl(assis) Brit(annicae)*: 'The length in feet built by the British fleet.'

As with the *civitates* inscriptions from the section of the Turf Wall, these stones may relate to the rebuilding in stone. That the *classis Britannica* was also involved with the Hadrianic construction is attested by the building slab (*RIB* 1340) from the portico of the granaries at the fort at Benwell.

A third building stone with the word *pedatura* comes from further west, at Drumburgh:

> *RIB* 2053 *pedatura Vindo moruci*: 'The length in feet built by Vindomorucus'.

Interestingly this is the only building stone from the Wall which refers to an individual, and, coincidentally, it can be linked by the terminology employed to one of the *civitas* stones. There is only one further inscription from the Wall with the word *pedatura*, *RIB* 1629 from Housesteads. It, too, may preserve part of a personal name:

> *RIB* 1629: *[pe]datura [. . .]uci* 'The length in feet built by . . .'

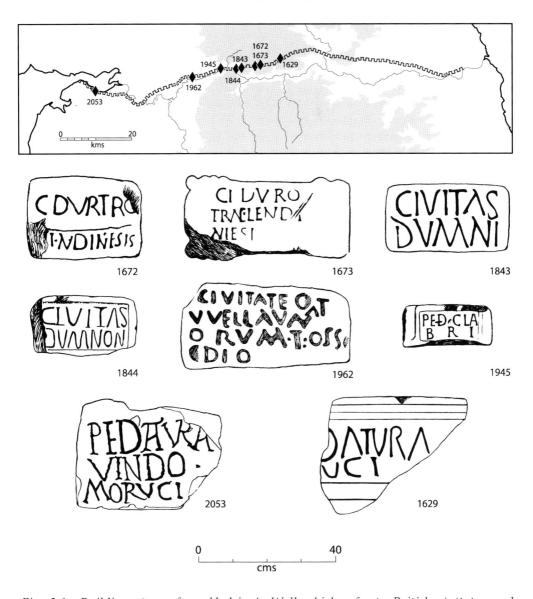

Fig. 3.1 Building stones from Hadrian's Wall which refer to British civitates *and individuals, together with their find-spots; and an inscription of the* classis Britannica

Discussion

All these inscriptions are undated, but the fact that some come from the western part, the area of the Turf Wall, implies that some, at least, are secondary to the Hadrianic construction and, at the earliest, might be associated with the rebuilding of the Turf Wall in stone. Thus Collingwood, as did Birley, believed that the inscriptions referred to the rebuilding of the Wall in the time of the Severus.[2] For Frere 'it is certain that the *civitates* took no part in the original building of the Wall under Hadrian, and that these inscriptions record a subsequent repair. But whether they should be ascribed to the Severan or Constantian reconstructions – or even to 369 – is not at all clear. They are usually taken to date to the time of Severus'.[3] Later in his account, however, he is inclined towards Stevens' argument: 'some of the actual work of rebuilding may have been carried out by corvées provided by the *civitates* of southern Britain . . . if the inscriptions . . . may be connected with a tradition preserved by Gildas'.[4] John Mann pointed out that when the work was undertaken, the southern *civitates* were likely to have been under the same civil authority as the Wall. This was true in the second century before the division of Britain, after which the southern *civitates* would have been in a separate province. However, in the fourth century all the provinces of the island were under the overriding authority of the *vicarius*.[5] All the inscriptions incorporating the term *pedatura* imply they are part of a larger project, where other organisations (such as the *centuriae*) also record distances. This would tend to place them in the context of the principal period of building of the Wall in the second century. This group includes the stones referring to the *classis Britannica* as well as to the individual(s), and to one *civitas*, that possibly referring to the Brigantes. Indeed, since the *classis Britannica* is the only military unit to employ the term, it is possible that the other groups associated with it by shared use of this word worked alongside the fleet, or under its supervision. The next question is whether the group can be expanded to include all the remaining *civitas* stones. The *classis Britannica* is not attested epigraphically after the mid-third century,[6] and there is nothing inherently 'late' in the character of any the inscriptions; they merge in style with the other building stones. There is thus no reason not to propose that all the named *civitates* are associated with the initial construction of the stone Wall and the replacement of the Turf Wall in stone, and that they belong to the second century, before the division of Britain into *Inferior* and *Superior*. Indeed in the general context and tradition of commemoration of building associated with Hadrian's Wall, the *civitates* stones make better sense when they are seen against that background. We have no other evidence for comparable, inscribed building stones (as opposed to formal building inscriptions) dedicated by military units from the Wall from the third and fourth centuries.

Given attempts to try and understand the scale of the work involved in the construction of Hadrian's Wall, and the very considerable demands that it would have made on the supply of suitable transport and materials, it is easy to see how the project could well have involved resources from the south of the province,[7] and indeed we know that the *classis Britannica* was involved from the outset, as the Benwell stone attests. One of the materials associated with the fleet is the production of iron from the Weald of south-east Britain, and it is reasonable to suppose that it was involved with supplying the project as well as taking part in the process of construction. On the basis of the pottery manufactured in the south-west of Britain and found in quantity on Hadrian's Wall (notably South-East Dorset BB1, but also

Severn Valley ware), it is clear that quite humble goods were being transported very great distances to the northern frontier, though not necessarily all by the fleet. However, there is the link provided by *pedatura* with one *civitas* and individual(s), and it is possible therefore that the fleet was made responsible for the supply of civilian workers to the project. If certain commodities were being transported long distances to the north, so, too, might groups of civilians have been brought in to help with the project.

We can only conjecture how the corvées were organised, but the assertion of local identity suggests a degree of independence. The presence of a named individual, Tossodio, in association with the Catuvellaunian stone, like the names of the centurions, suggests a foreman and a degree of local leadership. Whether this was established by the *civitas* before departure, or emerged later on the Wall, is not known, but the former seems more likely. We have no clue as to the range of skills among the civilian corvées, but they clearly included literacy. The early second century was a time of continuing capital investment into monumental buildings among the cities of the southern *civitates*, and it is possible that the *ordo* in question contracted with the fleet, or the provincial government, to supply a building team with foreman.

It is generally accepted that *RIB* 1672 and 1673 refer to Ilchester, Somerset, which is identified with the *Lindinis* of the Ravenna Cosmography, though there is no independent epigraphic evidence to confirm the association.[8] Bogaers dissented from the view that the inscription translated '*civitas* of the Durotriges of Lendiniae', arguing that here *civitas* should be translated as 'town'.[9] Whichever of these interpretations is favoured, there are interesting, and inter-connected, implications. First, if we accept a second-century date for these stones, it means that the *civitas* as tribal capital of the *Durotriges Lendiniensis* is also second-century in date, and is not a later sub-division of the *civitas* of the *Durotriges*, as was first suggested by Stevens.[10] This would make Ilchester the smallest *civitas* capital with a defended area at the end of the second century of some 25 acres (10 ha). This compares with *Moridunum*, *civitas* capital of the Demetae in south-west Wales, at 31 acres (13 ha), and *Venta Icenorum* at 35 acres (14.2 ha). If we follow Bogaers' interpretation of *civitas*, it would also be the smallest city in *Britannia*. We know very little about the internal organisation of the town, though there is some evidence to suggest a street grid and a large masonry building in the centre.[11] It clearly had attractions because it became the centre of a group of rich villas and itself doubled in size to about 50 acres (20 ha). As for the tribal area, the town commanded the low-lying lands of the Somerset Levels which add a geographical integrity to the proposed political entity of the *civitas Durotrigum Lendiniensis*.

Two further thoughts follow from a relatively early designation of the *civitas Durotrigum Lendiniensis*. First, future discoveries may define further early tribal *civitates* of relatively limited geographical extent. It has already been suggested on the basis of a milestone of the reign of the Gallic emperor, Postumus, discovered in 1964, that the *civitas* of the Carvetii was carved out of the territory of the Brigantes in the third century with its centre at Carlisle.[12] A more recent find of a second milestone now gives a *terminus ante quem* of 223 (the reign of Severus Alexander) for the creation of the *civitas*, and confirms Carlisle as the centre.[13] This date is now close to the second century! It also raises the question whether the Carvetii were an independent tribe, achieving self-governing status about the same time as the Brigantes. Carlisle brings another 'small town' to the rank of *caput civitatis* with, as yet, no convincing evidence for street planning or civic buildings.[14] Second, if *civitas* capitals include relatively small settlements, it raises questions about the appropriate accommodation of the *ordo*. Frere has sought the identification of the building in which the *ordo* of the *civitas* would meet in the basilica alongside the forum in the monumental complex we understand as the forum-basilica.[15] There is no difficulty in identifying monumental buildings in the centres of the larger towns which share similar characteristics in terms of their architecture, and which are interpreted as fora-basilicae, but there is no evidence for buildings on such a scale in the smaller towns. Partly this is a reflection of the overall lack of evidence from these settlements, but we might also be prepared to expect that the needs of the *ordo* could be accommodated in other ways than with the type of building conventionally known as the forum-basilica, and represented classically in cities such as Caerwent, London, Silchester and Wroxeter. Aerial photography of the 'small town' of Water Newton (*Durobrivae*), for example, reveals evidence of two large courtyard buildings, one reminiscent of the classic forum-basilica plan, and both potentially with sufficient accommodation to house the *ordo*. While the only direct evidence of the town's administrative status are the *mortarium* stamps with the legend *Cunoarus Vico Duro(brivae)* or similar, it has been suggested that it became a *civitas* capital. Notwithstanding its size (44 acres [17.8 ha] within the walls), however, unlike the towns whose status as *civitas* capitals is assured, there is no evidence of a regular street-grid or other public buildings.[16]

To conclude, there is no evidence to support a late Roman date for the building stones from Hadrian's Wall which give the names of *civitates* and personal name(s). They are best seen as part of the original construction or the replacement of the Turf Wall with stone in the second century. If the readings of *RIB* 1672 and 1673 are correct, there are implications for the chronology of the organisation of the province into *civitates*, and for the character of some of the urban centres which would have provided the accommodation for the *ordo* of the *civitas*. There may be more of a gradation rather than a clear-cut division in function and status between the planned and the unplanned town, and between the 'classic' forum-basilica and the possible public buildings identified from aerial photography at *Durobrivae*. In this respect the plan of the forum-basilica at *Venta Icenorum* does not measure up well in comparison with its counterparts at Caerwent, Silchester and Wroxeter. It may have more in common with the as yet unexplored buildings noted above at *Durobrivae*.

Notes

1. Stevens 1940, 148; 1941, 359.
2. Birley 1961, 210; Collingwood and Myres 1936, 136.
3. Frere 1999, 162.
4. Frere 1999, 349.
5. Mann 1974.
6. Cunliffe 1968, 261.
7. Hill 2004; Kendal 1996.
8. Rivet and Smith 1979, 392.
9. Bogaers 1967, 233.
10. Stevens 1952.
11. Burnham and Wacher 1990, 62–70.
12. Frere 1999, 178–9; Higham and Jones 1985, 9–14.
13. Edwards and Shotter 2005, 67–71.
14. Burnham and Wacher 1990, 51–8; McCarthy 2002, 67–92.
15. Frere 1999, 197.
16. Burnham and Wacher 1990, 81–91, fig. 18; Frere 1999, 201 with note; Fincham 2004, 28.

References

Birley, E. 1961: *Research on Hadrian's Wall*, Kendal

Bogaers, J. E. 1967: Review of J. S. Wacher (ed.), *The civitas capitals of Roman Britain: papers given at a conference held at the University of Leicester, 13–15 December 1963* (1966), JRS 57, 230–4

Burnham, B. C. and Wacher, J. 1990: *The 'Small Towns' of Roman Britain*, London

Collingwood, R. G. and Myres, J. N. L. 1936: Roman Britain and the English settlements, Oxford

Cunliffe, B. W. 1968: 'The British Fleet', in id. (ed), *Fifth report on the excavations of the Roman fort at Richborough, Kent* [Reports of the Research Committee of the Society of Antiquaries of London 23], Oxford, 255–71

Edwards, B. J. N. and Shotter, D. C. A. 2005: 'Two Roman milestones from the Penrith area', *Trans of the Cumberland & Westmorland Antiquarian & Archaeological Society* 5, 65–77

Fincham, G. 2004: *Durobrivae: a Roman town between Fen and Upland*, Stroud

Frere, S. 1999. *Britannia. A history of Roman Britain*, fourth edition, London

Higham, N. and Jones, B. 1985: *The Carvetii*, Gloucester

Hill, P. R. 2004: *The construction of Hadrian's Wall* [BAR British Series 375], Oxford

Kendal, R. 1996: 'Transport logistics associated with the building of Hadrian's Wall', *Britannia* 27, 129–52

McCarthy, M. 2002: *Roman Carlisle and the lands of the Solway*, Stroud

Mann, J. C. 1974: 'The northern frontier after AD 369', *Glasgow Archaeological Journal* 3, 34–42

Rivet, A. L. F. and Smith, C. 1979: *The place-names of Roman Britain*, London

Stevens, C. E. 1940: 'The British sections of the Notitia Dignitatum', *Archaeological Journal* 97, 125–54

Stevens, C. E. 1941: 'Gildas Sapiens', *English Historical Review* 56, 353–73

Stevens, C. E. 1952: 'The Roman name of Ilchester', *Proceedings of the Somerset Archaeological Society* 96, 188–92

Chapter 4

THE ROMAN FORT AT NEWSTEAD: THE WEAPONS AND THE GARRISONS

William Manning

I first met Sheppard Frere in 1956 when he came to lecture to the University of Nottingham Archaeological Society of which I was then Chairman. Two years later I became his student at the Institute of Archaeology of London University, and so began a friendship which has continued to the present day. This paper is essentially a statement of work in progress, part of a larger study of the ironwork from the fort at Newstead undertaken for the National Museums of Scotland. In writing it I have not attempted to place the Newstead weapons in the context of Roman weapons in general, but to provide a study of one of the most important and closely dated collections of spearheads from Britain; to have attempted more would have resulted in a paper of excessive length. I offer it to Sheppard as a token of my gratitude for half a century of help, encouragement and friendship.

The context

The fort at Newstead, near Melrose in the Scottish Borders, was at the centre of the systems of forts constructed in southern Scotland in the Flavian and Antonine periods. The site was extensively excavated under the direction of James Curle between 1905 and 1910, excavations which established the sequence of occupation and the general layout of the various forts.[1] Later excavations by Ian Richmond in the 1940s elucidated many of the problems which the earlier work had left open,[2] and Rick Jones and Simon Clarke have undertaken more recent work on the site.[3] In all there were four main phases of occupation:

1   The first fort was established by Agricola in *c.* AD 80. The defences were defined by Curle who showed that the fort had an area of 4.14 ha (10.25 acres). The only building known is a timber-framed structure, interpreted at the time as a stable. The suggested garrison, two *alae quingenariae*, is based entirely on the size of the fort.
2   This first fort was completely levelled in the late 80s and a new fort of 5.7 ha. (14.1 acres) was built on the same site, its size and strength making it the keystone in the military system of southern Scotland. Within it were barracks whose size suggests that they were intended for legionaries, probably brigaded with a cavalry unit. It was closed on the Trajanic withdrawal from Scotland in the early years of the second century.

3 With the move forward from Hadrian's Wall to the Antonine Wall at the beginning of the reign of Antoninus Pius *c.* AD 140, the site was reoccupied and a new fort of 5.9 ha. (14.6 acres) was built. The *praetentura* contained 12 barracks which were separated from *the retentura* by a stone wall, the suggested explanation for this division being that the *praetentura* held a legionary vexillation, the *retentura* an *ala* of auxiliary cavalry.

4 After a brief period of closure in the late 150s, when the frontier returned to Hadrian's Wall, the fort was reoccupied in *c.* 160. The dividing wall was demolished and new barracks and what have been interpreted as stables were built which have been identified as suitable for an *ala milliaria*.[4]

The date of the final closure remains uncertain for, as Brian Hartley pointed out, some of the samian ware from the site probably dates from after *c.* AD 163, when the other forts in southern Scotland appear to have been dismantled. This suggests that Newstead may have continued to be occupied until at least *c.* AD 180. Two coins, one of Faustina II and the other of Crispina, may support the evidence of the samian ware.[5]

Although the sequence of forts is firmly established, the evidence for their garrisons, as so often, is less secure. The excavations produced a number of inscriptions, mainly on altars, which establish some of the personnel, and presumably their units, in the fort at various times. They are:

1 An altar dedicated to Apollo by Lucius Maximus Gaetulicus, a legionary centurion,[6] from Pit LXXXIII in the South Annexe, which was dated to the Antonine period on ceramic evidence.[7] An inscription from Great Chesters reveals that Gaetulicus served in the Twentieth Legion.[8]

2 An altar dedicated to the Goddess of the Parade Ground by Aelius Marcus, decurion of the *ala Augusta Vocontiorum*. It was found in 1783, 200 yards east of the fort, presumably from a pit in the East Annexe. Richmond suggested that this unit was in occupation in the first Antonine phase (i.e. Phase 3).[9]

3–5 Three altars dedicated by Gaius Arrius Domitianus, centurion of the Twentieth Legion. The first, to Diana, came from the ditch of East Annexe;[10] the second to Jupiter Optimus Maximus,[11] and the third to Silvanus, both came from a well in the Antonine headquarters building.[12]

6 A fragment of an inscription apparently referring to the Twentieth Legion came from the well in the Antonine headquarters building.[13]

To these may be added *graffiti* on equipment and tools. Those on the cavalry helmets[14] add nothing to the evidence of the helmets themselves; both were found in late Flavian/early Trajanic deposits. Another on a spearhead from a late Flavian/early Trajanic pit[15] may refer to a *turma*, while a punched ownership *graffito* on an axe refers to a century.[16] More useful are a set of nine *phalerae* awarded to Domitius Atticus from Pit XXII, dated to the Flavian period,[17] for such decorations were awarded to legionaries rather than auxiliaries.[18] In addition to these we have a lead seal from the inner ditch of the west annexe which reads *Cohortis III Nerviorum*;[19] three camp-kettles, one with the *graffito* LVCANI T LVCANI ('*turma* of Lucanus', written twice), from the late Flavian/early Trajanic Pit XIV;[20] another, from the late Flavian/early Trajanic Pit X, refers to the century of SA . . . ;[21] while a third, with the punched *graffito turma Crispi / Nigri* ('*turma* of Crispus, (property) of Niger'), came from the Antonine Pit XCIX.[22]

A *dipinto* on the neck of an amphora from the late Flavian/early Trajanic Pit LXXVIII reads *Atti Secundi tr(ibuni) / lagunu(m) m(odiorum) iii*, '(Property) of Attius Secundus, tribune: a jar of three *modii*'.[23] Presumably it indicates the presence of a tribune at Newstead, and, as Frere and Tomlin note, 'this is the first epigraphic evidence of the Flavian garrison at Newstead . . . : it was commanded (?) by a tribune, and must therefore have included a milliary cohort or, more likely, a powerful legionary vexillation.'

Discussion

None of this material can be linked with the first, Agricolan fort, but the evidence for the garrison of the second, late Flavian, fort is far stronger. The cavalry helmets, the spearhead and the camp kettle with *graffiti* referring to *turmae* are all clear evidence for a cavalry unit at Newstead in that period. Alongside these are the references to centuries, probably, although not certainly, legionary, on the axe and another camp kettle;[24] the *phalerae* of Domitius Atticus and the *dipinto* of the tribune Attius Secundus, all suggest that there was also a legionary element in the late Flavian fort.

There is no firm evidence of this type for the garrison of the first Antonine fort, unless the camp kettle belonging to Niger came from this phase. Richmond assigned the altar erected by Aelius Marcus of the *ala Augusta Vocontiorum* to this fort, but firm evidence for this is lacking.

The altars erected by Gaius Arrius Domitianus of the Twentieth Legion imply the presence of a legionary vexillation in the final phase. Two of the altars were found in the filling of the well in the headquarters building, suggesting that they were in that building when it was demolished. Given the Roman custom of concealing such inscriptions when they abandoned forts, a custom particularly well illustrated on the Antonine Wall, it seems most unlikely that they would have been erected in Phase 3 and abandoned in the *principia* when that fort was dismantled. The discovery of the base of a Dragendorff 33 samian cup with the stamp of PROBVS in this well[25] suggests that it was not refilled at the end of Phase 3, for, as Hartley notes, 'whether the stamp could be quite as early as 160 is doubtful.'[26] Indeed, if Hartley is correct in suggesting that the fort continued to be occupied as late as *c.* 180, there is no obvious reason why the well should have been refilled before then. If so, the altars must imply the presence of legionaries at some time during the final phase.

The weapons

The spearheads

There are various ways of fighting with spears: they may be thrown; used in hand-to-hand combat, in effect as a form of long-handled sword; used by infantry as pikes against cavalry (in which case they are likely to have had long hafts); or they served as cavalry lances. Nor is the distinction between the smaller spearheads and the heads of large artillery projectiles, such as those discussed below, always completely clear. In the present context, we may probably ignore their use as pikes, for that form of warfare is not well attested in the Roman period. Such evidence as we have suggests that in the first and second centuries AD the normal legionary spear was the *pilum*, with its characteristic long iron shaft and small pyramidal head. Both auxiliary infantry and cavalry used spears, but differentiating between the various types is less easy. We may safely assume that the lance was not used by the infantry, but it is not really clear what a Roman lance-head looked like, and those shown on reliefs are usually too stylized to be useful. Similarly the infantry may have thrown their spears, but literary sources make it clear that in addition to their lance Roman cavalry also carried javelins which they too threw.[27] Although the idea that Roman cavalry used their lances to attack the enemy without dismounting has been questioned, the evidence of cavalry tombstones, which often show them doing just that, appears incontrovertible. There would be no point whatever in repeatedly showing cavalrymen doing something which everyone knew was never done.

Various attempts have been made to produce classifications of Roman spears,[28] but while all agree on a few basic divisions, attempts to refine the groups have been less successful. In a detailed discussion of the large assemblage of weapons from the Claudian fort at Hod Hill, Dorset, the writer divided them into four groups, using the form and size of the blades as the key criteria, in particular the ratio of the length and width of the blades, arguing that the blade is the functional part of the weapon and, therefore, the part most likely to reflect their intended use.[29] The quality of workmanship, and such features as whether the flanges forming the socket had been welded together or left open were ignored, as they do not affect its basic function. Most examples lacked distinct midribs.

Group I had small, leaf-shaped blades between 4.5 cm and 6.5 cm in length and 2 cm and 3 cm in width. The exact shape of the blade varied somewhat, but no more than might be explained by minor variations in the practices of different workshops or even individual smiths; functionally they were all the same (44 examples or 49.4%).

Group II comprised larger versions of Type I, with relatively slender blades between 8 cm and 10 cm in length and 2 cm to 3 cm in width (23 examples or 26%).

Group III was a smaller group with relatively long, narrow blades between 13 cm and 15 cm in length and 1.8 cm and 2.3 cm in width (6 examples or 6.7%).

Group IV contained the largest with blades between 17 cm and 25 cm in length and 3 cm to 4 cm in width. They were subdivided into three sub-groups:
  • *IVA* had narrow, leaf-shaped blades with gently curving shoulders and midribs of varying prominence (6 examples or 6.7%).

- *IVB* had narrow, slightly tapering blades with short, steep shoulders (6 examples or 6.7%).
- *IVC* differed from Type IVB in that the flanges forming the socket were not welded together (4 examples or 4.5%).

Thus Groups I and II accounted for 75% of the spearheads.

Of the thirty-two spearheads from Newstead which are included in this survey,[30] thirteen are of late Flavian or Trajanic date, four are probably Antonine and fifteen are unprovenanced. Unfortunately the 'Antonine' spearheads must be regarded with some suspicion. The Accession Register states that they all came from 'Pits LXX and LXXX combined' and gives an Antonine date, probably following Curle's report. All have unusually high accession numbers (FRA 3295–3299), suggesting either that they entered the collections at a late date, or that, for some reason, they were not accessed until many years after the rest of the collection, most probably the latter. Curle records that both pits were Antonine in date,[31] but in his detailed descriptions of the pits and their contents he makes no mention of their having produced spearheads, although he does record other small artifacts from them.[32] In fact the Register lists some sixteen iron objects from these two pits, all of them of recognizable types, which Curle almost invariably listed in his summaries of the pits and their contents. There is no obvious reason why he should have omitted these pieces, and the fact that the four spearheads are the only spearheads in the Newstead assemblage allegedly from an Antonine context makes their omission even odder. Both pits were quite deep, Pit LXX being 13 ft 3 in and Pit LXXX 12 ft, and iron artefacts from pits of this depth, which were effectively anaerobic, are usually well preserved, whereas the four spearheads in question show the corrosion more typical of unstratified finds. Taken together, these facts must cast some doubt on Pits LXX and LXXX being the true provenance of these spearheads. On the other hand, as Dr Fraser Hunter has pointed out to me, other pit groups are conflated (for example, Pits LV and LVI, LX and LXI, LXIII, LXIX and LXXIII, and LXIV and CV), and there is no obvious reason why these artefacts should have been assigned to these pits if this was not done on the excavations. The question is probably insoluble. However, if any one them came from Pit LXX they are likely to date from late in the final phase, for this pit produced one of the few stratified sherds of late Antonine Rheinzabern ware.[33]

Using the same criteria as were used for the Hod Hill spearheads, we may divide them into four main types (Fig. 4.1a), which are clearly defined in the chart which compares the length and breadth of the blades (Fig. 4.1b). All have relatively narrow, leaf-shaped blades, with their maximum breadth coming at a point between one quarter and one third of the way along the blade from the socket. The remarkable uniformity of their basic form is shown in Chart 2a (Fig. 4.2a), which relates the length of the blade to the distance of the maximum width from the tip. All have a thin, diamond-shaped cross-section without a distinct mid-rib. The edges of the flanges forming the socket are usually welded together for most of their length, often leaving a V-shaped gap at the mouth. Most, but not all, had nails just above the mouth of the socket. Other attempts to define meaningful groups,

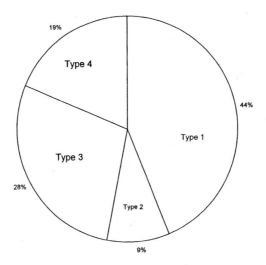

Proportions of Spearhead Types (Sample 32 Spearheads)

Chart 1

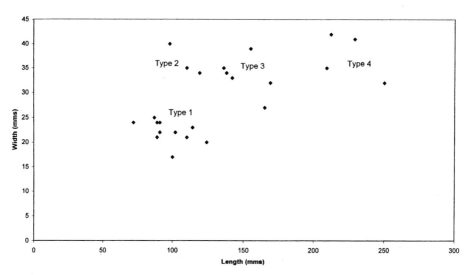

Spearheads: Length of Blade / Maximum Width of Blade

Fig. 4.1 (a) (above) Chart 1: Proportions of spearhead types; (b) (below) Chart 2: Ratio of the length to the maximum width of the blades

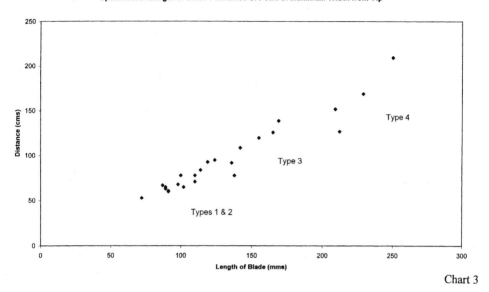

Chart 3

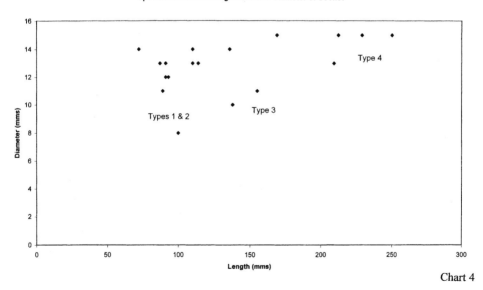

Chart 4

Fig. 4.2 (a) (above) Chart 3: Ratio of the length of the blade to the distance of the point of maximum width from the tip; (b) (below) Chart 4: Spearheads: ratio of the length of the blade to the internal diameter of the socket

William Manning

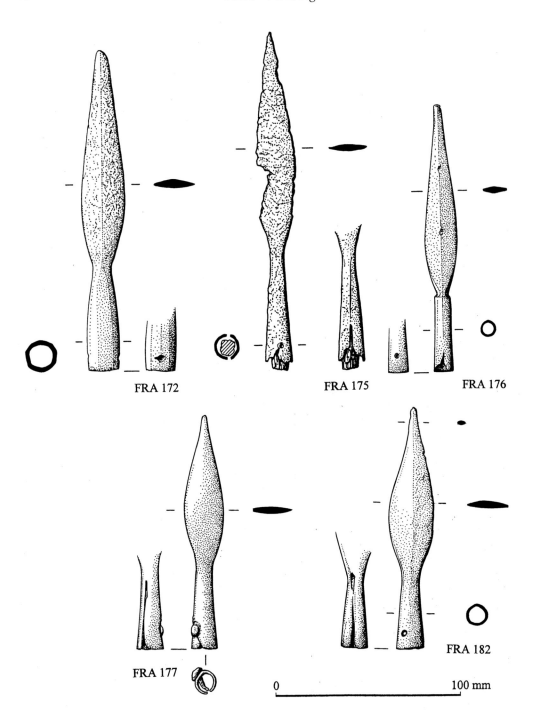

Fig. 4.3 Type-1 spearheads from Newstead

using such criteria as the ratio between the diameter of the socket and the length of the blade (Fig. 4.2b) reveal the same basic groups, although less clearly.

Type 1 (Fig. 4.3) has a relatively small, narrow, leaf-shaped blade with rounded shoulders and edges which are almost straight between the shoulders and the tip. The edges of some of those which are well preserved have a very flattened S-curve which creates an elongated tip (e.g. FRA 177, FRA 182). Although most are well-made, only one (FRA 176) has details which could be considered decorative. There are fourteen examples of this type, one of which is a slight variant (FRA 179). Seven are from late Flavian or early Trajanic contexts, two from the allegedly Antonine 'Pits LXX and LXXX combined', and five are unprovenanced.

Type 2 (Fig. 4.4) is a somewhat larger version of Type 1, with more angular shoulders. Their position on Chart 1b (Fig. 4.1b), which shows the ratio of the length to the breadth of the blades, confirms the visual impression that they are a distinct group, albeit a numerically small one with only three examples, all unprovenanced.

Type 3 (Fig. 4.5) has a larger blade, curved shoulders and a socket which, when com-plete, is relatively long and narrow in proportion to the overall size of the spear-head. There are nine examples of this type, one being a slight variant. All are unprov-enanced save for two which are attributed to Pits LXX and LXXX combined and so are probably of Antonine date. Whether their complete absence from the Flavian pits and the ditch of the early fort, which produced the majority of the examples of Types 1 and 4, indicates that they are of Antonine date is possible but far from certain.

Type 4 (Fig. 4.6) has a long, narrow blade with curved shoulders and edges which are straight between the shoulders and the tip. In their general appearance they are longer versions of Type 1, with relatively short and narrow sockets. All are extremely well made, and, as they all come from pits, they are extremely well preserved. There are six examples of this type, all from late Flavian or Early Trajanic contexts.

The most unusual feature of the Type-4 spearheads is that of the five where the tip survives, four, while having sharp edges, end not in points but in thickened, blunt tips. There can be no question of their being unfinished, or of the end having been blunted by impact; the quality of their preservation makes it quite certain that they are blunt by design. Of the other

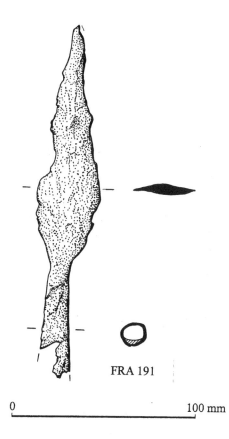

FRA 191

0   100 mm

Fig. 4.4 Type-2 spearhead from Newstead

spearheads in the collection which are not too corroded for the nature of the tip to be obvious, only one Type-1 spearhead has a similarly blunt tip (FRA 176: Fig. 4.3). A possible explanation of this feature is discussed below.

If we compare the Newstead spearheads with those from Hod Hill, we find both similarities and differences. Groups 1 are similar in their general proportions, and probably function, but the Hod Hill examples are generally wider in proportion to their length, very similar to the single Type-1 variant from Newstead. Groups 2 are remarkably similar in size and form in both cases. The spears in both Groups 3 are similar in length, but the Hod Hill spearheads are markedly narrower in proportion to their length than are the Newstead ones. Groups 4 are similar in size and proportions, but the Hod Hill examples are far inferior in the quality of their workmanship to those from Newstead and lack their blunt points. The most notable difference between the two groups is the almost complete absence from Newstead of the crudely-made spearheads which are so characteristic of the Hod Hill assemblage. A possible explanation may lie in the fact that Hod Hill was occupied in the opening years of the conquest; indeed the excavators suggested that it had been abandoned by AD 51.[34] At that time the Roman army was advancing on several fronts in a province too new for the normal system of supplies to have been established, and there may have been a shortage of expendable equipment such as spears, which had to be overcome by rapid, local manufacture, probably by the units themselves. By the late Flavian period, the economy of the province had developed, and the army would have established both the production centres and transport system necessary for its units to be well supplied from existing stocks.

Whether the relatively slight differences between the two groups reflect meaningful changes in the design of spearheads over the fifty to one hundred years which separate them is a question which only the discovery of other large assemblages will resolve.

Function
Although the division of the spearheads into four groups appears to be valid, it does not indicate which troops used them and how. Of the four types, Type 1 and Type 4 were in use in the Flavian phases, Type 1 certainly during the first phase, as four examples were found in the ditch of the early fort which was refilled in the late eighties. If the key pit-groups from the East Annexe were deposited on the closure of the second fort in the opening years of the second century, as seems probable although not certain, they were also used by the garrison of that fort. The Type-4 spearheads are all from late Flavian or early Trajanic pits. The three Type-2 spears are unprovenanced, as are the majority of Type 3, save for two from the probably Antonine 'Pits LXX and LXXX combined'. But when we try to link these types with the various possible garrisons we run into problems. There is no clear evidence for the garrison of the Period-1 fort. The suggestion of two *alae quingenariae* appears to have been based on the size of the fort, and there is no epigraphic evidence to support it. A legionary vexillation brigaded with a cavalry *ala* is the suggested garrison for the Phase-2 fort, and the artefactual evidence would certainly support at least the auxiliary element. The well-known parade helmet and curb-

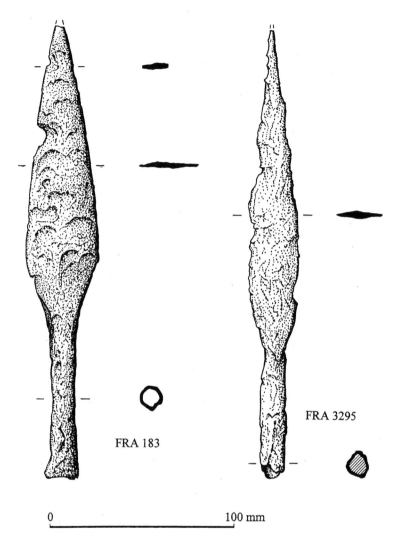

FRA 183

FRA 3295

0   100 mm

Fig. 4.5 Type-3 spearheads from Newstead

bits from Pit XXII,[35] the set of saddle-horn plates from Pit XXII,[36] the harness mounts and fittings,[37] the copper-alloy cooking vessel with the *graffito* of the *turma* of Lucanus from Pit XIV,[38] and the Type-4 spearhead from Pit XVI with an ownership *graffito* apparently referring to a *turma*,[39] all confirm the presence of a cavalry unit in the fort in its second phase. The altar to the Goddess of the Parade Ground dedicated by Aelius Marcus, decurion of the *ala Augusta Vocontiorum*,[40] may have originated in the Flavian period or the later Antonine fort as Ian Richmond supposed. There is less evidence for legionaries in either of the Flavian phases; certainly the kind of equipment usually associated with legionaries is extremely rare, and there are no certain legionary inscriptions or *graffiti* from this period; only the two *gladii* from Pit LVII can be claimed as legionary equipment. Perhaps the best artefactual evidence is the set of nine *phalerae* awarded to Domitius Atticus from Pit XXII,[41] a type of decoration awarded to legionaries rather than auxiliaries,[42] and the *dipinto* referring to the tribune Attius Secundus from Pit LXXVIII.[43] A man of his rank would not have been in command of an auxiliary unit unless it was a milliary *cohort*, which is highly unlikely to have been found at Newstead in the Flavian period; this leads to the assumption that he was commanding a substantial legionary vexillation.

Of course, absence of evidence is not evidence of absence, but there is a notable lack of material which can certainly be associated with an auxiliary infantry unit, in which case we may probably identify most of the spearheads from the Flavian forts as being cavalry weapons. Ancient references to cavalry using spears or lances is limited, although Josephus refers to Roman cavalry having a spear and several lighter javelins in a quiver.[44, 45]

Most reliefs showing auxiliary cavalry are on tombstones, and a high proportion follow a conventional design with the man on his horse spearing a crouching enemy, suggesting that this was one of the favoured techniques when fighting infantry. There is no evidence whatsoever that Roman cavalry ever used their lances against enemy cavalry in the manner of a medieval tournament. If we take the reliefs and Josephus' comment into account, it seems likely that cavalrymen will have carried a spear suitable for use as a lance against infantrymen, which, like his sword, he would normally retain, and others which could be thrown and which would probably be regarded as dispensable. The Type-1 Newstead spearheads would seem to be well-suited for throwing spears; the Roman throwing-spear *par excellence*, the *pilum*, had a very small head. On the other hand, the Type-1 spears would also appear to be suitable as lance-heads. The cavalryman has the advantage of height when dealing with infantry, and under those conditions a relatively small head, which would penetrate the enemy's body but which could be withdrawn relatively easily, is ideal. The truth may well be that they served both functions, and that the main difference was the longer haft necessary when the head was mounted as a lance.

Although slightly larger than the Type-1 weapons, the Type-2 spearheads can probably be regarded as minor variants of Type 1, and are equally well suited for use as either a spear or lance. The Type-3 heads are more of a problem: most are badly corroded, but in the absence of any evidence for auxiliary infantry at Newstead, except possibly in Period 1, we must accept them as probably cavalry weapons.

Type 4 is another matter. If the ownership *graffito* on FRA 171 does refer to a *turma*, it must have been a cavalry weapon. It appears to have two ownership inscriptions on one side of the blade, while on the other is a dotted X, almost certainly the mark of a third owner. All of these spearheads are of excellent workmanship, with carefully forged details, and they do not have the appearance of weapons which were designed to be used and discarded, an argument which, admittedly, is not conclusive as *ballista* heads often show a surprisingly high finish.

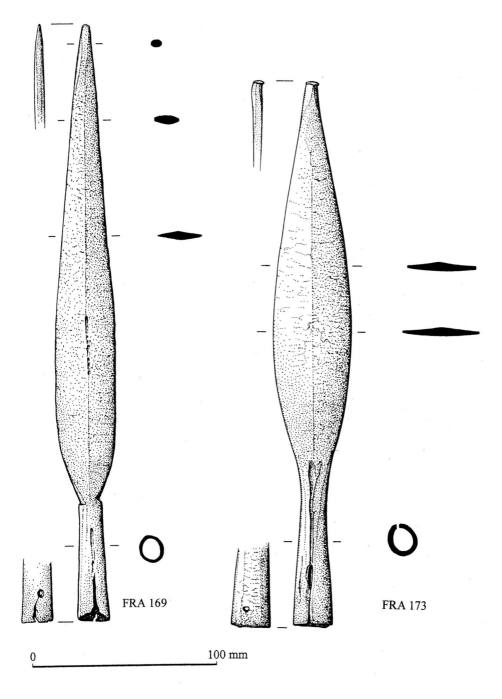

Fig. 4.6 Type-4 spearheads from Newstead

Nonetheless, the fact that the spear had been owned by three troopers is convincing evidence that it was a weapon which they regarded as their own, and which was probably in use for some years. All of this would suggest that we are dealing with a lance rather than a throwing spear. But it is a lance with an intentionally blunt tip, and one of a distinct group of equally blunt weapons. What then was the function of these weapons? Their condition is such that it allows us to say that it is absolutely certain that they are not unfinished, and that their bluntness is not the result of impact. Were they intended to be functional, or are they another aspect of the parade armour so graphically illustrated by the parade helmets from the fort, intended for use in exercises where they would not injure another contestant if they accidentally struck him? The answer is probably no. The tips, though blunt, are not so broad as to prevent penetration and the edges below the tip are very sharp. The explanation may lie in the fact that in a province such as Britain, enemy soldiers were either likely to lack body armour or be wearing chain-mail, and the latter might well be sufficiently robust to turn the point of a normal spear, whereas the strong tip of our Type-4 spearheads could be driven through the mail, after which the edges would do the real damage. Clearly we cannot be certain on such a point, but the discovery of four of these weapons at Newstead indicates that they were an accepted type, and, if the *graffiti* have any meaning, one at least was used by cavalrymen.

Pilae

Given the epigraphic evidence for legionaries at Newstead, the total lack of certain examples of *pilum* heads in the collection is surprising. Indeed the only evidence for the *pilum* from the site is a single example of the truncated pyramidal collars which strengthened the top of the *pilum* shaft from the Flavian/Trajanic Pit XVI.[46]

Boltheads

There are thirteen *ballista* boltheads from Newstead, all of the normal type, with conical sockets and elongated, pyramidal heads (FRA 201, FRA 205 and FRA 210); two others, which are larger and have heads of triangular cross-section (FRA 3299), may or may not be boltheads (Fig. 4.7). As the Charts (Fig. 4.8a and b) show, all of the main group are very similar in size, weight and, if the diameter of the mouth of the socket reflects their calibre, in that as well. The one outlier of this type on the charts (FRA 198, with a length of 62 mm) is almost certainly damaged, and originally was similar to the others. Where their context is recorded it is almost always Flavian or Flavian/Trajanic in date; two have contexts which could be either Flavian/Trajanic or Antonine (FRA 198 from the baths and FRA 210 from the *principia*), and three have no meaningful context. Three came from the ditch of the first Flavian fort, and five from Flavian/Trajanic pits.

It is usually assumed, probably mainly on the evidence of Trajan's Column and the large numbers of boltheads found on legionary sites, that the *ballista* was a legionary weapon. If the Flavian/Trajanic pits which produced the bulk of the heads were refilled in the closure phase, the boltheads will have originated in the

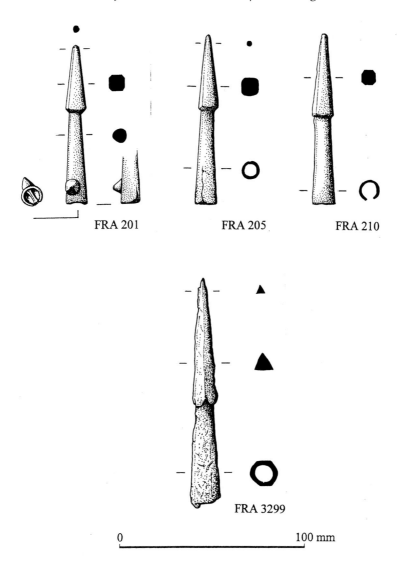

FRA 201

FRA 205

FRA 210

FRA 3299

0   100 mm

Fig. 4.7. Boltheads from Newstead

second Flavian fort which is thought to have had legionaries in its garrison. The three from the ditch of the first fort, which is not usually regarded as having legionary troops, create a slight problem, which is amplified by the discovery of five bolt-ferrules in the same ditch. But, in reality, the evidence for the garrison in this phase is too slight to exclude the possibility of some legionaries forming part of it, while a handful of *ballista* bolts could have probably been found in any auxiliary fort.

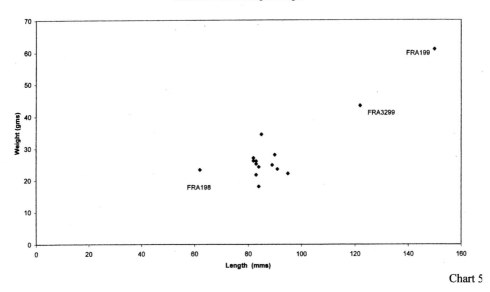

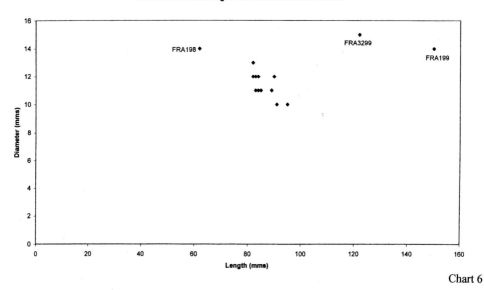

Fig. 4.8 (a) (above) Chart 5: Boltheads: ratio of the overall length to the weight; (b) (below) Chart 6: Boltheads: ratio of the overall length to the external diameter of the sockets

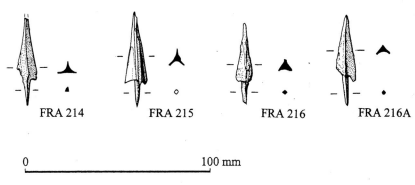

Fig. 4.9 Arrowheads from Newstead

Possible boltheads

Of the larger type of possible bolthead, one (FRA 3299: see Fig. 4.7) is recorded as coming from the combined Pits LXX and LXXX; the other (FRA 199) has no recorded context. The Accession Register suggests that they may have been *pilum* heads, but they lack the long iron shank which characterises the true *pilum*, and most *pilae* have square-sectioned heads. They could, of course, have been a form of spear or lance-head, but they are sufficiently similar to the normal *ballista* bolthead to suggest that is what they are, and this identification is supported by the fact that their socket-mouths are only marginally larger than those of the other boltheads.

Arrowheads

The only arrowheads from the site are a small group of seven (four are shown in Fig. 4.9), all of the normal type – tanged with a triple-flanged head; all come from Pit I, the Antonine well in the *principia*.[47]

Swords

There are eight swords, either fragmentary or complete, from Newstead.[48] Of these four are *spathae*, two *gladii* and two 'Celtic', with blades which are thinner than those of the *spatha* and have hilt-guards of native types. With the exception of one of the *spatha* fragments, all come from late Flavian/Trajanic contexts, the two *gladii* being found with one of the *spathae* in Pit LVII. If we accept the traditional view that the *gladius* was used by legionaries and the *spatha* by auxiliaries, the discovery of two *gladii* in a context which relates to the second Flavian fort is of importance in providing some artefactual evidence for the presence of legionaries in the fort at that time. Unfortunately, as Valerie Maxfield and others have argued,[49] such certainty is impossible, and while the older view may reflect their normal use, it was probably far from invariable. The 'Celtic' swords could be captured booty, or, perhaps more probably, have been used by some of the auxiliaries.

Helmets and armour

The helmets and *lorica* fragments from the site, although exceedingly interesting in themselves, largely confirm the other evidence for the garrisons of the various phases. In all there are parts of four helmets: an iron parade helmet with its mask,[50] another helmet in copper alloy,[51] a copper-alloy mask,[52] and a plain iron cavalry helmet.[53] All come from late Flavian/Trajanic contexts, the three helmets being found together in Pit XXII and the mask in Pit LVII. Almost all of the armour – *lorica segmentata, lorica hamata* and *lorica squamata* – came from the Antonine well (Pit I) in the *principia*[54] and so may date from as late as *c*. AD 180.

Other equipment

There are a number of other military fittings – horse-gear, saddle-mounts, fragments of shield-fittings and the like – from Newstead, but it is beyond the scope of this paper to discuss them all. What can be said is that they accord with the evidence from the other equipment on the types of unit in garrison in the various phases of the site.

Acknowledgements

In writing this paper I have received advice and information from Drs Fraser Hunter, Roger Tomlin and Peter Webster to whom I am most grateful, as I am to Ms Marion O'Neil for the drawings of the weapons.

Appendix

Contexts of spearheads, boltheads, and arrowheads at Newstead

Spearheads
Type 1

FRA 96a	Pit X	Late Flavian / Early Trajanic
FRA 172	Pit XVI	Late Flavian / Early Trajanic
FRA 175	Unprovenanced	
FRA 176	Ditch of Early Fort	Late Flavian
FRA 177	Ditch of Early Fort	Late Flavian
FRA 181	Ditch of Early Fort	Late Flavian
FRA 182	Ditch of Early Fort	Late Flavian
FRA 189	Unprovenanced	
FRA 192	Unprovenanced	
FRA 193	Unprovenanced	
FRA 197	Unprovenanced	
FRA 3296	Pits LXX and LXXX (combined)	Antonine
FRA 3297	Pits LXX and LXXX (combined)	Antonine
Variant		
FRA 179	Pit X	Late Flavian / Early Trajanic

Type 2

FRA 186	Unprovenanced	
FRA 190	Unprovenanced	
FRA 191	Unprovenanced	

Type 3

FRA 183	Unprovenanced	
FRA 184	Unprovenanced	
FRA 185	Unprovenanced	
FRA 188	Unprovenanced	
FRA 195	Unprovenanced	
FRA 196	Unprovenanced	
FRA 3295	Pits LXX and LXXX (combined)	Antonine
FRA 3298	Pits LXX and LXXX (combined)	Antonine
Variant		
FRA 194	Unprovenanced	

Type 4

FRA 168	Pit XVI	Late Flavian/Early Trajanic
FRA 169	Pit XVI	Late Flavian/Early Trajanic
FRA 171	Pit XVI	Late Flavian/Early Trajanic
FRA 173	Pit XVI	Late Flavian/Early Trajanic
FRA 174	Pit LIV	Late Flavian/Early Trajanic
FRA 180	Pit LV	Late Flavian/Early Trajanic

Boltheads

FRA 198	Baths	Uncertain date
FRA 201	Pit VII	Late Flavian/Early Trajanic
FRA 202	Pit LV	Late Flavian/Early Trajanic
FRA 203	Pit LV	Late Flavian/Early Trajanic
FRA 204	*Praetentura*	Uncertain date
FRA 205	Ditch of Early Fort	Late Flavian
FRA 206	Pit LV	Late Flavian/Early Trajanic
FRA 207	Ditch of Early Fort	Late Flavian
FRA 208	Ditch of Early Fort	Late Flavian
FRA 209	Pit VII	Late Flavian/Early Trajanic
FRA 210	*Principia*	Antonine?
FRA 210a	Unprovenanced	
FRA 3390	Unprovenanced	

Anomalous boltheads

FRA 199	Unprovenanced	
FRA 3299	Pits LXX and LXXX (combined)	Antonine

Bolt ferrules

FRA 219	Ditch of Early Fort	Late Flavian
FRA 220	Ditch of Early Fort	Late Flavian
FRA 221	Ditch of Early Fort	Late Flavian
FRA 222	Ditch of Early Fort	Late Flavian
FRA 223	Ditch of Early Fort	Late Flavian

Arrowheads (triple-flanged)
FRA 211   Pit I *Principia*   Antonine
FRA 212   *Principia*   Antonine?
FRA 213   Pit I   Antonine
FRA 214   Pit I   Antonine
FRA 215   Pit I   Antonine
FRA 216   Pit I   Antonine
FRA 216a   Unprovenanced

Notes

1. Curle 1911.
2. Richmond 1950.
3. Clarke and Jones 1996.
4. The sequence is conveniently summarized in Steer 1976.
5. Curle 1911, 399, nos 117 and 118; Hartley 1972, 53–4. Unfortunately, with the exception of sherds from Pit 70 (Hartley 1972, 54, no. 4) and the inner ditch of the later fort (Curle 1911, 218; Hartley 1972, 54, no. 4), none of the late material is from recorded contexts.
6. *RIB* 2120.
7. Curle 1911, 135.
8. *RIB* 725.
9. *RIB* 2121.
10. *RIB* 2122.
11. *RIB* 2123.
12. *RIB* 2124.
13. *RIB* 2127.
14. *RIB* II.3, 2425.4 and 2524.5.
15. *RIB* II.3, 2427.3.
16. *RIB* II.3, 2428.4 .
17. *RIB* II.3, 2427.4–12.
18. Maxfield 1986, and personal information from Professor Maxfield.
19. *RIB* II.1, 2411.142.
20. *RIB* II.2, 2415.65.
21. *RIB* II.2, 2415.66.
22. *RIB* II.2, 2415.68.
23. *RIB* II.6, 2492.7.
24. Dr Roger Tomlin informs me that while the letters SA, which begin the name of the centurion referred to on the camp kettle (*RIB* II.2, 2415.66), may suggest some common Latin *cognomina*, e.g. Sabinus, Salvius or Saturninus, they could also relate to two favourite Gallic/Celtic name-forms, Sacer and Sanctus. 'Compitalicus', the name of the owner of the axe, is very unusual (*RIB* II.3, 2428.4). It seems to be derived from Compitalia, an ancient festival revived by Augustus, and its very obscurity makes it difficult to imagine an auxiliary bearing such a name. The centurion's name, Barrus, is a Celtic name-element: witness the lead tank-maker, Cunobarrus (*RIB* II.2, 2416.4). But it is also a rare Latin *cognomen*, apparently restricted to Picenum (Cicero, *Brut.* 46, 169, with *CIL* IX.3455). Horace uses it (*Serm.* I.6.30) as the typical name of a political '*arriviste*/carpet-bagger'. A firm decision is impossible, but the balance of probability

tilts a little in favour of a legionary origin for both men.
25. Curle 1911, 116.
26. Hartley 1972, 51.
27. Bishop and Coulston 2006, 76–8.
28. Brailsford 1962, Scott 1980, Marchant 1990 and others.
29. Manning 1985, 160–70, pls 76–81.
30. A small number have been omitted from this survey, either because their date is uncertain or because they were too damaged for a type to be assigned.
31. Curle 1911, 112 and 113.
32. Curle 1911, 132, 135.
33. Hartley 1972, 54, no.5.
34. Richmond 1968, 119.
35. Curle 1911, 168 and 296.
36. Curle 1911, 177.
37. E.g. Curle 1911, 298, from Pit LV; 300, from Pit LXXVIII.
38. *RIB* II.2, 2415.65.
39. *RIB* II.3, 2427.3.
40. *RIB* 2121.
41. *RIB* II.3, 2427.4–12.
42. Maxfield 1981, 91–5 and personal information.
43. *RIB* II.6, 2492.7.
44. Bishop and Coulston 2006, 78.
45. Pliny the Younger records that his uncle, Pliny the Elder, had written a manual on *De iaculatione equestri* ('The art of using a javelin on horseback') when he commanded a cavalry unit (*Letters* III.5).
46. Curle 1911, 288.
47. Curle 1911, 189.
48. Curle 1911, 183.
49. Maxfield 1986.
50. Curle 1911, 168.
51. Curle 1911, 166.
52. Curle 1911, 170.
53. Curle 1911, 164.
54. Curle 1911, 156.

References

Bishop, M. C. and Coulston, J. C. N. 2006: *Roman military equipment: from the Punic Wars to the Fall of Rome,* second edition, Oxford

Brailsford, J. W. 1962: *Hod Hill. Volume One. Antiquities from Hod Hill in the Durden Collection,* London

Clarke, S. and Jones, R. 1996: 'The Newstead pits', in van Driel-Murray 1996, 109–24

Curle, J. 1911: *A Roman frontier post and its people. The Roman fort of Newstead,* Glasgow

Hanson, W. S. and Keppie, L. J. F. (eds) 1980: *Roman Frontier Studies 1979* [BAR International Series 71], Oxford

Hartley, B. R. 1972: 'The Roman occupation of Scotland: the evidence of samian ware',

Britannia 3, 1–55

Manning, W. H. 1985: *Catalogue of the Romano-British tools, fittings and weapons in the British Museum*, London

Marchant, D. 1990: 'Roman weapons in Great Britain, a case study: spearheads, problems in dating and typology', *Journal of Roman Military Equipment Studies* 1, 1–6

Maxfield, V. A. 1981: *The military decorations of the Roman army*, London

Maxfield, V. A. 1986: 'Pre-Flavian forts and their garrisons', *Britannia* 17, 59–72

Richmond, I. A. 1950: 'Excavations at the Roman fort of Newstead 1947', *Proceedings of the Society of Antiquaries of Scotland* 84 (1949–50), 1–37

Richmond, I. A. 1968: *Hod Hill. Volume Two. Excavations carried out between 1951 and 1958*, London

Scott, I. R. 1980: 'Spearheads of the British *limes*', in Hanson and Keppie 1980, 33–43

Steer, K. A. 1976: 'Trimontium', in Stillwell *et al.* 1976, 935

Stillwell, R., MacDonald, W. L. and McAllister, M. H. (eds) 1976: *Princeton Encyclopedia of Classical Sites*, Princeton

Van Driel-Murray, C. (ed.) 1996: *Military Equipment in Context. Proceedings of the Ninth International Military Equipment Conference, Leiden, 1994*, Oxford

Chapter 5

MILITARY *VICI* IN ROMAN BRITAIN REVISITED

C. Sebastian Sommer

It is now almost 25 years ago, in September 1981, that I met Sheppard Sunderland Frere for the first time during one of his later excavation campaigns at Strageath.[1] Not long afterwards I introduced myself to him formally as his new student at the Institute of Archaeology in Oxford. When I explained that I had been awarded a two-year-scholarship[2] and that I was interested in the military vici *of Roman Britain, I was immediately stuck with my topic. "That's good, you can write a Master's dissertation on that", he said, with his pipe as usual in the mouth; and that was precisely what I did.[3] Since then, frequent contact and discussions with British colleagues at the International Congresses of Roman Frontier Studies, occasional private visits to Britain, invitations to conferences on the Island as well as a subscription to the journal* Britannia, *and an occasional book order as well, have kept me in touch with the topic. However, the invitation at the suggestion of David Breeze to speak at a one-day seminar at the University of Lancaster's Centre for North-West Regional Studies in 2005, in conjunction with the Cumberland and Westmorland Antiquarian and Archaeological Society, at Newton Rigg, North Penrith (and, as it turned out, also at the Senhouse Roman Museum, Maryport, on the preceding evening), forced me to re-examine the subject. The reactions I had from Professor Frere both before and after these talks – being a Friend of the Senhouse Museum he had received invitations to the events – as well as the positive comments of D. J. Breeze, have encouraged me to present here some thoughts about questions both old and new on the military* vici *of Roman Britain.*

Introduction

In recent years, in a number of papers, I have tried to summarize the present state of knowledge about the military *vici* on the Continent.[4] They were based primarily on the evidence of southern Germany, in particular those of the final *limes* forts, and also the settlements founded at fort-sites located along previous fortification lines in the provinces of Upper Germany and Raetia – a frontier defence-system which is now a 'World Heritage Site' in its own right. My aim was to consider the general lay-out, typology, building regulations and the reconstructions of the houses of these settlements, as well as the relationship between the forts and the *vici's* inhabitants, i.e. the soldiers on the one hand, and the military *vici* and their occupants (the camp-followers) on the other. Quite a number of these topics addressed questions which I raised 25 years ago about the military *vici* of Roman Britain – when it was realised for the first time that they formed a distinctive group of Roman settlements – and such themes were followed up and enlarged upon by my later studies of the *vici* in southern Germany.[5] In the event, despite the presence of the English Channel dividing the two areas, and despite different historical developments, different troops and different commanders, the discoveries, and the problems they pose, in the one region are clearly highly relevant to our understanding of the *vici* in the other. Therefore, it seems appropriate for me to look once again at my original field of research in Britain, now with the benefit of new knowledge derived from more recent study of the Continental examples.

A fresh look at old sites is particularly worthwhile, since we are now faced with a whole battery of new evidence. The studies of the 1980s were triggered by 'research-driven' excavations at places like Vindolanda in Britain with its fascinating results – even though the latter lacked proper detailed publication for a long time[6] – and by a number of large-scale rescue-excavations of military *vici* in Baden-Württemberg[7] (most importantly at Bad Wimpfen,[8] Böbingen-Unterböbingen,[9] Buch,[10] Jagsthausen,[11] Köngen,[12] Ladenburg,[13] Osterburken,[14] Rottweil,[15] Sulz[16] and Walheim[17]), and to a lesser extent in Bavaria (Aislingen,[18] Künzing,[19] Regensburg-Kumpfmühl,[20] Straubing[21] and Weißenburg[22]) and Hesse (Groß-Gerau[23] and Heldenbergen[24]), together with their first preliminary reports.[25] However, without the enormous amount of evidence gathered by aerial survey both in Britain and on the Continent, the arbitrary nature of rescue excavation would have allowed only a very partial and piecemeal view of military *vici* across the Empire. Only with the possibility of understanding whole settlements as revealed by aerial photography could many aspects of settlement morphology become clear, enabling us to make general statements about their nature and lay-out with greater confidence.[26] Over subsequent years our picture has became richer and more detailed as more and more sites have had to be excavated in advance of destruction, and the number of places under aerial surveillance has also increased. Fortunately, in Britain, as well as in Germany, military *vici* have become of interest to increasing numbers of researchers.[27] As a consequence, several mostly local and regional studies of military *vici* have been published in detail (and I may not be aware of them all). [28] This research has also been influenced by the study of the so-called 'small towns', which the larger *vici* virtually are. The interesting theoretical approach of S. James' recent paper on the inter-relationship between soldiers and civilians also deserves a mention, as it not only throws light on many topics which have been discussed in previous years, but also opens up fresh perspectives.[29]

But the most exciting development of the last few years is the dramatic expansion in our knowledge provided by geophysics. Many of the places which had 'resisted' aerial reconnaissance, whether through unfavourable local geology or the problematic nature of the crops being grown on them, have revealed their secrets through this equally non-destructive technique (although of course much more physical effort is required to produce results than is the case with aerial photography). In particular, magnetometry, with its wide range of equipment, ranging from simple-to-use machines (such as the Fluxgate Gradiometer) to highly complicated, extremely sensitive equipment (such as the Caesium-magnetometer),[30] has been applied to many sites in large-scale operations,[31] providing us with a wealth of new evidence. This research enables us to analyse and understand in detail many more *vici*, or at least test previous theories about them against new information. For Britain the work of J. A. Biggins and D. J. A. Taylor in the north of England, and of D. Hopewell in Wales, is of particular significance. Whereas Biggins, Taylor and their collaborators have worked on the basis of individual contracts and funding at specially selected sites,[32] Hopewell and his colleagues work exclusively for CADW, the Welsh Heritage Agency.

To exploit the new technical possibilities of geophysical research, a unique programme in Wales called 'The Roman Fort Environs Project' was set up to investigate the forts and their surroundings. One aim was to gain better under-standing of the sites for their own protection.[33] Just as, many years ago, most large-scale excavations and aerial photographs were made accessible early on through preliminary reports and the photographs themselves without full interpretation, so the primary results of many of the geophysical surveys are now often also published before there has been time to accompany them with detailed individual inter-pretation. We are fortunate that our colleagues share their knowledge so freely and accessibly by doing so. The thoughts that appear below on the military *vici* of Roman Britain are very much based on their results (Appendix 1) – I am of course very much indebted to those who have carried out and published these geophysical surveys[34] – as well as on their most recent papers.[35]

Typology of military vici

Street-type

Nowadays there is no doubt at all about the truth of the generalisation that every independent auxiliary fort of a certain size was accompanied by a military *vicus*. We can also say without hesitation that the most typical type of lay-out of military *vici* on the Continent, that is, the 'through-road type'[36] (perhaps better called the 'street-type', or 'ribbon-type'[37]), is also the one most commonly found in Roman Britain. Looking at different sites, like Brougham in the north-west,[38] Caerhun in Wales[39] (Fig. 5.1 and 5.2), or Maryport on the Cumbrian coast (Fig. 5.3),[40] we can see that in each case a main road approaching the fort is accompanied by the buildings of the *vicus* on either side. One gets the impression that the parts most easily recognisable indeed make up the core of each *vicus*. Typically, in a 'street-type' *vicus* (as in the examples just listed), the settlement is found along a road leading to one or both of the *portae principales*. In fact, settlements appear to be located in front of the *porta principalis dextra* more often than not,[41] as for example at Maryport. That the right-hand side has a certain prominence in Roman military architecture in general can be seen from the lay-out of the forts themselves, where the *praetorium* is generally situated on the right-hand side of the *principia*. The

Fig. 5.1 Caerhun, aerial photograph of the fort and its surroundings (K17-AI 182, 7th July 1975. Copyright reserved. Cambridge University Collection of Air Photographs)

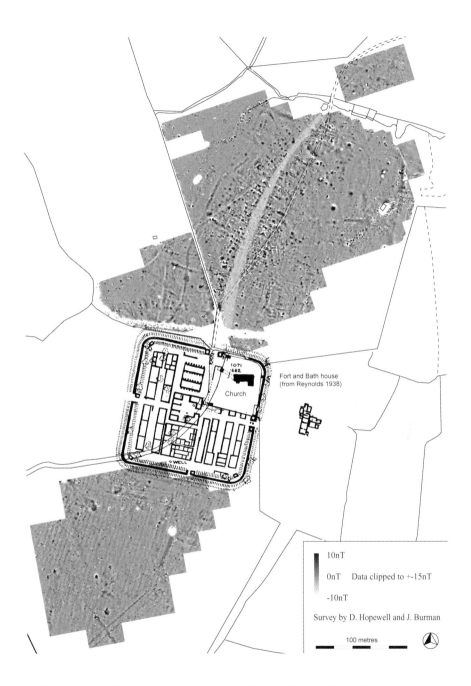

Fig. 5.2 Caerhun, gradiometer survey to the north and the south of the fort

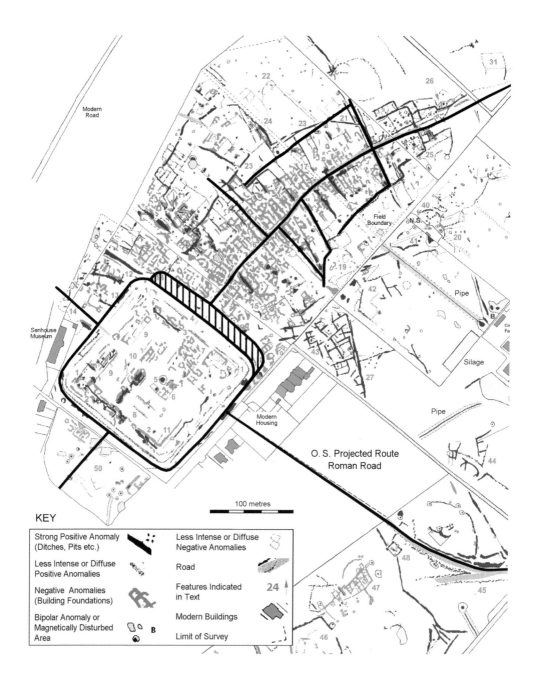

Fig. 5.3 Maryport, interpretation of the geophysical survey with reconstruction of the street-system

distribution of baths in Upper Germany shows a similar preference for the right-hand side. The existence of a military *vicus* in front of the fort, outside the *porta praetoria*, is often connected, in fact, with the location of the garrison bath-house there (this in turn is dependent on the standard direction of the fort towards the lowest-lying ground, since the *porta decumana* should in theory be located on the highest ground). The greatest likelihood, therefore, of providing an adequate water supply for the baths was to bring water directly from fountains or springs and to lead it via pipes in a gently downhill direction, usually to the area in front of the *porta praetoria*.[42] As a *vicus* here is almost always found in combination with a bath-house, it is obvious that this was a prime position for the location of military *vici*.

An apparent exception is Caerhun (Fig. 5.2), where the main *vicus* lies in front of the left gate (*porta principalis sinistra*). Its unusual location can be explained by the importance of the road leading north. Whereas the latter either led directly to the legionary fortress of Chester, or at any rate connected the fort to the Chester–Caernarfon road (one of the most important routes in the north of Wales), the road towards the south (in the direction of the forts at Bryn-y-Gefeiliau and Tomen-y-Mur) is likely to have been of much lesser importance.[43] The east-facing direction of the fort at Caerhun, where the usually less prominent *porta principalis sinistra* is located on the north side, was in turn due to the presence of sloping ground on the east side towards the river Conway.

The situation at Hindwell in Wales is similar. If, as has been suggested, the long-distance road passed the fort to the north, the shortest link with the fort was probably provided by a road leading to the *porta decumana*. From geophysical survey, however, it is clear that the military *vicus* was located along a road which approached the fort from the east, in other words in the direction of the *porta principalis sinistra*.[44]

From the lay-out of the sites mentioned so far, as well as in the case of many others, it is clear that long-distance roads did not usually by-pass forts. Instead, they end at the fort gate(s), or rather they lead through the fort itself by means of the *via principalis* (and sometimes the *via praetoria* too). The geophysical plots of Caerhun, Hindwell and Llanfor,[45] as well as those at Maryport and Birdoswald (Figs 5.3 and 5.5), for example, only leave space (if they leave any at all) for a local perimeter road immediately outside the edge of the outermost fort ditch. Whether that traffic which was not due to terminate (or indeed start) at the forts was actually directed through the middle of the forts, or had to move around them on some other complicated route, is a matter for speculation. However, as the perimeter roads in many cases did not have a major influence on the lay-out of the military *vici*, the overall general impression that they had a secondary importance is clear: even through-traffic generally seems to have been directed through the fort, perhaps for reasons of control.

Most of the military *vici* in Britain belong to the 'street-type'. The principle certainly seems to have been favoured at most forts in Wales and also along Hadrian's Wall, and the sites discussed above could be said to be 'typical', because of their similarity to one other and indeed to so many other military *vici*.[46]

Fig. 5.4 Old Carlisle, aerial photograph of the fort and its surroundings (K17-AI 145, 1st July 1975. Copyright reserved. Cambridge University Collection of Air Photographs)

Tangent-type

Another, though much less frequent, type of military *vicus* is what I have called the 'tangent-type'. Here the major road had to by-pass the fort for topographical reasons, usually because the latter was situated on a promontory, so making it difficult to approach the fort through more than one gate. The most obvious example of this type in Britain is Old Carlisle in Cumbria. Marvellous old aerial photographs (e.g. Fig. 5.4) show the Carlisle–Papcastle road by-passing the fort at some distance to the south-east, with densely-packed strip-buildings lining the road over several hundred meters. Another road, branching to the north towards Kirkbride, similarly by-passes the fort, although this time it passes directly in front of it. Along its southern part, as well as along an additional short road connecting the long-distance highway with the *porta principalis dextra*, more buildings can be seen. Clearly of lesser importance was a branch off the main road from Carlisle which led directly to the *porta praetoria* as well. The explanation of this lay-out lies in the fairly steep slopes which exist directly to the north and the west of the fort, where the land drops away by more than ten metres into the narrow cutting occupied by the Wiza Beck.

The newly-discovered site of Roecliffe, where the fort was connected with Dere Street via the north gate (which was, I suggest, the *porta principalis dextra*), seems to be of the same 'tangent' type as well.[47] Based on the evidence of Vindolanda, Carvoran and the overall direction of the Stanegate road, I assume that most of the military *vici* along that road belong also to this type.[48] Apart from Roecliffe, the *vicus* arrangments at High Rochester, Catterick, Piercebridge and Greta Bridge[49] all point to the conclusion that this may have been the standard type for most of the forts located on the road-system of northern Britain.

Ring-type

A third type of military *vicus* identifiable on the Continent is the 'ring-type'. Here the buildings are situated along the far side of a road running all the way round the fort, at quite a distance from the latter's ditch(es). To date, this has been found only at forts with an equestrian garrison (not necessarily only cavalry *alae*, but also at those designed for part-mounted *cohortes equitatae*). The reason for this may have been the need to provide exercise grounds for the horses close to the fort. I am not aware that this type been yet has been found in Britain. Although separate and clearly distinguishable parade-grounds have occasionally been identified in Britain, there may have been no need there for the 'ring-type' of *vicus* lay-out.[50]

Internal structure

Street-system

Within those military *vici* which are based on a street-system arrangement, we can usually distinguish between the main part of the *vicus* and one or several parts which are of lesser importance, on the basis of their extent and sometimes their position. Without doubt, the long-distance road formed the most prominent structural feature in the main part of any *vicus*, providing as it did the easiest route of access to the fort. The greatest density of housing can usually be found here, as well as the bath-house and/or a *mansio* (if for topographical reasons they were not located directly in front of the *porta praetoria*). In general, the main part of a street-type *vicus* runs for several hundred meters in length. A good example is that at Maryport, which extends for about 350 m north of the fort (Fig. 5.3).[51]

The lay-out of a military *vicus* was rarely, however, completely clear-cut and straightforward. Quite often the basic plan is obscured by additions. For example, the *vicus* of Old Carlisle (Fig. 5.4), besides the main features of the tangent-type which it displays, contains also some elements of the 'street-type' *vicus*, both along the road leading directly to the *porta praetoria*, and along the (side) road to the *porta principalis dextra*. At Caerhun (Figs 5.1 and 5.2), the position of the bath-house and especially of the stone buildings north of it (possibly a *mansio*) required access via a road which led around the north-eastern corner of the fort. At Maryport (Fig. 5.3), the various parts of the *vicus* on all sides of the fort, although each of them individually may have had the structure of a street-type *vicus*, must also have had a linking road leading around the perimeter of the fort ditches.

Unfortunately, without excavation and proper dating evidence, we cannot determine which of these suspected 'additional' elements were in fact part of the original lay-out, and which were added later, either in the course of the continuous development of the *vicus* over the years, or as part of some kind of new lay-out. The latter, for example, might have occurred when a new garrison arrived with its own camp-followers, who might have had different needs or different ideas about the set-up of a military *vicus*.[52]

In order to understand the structure of military *vici* better, it is worth looking at some of them in more detail. At Caer Gai in Wales, we can see from both aerial photographs and the magnetometry plot that at least three additional roads branch off the main roads at right-angles: one even has another branch parallel to the main road, forming a sort of a street-grid.[53] Furthermore, at least a minor road is needed to provide a link with an isolated building about 60 m north of the road leading to the east.

Maryport

At Maryport we can reconstruct with some certainty the whole complexity of a larger military *vicus* (Fig. 5.3). As already mentioned, the long-distance road from the north-east formed the core of the *vicus* with a length of more than 300 m. This road ended in an open space, without any geophysical anomalies, which runs along the full length of the north-eastern side of the fort, directly beyond its outermost ditch (*c.* 200 m by 22 m; Fig. 5.3, hatched area). The area may have served as a market-place (see below, p. 118). From there, narrow roads ran around the fort's corners to the north-west and the south-east, to connect with one road coming from Papcastle and another heading towards the sea. The geophysical survey hints at the presence of a considerable number of buildings along the perimeter road. Their orientation at right-angles to the ditches suggests that they fronted this road. The road probably continued around the south-west of the fort, giving access to those parts of the *vicus* in front of the *porta principalis sinistra*, as well as to the parade ground which is known to lie under modern housing on this side of the fort. It seems likely that the road then ran around the western corner, forming a sort of ring road around the entire fort.

There might also have been further houses along the road which approaches the fort from the south-east, but here the ground is now covered by modern buildings. Certainly there were structures lining the road leading to the sea on the north-west side. On the assumption that the *porta praetoria* was the main gate, Biggins and Taylor have suggested that we need to reconstruct a considerable amount of ground in front of the fort on this side, which has now been lost either by quarrying or through erosion caused by the sea. As mentioned above, the orientation of the fort towards the sea seems to be a side effect of the desire to let the main traffic run through the fort in the easiest way possible, i.e. along the *via principalis.* However, another consequence was that the lowest ground in the immediate proximity of the fort was also situated on that side. For that reason I believe that we have to locate the garrison bath-house here, which was not detected with any certainty elsewhere in the extensive geophysical survey.[54] This would be according to the 'rules' (see above, p. 101).

This is not, however, the end of the road-system. Without doubt the religious precincts behind the building plots (Fig. 5.3, nos 19, 40, 21: see below, p. 108) had to be connected to the main road to provide access for worshippers. Narrowly-spaced, linear features, parallel to one another, suggest secondary tracks. On the north-east side these would also have formed the boundary between the *vicus* proper and the cemetery. Further lanes would be appropriate in the sector of the *vicus* close to the fort, but their positions cannot be determined at present. Furthermore, on the basis of the magnetometry results, lanes roughly parallel to the main road can be suggested which formed the connection between the temples and the access lanes described. These may have served for some distance as back lanes.[55]

Vici *in Wales*

The situation in the north-eastern part of Cefn Caer is similarly complex (Fig. 5.6). From the most prominent part of the *vicus* on the north-east side, a road seems to run around the northern corner of the fort. Although Hopewell did not interpret the anomalies which clearly occur along its course, I think that they are evidence of buildings set at right-angles to this street, directly opposite the outermost ditch. There is in addition a road parallel to the fort's north-western side at a distance of 60 m from it: this branches off the road from the *porta principalis dextra*. Unfortunately the further course of this road lies outside the survey area. It is unclear whether it connects with the road off the *porta decumana* (as I believe it does), and if so precisely where. Unlike the main roads here, this road of secondary importance shows occupation only on the side opposite to the fort (this may suggest that the plots fronting the road around the fort's northern corner extend over the whole width of 60 m up to that side road). Unlike the geophysical surveyors who claim it to be so, I cannot see a Roman origin for the curving 'road' at the far west of the survey, which meets the road off the *porta principalis dextra* at a 45 degree angle.[56] All the anomalies here are set invariably at right-angles to the main road, and seem to have no relation at all to the feature just discussed. Also such a road would conflict with the possible *mansio*, the strong rectangular feature directly north-west of the modern farm-buildings. Furthermore, it is difficult to interpret the anomalies beyond as graves (*busta*)[57] because of their proximity to the fort. They are surely rather to be seen as remains of buildings (hearths?).[58] The picture is again that of a multi-faceted *vicus* structure with some form of street-grid in front of the right-hand side of the fort.

At Caerhun (Fig. 5.1 and 5.2), the structure of the *vicus* appears at first glance to be straightforward. No additional roads are visible on the geophysical plot.[59] The aerial photographs, however, suggest a road parallel to the northern side of the fort, running towards the river and passing a stone building on the north-east (possibly a *mansio*). Secondly, the bath-house in front of the *porta praetoria,* identified by excavation, and the *mansio* (?) north of it needed a direct link. I suggest that they were reached by a road which runs parallel to the eastern side of the fort: a link between the extension of the *via praetoria* and the road on the north-east is in fact suggested by the aerial photographs. The equidistant positioning of the buildings in relation to the fort, including stone buildings 4 and 5 as suggested by the geophysical survey, make it possible to reconstruct this road at a distance of *c.* 35/ 40 m from the outer side of the ditch, immediately west of the bath-house. This would leave an open space between the ditch and the fort similar to the ones mentioned above for forts with a ring-type military *vicus*; that in turn implies that the different barracks of the fort can be interpreted simply as those of a *cohors equitata*, with the mounted part housed in the *retentura*: the latter was situated closest to the open space outside for exercising the horses.

The hypothetical road may have continued around the south-eastern corner of the fort, perhaps even around the annexe seen on the south-west by Reynolds. Unfortunately, since modern agricultural activity has either destroyed, or at any rate obscured, Roman structures on the south side, we cannot be sure whether another portion of the *vicus* originally existed in front of the *porta principalis dextra*; certainly the existence of further *vicus* development there would be entirely plausible. On the other hand, a Roman origin for roads 7 and 8, claimed in the interpretation of Hopewell as leading 'diagonally' to the former docks area, seems to me to be highly unlikely. Everything in the *vicus* of Caerhun points to a more or less rectangular lay-out for its component parts.

A complex rectangular system is evident also for Caersws. Here a recent plan compiled mainly from aerial photography shows not only the principal roads, but also lesser roads branching off them at right-angles, as well as the beginning of a road leading around the fort.[60] All the roads in front of the *porta principalis sinistra* and the *porta praetoria* were accompanied by dwellings (and the bath-house and a possible *mansio* can be located immediately to the right of the *porta praetoria*).

Vici *on Hadrian's Wall*

If we compare the results from both geophysical survey and aerial photography with the military *vici* which have been most extensively excavated in Britain, those of Vindolanda and Housesteads, it becomes evident that the latter are representative examples of their type. At Vindolanda the most recent plan[61] shows not only some buildings along the Stanegate, the long-distance road which by-passes the fort (so making Vindolanda an example of the tangent-type of *vicus*),[62] but also a ribbon-like settlement along a road which leads to the *porta principalis sinistra* of the fort. It has been suggested that this road picked up the line of the *via principalis* of the 'large early timber fort'.[63] Unfortunately, the point where this road branched off the Stanegate has not yet been established. A further complication is that part of the *vicus* was laid out on a grid-like system towards the south: this was centred on a road which met the fort at a position even further south than the *porta principalis dextra* of the first stone fort.[64] Recent excavations have discovered an area built up along a road connecting this part of the *vicus* with the Stanegate further west. Last but not least, there is a ring-road leading around the western part of the fort directly beyond its walls, apparently overlying the ditch for some of its course.[65] Especially on the south-west side, the buildings of the *vicus* certainly focus their attention on this road.

At Housesteads, densely-packed buildings line the road leading south from the *porta principalis dextra*, partially confined by a further road which departs directly from the gate in a south-westerly direction.[66] Buildings are also attested along a road off the *porta praetoria* as well as lining another road running around the fort. As at Vindolanda, the latter road was partly established over the former line of the fort ditch. Geophysical results suggest the presence of more buildings to the south-west and west of the fort, along the line of the extension of the *via decumana*,[67] in most places just as densely packed as at Vindolanda.

Apart from their general similarity to other sites, the plans of the *vici* at Vindolanda and Housesteads present us with a number of peculiarities. Firstly, almost none of the houses seem to have had any kind of back yard. House- and plot-sizes appear to have been almost identical, but the situation may be complicated by the fact that the chronology of the various buildings uncovered was not precisely established.[68] Secondly, the very close proximity of *vici* to forts, so close that it allows no space for the ditch(es) on most sides of the latter, is to my knowledge unparalleled. This seems peculiar, as at Vindolanda the presence of extensive flat grounds on both the west and the north-west sides of the fort did not make a lay-out like this absolutely necessary. At Housesteads, however, the available ground seems to have been limited for topographical reasons. Perhaps what we have here is a great number of late Roman features in the plans, which have complicated our understanding of the original arrangement. We have to admit, in fact, that unfortunately we do not know very much at present about the military *vici* of the late Roman Empire. It would appear that at some stage the fort ditches did not serve a useful function any more, and that even greater proximity between the two 'partners', i.e. the fort and its attendant *vicus*, was felt to be necessary and indeed desirable, even more so than in earlier times. Thirdly, at Vindolanda it is highly unlikely that the timber fort, into which the famous writing tablets provide so much insight, did not itself have a military *vicus*, even though any knowledge about this early (timber) phase of the settlement is entirely lacking.

The discoveries at Chesters likewise pose many questions.[69] The area in the vicinity of the fort to the east was limited by the river North Tyne. Although aerial photographs suggest a certain importance for the road leading from the *porta decumana* as well as another curving around the fort from the north-west, it is hard to distinguish individual structures or other features. What we can see seems to be the effect of the long-term use of a limited space, which makes it difficult to disentangle the superimposed features and to determine the original lay-out.

Temples and shrines

With regard to the overall picture, it would be good to know why and how the original lay-out and street-system were expanded as each settlement grew in size. In some cases a special function for specific parts of the *vicus*, such as has been noted above in the context of bath-houses and *mansiones*, may have been the driving force. At Caer Gai, geophysical anomalies hint at an isolated building on the northern periphery of the *vicus*, situated at some distance from the densely built-up area along the main road. Unfortunately, limited trial excavations there were not able to reveal the character of the anomaly, although its interpretation as a building is indisputable.[70] However, in line with the evidence from the geophysical survey, but in contrast to the interpretation proposed in the original publication, I suggest a different type of building here, with a size of about 20 m by 10 m. I believe that the southern part of feature 43 was the northern edge of this edifice. This leads to the possible reconstruction of a three-aisled building with the parts shared between features 30 and 35, with 43 and 44/45 forming the aisles, and the part between 30 and 44/45 the nave. By analogy with Carrawburgh and – more importantly because of its almost identical peripheral position within the military *vicus* – with Künzing on the Danube,[71] the interpretation of this structure as a *mithraeum* seems conceivable.

A similar position within the *vicus* is taken by the temple (for which the interpretation of a *mithraeum* seems possible, too) and the circular building at Maryport, excavated in 1880 together with two altars (Fig. 5.3, no. 19).[72] Behind the regular construction south of the main road, the area set aside for religious purposes seems to have been assigned in such a way that no interference with the regular building-plots was necessary. Equally, an irregular circular enclosure, which probably represents the place where in 1870 seventeen altars were excavated,[73] and a triangular plot close to the spot where the so-called 'serpent stone' was found, together with anomalies interpreted as graves to the north of the road,[74] all lie behind the regular buildings (Fig. 5.3, nos 40 and 21). These may be interpreted as secondary arrangements, which developed after the original foundation of the *vicus*, although it should also be noted that both the religious sites to the south of the road were located on the highest points of the ridge on which the Maryport fort and its *vicus* were constructed. Visibility from a distance as well as from all directions was therefore guaranteed.[75]

This is also in line with the discoveries from many other military *vici*.[76] With the exception of a stone building at Ruffenhofen at the Raetian *limes* in Bavaria, which has a rectangular recess and a *porticus* facing onto the short road connecting the fort with a tangent road,[77] I know of no evidence for a temple or other religious precinct site within the regular lay-out, or indeed at the centre, of a military *vicus*. In fact the same is true of 'normal' civilian *vici* as well. We have, therefore, to conclude that temples, *mithraea* and religious precincts in general (occasionally connected with cemetery areas) were not part of the original lay-out, but resulted from the later development of these settlements. The reason may be that the Romans had no imposed 'state' religion, and dedications and donations were therefore a matter for independent action on the part of individuals. This would imply that roads or lanes connecting these sites to the main roads either had to be laid in a secondary period as well, or that the position of the temples was determined by the prior existence of an access road.

Amphitheatres

Judging by their position within military *vici*, amphitheatres were not part of the primary lay-out either. At Forden Gaer,[78] Inveresk,[79] Newstead,[80] Newton Kyme,[81] Richborough,[82] and Tomen-y-Mur,[83] the amphitheatres, still sometimes visible on the surface, are situated to one side or at the far end of the military *vicus*, or even lie beyond its limits. This makes the notion of the site of an amphitheatre being chosen in a secondary period, and the structure duly erected, highly plausible. This view is supported by the fact that in none of the military *vici* which have seen intensive geophysical survey have the remains of an amphitheatre been detected. That of Tomen-y-Mur may be truly unique for Wales.[84] Although the surprising find of a timber amphitheatre at Künzing on the Danube in 2003[85] on the very edge of a ring-type *vicus*, and the rediscovery of an amphitheatre with a stone wall around the arena at Arnsburg in Hesse,[86] which lay well beyond the built-up area of the military *vicus*, might suggest otherwise, it seems highly unlikely that amphitheatres are installations that should be found outside virtually every fort, like bath-houses for example. Instead, it looks as if they were erected at certain places for specific occasions, and were not necessarily used for long afterwards.[87] Perhaps the situation at Zugmantel in Upper Germany, where not one but two amphitheatres are known 200 m north and 350 m east of the fort, both some way away from the *vicus* proper,[88] supports this interpretation. When, in the course of the life of a military *vicus*, an amphitheatre became necessary, a suitable site had to be found. Usually by that time only locations on the perimeter of existing settlements were available for such a large and new facility.

Cemeteries

No settlement would be complete without one or several cemeteries. Usually they were positioned at a discrete distance from the fort's ditches, leaving enough space for the military *vicus* and its buildings.[89] The interpretation, therefore, of a line of strong anomalies in the geophysical survey at Bryn-y-Gefeiliau as a line of burials, directly in front of the *porta praetoria* and parallel to the road leading east,[90] seems to me highly unlikely in view of their position; the same is true of the somewhat similar features along the road leading north from the *porta principalis dextra* at Cefn Caer, also interpreted as graves (*busta;*[91] Fig. 5.6). On the other hand, the circular features considered to be tombs at Cefn Caer behind the southern annexe (Fig. 5.2), and at Caer Gai along a road leading to the north,[92] are in positions that are much more plausible for cemeteries. More typical, however, are the locations of the presumed cemeteries at Caerhun (Figs 5.1 and 5.2), immediately beyond the main part of the military *vicus* at a distance of about 300 m from the fort,[93] at Birdoswald, at a distance of about 400 m to the south-west of the fort,[94] and at Maryport, where the burial ground lies some 300 m from the fort, within small ditched enclosures directly beyond the *vicus* (Fig. 5.3, between 21 and 26).

'Fixed' forts

So far we have been dealing mostly with forts and their *vici* which were located on carefully-chosen sites in the countryside, according to the dictates of military strategy and topography. However, a particular feature of Roman Britain are the 'fixed' forts on Hadrian's Wall and the Antonine Wall, where the close relationship between the forts themselves and the respective Wall of which they were an integral part left Roman surveyors and *architecti* with much less opportunity for a generous and systematic *vicus* lay-out. This is particularly true of the forts on Hadrian's Wall, where in some cases a third of the fort projected beyond the line of the Wall, and where the presence of the Vallum to the south further narrowed the range of options.

As with the sites already mentioned (Housesteads, Vindolanda), the buildings of the *vici* often started immediately outside the outer edge of the outermost ditch. Nowhere are there signs of a glacis, or any other special means to keep the civilians away from the fort. This to me is a clear sign that Roman surveyors, among others, thought of the military *vicus* as playing a key role for each fort as part of a symbiotic relationship. It also shows that one suggested function of the Vallum, to keep the civilians away from the forts themselves and from Hadrian's Wall,[95] cannot have been directed at the camp-followers, because they of course were originally living in the zone between Wall and Vallum, until in many cases the expanding *vicus* was in time built over the filled-in Vallum.

Halton Chesters

At Halton Chesters,[96] for example, densely-packed buildings are clearly distinguishable to the south of the fort between the latter's ditch and the Vallum, which swerves to avoid the fort by means of clear, angled changes in direction. These buildings seem to give onto a road leading around the fort along the edge of its ditch, leaving only 20 m to 25 m for building plots before the beginning of the northern mound of the Vallum. As Halton Chesters is one of those forts where the *portae principales* opened their gates beyond the Wall, streets beginning there could not be used as an orientation for the military *vicus*. To give access to the area behind the Wall other than through the *porta decumana*, Halton Chesters as well as similar forts which projected north of Hadrian's Wall were provided with an additional set of gates, at either end of the *via quintana*. One of these gates served as the focus for at least a prominent part of the military *vicus* to the east (the area outside the lesser west gate at Halton Chesters has not yet been surveyed or published). The road starting here became the backbone of the *vicus*, like the road off a *porta principalis dextra* elsewhere, with regular strip-buildings on both sides of it. An additional, parallel road, about 10 m north of the ditch of the Vallum, may be of a later date, as it must have been on the same alignment as the original northern mound of the latter. Nevertheless, some buildings seem to have existed parallel to it to the south, squeezed in between this road and the ditch of the Vallum.

Directly in conflict with the Vallum at Halton Chesters, on the other hand, or rather actually overlying it and therefore not contemporary with it, is a street-type part of the *vicus* stretching for about 200 m to the south from the *porta decumana*; it started just beyond the buildings to the south of the fort mentioned above. As the interpreters of the geophysical survey suggest that this road was shifted eastwards by approximately 10 m at some point, this probably indicates that there were consecutive phases of the *vicus*, the street-type-part to the south being probably laid out sometime after the reoccupation of the Wall in the 160s, perhaps as late as the third century after the Vallum had finally been abandoned. This opened up new opportunities of space and afforded the possibility of a 'proper' laying-out of a new-style military *vicus*.

Birdoswald

The situation at Birdoswald is somewhat similar (Fig. 5.5).[97] Again, we have to consider not only the restrictions on space imposed by the fort's 'fixed' position on Hadrian's Wall, but also the complexity of a multi-phased development. Originally, the fort was connected to the Turf Wall with the *praetentura* projecting beyond it, as at Chesters and Halton Chesters on the Stone Wall.[98] That implies that those parts of the military *vicus* north of the line of the Turf Wall which are visible in the geophysical survey must be a development of a somewhat later stage, after the line of the Wall was altered to run up to the north wall of the fort. It also means that the area of the original military *vicus* must have been extremely limited, because the ground falls precipitously away immediately south of the fort, even if the earliest fort on this site may have been slightly shorter than its later stone successor.[99] Consequently, we have to look again at the sequence of buildings and ditches to the south of the fort – and ask how many of those unearthed in the 1930s belonged to a pre-Vallum timber-fort phase.[100] Once the Stone Wall was built on the more northerly alignment, the amount of space available for a *vicus* was considerably enlarged, and – as can be seen from the results of the survey – was indeed used.

Interestingly, on the east side, the Turf-Wall ditch as well as the ditch of the Vallum were only back-filled up to a point approximately 200 m from the fort.[101] Apparently, a distance of 200 m in the immediate environs of the fort was considered sufficient for the development of the *vicus*.

It is difficult now to disentangle the development of occupation to the east of the fort since several different and successive phases are clearly present. The main feature here is the road leading from the *porta principalis dextra* to the east, running in its western part on top of the line of the former Turf Wall. Over a length of *c.* 70 m to the north of this road and for some 40 m to the south, we can distinguish structures set at right-angles to it. Whether all the buildings observed along its course are of Roman date is open to debate. Most likely there existed a road parallel to the one already noted leading to the east from the *porta quintana,* similar to the one discussed above at Halton Chesters. The latter could have formed the core of the eastern *vicus* during the Turf-Wall phase.

A prominent ditch between 60 m and 70 m east of the fort probably limited the buildings on this side. It has been compared with a fifth-century defensive ditch cutting through earlier buildings in the *vicus* at Malton.[102] Despite the less regular appearance of this area by comparison with the western parts of the fort, the interpretation of differing military influence for the two areas is in my opinion far-fetched, unless the ditch is part of an annexe, as has also been suggested.[103] The differing appearance of the two areas is probably due to the fact that more building phases occurred in the eastern sector of the *vicus*.

To the west of the fort, the geophysical survey shows a regular, almost typical street-type-*vicus* appearance along the road leading out of the *porta principalis sinistra,* so this area was definitely settled at a period later than that of the Turf Wall. Its length amounts to approximately 200 m, and the widening of the road suggest the existence of a market-place here (see below, pp. 117–18).

The discovery of occupation to the north of the fort, i.e. north of Hadrian's Wall, for approximately 100 m along the road (the Maiden Way) in the direction of the outpost fort of Bewcastle, is fascinating (Fig. 5.5, 42–45). A large area on some kind of platform to the north-west, also beyond the Wall, has been suggested as a possible parade-ground.[104] Unfortunately, being not very clear, these results cannot add further evidence on the question of the lay-out of *vici,* although they are able to show the complexity and range which a developed military *vicus* demonstrates.[105]

How did the development of the Birdoswald *vicus* take shape? First of all, we have to look for a pre-Vallum phase, as there is no reason to assume that the first soldiers arrived at this spot without their camp-followers. The slight adjustment of the line of the frontier northwards from that taken by the Turf Wall can be seen as providing the possibility of creating new space and a fresh laying-out of the *vicus.* Indeed the decision to change the alignment of Hadrian's Wall here may have been prompted by the need to provide more space around the fort. In any case, the changes within the settlement must have been immense. My guess is that it happened in combination with a change of garrison (and consequently a change of *vicus*-inhabitants).

It would be of great interest if the date of the features to the north of the Wall

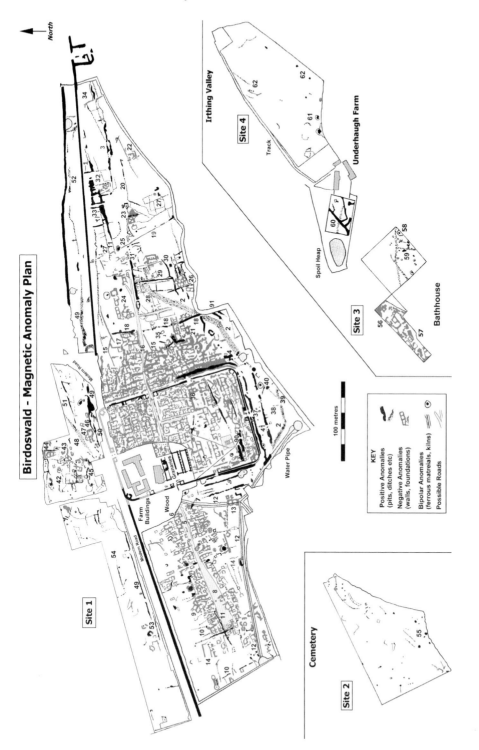

Fig. 5.5 Birdoswald, interpretation of the geophysical survey

could be established. Apparently, at some point, the Wall was no longer seen as a dividing line, and civilian settlement became possible on both sides of it. That would be no surprise if this part of the *vicus* was actually built while the Antonine Wall was in use; but Birdoswald was not garrisoned at that time. More likely a pragmatic view was taken that the fort at Bewcastle, and the road leading towards it, including its immediate environs, were seen as counting as a proper part of the Roman Empire, or at least as an area not in danger and so suitable for civilian settlement.[106]

Carvoran

It is rather strange at first sight that the geophysical survey of Carvoran and its surroundings shows a picture not dissimilar to that of Halton Chesters and Birdoswald, although this fort originally belonged to the Stanegate line. It was not, therefore, physically attached to Hadrian's Wall, despite its close proximity to the Wall, and its continued use, therefore, in its new role as a Wall fort.[107] Traces of a complex military *vicus* with a mixture of ribbon-like- and ring-road-appearance types are apparent along the line of the road which marks a continuation of the *via principalis* to the east and west of the fort. Particularly striking are the strong linear anomalies to the south of the fort, extending for between 50 m and 60 m, and lying approximately at right-angles to the fort's defences. These structures seem to continue for more than 200 m to the east, on a line south of the southern defences. The backbone was provided by the Stanegate road, by-passing the fort between the southern defences and the southern *vicus* anomalies, and continuing between parts of the south-eastern *vicus*. The question of why the anomalies along the Stanegate seem to be so much stronger and more clearly structured than those to the east and west of the fort is an interesting one, so far unexplained.

Castlesteads

With these images in mind, the results of the geophysical survey at Castlesteads are somewhat surprising.[108] Unfortunately, because the area of the fort itself lies in private parkland and was not suitable for geophysical examination, the fort-site itself could not be surveyed; therefore the picture of the *vicus* that we have here is somewhat 'hanging in the air', divorced from the fort to which it belonged.

At the northern edge of the area surveyed, a large ditch following the suggested line of the Vallum is detectable. South of this there is an area between 30 m and 40 m across with anomalies which look more or less like typical *vicus* buildings, bounded by another strong feature with two distinct corners. A pair of double-lined linear features, probably roads, approach very prominently from the south-south-west, and (in the form of a narrower road) from the east: they appear to be heading for these ditch corners. Another lane coming from the south-west meets at a sharp angle the south-western road shortly before the ditch. There are two additional curvilinear features further east. Several minor double lines suggest connecting lanes between the roads. All these roads and lanes are accompanied on both sides by a series of sub-rectangular (to the west) and more 'devious' (in the east) ditched enclosures with some compression of features in the centre, forming something which can best be described as a Romano-British field-system.[109]

Biggins' interpretation of this was that 'there can be no doubt that the fort and *vicus* were founded on a Romano-British settlement, and that the field-system continued to be maintained'. This would be a rare – if not indeed unique – example in the later first and second centuries AD where a Roman fort was positioned within an existing settlement.[110]

I propose an alternative interpretation. Considering the regularity of the southernmost ditch, which apparently takes its reference from the suggested position of the fort, this feature may in fact represent the Vallum. The features north of it would be the traces of an earlier military *vicus*, regularly laid out, such as we have seen at Halton Chesters and Birdoswald. I have no explanation for the inner ditch, except that this may perhaps be 'the watercourse shown on Henry MacLaughlan's map'.[111] Most important is, however, the close relationship between the ditch interpreted as part of the Vallum, and the roads and lanes within the field-system to the south. They directly relate to that ditch. This strongly suggests that first the ditch and then the roads were built. There is no evidence for a post-Roman dating of the enclosures. I think, therefore, that we have to understand the 'field-system' as belonging to the Roman settlement, i.e. as part of an enlarged military *vicus*.

Carriden

Although Carriden at the eastern end of the Antonine Wall is not generally considered a 'fixed' fort, a discussion of its *vicus* should be added here because the picture seen in aerial photographs is comparable with that at Castlesteads (Fig. 5.7).[112] From the fort's south-eastern gate (*porta principalis sinistra?*) and from its north-eastern corner, roads lead eastward, accompanied by roughly regular, sub-rectangular ditched enclosures, for approximately 500 m. About 100 m east of the fort, a crossroads has been detected, connecting the two main roads and continuing to the south, thus forming the beginning of a street-grid. The famous stone attesting *vicani consistentes* at the fort of *Velunia* or *Veluniate* was found within the northern part of this system.[113] This and the direct relationship of fort to street-system leave no doubt that fort and field-system were contemporary, thus leading to the interpretation of the field-system as being part of the military *vicus*. At Inveresk, at the end of Dere Street, we find a similar lay-out.[114] As at Castlesteads it may be secondary, however, since it lies more than 600 m from the fort, and excavation has detected traces of regular strip-houses closer to the fort. However, their proximity to the amphitheatre suggests that the fort and at least some parts of the field-system are contemporary.

Discussion

The question arises as to why there is such a discrepancy between the various parts of the *vicus* within the overall lay-out (at Castlesteads and perhaps at Inveresk). The answer might lie in the chronology. As at Halton Chesters and Birdoswald, where a new phase of development after the abandonment of the Vallum is the most likely explanation, I proposed an earlier dating for the features within the outer ditch at Castlesteads. The other parts would be a later addition. But how can the field-systems as such be explained? They very much resemble settlement patterns typical for the south-east of Britain, but which can also be found to a certain extent in lowland Scotland as well.[115] In particular, one should bear in mind the striking plan of Brancaster in Norfolk, where a vast series of ditched enclosures, connected and made accessible by road-like features, were oriented solely and exclusively by reference to the *portae principales* of the large fort in its centre: the settlement on either side without doubt represents the military *vicus*.[116]

An explanation for this adoption of southern, or at any rate lowland, structures in the north on Hadrian's Wall and even in Scotland is that the units and their camp-followers, occupying forts such as Castlesteads, may have come from the south and brought with them their own special traditions, or else had been newly recruited in the south. They would have started the expansion of the *vicus* in the way they were used to, that is, in the 'Romano-British lowland way'.[117] The time for this would be immediately after the abandonment of the Vallum, after Hadrian's Wall was reoccupied in the 160s, after the abandonment of the Antonine Wall. Initially it is thought that the Vallum was re-commissioned at this time, but certainly by the early third century it seems to have fallen into disuse. For the places in Scotland I suggest a similar development. The position of the fort at Carriden, as well as at Inveresk in the far north, and also the relationship between forts and military *vici* in general, make it most unlikely that the inhabitants of the plots in these field-systems came from the immediate vicinity.

We have to conclude that, despite certain differences, the evidence from Benwell, Housesteads, Birdoswald, Castlesteads, Chesters and other places on Hadrian's Wall shows, not only in the hinterland but also in the military zone of Hadrian's Wall itself, that military *vici* not only existed but also had in general a similar structure and size to those of *vici* in other areas. On Hadrian's Wall, the close relationship between the forts and the Wall itself, and the temporary constraints on space at first because of the construction of the Vallum, may have been responsible for some irregularity in the lay-out of these settlements. However, in principle there is nothing to suggest that the relationship between the forts here and their *vici* was different from anywhere else. For some time the Wall even seems to have lost its function as a divider. The evidence from Housesteads and Vindolanda, as well as probably from Chesters at a later date, shows that this relationship became even closer as parts of the ditch-systems were given up and taken over by roads leading around the forts, roads which connected different parts of the *vici* and provided access to the buildings themselves.

The question as to whether sites on the Antonine Wall 'functioned' in a similar way is an interesting one. Unfortunately, we still do not know very much about their surroundings. Recent geophysical work at Bar Hill and at other forts on the Antonine Wall, in preparation for its nomination as a World Heritage Site, seems to have yielded inconclusive, or perhaps even negative, results.[118] Below (pp. 122–3) I shall argue that here the enlarged 'annexes' may have housed civilians. That a northern location was not considered unsuitable for camp-followers in general can be seen at Bewcastle, High Rochester (see above) and, as mentioned earlier, even Inveresk and Carriden, where an inscription provides evidence for the existence there of a body of *vicani*.[119]

Market-places

On the Continent it has been noted that in quite a number of *vici*, the main road was laid out in such a way that it was wide enough to form a piazza-like structure, usually interpreted as a market-place.[120] Buildings here, in general simple strip-houses with various functions, were often provided with a *porticus*, giving them a more conspicuous appearance, as well as providing protection to passers-by.

At Caerhun in Wales, aerial photographs suggest a widening of the road running north from the *porta principalis sinistra*, the road which forms the core of the military *vicus* (Fig. 5.1). On the basis of this widening, Davies had mentioned in an earlier publication the possible presence of a market-place here.[121] This impression is strongly supported by the new evidence from the geophysical survey (Fig. 5.2). Low or no anomalies represent the road for a length of *c.* 120 m, with a width of up to *c.* 14 m before it gradually narrows to perhaps 7 m.[122] Including possible porticoes in front of the buildings, which may legally have been considered as part of the public area of the market-place,[123] an 'official' width of around 18 m may be surmised, the equivalent of half an *actus*.

At Caer Gai the question needs to be asked as to whether the road leading north-eastwards, most likely from the *porta principalis dextra*, also formed a market-place. Over a length of *c.* 100 m and with a width of approximately 15 m, the suggested line of the road is without any anomalies. Even beyond this area, excavation showed a width of nearly 10 m for the road, which looked much narrower on geophysical evidence.[124] Equally, at Cefn Caer, the road leading to the north-west from the *porta principalis dextra* (Fig. 5.6) clearly widens beyond the rectangular building complex which has been interpreted as a *mansio*.[125] The recent survey which has extended the evidence further to the north-west supports this interpretation.[126] Again, a width of about 15 m is most likely for the open part, not counting flanking porticoes. Whether the area directly in front of the gate and the '*mansio*', equally 'calm' in geophysical terms, forms a rectangle of approximately 30 m by 30 m and represents another open space cannot be determined, since this zone was only partially surveyed. Despite the impression that the part of the *vicus* which lies behind the *porta decumana* is the larger, the presence of an open market-place would define the *vicus* to the north-west as the main constituent part.

A market-place was undoubtedly the centre of the western *vicus* at Birdoswald on Hadrian's Wall (Fig. 5.5). The road leading from the *porta principalis sinistra* widens after *c.* 90 m to an open triangular space, approximately 90 m in length and *c.* 18/20 m in width, with only a few anomalies in the middle (Fig. 5.5, nos 8–11).[127]

The end of this widened stretch can be seen at the forking of the road, with one branch going off towards the south-west to reach a cemetery,[128] and the other continuing westwards as the military road. The traces of habitation facing onto this road and the market-place are typical, and can easily be interpreted as the remains of strip-buildings.

The situation at Maryport, however, appears to be different. No particular 'treatment' of the main road can be detected. However, it ends in a space without any geophysical anomalies which runs along the whole length of the north-eastern side of the fort, directly beyond its outermost ditch (c. 200 m by 22 m: Fig. 5.3, hatched area). As this area is too small to be used as an exercise ground for horses, in the sense of the ring-type *vicus* (see above, p. 103), and since a parade ground is known to have existed to the south-east of the fort, I suggest that this other area be interpreted as a market-place. However, if this interpretation is correct, its lay-out would be unique.

Perhaps Newstead had a market-place as well. On the basis of the width of the earlier of the superimposed roads to the south (up to 13 m), the distance the excavated houses kept from its edge (approximately 5 m), as well as the distance of the road from a large drain on the other side, an *agger* of c. 27 m, probably three quarters of an *actus*, can be reconstructed.[129] This would have provided more than enough space for market functions.

The proximity of the market-places to the forts and their gates clearly points to their military role, and to the soldiers as being their primary target in marketing terms. The role of such markets in the life of the wider area around the forts and in that of the (native) population living in the environs is a topic for discussion. Perhaps to a certain extent regional products were offered, so long as the military authorities themselves, and in particular the spending power of soldiers on a salary, created and maintained a market.[130] This may have led to a certain mixing of the military and civilian/native population. But, in general, the picture of an 'inter-woven' society such as that depicted by S. James[131] seems to have existed only in the lowlands, if at all. In Wales and the northern military zone, the military *vici* must have had only limited functions for the natives' needs. Otherwise the *vici* would have continued to exist after the withdrawal of the garrisons. This observation implies, furthermore, that as a general rule the movement of people from the neighbourhood surrounding forts into the *vici* themselves must have been marginal.

Military vici and annexes

Annexes and their relation to the military *vici* need also to be discussed, since they are regular features outside British forts. In the past relevant evidence was scarce, and the question therefore of their possible identity and function had to be left open. In 1984, however, I ventured to express the opinion that they 'were not merely intended as protection for official buildings like baths and *mansiones* as well as for the baggage train, but also gave shelter to camp-followers and traders'.[132]

Roman road

Roman road

Roman road and market place

Cefn Caer farm and outbuidings

Modern road

Sunken lane

8nT

0nT   Data clipped to +-15nT

-8nT

Survey by D. Hopewell and J. Burman

100 metres

Fig. 5.6 Cefn Caer, Pennal, gradiometer survey of the fort with annexes and its surroundings

Breeze, on the other hand, wrote in the same year that 'excavations, admittedly limited in extent . . . have failed to produce evidence of civilians in the annexes, and it seems probable that they were purely military in function, serving as defensive enclosures for semi-military activities'.[133] Recently Biggins and Taylor considered annexes as usually containing 'the bath-house, and other military buildings which could not fit comfortably within the ramparts'.[134] Davies wrote in even more detail about 'buildings and structures within annexes, such as the bath-house and the tile/pottery kiln at Gelligaer . . . most likely [they] represent a specifically military adjunct, comprising structures which could not be accom-modated within the fort by reason of space, safety or noxious smell;'[135] and he further added, two years ago, that annexes were 'sometimes housing complex, stone courtyard buildings termed *mansiones*, almost certainly linked to the operation of the *cursus publicus*.[136] This generally-held view seems supported by the few excavations which have taken place within annexes, such as that at Bearsden on the Antonine Wall, where Breeze unearthed a bath-house with accompanying installations.[137]

If lack of space for such buildings was indeed the case, however, why did *architecti* simply not make the fort larger? Why were bath-houses and *mansiones* in some cases considered to be endangered and placed within an annexe, while at other places they were 'regularly' – in a Continental sense – integrated into the planning and construction of the *vicus*? Why should the smells of ovens and kilns bother the soldiers more or less when they were set within an annexe or in the *vicus* rather than in the fort? In my opinion, we are far from understanding the function of the annexes, or the reasons why they are common in Britain and almost non-existent in Germany.

In contrast to 1984, we can now look at quite a number of sites where we know about the existence of either an annexe or a military *vicus*, or in some cases both. At the small annexe to the south-west of the *porta principalis dextra* at Caerhun, the excavator saw evidence of civilian habitation.[138] We now know that this enclosure is situated opposite the main part of the *vicus*. However, due to its limited size and the location of both bath-house and *mansio* in front of the fort, it cannot have played a major role for civilians (Fig. 5.2). At Caersws a small annexe at the *porta decumana* is separated in the same way from the *vicus* by the fort, as also at High Rochester[139] and Carriden (Fig. 5.7). At Caer Gai, the most recent geophysical survey, conducted by Hopewell and Burman, shows a large annexe along the whole length of the south-eastern defences: it contains a huge courtyard building to the south of the road leading from the fort, and very strong and complex anomalies, most probably representing the bath-house, to the north of it. Again, the annexe apparently did not interfere directly with the lay-out of the *vicus* situated to the north-east and to the south-west. However, it cannot be excluded that the annexe is secondary, as it may have cut a perimeter road leading around the southern corner of the fort, where there was a certain amount of habitation. It is also possible that the *vicus* was later extended around the annexe.[140] At Dinefwr Park, Llandeilo, the interpretation of the system of ditches along the right-hand (south-eastern), side of the fort, either as belonging to an earlier fort[141] or else as an annexe, is ambiguous. In any case, there is a clear distinction between the anomalies of the military *vicus* in front of the fort, and some ribbon-like anomalies along the continuation of the road coming from the *porta principalis dextra* within the annexe.[142] This is best interpreted as a 'typical' military *vicus* immediately beyond the ditch(es) of an annexe.[143]

The situation at Birdoswald is less certain. Interpretations of the ditch to the east of the fort, an area which contains densely-packed structures, is that it is either 'late' or 'limiting a possible annexe'.[144] If the latter were the case, the annexe was clearly located opposite the *vicus* proper. The annexe at Bryn-y-Gefeiliau, by contrast, which is set directly behind the *principia* of the fort, seems to be the result of a reduction in the size of the fort. Traces of occupation with two different alignments would point to different phases of use. However, as the structures

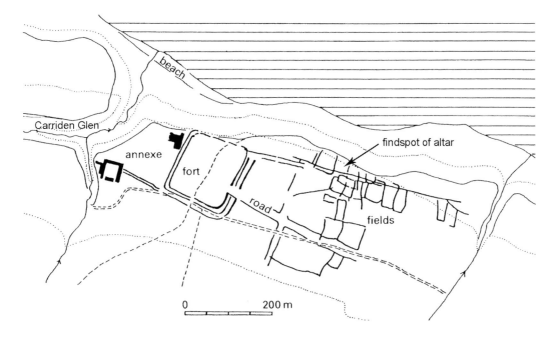

Fig. 5.7 Carriden, line drawing of the results of aerial photography

which are set at an oblique angle to the buildings inside the fort and its defences are known mostly from excavations in the 1920s, the plan may be misleading, and the different orientation the result of a surveying error. Accurate interpretation of these features therefore remains problematical. The excavators suggested that the remains belonged to either a bath-house or a *mansio*.[145]

In general, we see a tendency in Roman Britain to distinguish between military *vici* and their buildings on the one hand, and annexes on the other. The two components are usually located on different sides of the fort. Whereas annexes appear to be either empty or densely-packed, *vici* generally have a regular ribbon-like structure, as described above. If we bear in mind that baths (and perhaps also *mansiones*) are normally found in front of the *porta praetoria* where they often were not an integral part of the main *vicus*, we can assume for these buildings a somewhat closer connection with the forts, or rather with the military administration, perhaps resulting – for whatever reasons – in the placing of these installations within an annexe, whenever, that is, an annexe was thought necessary.

The difference between annexes and military *vici* can be seen most clearly in the fascinating surroundings of the fort of Cefn Caer (Fig. 5.6). The geophysical survey here revealed the presence of an annexe extending across the entire width of the fort in front of the *porta praetoria*. Originally it seems to have had a depth of *c*. 50 m, but the evidence suggests that it was later enlarged to sub-rectangular form with dimensions of 110 m by 75 m. It contained an area with quite strong anomalies, measuring some 40 m by 40 m: it is uncertain whether this area included a *mansio* as well as what were probably the baths, or just a large bath-building.[146] In front of the *porta principalis dextra* the road had been widened to *c.* 15 m to form a market-place (see above), defining that part as the centre of the military *vicus*; its expansion was, however, limited by a little creek on the north-west.[147] The geophysical survey shows that the area in front of the *porta principalis sinistra* seems not to have been used for *vicus* purposes, perhaps due to its proximity to boggy ground towards the south. The only direction for the *vicus'* expansion was therefore in front of the *porta decumana.* Perhaps an increasing importance of the link towards the north-east, to the next fort at Brithdir, made this position attractive. In fact, a sizeable part of the military *vicus*, with a length of possibly more than 200 m, was found on this side of the fort.

A unique feature at Cefn Caer is the fact that the road which forms the core of this part of the *vicus* did not lead directly to the *porta decumana* or to the gap in the ditches, but reached the ditches more than 20 m north of this position. It then took a sharp bend to the left, continued along the edge of the ditch, and then entered the fort via another 90-degree bend to the right. The reason for this is obvious: the military *vicus* had to avoid another two-phased annexe at the eastern part of the rear of the fort. The *porta decumana* opened into both annexes, which had dimensions of 40 m by 70 m and 70 m by 80 m respectively. No trace of occupation in either annexe was revealed by the geophysical survey, so they have been interpreted as storage compounds.[148] As a result of this competition for space, the elongated buildings, or rather the plots of the *vicus* located between road and annexe, were limited to a length of approximately 22 m.[149] Nevertheless, the existence of a regular lay-out of plots there is indisputable. As none of the features seems to extend over the ditch of the neighbouring annexe, it is clear that the military *vicus* and annexe were both in use at the same time, at least for a while.

This clear 'contradiction' of annexe and military *vicus* proves that annexes in general were not militarized or fortified versions of civilian settlements. Rather, annexes and military *vici* seem to have had little in common with one another except in their proximity to forts and, occasionally at least, in the location of the bath-house as well as possibly a *mansio*, which are sometimes found within the annexe if there is one.

Elginhaugh, Newstead and the forts on the Antonine Wall may be considered to be possible exceptions to this generalization. At Elginhaugh the buildings partially excavated are certainly strip-houses,[150] perhaps even with porticoes. However, the limited extent of the excavation leaves room for debate as to whether these buildings did indeed belong to the same phase as the 'annexe ditches', especially as similar constructions probably continued beyond those ditches. What is clear is that at some point the buildings were abandoned, and subsequently were cut by a new (and extraordinary) funnel-shaped ditch-system.

At Newstead, the southern annexe probably comprised between about 80 and 100 'civilian' buildings, although the evidence is apparently not undisputed.[151] The published plans of the details of this *vicus* known to me clearly show strip-houses (see below, p. 124).[152] The eastern annexe contained buildings on either side of the road over a length of 80 m. The size of these annexes is exceptional.[153] Perhaps the two systems should better be interpreted not as annexes but as defences of the military *vicus* (see also below, p. 130).

In the same context it is worth considering again the forts on the Antonine Wall, for most forts here, if not all of them, had an annexe. That in itself is significant, especially since the forts on Hadrian's Wall, and earlier forts in general, usually had none. By comparison with other annexes, the ones on the Antonine Wall are fairly large, usually only a little smaller than the forts to which they belong.[154] In addition, it is worth noting that these annexes usually lay on one or other side of the fort, with the extension of the *via principalis* as the long-distance road leading through them. Recent geophysical survey on the Antonine Wall has had difficulty finding outside these annexes any traces of civilian occupation at all in the sense discussed above.[155] It seems therefore as if the annexes on the Antonine Wall took over the role and positions of military *vici* elsewhere. If that is right, the defences have to be seen as being necessary for their protection. The *vici* themselves would also have been rather small; but the forts themselves on the Antonine Wall were quite small, and were often garrisoned only by part-units.[156] It is not surprising, therefore, that many of the bath-houses were not very large either.[157] This would imply that the creation of the Antonine Wall and the garrisoning of a number of forts there with only part-units must have provided less attraction to a substantial part of the unit's camp-followers. This in turn would suggest that the previous places they occupied, at the forts on Hadrian's Wall or in its hinterland, for example, must have retained some importance in their respective areas, despite the withdrawal of the troops from the adjacent forts. Another possibility is that the previously-occupied forts were not completely abandoned: the inhabitants of the old military *vici* would then have had the choice of either following the unit to its new base or staying put, and it seems that quite a number may have chosen the latter option.[158] It appears that the military felt responsible for the protection of those who followed them. Defended areas which have the appearance of large annexes were, therefore, built on the Antonine Wall to protect these civilians.[159]

Individual buildings

This is not the place to discuss in detail the individual buildings of the military *vici* of Roman Britain. Bath-houses, *mansiones* and other complex structures not only served important functions for the military in general and for soldiers individually, but often also provided the starting-point for the overall lay-out of a military *vicus*. In particular the baths formed a focus of life within the *vici*.[160] As there is so much new evidence, in particular from geophysics, and as these buildings form such prominent features, it would be worth singling them out for an independent study.

As for living quarters, the most common type of house in the military *vici* of Britain, as indeed it is on the Continent, was the strip-house.[161] Its narrow, elongated form enabled many houses to enjoy the advantage of comparative proximity to the fort: 'open' fronts gave easy access to shops or *tabernae* in the front part of these buildings, and, as the roof rested on the long outside walls generally without internal supports, the interior afforded great flexibility both in plan and function. Generally erected on elongated plots, these buildings could easily be altered by additions to both front (e.g. the provision of a *porticus*) and rear.[162]

The buildings excavated at Newstead are quite small. Buildings of up to only 10 m by 4.5 m, each erected separately, have for example been found within the southern 'annexe'.[163] At Elginhaugh the buildings partially excavated appear to be strip-houses measuring up to 17 m by 6 m,[164] some perhaps even with porticoes. An equally good, representative example of a strip-house is building 722 at Ribchester.[165] Measuring 15 m by 5 m it displays the main characteristics of these buildings, viz. not only an elongated form, but strong, stable outer walls, a more or less open front, flexible internal divisions and varied use. A long succession of hearths and possible evidence for industrial production does not necessarily mean that the structure in question was a *fabrica*; rather such activity in general is commonplace in strip-buildings.

The buildings excavated at the 'industrial settlement' of Walton-le-Dale are among the most typical strip-buildings I know.[166] Again, several contained evidence for processes involving heat. Behind the buildings up to 20 m in length, the plots continued for at least the same distance again, divided by lanes, possible fences and perhaps limited by a ditch. In at least one instance two stone buildings shared a common wall, and another timber building followed without a gap. Certainly the buildings of period 3 had porticoes in such a way that they formed a continuous structure along the road, interrupted only by side lanes.[167] A military function has been suggested for the settlement at Walton-le-Dale, and the most likely interpretation of the settlement is that it is indeed a military *vicus*. The implication is that an adjacent fort should be sought, probably to the south of the excavated area, if the *vicus* was of the street-type, or else somewhere to one side, if the settlement was an example of the tangent-type.

Twenty-five years ago it was thought that strip-houses in Roman Britain were generally smaller than those on the Continent.[168] The more recent discoveries mentioned above still support this original conclusion. At Cefn Caer, for example, building lengths of between 10 m and 15 m and widths of between 5 m and 6 m have been suggested on the basis of the geophysical evidence, although in excavation they turned out to be much larger than originally thought (18 m by 8 m and possibly 15 m by 7 m instead of 10 m to 15 m by 5 m to 6 m).[169] In other recent work at Birdoswald, Halton Chesters, Castlesteads and Carvoran, building widths of about 7 m and lengths of less than 20 m were seen as normal.[170]

This compares with the few results from the *canabae* of legionary fortresses. The buildings excavated at Caerleon in 1985 range in size from 16 m to 17 m in length and from 5 m to 7 m in width (the size 11 m by 7 m, mentioned in the publication, does not conform to the plan).[171] The fronts of at least two of the houses were constructed in a different way from the main walls, and therefore can probably be interpreted as having open fronts. One building was clearly provided with a *porticus*, with posts set on individual stone slabs; that in the centre has a socket hole.

In complete contrast to the dimensions listed above, excavated buildings of Flavian and later date on the Continent show lengths starting at 22 m and going up to 40 m.[172] Widths between *c.* 6 m and 9 m are normal. Only buildings of Claudian or earlier origin appear to have been in general smaller.[173] In this context it is interesting that some of the buildings recorded at Maryport by geophysical survey were considered as being 'very large'.[174] Biggins and Taylor mention sizes of 26 m and 30 m by 11 m as well as 21 m by 8 m and 28 m by 19 m.[175] Although there is reason to be sceptical about the interpretation of individual building details from geophysical plots, the general outline must be accurate. A comparison, therefore, of geophysical evidence with the results from large-scale excavations where several building plots have been uncovered is interesting. A comparison of just one part of the plan of the Maryport *vicus* with those of excavated houses at Ladenburg and Walheim in Upper Germany[176] (Fig. 5.8) shows a close resemblance in dimensions. This suggests that the buildings at Maryport were actually of similar size as those in Ladenburg, and indeed larger than British *vicus* buildings in general. Equally, the features behind the buildings, most probably to be interpreted as boundary lines, bear close resemblance to similar features on the Continent. At Maryport distances between these lines of less than 10 m, between 15 m and 20 m, and even between 25 m and 30 m, can all be distinguished. Comparing this with examples from southern Germany, one might interpret the evidence from Maryport as representing single, double and triple plots, in the latter cases filled with either a single building, a complex building, or 'groups' of buildings.[177] Nevertheless, as I have argued elsewhere,[178] regularity in lay-out and plot-widths cannot be taken as evidence of direct military interference, with the possible exception of the initial laying-out of building-plots lining the principal roads.

The concept behind the structures at Maryport, with its dense sequence of buildings (some houses even share party walls with their neighbours), is similar to that seen in excavations on the Continent. Not dissimilar is the picture from Vindolanda and Housesteads, despite the queries noted above about absent courtyards and the problems posed by what may possibly be late structures. The same impression of dense habitation can also easily be seen in most of the geophysical surveys discussed here. In complete contrast, however, is the apparently generous spacing of houses suggested by several recent excavations. At Caerleon, for example, gaps of between 5 m and 6 m have been noted between each house, partially filled by metalled lanes between them.[179] Nevertheless, I get the impression that the 'densely-packed' aspect of strip-buildings is sometimes ignored when interpreting limited areas of actual excavation. For example, the fact that only a few houses were directly identifiable by the geophysical survey at Cefn Caer (Fig. 5.6) has apparently influenced the interpretation of the results of a trial trench (no. 1): only a single timber building was identified, with post construction as its framework, and additional planking on sleeper beams as its vertical wall construction.[180] But, if we make the assumption (which I think more probable) that a compact construction was used, as suggested by the density of linear anomalies over most of the magnetometer plot (and supported by excavated examples on the Continent), it appears better to interpret the excavated remains as consisting of two houses (not one) immediately next to each other, the first with a post-type construction (and walls of wattle and daub), and a second, possibly more lightly constructed, which was set on a sleeper-beam foundation, perhaps again with walls of wattle and daub. The fact that remains of wattle and daub were not found in the excavation is not surprising, since the report mentions plough grooves cutting into the clay floors: site preservation was clearly poor.

The results of a second trench (no. 2) further east in the *vicus* of Cefn Caer reveal a similar situation. Although the excavation was carried out believing that two overlapping and consecutive buildings would be found, on the basis of the interpretation of results from high-resolution geophysics, the features unearthed should probably rather be interpreted as belonging to two more or less parallel buildings, approximately 2.5 m apart.[181] Looking at the size of the posts, row 06–36 seems to represent an outer wall (the western wall of building II) rather than an interior division. This is supported by the fact that the position which was considered to be the outer wall from the geophysical survey further west corresponds exactly with the line of the eastern wall of building I in the excavation (feature 45/52).[182] As a result, the sequence of buildings and their dating put forward by the excavators is in my view questionable.[183]

The excavation of Trench 2 at Cefn Caer was unfortunately never finished. It cannot therefore be determined whether an area more than 2 m wide consisting of 'silt containing stones' (30),[184] located between the road and the proposed façade of the building partially excavated (building II), was part of the road or – in my opinion – evidence for some kind of *porticus* in front of the house, continuing to the neighbouring building. The necessary posts may have rested on large stone slabs similar to those used in hearth 12, or on the cobbling of the street itself. Just as modern agricultural activity seems to have damaged other parts of the street, these stones may simply have been ploughed away.

In my opinion 'Continental'-type strip-houses with *porticus* were much more common in British military *vici* than has hitherto been realized. Looking at Greta Bridge, for example, I think that the features discovered and recently presented as a phase-II timber building have to be reconstructed as two strip-houses, rather than as a single, exceptional courtyard house. The plan as published ignores the unexcavated parts and also certain differences in the posts forming the *porticus*, as well as in buildings lines.[185] The result is unnecessarily complicated, and does not explore the possible options which might have presented themselves had the areas destroyed by a later stone building been preserved.

The excavated features at Greta Bridge can be reconstructed more easily, in my view, in the following way (Fig. 5.9). A northern building would have broadened over its length of 14 m from 5.6 m wide in the front to approximately 6.3 m wide at the back. The back of that building does not have to be on exactly the same line as that of its southern neighbour. In front of the building proper, a *porticus* with a depth of 2.2 m was added, most likely a five-post construction. In the central part of the building there was a hearth in a similar position as in the southern building (interpreted in the report as a bread-baking oven in the 'courtyard'). The southern building may have had a common wall with its northern neighbour (107). Along

Fig. 5.8 Maryport, overlay of an excerpt of the magnetometer plot of the main vicus *with plans of phase 2 West of Ladenburg and Walheim, Germany*

this wall a narrow corridor, 0.6 m wide, would have given access to the main part of the house. Another possibility is an independent building divided from the southern one by a gap of 0.6 m. The evidence for the back part of this house will have been destroyed by the construction of the later stone building. The cobbles in the central part suggest that the former option is more likely to be the correct one, since they extend a little way beyond the presumed northern limit of that house. The façade of the southern house is set back slightly by comparison with the northern one. It was fronted by a *porticus* a little less than 2 m deep. This was carried on three front posts (one has to be reconstructed outside the limits of the excavation) and had a support in its middle. In both cases, the porticoes of the two houses were erected separately and belonged independently to each building.

The situation on the street front reconstructed here for Greta Bridge is almost identical to that at Ladenburg (phase-2 West, buildings A and B).[186] There, the occurrence of two *porticus* posts next to each other, one exactly on and one slightly off the boundary line, was explained by supposing the existence of legal regulations giving rights over the boundary line only to one of the neighbours (in the case of Greta Bridge, that would be to the owner of the more northerly plot).[187] Each of the proposed buildings at Greta Bridge had a typical strip-house plan: there were two *taberna*-like rooms at the front behind the *porticus*; then a narrow corridor giving access to a large 'common room' with hearth or oven in the middle. In the southern building the 'common-room' was accompanied by two small rooms on one side, in the northern building perhaps by just one side room; and finally one large or two smaller rooms at the end of each house. Apparently the area of the front porticoes was more public than private, since the cobbling of the street extended without a break under the porticoes, directly up to the front walls proper of the houses. Again this is a feature found at Ladenburg (for example), where the fronts of the houses remained the same throughout all building phases, while the porticoes themselves were often moved both forwards and backwards.[188]

Limits of military vici

If we are to understand military *vici* as settlements in their entirety, one has to ask where exactly their limits were set. Usually the areas opposite the forts along the long-distance roads were bounded by cemeteries. These must have been properly established at the time of the initial laying-out of the *vicus* (by the military?), and many *vici* came to fill the whole of the space between fort and cemetery. The area of the cemetery was always respected, and no example is known where a cemetery is overlain by parts of the *vicus*. This arrangement of space is perhaps the most important single factor which defined the size of military *vici*.[189]

On the edges of settlements, the visible utilisation of the plots often seems to end at a definite line.[190] Sometimes this line is clearly defined. At Hindwell in Wales, the structures detectable in the geophysical survey and attributable to the military *vicus* end on the south side with a linear feature interpreted as a fence,[191] although the distance of only 30 m from here to the front of the buildings seems rather short. On the other hand, there is a vague impression of a parallel feature a little further south of the suggested fence-line, as well as a few additional anomalies beyond. This may suggest the presence of a back road here, running roughly parallel to the main road.

At Caerhun (Fig. 5.2), the ditch-like feature beginning at the north-west corner of the fort and running roughly parallel to the main road for 260 m, separated from it by a distance of about 50 m, can be understood as marking the boundary of the

Fig. 5.9 Greta Bridge, alternative reconstruction of phase-II timber buildings as strip-houses with porticoes

military *vicus* on the west and north sides, although it is not clear whether the northern part bends back south at some point or extends towards the river.

A similar feature can be seen in the geophysical survey of Cefn Caer, to the south of the road leading in a north-easterly direction (Fig. 5.6). A ditch-like feature runs roughly parallel to the road, separated by a distance of approximately 40 m,[192] and is connected to two ditches at right-angles to the road. These may be interpreted as boundary lines between individual plots.

The results from the Maryport survey in this context are fascinating (Fig. 5.3). The main part of the *vicus* here extending along the trunk road heading north-eastwards was limited by ditches, which had been partially re-cut in subsequent phases.[193] As they were connected to features at right-angles to them and to the road, which were therefore interpreted as boundary lines between the individual plots (see above), the original view that they define the outer limits of the building plots is plausible. It is interesting that these plots extend to a length of around 80 m for the first 150 m from the fort. They are then reduced to about 60 m in length. A further reduction to perhaps only 25 m to 30 m at the far end of the *vicus* should not be seen (in my opinion) as enclosing further habitation, but as defining the limits of the principal cemetery. The distinction between the areas of the living and the zone reserved for the dead is emphasized by a double line, which is suggestive of a lane. Including a further reduction to only 10 m at the far edge of the *vicus*, there would have been room for about 100 m of burial ground on both sides of the road. Again, none of these ditch-like features seem substantial enough to be interpreted as having a defensive character. In some parts a double line may suggest even a back lane. Whether the curving ditch a little further north (Fig. 5.6, 23) had a similar function is a matter for speculation.

Whereas the features apparently limiting military *vici* so far discussed are most probably to be interpreted as marking the end of individual plots rather than having a defensive capability, the ditches found at Birdoswald at both edges of the military *vicus* (Fig. 5.5, no. 10 on the west and no. 18 on the east) may indicate another purpose altogether. To the north the limits of the building lots were probably provided by Hadrian's Wall itself, and to the south by the precipitous end to the flattish area of ground. The ditches, on the other hand, clearly mark the limits of the dense settlement-pattern on either side of the fort. Their size seems to point clearly to their having 'defensive' function, but the alleged 'late' date[194] assigned to them is questionable. Also the possibility of an annexe here has been mentioned.[195] It should, however, be noted that the remains of possible further buildings have been detected beyond both of these boundary ditches, suggesting later expansion of the *vicus*, beyond the limits originally envisaged for it. The debate about the evidence at Newstead is similar (see above, pp. 122–3). Due to their overall sizes and the nature of the buildings within the annexes, these latter may be understood as defended military *vici*.[196]

With the exception of the few examples listed above where a defensive ditch (and accompanying rampart?) seems possible,[197] and those on the Antonine Wall, where the 'annexes' may have housed (small) military *vici* (see above, p. 123), the settlements outside Roman forts were generally not defended. The possibility, however, of physical limits existing in the sense of boundary lines nevertheless seems plausible, separating the *vici* as such from their surroundings. The legal status of military *vici* as such cannot be discussed here. One should consider the possibility, however, that lands adjacent to auxiliary forts were specifically designated as being set aside for the use of military *vici*, in much the same way as the area *intra leugam* (attested for the legionary fortress of Carnuntum on the middle Danube) was defined.[198] A similar situation has also been suggested at many other sites.

One outstanding question concerning military *vici* is the identity of the owner of the lands immediately beyond the fort and *vicus* – or rather who had the right to use them. Were they *prata auxiliaria* assigned for strictly military use? At Maryport this area may have been limited by a curvilinear ditch some 600 m to 700 m beyond the fort to the east, clearly related to the Roman road to Carlisle. Biggins and Taylor, on the other hand, considered this as marking a possible limit to 'the *vicus* and farming lands in its environs'.[199] But whose land lay beyond that?

The end of the military vici

The chronological end of the military *vici* of Roman Britain is also a matter on which more research is needed. The new evidence from Wales underlines the very close proximity, often discussed, of forts and their garrisons on the one hand, and the *vici* with their camp-followers on the other. For most of the Welsh forts the evidence is becoming increasingly strong that the *vici* were greatly reduced in size more or less at the same time as the removal of the garrisons: this was because of the 'symbiotic existence', which was the essence of the fort-*vicus* relationship.[200] At the latest, the *vici* were abandoned one or two generations after the withdrawal of the fort's garrison. In the true sense of the word most of the inhabitants of *vici* remained 'camp-followers', and therefore accompanied the transferred troops to their new place of garrison. Apparently the surrounding areas of most of the Welsh forts did not need focal points afterwards. This can be deduced from the fact that in contrast to so many formerly military *vici* in the British Lowlands and on the Continent, which continued in existence as civilian settlements, sometimes developing into 'small towns' or even into *civitas* capitals, few of the Welsh *vici* (Carmarthen is the obvious exception) developed an independent civilian identity in the Roman period. On rare occasions, however, the maintenance of a *mansio* may have led to a continuation of life on a small scale in Wales into the later second and third centuries AD, within the otherwise mostly-abandoned *vici*.[201]

That *vici* could be further developed if an adequate hinterland existed, and take on new functions and responsibilities, can be seen, for example, at a place like Catterick. Although the second-century fort and its *vicus* are only vaguely known, there is no doubt that the later town was built on the structures of a predecessor. Its original function was revived when, in the fourth century, a new fort was erected next to the town, and so the town served again as a kind of military *vicus*. The place must have originated as a tangent-type military *vicus* based on Dere Street (as the main road by-passing it), to which it was connected by a road running towards the east gate (in the fourth-century fort, the *porta praetoria*). The original T-junction developed into a crossroads, and from there it was not long before an early street-grid developed which can still be detected in the overall plan.[202]

Conclusion

Military *vici* are a fascinating type of Roman settlement. Knowledge about them helps us to understand auxiliary forts and the functioning of the Roman military in general. Although in recent years geophysical evidence has shed much light on many sites, we are still far from obtaining a complete picture. Many older questions still remain unanswered, while new ones have been raised by the latest research.

The differentiation, for example, between the role of the military as such, on the one hand, and that of civilians on the other in the day-to-day management of *vici* remains unclear. Using similar evidence from different sites, or even the same evidence from a single site, various models can be constructed which are completely different from one another. At Ribchester, for example, evidence of 'industrial functions' in an elongated building led to its identification as a _fabrica_. This in turn was seen as evidence for a strong military interference in extramural affairs.[203] According to an alternative hypothesis, however, the building was an ordinary strip-house, and was part of a military _vicus_, producing metal objects for perhaps both the military and the civilian market.

Our knowledge about the population of military _vici_ is in its infancy. Questions can be asked (but not answered on present evidence) about recruitment from and the interaction with the (native) population in the fort's immediate hinterland, as well as the overall importance of _vici_ in the socio-economic fabric of the micro-region which they served.[204]

Further discussion is also needed of the primary evidence for the structural relationship between forts and their attendant _vici_. Some of the hypotheses raised here concerning chronological and/or regional distinctions need to be tested by further research, and either confirmed or rejected. In Wales and on Hadrian's Wall, for example, 'street-type' military _vici_ seem to be the rule, whereas on the Stanegate and on Dere Street the tangent-type appears to be the most common lay-out. On the Antonine Wall enlarged 'annexes' may have formed small, defended military _vici_. Later _vici_, as at Housesteads, Vindolanda and perhaps Chesters, present us with a picture of rather dense and crowded occupation in such settlements. Across the whole Roman Empire, it is important to know to what extent differences between _vici_ are due to differing ideas of individual provincial governors, differing provincial policies, or even differing instructions in military handbooks; or are the varieties due rather, perhaps, to socio-economic factors, which naturally vary from province to province and even from micro-region to micro-region ?

What was the significance of the military _vici_ for the economy of the provinces? Were they a significant factor? The questions which M. Millett has raised for urban sites, concerning the need to compare the pattern of small finds within different types of settlement, is valid also for military _vici_, as they too were an integral part of Romano-British society.[205] It would, therefore, be very interesting to study the use of a material like samian pottery in the forts, and then compare it with its frequency in military _vici_ and small towns. Did different places in the same category receive different goods, and, if so, why did this happen?[206] Perhaps the forthcoming study of J. Evans will provide a first step towards answering these questions.[207] Without detailed knowledge of the relative chronology, however, the conclusions to be drawn from the study of small finds will always be piecemeal. And it is important to stress also that equally important for the understanding of British military _vici_ is their comparison with Continental examples.

Undoubtedly what we need in the future is not only evidence from aerial photography and geophysical survey, but also from archaeological fieldwork too. Whereas trial trenches may confirm, correct, or add to an interpretation drawn from finds-distribution and other non-destructive research, and can also show stratigraphic sequences and provide limited dating evidence (unfortunately, of course, only for one particular location),[208] it is only large-scale excavation which can reveal details of the construction, use and function of individual houses,[209] their position within settlements, the dynamics of a *vicus*, and all the other aspects of a settlement's relationship with the forts they served. Considering the limited amount of evidence which has been preserved, and the need for its conservation (together with the enormous resources that such conservation entails), the results of past excavations cannot be valued highly enough. Even if the excavation techniques of earlier days seem in part, at least, outmoded from our present perspective, the results from places like Vindolanda are extremely important. An examination of their buildings' stratigraphy, and of their relative and absolute chronologies, just by studying and presenting the features and finds already discovered, would enable further advances to be made in the study of the military *vici* of Roman Britain.

Appendix 1

Recent geophysical surveys with interpretable results and larger scale excavations in British military *vici*:

Bewcastle (*Britannia* 32 [2001], 336)
Birdoswald (Biggins and Taylor 1999 and 2004b; *Britannia* 32 [2001], 331, fig. 11)
Brecon Gaer (*Britannia* 36 [2005], 390)
Bryn y Gefeiliau (Hopewell 2005)
Caergwanaf (*Britannia* 36 [2005], 390–2, with fig. 4)
Caerau (*Britannia* 36 [2005], 390)
Caer Gai (Hopewell 2005)
Caergwanaf (*Britannia* 35 [2004], 263–4)
Caerhun (*Britannia* 34 [2003], 295, with fig. 2; Hopewell 2005)
Caersws (*Britannia* 36 [2005], 389–90)
Carvoran (*Britannia* 32 [2001], 330–1, with fig. 10; *Britannia* 31 [2000], 391)
Castlesteads (Biggins and Taylor, forthcoming; *Britannia* 32 [2001], 333, with fig. 12)
Cefn Caer, Pennal (Hopewell 2005; *Britannia* 32 [2001], 313, with fig. 2)
Chesters (*Britannia* 35 [2004], 273, with fig.8)
Colwyn Castle (*Britannia* 36 [2005], 390)
Dinefwr Park, Llandeilo (*Britannia* 35 [2004], 254–6, with fig. 2)
Drumlanrig (*Britannia* 36 [2005], 401–2, with fig. 9)
Drumquhassle (*Britannia* 36 [2005], 395–8, with fig. 8)
Fendoch (*Britannia* 36 [2005], 395, with fig. 7)
Halton Chesters (*Britannia* 32 [2001], 328, with fig. 8; Bidwell 1999, 109–10, with fig. 27)
High Rochester (*Britannia* 36 [2005], 408; Bidwell 1989, 188–95, with fig. 63)
Housesteads (*Britannia* 36 [2005], 406; J. A. Biggins and D. J. A. Taylor, *Archaeologia Aeliana* 5th series, 33 [2004], 51–60)
Inverquharity (*Britannia* 34 [2003], 300–02, with fig. 4)
Llandovery (*Britannia* 36 [2005], 385–6, with fig. 2)
Llanfor (*Britannia* 34 [2003], 296, fig. 3; *Britannia* 29 [1998], 368, with fig. 3; Hopewell 2005)
Maryport (Biggins and Taylor 2004a; Hopewell 2004; *Britannia* 32 [2001], 337–9, with fig. 13)
Newstead (*Britannia* 26 [1995], 337–41, with figs 8–9; *Britannia* 24 [1993], 282–3, with figs 9 and 10)

Pen Llystyn (Hopewell 2005)
Pumpsaint (*Britannia* 31 [2000], 372, with fig. 2)
Richborough (Linford *et al.* 2004)
Roecliffe (Bishop 2005)
Vindolanda (*Britannia* 32 [2001], 330; *Britannia* 36 [2005], 407, with fig. 11)

Notes

1. Frere and Wilkes 1989. I am also grateful to Susanne Scherff, of the Bayerisches Landesamt für Denkmalpflege, who made the additions in Figs 5.2–5.9.
2. I am grateful that the Deutsche Akademische Austauschdienst (DAAD) recommended me to the Dulverton Trust, which in turn granted me a Michael Wills Scholarship. St Antony's College provided me with hospitality at Oxford. The consequence of both are not only my M. Phil. degree, but also a life-long scholarly friendship with Professor Frere, lasting friendships with several of my co-students, and, last but not least, my marriage to Mary Wong, M. Phil. I am also grateful to my wife for yet another attempt to make my English text comprehensible, and also to the Editor of this volume who took a great deal of time and trouble in making further extensive revisions to my English text, to its great advantage.
3. At Professor Frere's suggestion, it was accepted by British Archaeological Reports, and published as Sommer 1984.
4. Sommer 1997; 1999; in press.
5. Sommer 1988.
6. Birley 1977. Unfortunately the military *vicus* is still without any proper site report or final publication.
7. For a summary, see Rabold, Ronke and Seitz 1988.
8. Filgis 2005.
9. Rothacher 2005.
10. The latest publication is Greiner 2002.
11. Thiel 2005.
12. Cf. now Luik 1996 and 2004.
13. Cf. now Kaiser and Sommer 1994; Schmidts 2004.
14. Cf. Landesdenkmalamt Baden-Württemberg 1994; the final publication is in press (by E. Schallmayer and S. Huther).
15. Summarized in Sommer, Kortüm and Fecher 2005.
16. Summarized in Sommer 2005.
17. Cf. now Kortüm and Lauber 2004.
18. Czysz 1990; Kainrath, forthcoming.
19. Ganslmeier and Schmotz 2003; the most recent plan is in Schmotz 2005.
20. Cf. Faber 1994.
21. For a summary see Prammer 1998.
22. There is only a short preliminary report: Dinkelmeyer, Erdrich and Klein 1988.
23. For a short preliminary report, Hanel 1992; a final report by C. Wenzel is in preparation.
24. Czysz 2003.
25. For the state of knowledge at the time (the 1980s), see the bibliographies in Sommer 1988, 648–703, for southern Germany, and in Sommer 1984, 62–101, for Britain.
26. I am grateful for permission to look through all the relevant photographs in the

Cambridge University Collection of Air Photography, taken mostly by the late J. K. S. St Joseph, as well as for the chance to get many copies of photographs of German sites from the archives of aerial photography held by the Bayerische Landesamt für Denkmalpflege (Munich), and the Landesdenkmalamt Baden-Württemberg (Stuttgart), taken mostly by O. Braasch and R. Gensheimer.

27. E.g. Blagg and King 1984, with several relevant articles.
28. Britnell 1989; Buxton and Howard-Davis 2000; Davies 1990; Davies 2004 (using already a great deal of geophysical evidence); Dearne 1993; Ferris and Jones 1991; Hanson and Macinnes 1991; Higham 1991.
29. James 2001. For 'small towns', cf. Burnham 1987; Burnham 1988; Smith 1987; Burnham and Wacher 1990.
30. See (e.g.) Becker and Fassbinder 2001; Biggins and Taylor 2004b, 161; Clark 1990; David 1995; and Fassbinder and Irlinger 1999.
31. E.g. at Maryport a stunning 67 ha have been surveyed (Biggins and Taylor 2004a, 102).
32. Biggins and Taylor 2004b, 99.
33. Hopewell 2005, 225. It is most interesting that much of the work then (aerial photography in Germany) and now (geophysics in Wales) was not primarily research-driven, but was part of heritage management; it was financed with the goal of gaining more information about the location and quality of preservation of the sites, in order to establish a better basis for their scheduling as ancient monuments, and to increase and promote the potential for the use of these sites.
34. To this note of thanks I would like to add the name of D. J. Breeze, who first pointed me in the direction of a considerable number of these articles; he also forwarded information to me in advance of publication, and has always generously shared his thoughts, with me as with others – and not only on this topic.
35. Biggins and Taylor 2004a; Biggins and Taylor 2004b; Hopewell 2005.
36. Sommer 1999, 81.
37. The latter can be deduced from the description of 'ribbon development' (Hopewell 2005, 266; however, I am not really sure where in Sommer 1984 I wrote that this type is exceptional in Roman Britain!), and the 'ribbon-like appearance' (Sommer 1999, 81) along the main roads.
38. Sommer 1984, plate 3.
39. Hopewell 2005, 242–6.
40. Sommer 1984, pl. 22; Biggins and Taylor 2004a.
41. Sommer 1984, 15; 42–3 and fig. 22; Sommer 1988, 550–4 and figs 18 and 31.
42. Sommer 1984, 43, figs 21 and 22; Sommer 1988, 528–47; baths: 548–50 with fig. 18.
43. Hopewell 2005, 242.
44. H. Becker, in Gibson 1999, 66, particularly figs 24 and 35; J. Davies, in Gibson 1999, 70 (strangely, although the road approaching the *porta decumana* in a slight curve from north-north-east is most prominent in the magnetometer readings, it is not mentioned in the text or interpretation). The clear continuation of the Roman road west of the fort (Gibson 1999, fig. 17) makes in my view the assumption that a road by-passed the fort to the north rather doubtful.
45. Hopewell 2005, fig. 12. From the geophysical survey it appears that an extensive civil settlement existed to the north (*porta principalis sinistra*) of the fort at Llanfor, perhaps including habitation along a parallel road to the north-west, as well as outside both the east gate (*porta praetoria*) and most probably also the south gate (*porta principalis dextra*). Concerning the interior of the fort, I disagree with the interpretation of the geophysical survey for the *retentura* as given by Hopewell 2005, fig. 12. From his fig.

11, it becomes apparent that each and every one of the strong geophysical anomalies on the outside of each barrack are not in alignment with one another. This suggests not a typical layout of *arma* and *papilio,* but rather a strong representation of gullies in the front rooms, as detected in so many forts with an equestrian garrison (Sommer 1995, 158–63; Hodgson 2003, 37–90). The length of the barracks at around 60 m equally points to cavalry sub-units as their most likely occupants. If similar features existed in the barracks of the left *praetentura* (here the magnetometer reading is not so clear), the fort could have housed at least 18 *turmae* of an *ala* as garrison.

46. *Contra* Davies 1990, 65.
47. Bishop 2005, in particular figs 3 and 39.
48. *Britannia* 36 (2005), 407, fig. 11; *Britannia* 32 (2001), 330; *Britannia* 32 (2001), 330–1, fig. 10.
49. Bidwell 1999, 188–95, with fig. 63; Millett 2001, fig. 21; Wilson P. R. 2002; Fitzpatrick and Scott 1999, in particular fig. 2 (the position of the late fort can hardly have been conceived without the earlier structures underlying it determining its site); Casey and Hoffmann 1998, particularly fig. 1.
50. Perhaps the 'magnetically quiet' area (Hopewell 2005, 228) between the two outer ditches and the inner ditch at Cefn Caer in Wales, with a width of 15 m to 20 m to the north-east and south-east (Fig. 5.6) served as exercise areas, since that gap was apparently not built over by the military *vicus* of the later fort (the outer ditches are thought to go back to an early phase). However, the size of the barracks, with a maximum length of approximately 50 m, as well as the overall size of the fort, speak against a (partial) equestrian occupation (see Sommer 1995, 156–8, for the discussion of barrack sizes and garrisons).
51. Biggins and Taylor 2004a, 113.
52. A proper change of layout is suggested at Llanio, where a road overlies earlier *vicus* buildings (Davies 2004, 100). Even stronger is the complete change of plans suggested at Vindolanda (Birley 1977, 70–2; Bidwell 1985, 88–92; Bidwell 1999, fig. 38).
53. Hopewell 2005, fig. 4; Sommer 1984, pl. 9.
54. Wilson 2004, 31, suggests that it may have stood at the fort's north angle where Biggins and Taylor think there was a *mansio*: Biggins and Taylor 2004a, 126. For loss of ground on the fort's north-west side through erosion and quarrying, Biggins and Taylor 2004a, 125.
55. Biggins and Taylor 2004a, 127.
56. Hopewell 2005, 232.
57. Hopewell 2005, 232.
58. This interpretation is supported by the results of an additional survey towards the north-west. I am indebted to D. Hopewell for providing me with a preliminary print-out of these unpublished results.
59. Hopewell 2005, 247.
60. Davies 2004, fig. 7.8.
61. *Britannia* 36 (2005), 407, with fig. 11.
62. In Sommer 1999, 83, however, I wrote about a predominance of the street-type-parts and the ring road.
63. Bidwell 1999, fig. 132.
64. Bidwell 1985, 92.
65. For the relationship between buildings and ditches just outside the west gate, compare *Britannia* 33 (2002), 295–8, with fig. 11.
66. Crow 2004, 71–88 with figs 33 lower and 40.

67. Biggins and Taylor 2004c.
68. The latter seems supported by the fact that for Vindolanda a detailed plan of the excavations of the *vicus* has never been published, and phasing can be no more than provisional (Bidwell 1985, 88–92, with fig. 37). For an earlier excavation, the Housesteads plan may well show similar problems.
69. *Britannia* 35 (2004), 273 with fig. 8; Bidwell 1999, 114–17, with fig. 32.
70. Hopewell 2005, 262–5, with figs 4 and 17.
71. Schmotz 1999; Schmotz 2005, fig. 1.
72. Biggins and Taylor 2004a, 115. The interpretation of the rectangular temple as a *mithraeum* is, however, disputed by Wilson 1997b, 30–2, who suggests that this may be the temple of Jupiter Optimus Maximus named in the many altars from the site.
73. Biggins and Taylor 2004a, 119–21.
74. Biggins and Taylor 2004a, 116.
75. Compare (e.g.) the position of the Gallo-Roman temples at Rottweil in Upper Germany (Sommer, Kortüm and Fecher 2005, plan on p. 298).
76. E.g. the Romano-Celtic temple discovered at Vindolanda, dated to the late first and second centuries, and the cremations in its vicinity, which were situated 'close to the Stanegate road at the north-west corner of the *vicus*' (*Britannia* 33 [2002], 295–7, with fig. 10); the possible Dolichenum at Piercebridge behind the buildings close to the river (Fitzpatrick and Scott 1999, fig. 2); or the shrine at Housesteads behind regular houses (Crow 2004, with fig. 40 on 74).
77. Sommer 2004b, fig. 1; Becker and Fassbinder 2001, 6–13, fig. 7. I would not exclude the possibility that this building should be identified as a *schola*.
78. Frere and St Joseph 1983, 104 with fig. 58 (200 m north-east of the fort).
79. Breeze 2006, 87 (700 m east of the fort).
80. *Britannia* 27 (1997), 412, figs 9–10; *Britannia* 24 (1993), 282–3 (at the north-eastern edge of the plateau).
81. Frere and St Joseph 1983, 112–13 with fig. 63 (a late Neolithic henge monument perhaps re-used as an amphitheatre, independent of the street- and field-system to the south-east of the fort).
82. Linford *et al.* 2004 (400 m to the side, away from the *vicus*' road-system; note that this amphitheatre is of a similar size to legionary and/or civilian ones, and built in stone).
83. Nash-Williams 1969, 113 with fig. 60; Wilson, R. J. A. 2002, 339 with fig. 73; Frere and St Joseph 1983, 109 (300 m off the *porta principalis sinistra*, beyond the parade-ground).
84. Davies 2004, 98.
85. Schmotz 2005; Schmotz 2006.
86. Bender 2005.
87. Schmotz 2006, 112–16; Waldherr 2006.
88. Sommer 1988, fig. 5 (detached folding plan).
89. Sommer 1988, 556–61 with fig. 33.
90. Hopewell 2005, 241, fig. 7 (feature 20).
91. Hopewell 2005, 232.
92. Hopewell 2005, 232 and 235, with fig. 4 on 234.
93. Hopewell 2005, 246.
94. Biggins and Taylor 2004b, 168, fig. 1.
95. For earlier discussions of this problem, cf. Sommer 1984, 15–17; Breeze and Dobson 2000, 56–9 (proposing the function of the Vallum as being to control the movement of people).
96. *Britannia* 32 (2001), 328, fig. 8.

97. Biggins and Taylor 2004b.
98. Biggins and Taylor 2004b, 164.
99. Biggins and Taylor 2004b, 174–5.
100. Simpson and Richmond 1933 and 1934; Sommer 1984, 65, fig. 2; Biggins and Taylor 2004b, 175; compare also Wilmott 1997. Note that one of the results of the research at Birdoswald is that a significant part of the southern plateau, including the *vicus* there, has been lost through erosion, not only over the centuries but even since the last excavation in the 1930s (Biggins and Taylor 2004a, 174).
101. Biggins and Taylor 2004a, 164.
102. Biggins and Taylor 1999, 107.
103. Biggins and Taylor 2004b, 176; Biggins and Taylor 1999, 107–8.
104. Biggins and Taylor 2004b, 176.
105. I would like to follow Biggins and Taylor 2004b, 177, who suggest that the position of the missing bath-house was south of the present escarpment, now lost through centuries-long erosion.
106. On this interpretation, it is surprising to see that Bewcastle on the Maiden Way appears to lack a military *vicus*, or at least in the expected area for it between this long-distance road by-passing the fort and the fort itself, as was suggested by a geophysical survey there (*Britannia* 32 [2001], 336).
107. *Britannia* 32 (2001), 330–1 with fig. 10.
108. *Britannia* 32 (2001), 333 with fig. 12. As the surveyors are preparing an extensive article on their results (Biggins and Taylor, forthcoming), the plot of the magnetometer results was not available for re-publication here.
109. A. Biggins, in *Britannia* 32 (2001), 333.
110. Sommer 1988, 488–9; Sommer 1999, 90–2.
111. A. Biggins, in *Britannia* 32 (2001), 333.
112. *Britannia* 26 (1995), 332–3.
113. *JRS* 47 (1957), 229–30; Sommer 1984, 22–3; Hanson and Maxwell 1986, 188–9, with pl. 9.2; Keppie 2001, 37.
114. Hanson and Maxwell 1986, pl. 9.5; Breeze 2006, fig. 74.
115. Compare (e.g.) Frere and St Joseph 1983; Hanson and Maxwell 1986, 14, pl. 1.4.
116. Sommer 1984, fig. 3; Hinchcliffe and Green 1985, 176–81 with fig. 2 facing p. 2. It should be noted that the fort here is a foundation of the late second century, but it continued in occupation later as part of Saxon Shore fort defences.
117. Unfortunately the precise sequence of garrisons at Castesteads is rather uncertain: Breeze and Dobson 2000, 260 and 271.
118. D. J. Breeze, personal communication.
119. *JRS* 37 (1947), 229–30. For the administration of military *vici*, see Sommer 1984, 22–9; Sommer 1988, 622–7; Sommer 1999, 87–9; and Sommer, in press.
120. Kaiser and Sommer 1994, 380–7; Sommer 1997, 47; Sommer 1999, 86.
121. Davies 1990, 67, after a suggestion by G. D. B. Jones.
122. The continuing use of part of that road into the 1970s, and possible resurfacings associated with it, may account for the likely destruction of features; that in turn may account for the fact that the anomalies representing what was surely dense habitation along this road are quite small (Hopewell 2005, 243).
123. Kaiser and Sommer 1994, 380; see also Sommer 1999, fig. 6.
124. Hopewell 2005, 260, figs 4 and 16. From the description, trench 1 was intended to provide a sample of the area of high anomalies seen by the geophysical survey to the north of the road; however it appears (ibid. fig. 16) that the position of the trial

excavation is marked too far south-east in relation to the high-resolution area of the geophysics plot.

125. Hopewell 2005, 232.
126. I am indebted to D. Hopewell for providing me with a preliminary print-out.
127. The width of 30 m as given by Biggins and Taylor 2004b, 165, seems excessive. The authors see this area as elliptical, and also discuss the possibility of a ceremonial purpose for it (ibid. 176).
128. Biggins and Taylor 2004b, 164.
129. *Britannia* 24 (1993), 282, fig. 10.
130. Davies 1990, 67.
131. James 2001, in particular fig. 22.
132. Sommer 1984, 18–22, in particular 22.
133. Breeze 1984a, 48.
134. Biggins and Taylor 1999, 106.
135. Davies 1990, 65; cf. also E. W. Black in *Britannia* 24 (1993), 249–54.
136. Davies 2004, 97–8.
137. Breeze 1984a, 47–55.
138. Hopewell 2005, 242.
139. Davies 2004, fig. 7.8; Bidwell 1989, 188–95, with fig. 63.
140. See note 127. For preliminary results, see Hopewell 2005, fig. 4, with similar evidence from aerial photographs.
141. *Britannia* 35 (2004), 254, fig. 2.
142. The interpretation of a large anomaly 230 m north-west of the fort as a bath-house seems to me rather unlikely, as there is no connection apparent in the geophysical survey between it and the *porta principalis sinistra*.
143. *Britannia* 36 (2005), 385–6, fig. 2.
144. Biggins and Taylor 1999, 107–8.
145. Hopewell 2005, 238 and 241, with figs 6 and 7.
146. Hopewell 2005, 229.
147. Nash-Williams 1969, 104–6 with fig. 55.
148. Hopewell 2005, 229.
149. Hopewell 2005, fig. 13.
150. *Britannia* 19 (1988), 429, fig. 9.
151. Clarke 1996; Biggins and Taylor 1999, 108.
152. *Britannia* 24 (1993), 282, fig. 10.
153. *Britannia* 26 (1995), 337–41, with figs 8 and 9; *Britannia* 24 (1993), 282–3, with figs 9 and 10.
154. Hanson and Maxwell 1986, 92, with figs 5.3 and 5.4; Keppie 2001, 35 (with the most recent and up-to-date plans throughout the book); *Britannia* 27 (1996), 398, fig. 5 (Mumrills).
155. D. J. Breeze, personal communication; Breeze 1984a, 58; compare the catalogue in Sommer 1984, with somewhat 'strained' evidence.
156. Hanson and Maxwell 1986, table 8.1.
157. Hanson and Maxwell 1986, fig. 9.4.
158. Except for Carriden at the eastern end, only a limited amount of (non-structural) evidence for the presence of non-military persons is known from the Antonine Wall (a few inscriptions, and women's and children's shoes: Hanson and Maxwell 1986, 183–90).
159. In this sense, *contra* Hanson and Maxwell 1986, 188, and Keppie 2001, 36.

160. See above, p. 104.
161. Kortüm and Lauber 2004, 457–61; Sommer 1984, 47–8; Sommer 1991; Kaiser and Sommer 1994, 370–6; Sommer 1997, 45–6; Sommer 1998, 89.
162. Compare Kortüm and Lauber 2004, 452–64 too.
163. *Britannia* 24 (1993), 282, fig. 10.
164. *Britannia* 19 (1988), 429, fig. 9.
165. Buxton and Howard-Davis 2000, 103–26.
166. *Britannia* 29 (1998), 388–9 with fig. 8; *Britannia* 15 (1984), 284–6, with figs 6 and 7.
167. Originally, the posts in question were interpreted as having held doors.
168. Sommer 1984, 48.
169. Hopewell 2005, 232, 256 and 259, with figs 14 and 15. As pointed out above, I believe that building II may be of a different type.
170. Biggins and Taylor 2004a, 115, with further references.
171. *Britannia* 17 (1986), 366–9, with fig. 4.
172. Kaiser and Sommer 1994, fig. 375; Kortüm and Lauber 2004, tab. 46, fig. 191.
173. E.g. Aislingen on the early Danube *limes* (Czysz 1990; Kainrath, forthcoming).
174. Biggins and Taylor 2004a, 113–15.
175. Biggins and Taylor 2004a, 115. Strip-houses at Caerwent appear equally large (Kortüm and Lauber 2004, fig. 191).
176. Kaiser and Sommer 1994, fig. 263a, b and n, and fig. 264h.; Kortüm and Lauber 2004, fig. 192. The comparison between the size of some buildings in the Maryport *vicus* and those at Walheim has already been pointed out by Wilson (2004, 29–30).
177. Kaiser and Sommer 1994, 377–9, fig. 264; Kortüm and Lauber 2004, 462–4.
178. Sommer 1999, 88; *contra* Biggins and Taylor 2004a, 126.
179. *Britannia* 17 (1986), 366–9, with fig. 4.
180. Hopewell 2005, 256, fig. 14.
181. Hopewell 2005, 257–9, with fig. 15.
182. This may warn us not to go into too much detail when interpreting geophysics.
183. Accordingly, the strong anomalies in the geophysical plot, considered by Hopewell to belong to another phase of the *vicus* on a different alignment (Hopewell 2005, 232 and 257), probably have to be interpreted differently, e.g. as evidence for a later field-system (Fig. 5.6).
184. Hopewell 2005, 259, fig. 15.
185. Casey and Hoffmann 1998, 114–20, with figs 2–4.
186. Kaiser and Sommer 1994, 354–5, Beil. 28a; Sommer 1991, fig. 93.2.
187. Kaiser and Sommer 1994, 388–91; Sommer 1991, 475; Sommer 1999, 88.
188. Kaiser and Sommer 1994, 177–8; cf. also 380–3.
189. Sommer 1988, 556–64. Unfortunately shortage of time prevented more work in this paper on the relative sizes of the military *vici* in Roman Britain.
190. Sommer 2004b, 109–10.
191. H. Becker, in Gibson 1999, 49 and 66.
192. Hopewell 2005, 232.
193. Biggins and Taylor 2004a, 116.
194. Biggins and Taylor 2004b, 165 and 176.
195. Biggins and Taylor 1999, 107–8.
196. *Britannia* 26 (1995), 337–41, with figs 8 and 9; *Britannia* 24 (1993), 282–3, with figs 9 and 10.
197. A few more may be added in Britain (Sommer 1984, 48–9, is in need of updating in that respect), and in Germany (Sommer 2004b, 108).

198. Piso 1991; Sommer 2004c.
199. Biggins and Taylor 2004a, 127–8, fig. 5.6, no. 32 (beyond the range of my Fig. 5.3). Generally, the evidence for farming in the immediate surroundings of *vici* by the *vicani* is rather limited (Sommer 1988, 598–603).
200. Hopewell 2005, 227, 256, 259, 262, 265 and 267; Davies 1990, in particular 70 and 72; Davies 2004, in particular 109. However, I wonder how much room for debate there is on the dating of the withdrawal of troops from the forts, since very little evidence seems to have come from modern excavation within the forts themselves.
201. Hopewell 2005, 267 with reference to Davies 2004, 100.
202. Millett 2001, fig. 21; Wilson, P. R. 2002.
203. Buxton and Howard-Davis 2000, 414–21.
204. Breeze and Dobson 2000, 203–07; Keppie 2001, 35–9.
205. Millett 2001, 66. Only at proof-stage did I realise that it would have been worthwhile to discuss in addition the transition from fort and military *vicus* to 'small town', and even (in some cases) to *civitas* capital. A particularly good example showing the direct influence of forts and military *vicus* lay-out in the structure of a later civilian settlement is Corbridge (Bishop and Dore 1988).
206. Cf., for the middle Danube region, Moosbauer 2002.
207. Evans, forthcoming.
208. Hopewell 2005, 253–9.
209. Cf. Davies 1990, 66 and 72–3; Davies 2004, 109; Buxton and Howard-Davis 2000.

References

Becker, H. and Fassbinder, J. W. E. (eds) 2001: *Magnetic prospecting in archaeological sites* [ICOMOS Monuments and Sites 6], Munich

Bender, S. 2005: 'Ein Amphitheater im Lagerdorf des Kastells Arnsburg – Wiederentdeckung und Deutung einer Entdeckung', *Hessen Archäologie 2004*, 100–03

Bidwell, P. T. 1985: *The Roman fort of Vindolanda* [Historic Buildings and Monuments Commission for England, Archaeological Report 1], London

Bidwell, P. T. (ed.) 1999: *Hadrian's Wall 1989–1999*, Carlisle

Biggins, J. A. and Taylor, D. J. A. 1999: 'A survey of the Roman fort and settlement at Birdoswald, Cumbria', *Britannia* 30, 91–110

Biggins, J. A. and Taylor, D. J. A. 2004a: 'The Roman fort and *vicus* at Maryport: geophysical survey, 2000–2004', in Wilson and Caruana 2004, 102–33

Biggins, J. A. and Taylor, D. J. A. 2004b: 'Geophysical survey of the *vicus* at Birdoswald Roman fort, Cumbria', *Britannia* 35, 159–78

Biggins, J. A. and Taylor, D. J. A. 2004c: 'A geophysical survey at Housesteads Roman fort, April 2003', *Archaeologia Aeliana*[5] 33, 51–60

Birley, R. 1977: *Vindolanda. A Roman frontier post on Hadrian's Wall*, London

Bishop, M. C. 2005: 'A new Flavian military site at Roecliffe, North Yorkshire', *Britannia* 36, 135–223

Bishop, M. C. and Dore, J. N. 1988: *Corbridge. Excavations of the Roman fort and town, 1947–80* [Historic Buildings and Monuments Commission for England, Archaeological Report 8], London

Blagg, T. F. C. and King, A. C. (eds) 1984: *Military and civilian in Roman Britain. Cultural relationship in a frontier province* [BAR British Series 136], Oxford

Breeze, D. J. 1984a: 'The Roman fort on the Antonine Wall at Bearsden', in Breeze 1984b, 32–68

Breeze, D. J. (ed.) 1984b: *Studies in Scottish antiquity presented to Stewart Cruden*, Edinburgh

Breeze, D. J. 2006: *Roman Scotland. Frontier country*, London

Breeze, D. J. and Dobson, B. 2000: *Hadrian's Wall*, fourth edition, London

Britnell, J. 1989: *Caersws vicus, Powys. Excavations at the Old Primary School, 1985–1985* [BAR British Series 205], Oxford

Burnham, B. C. 1987: 'The morphology of Romano-British 'Small Towns'', *Archaeological Journal* 144, 156–90

Burnham, B. C. 1988: 'A survey of building types in Romano-British 'Small Towns'', *Journal of the British Archaeological Association* 141, 35–59

Burnham, B. C. and Davies, J. L. (eds) 1990: *Conquest, co-existence and change: recent work in Roman Wales* [Trivium 25], Lampeter

Burnham, B. C. and Wacher, J. S. 1990: *The 'Small Towns' of Roman Britain*, London

Buxton, K., and Howard-Davis, C. 2000: *BREMETENACUM. Excavations at Roman Ribchester 1980, 1989–1990* [Lancaster Imprints Series Number 9], Lancaster

Casey, P. J., and Hoffmann, B. 1998: 'Rescue excavations in the *vicus* of the Roman fort at Greta Bridge, Co. Durham, 1972–4', *Britannia* 29, 111–83

Clark, A. 1990: *Seeing beneath the soil. Prospecting methods in archaeology*, London

Crow, J. 2004: *Housesteads: a fort and garrison on Hadrian's Wall*, Stroud

Czysz, W. 1990: 'Rettungsgrabungen im Vicus des frührömischen Kastells Aislingen', *Das archäologische Jahr in Bayern 1989*, 114–18

Czysz, W. 2003: *Heldenbergen in der Wetterau. Feldlager, Kastell, Vicus* [Limesforschungen 27], Mainz-am-Rhein

Czysz, W., Hüssen, C.-M., Kuhnen, H.-P., Sommer, C. S. and Weber, G. (eds) 1995: *Provinzialrömische Forschungen. Festschrift für Günter Ulbert zum 65. Geburtstag*, Espelkamp

David, A. 1995: *Geophysical survey in archaeological field evaluation* [Ancient Monuments Laboratory, English Heritage], London

Davies, J. L. 1990: 'Military *vici*: recent research and its significance', in Burnham and Davies 1990, 65–74

Davies, J. L. 2004: 'Soldier and civilian in Wales', in Todd 2004, 91–113

Dearne, M. J. 1993: *Navio. The fort and vicus at Brough-on-Noe, Derbyshire* [BAR British Series 234], Oxford

Dinkelmeyer, M., Erdrich, M. and Klein, M. 1988: 'Ausgrabungen im römischen Kastellvicus von Weißenburg i. Bay.', *Das Archäologische Jahr in Bayern 1987*, Stuttgart, 114–18

Evans, J., forthcoming: *Roman pottery from Cefn Caer and Caer Gai* [quoted by Hopewell 2005]

Faber, A. 1994: *Das römische Auxiliarkastell und der Vicus von Regensburg-Kumpfmühl* [Münchner Beiträge zur Vor- und Frühgeschichte 49], Munich

Fassbinder, J. W. E. and Irlinger, W. E. (eds) 1999: *Archaeological prospection. Third International Conference on Archaeological Prospection* [Arbeitshefte des Bayerischen Landesamtes für Denkmalpflege 108], Munich

Ferris, I. M. and Jones, R. F. J. 1991: 'Binchester – a northern fort and *vicus*', in Jones 1991, 103–09

Filgis, M. N. 2005: 'Bad Wimpfen im Tal. Kohortenkastell und Vicus am Neckarlimes', in Planck 2005, 22–7

Fitzpatrick, A. P. and Scott, P. R. 1999: 'The Roman bridge at Piercebridge, North Yorkshire – County Durham', *Britannia* 30, 111–32.

Frere, S. S. and St Joseph, J. K. S. 1983: *Roman Britain from the air*, Cambridge

Frere, S. S. and Wilkes, J. J. 1989: *Strageath. Excavations within the Roman fort, 1973–1986*

[*Britannia* Monograph 9], London

Ganslmeier, R. and Schmotz, K. 2003: *Das mittelkaiserzeitliche Kastell Künzing* [Archäologische Denkmäler im Landkreis Deggendorf 8], Deggendorf, 28–32

Gibson, A. 1999: *The Walton Basin, Powys, Wales. Survey at the Hindwell Neolithic Enclosure*, Welshpool

Goldsworthy, A. and Haynes, I. (eds) 1999: *The Roman Army as a community* [*JRA* Supplementary Series 34], Portsmouth, Rhode Island

Greiner, B. A. 2002: 'Der Kastellvicus von Buch: Siedlungsgeschichte und Korrektur dendrochronologischer Daten', in Wamser and Steidl 2002, 83–9

Hanel, N. 1992: 'Neue Ergebnisse zur römischen Besiedlung bei Groß-Gerau', *Denkmalpflege in Hessen* 1992.2, 24–9

Hanson, W. S. and Macinnes, L. 1991: 'Soldiers and settlement in Wales and Scotland', in Jones 1991, 85–92

Hanson, W. S. and Maxwell, G. S. 1986: *Rome's North West Frontier. The Antonine Wall*, Edinburgh

Higham, N. J. 1991: 'Soldiers and settlement in Northern England', in Jones 1991, 93–101

Hinchcliffe, J. and Green, C. S. 1985: *Excavations at Brancaster 1974 and 1977* [East Anglian Archaeology Report 23], Norwich

Hodgson, N. 2003: *The Roman fort at Wallsend (Segedunum). Excavations in 1997–8* [Tyne and Wear Museums Archaeological Monograph 2], Newcastle upon Tyne

Hopewell, D. 2005: 'Roman fort environs in North-West Wales', *Britannia* 36, 225–69

James, S. 2001: 'Soldiers and civilians: identity and interaction in Roman Britain', in James and Millett 2001, 77–89

James, S. and Millett, M. (eds) 2001: *Britons and Romans: advancing an archaeological agenda* [CBA Research Report 125], York

Jones, R. F. J. (ed.) 1991: *Britain in the Roman period: recent trends*, Sheffield

Kainrath, B., forthcoming: *Der Vicus des frührömischen Kastells Aislingen an der Donau* [Materialhefte zur Vor- und Frühgeschichte in Bayern], Munich

Kaiser, H. and Sommer, C. S. 1994: *Lopodunum I. Die römischen Befunde der Ausgrabungen an der Kellerei in Ladenburg 1981–1985 und 1990* [Forschungen und Berichte zur Vor- und Frühgeschichte in Baden-Württemberg 50], Stuttgart

Keppie, L. (ed.) 2001: *The Antonine Wall. A handbook to the surviving remains*, fourth edition, Glasgow

Kortüm, K. and Lauber, J. 2004: *Walheim I. Das Kastell II und die nachfolgende Besiedlung* [Forschungen und Berichte zur Vor- und Frühgeschichte in Baden-Württemberg 95], Stuttgart

Landesdenkmalamt Baden-Württemberg (ed.) 1994: *Der römische Weihebezirk von Osterburken II. Kolloquium 1990 und paläobotanische-osteologische Untersuchungen* [Forschungen und Berichte zur Vor- und Frühgeschichte in Baden-Württemberg 49], Stuttgart

Linford, P., Linford, N., Martin, L. and Payne, A. 2004: 'Geophysics: Richborough. Characterising the Roman remains', *Conservation bulletin* 45, 14–15

Luik, M. 1996: *Köngen–Grinario I. Topographie, Fundstellenverzeichnis, ausgewählte Fundgruppen* [Forschungen und Berichte zur Vor- und Frühgeschichte in Baden-Württemberg 62], Stuttgart

Luik, M. 2004: *Köngen–Grinario II. Grabungen des Landesdenkmalamtes Baden-Württemberg, Historisch-Archäologische Auswertung* [Forschungen und Berichte zur Vor- und Frühgeschichte in Baden-Württemberg 82], Stuttgart

Maxfield, V. A. and Dobson, M. J. (eds) 1991: *Roman Frontier Studies 1989*, Exeter

Millett, M. 2001: 'Approaches to urban societies', in James and Millett 2001, 60–6

Moosbauer, G. 2002: 'Belieferungsstrukturen Ostraetiens und Westnoricums: Kastelle und Lagerdörfer im Vergleich', in Wamser and Steidl 2002, 201–06

Nash-Williams, V. E. 1969: *The Roman Frontier in Wales*, second edition (ed. M. G. Jarrett), Cardiff

Piso, I. 1991: 'Die Inschriften vom Pfaffenberg und der Bereich der *Canabae legionis*', *Tyche* 6, 131–69

Planck, D. (ed.) 2005: *Die Römer in Baden-Württemberg*, Stuttgart

Prammer, J. 1998: 'Der Kastellvicus von Sorviodurum-Straubing. Ein Zwischenbericht', *Vorträge des 16. Niederbayerischen Archäologentages*, Rahden/Westfahlen, 193–207

Rabold, B., Ronke, J. and Seitz, G. 1988: *Römische Städte und Siedlungen in Baden-Württemberg* [Archäologische Informationen aus Baden-Württemberg 8], Stuttgart

Reddé, M., Brulet, R., Fellmann, R., Haalebos, J.-K. and von Schnurbein, S. (eds) in press: *Manuel d'architecture gallo-romaine I. Les fortifications militaires*, forthcoming

Rothacher, D. 2005: 'Böbingen. Limeskastell und Siedlung', in Planck 2005, 43–5

Ruscu, L., Ciongradi, C., Ardevan, R., Roman, C. and Gazdac, C. (eds) 2004: *Orbis Antiquus. Studia in honorem Ioannis Pisonis* [Bibliotheca Musei Napocensis 21], Cluj-Napoca

Schmidts, T. 2004: *Lopodunum IV. Die Kleinfunde aus den römischen Häusern an der Kellerei in Ladenburg (Ausgrabungen 1981–1985 und 1990)* [Forschungen und Berichte zur Vor- und Frühgeschichte in Baden-Württemberg 91], Stuttgart

Schmotz, K. 1999: 'Ein Mithrasheiligtum in Niederbayern', *Das Archäologische Jahr in Bayern 1998*, Stuttgart, 94–6

Schmotz, K. 2005: 'Erste Arbeitsergebnisse zum Amphitheater von Künzing, Lkr. Deggendorf', *Vorträge des 23. Niederbayerischen Archäologentages*, Rahden/Westfahlen, 149–66

Schmotz, K. 2006: 'Das hölzerne Amphitheater von Künzing, Lkr. Deggendorf. Kenntnisstand und erste Rekonstruktionsansätze nach Abschluss der Geländearbeiten im Jahr 2004', *Vorträge des 24. Niederbayerischen Archäologentages*, Rahden/Westfahlen, 95–118

Simpson, F. G. and Richmond, I. A. 1933: 'Birdoswald', *Transactions of the Cumberland and Westmorland Antiquarian and Archaeological Society*, second series, 33, 246–62

Simpson, F. G. and Richmond, I. A. 1934: 'Birdoswald', *Transactions of the Cumberland and Westmorland Antiquarian and Archaeological Society*, second series, 34, 120–30

Smith, R. F. 1987: *Roadside settlements in lowland Roman Britain* [BAR British Series 157], Oxford

Sommer, C. S. 1984: *The military* vici *in Roman Britain. Aspects of their origins, their location and layout, administration, function and end* [BAR British Series 129], Oxford

Sommer, C. S. 1988: 'Kastellvicus und Kastell. Untersuchungen zum Zugmantel im Taunus und zu den Kastellvici in Obergermanien und Rätien', *Fundberichte aus Baden-Württemberg* 13, 457–707

Sommer, C. S. 1991: 'Life beyond the ditches: housing and planning of the military *vici* in Upper Germany and Raetia', in Maxfield and Dobson 1991, 472–6

Sommer, C. S. 1995: '"Where did they put the horses?" Überlegungen zu Aufbau und Stärke römischer Auxiliartruppen und deren Unterbringung in den Kastellen', in Czysz et al. 1995, 149–68

Sommer, C. S. 1997: 'Kastellvicus und Kastell – Modell für die Canabae legionis?', *Jahresberichte der Gesellschaft pro Vindonissa 1997*, Brugg, 41–52 (reprinted in *In memoriam Dumitru Tudor* [Bibliotheca Historica et Archaeologica Universitatis Timisiensis 4], Timişoara 2001, 47–70)

Sommer, C. S. 1999: 'The Roman army in SW Germany as an instrument of colonisation: the relationship of forts to military and civilian *vici*', in Goldsworthy and Haynes 1999, 81–93

Sommer, C. S. 2004a: 'Kastellvicus Ruffenhofen – Aufbau und Struktur einer Marketendersiedlung am raetischen Limes', in M. Crînguş, S. Regep-Vlascici and A. Ştefanescu (eds), *Studia Historica et Archaeologica in honorem Magistrae Doina Benea* [Bibliotheca Historica et Archaeologica Universitatis Timisiensis 6], Timişoara, 345–60

Sommer, C. S. 2004b: 'Anfang und Ende – Anmerkungen zur Ausdehnung und Begrenzung der Kastellvici' [Saalburg-Schriften 6], Bad Homburg v.d.H., 107–113

Sommer, C. S. 2004c: 'Intra leugam, Canabae, Kastellvici und der obergermanisch-raetische Limes', in Ruscu *et al.* 2004, 312–21

Sommer, C. S. 2005: 'Sulz. Kastell und Kastellvicus/Vicus', in Planck 2005, 332–5

Sommer, C. S., in press: '*Canabae et vici* militaires', in Reddé *et al.*, in press

Sommer, C. S., Kortüm, K. and Fecher, R. 2005: 'Rottweil. Kastelle und Stadt Municipium Arae Flaviae', in Planck 2005, 292–302

Thiel, A. 2005: *Das römische Jagsthausen – Kastell, Vicus und Siedelstellen des Umlandes* [Materialhefte zur Archäologie in Baden-Württemberg 72], Stuttgart

Todd, M. (ed.) 2004: *A companion to Roman Britain*, Oxford

Waldherr, G. 2006: 'Ein hölzernes Amphitheater in Künzing. Anmerkungen eines Alt-historikers', *Vorträge des 24. Niederbayerischen Archäologentages*, Rahden/Westfahlen, 119–34

Wamser, L. and Steidl, B. (eds) 2002: *Neue Forschungen zur römischen Besiedlung zwischen Oberrhein und Enns* [Schriftenreihe der Archäologischen Staatssammlung 3], Remshalden-Grunbach

Wilmott, T. 1997: *Birdoswald. Excavations of a Roman fort on Hadrian's Wall and its successor settlements: 1987–92* [English Heritage Archaeological Report 14], London

Wilson, P. R. 2002: *Cataractonium: Roman Catterick and its hinterland. Part 1: excavation and research 1958–1997* [CBA Research Report 129], London

Wilson, R. J. A. (ed.) 1997a: *Roman Maryport and its setting: essays in memory of Michael G. Jarrett* [Cumberland and Westmorland Antiquarian and Archaeological Society Extra Series 28], Kendal

Wilson, R. J. A. 1997b: 'Maryport from the first to the fourth centuries: some current problems', in Wilson 1997a, 17–39

Wilson, R. J. A. 2002: *A guide to the Roman remains in Britain*, fourth edition, London

Wilson, R. J. A. 2004: 'Introduction: the Roman frontier on the Solway', in Wilson and Caruana 2004, 19–38

Wilson, R. J. A. and Caruana, I. D. (eds) 2004: *Romans on the Solway. Essays in Honour of Richard Bellhouse* [Cumberland and Westmorland Antiquarian and Archaeological Society Extra Series 31], Kendal

Chapter 6

SAMIAN CUPS AND THEIR USES

Geoffrey B. Dannell

> 'Fill high the cup with Samian wine!'
> Byron, *'Don Juan'*

It will be 50 years this summer since I first started to excavate for Sheppard, at Verulamium. He introduced me to Brian Hartley, and encouraged me to learn more about samian ware in the service of Roman archaeology. Sheppard was a forbidding figure at that time. He was given to stern discipline (when we asked if we could wash in the changing rooms behind the Verulamium Museum, he pointed out sharply that the river Ver was perfectly serviceable!), but he was revered for his weekly site tours – ever the teacher, ever explicit and informative, and capable, as many today are not, of interpreting the evidence as it accumulated on the site, and not months later in an office.[1] Once, Sir Mortimer Wheeler visited the site, and without invitation gave an impromptu lecture over the trenches; Sheppard seethed. But to Wheeler's consternation, the assembled multitude greeted his peroration with undisguised laughter, for behind him, in the site-hut window, dangled an articulated skeleton dancing in perfect mimicry of the great man's gestures. It was an ample demonstration of our real regard for Sheppard, and I feel privileged to be able to offer these thoughts as a 90th birthday present.

Introduction

The introduction of vessels made with samian technology to Britain is known to have begun around the beginning of the first millennium AD. At many of the Iron Age cantonal and sub-cantonal capitals,[2] sites in southern Britain, and as far north as North Ferriby,[3] Italian products have been found as part of assemblages, including other exotic imports such as *terra rubra* and Central-Gaulish fine wares. In character, these vessels represent a totally alien tradition to indigenous ceramics.[4] The recent discovery of a ditch, perhaps associated with a putative Roman trading post, at Fishbourne which has a significant quantity of such material in its filling,[5] and the large quantity of vessels recorded from Camulodunum, suggest that samian was a valued commodity in Britain well before the Claudian conquest. Black Campanian gloss-ware, made in the same region as the early Dressel 1A wine amphorae, is not represented as an import, which implies that the use of fine table-wares in Britain was associated with cultural and commercial developments in the later Augustan period.

The contrast between the samian repertoire and contemporary native products is striking. However, it is the purpose for which samian was used which is important, as well as the social implications which stem from its employment. We have no literary sources to tell us what was going on in this respect at the time, and it may be dangerous to draw parallels with developments in Gaul, but on the other hand we know of affinities between the British and continental tribes.[6] It would seem that there was an increasing level of political and commercial relationship between Britain, Rome, and Romanised Gaul and Germany.[7] However, the fact that Britain was broadly left to its own devices between Caesar's incursions, and that of Claudius, spanning the period within which red-slipped Italian wares, and the earliest imitations from Gaul were produced, means that Britain was a sort of *tabula rasa* for the introduction of Roman dining and culinary habits. Three broad classes of vessels were imported: 'dishes', with upturned rims; smaller containers, which are usually called 'cups'; and 'bowls', which vary from plain, deep developments and variations on the shapes of the 'dishes', through to more specialised forms like the decorated vessels. Taken together, they have been classed as table-ware; they introduced new concepts, such as the foot-ring, to Britain.

These imports were not simply a matter of wealthy aristocracies and their associates purchasing luxury items in order, metaphorically, to decorate their sideboards. The proof that they were used for the purposes for which they were intended is marked by the appearance of the coarse-pottery *mortarium* in pre-conquest deposits.[8] The importation of such vessels implies the utilisation of a Romanised cuisine and almost certainly an accompanying dining ritual.[9] Since drinking was at the core of those customs, this paper reassesses the wide use of the word 'cup' to describe a number of the standard samian shapes.

The highly-fired surface of samian is resistant to residue analysis, so it is less likely, than as with coarse pottery, that one can discover what foodstuffs were associated with which vessels. However, it can be said that the growing amount of importation, most striking in the Neronian period (AD 54–68) and thereafter,[10] reveals a change of consumption habit, and therefore food preparation, which profoundly affected society.[11] The cultural rationale for buying a samian vessel for use in the deepest part of the Fens of East Anglia may not have been that of the sophisticated buyer in London, but the acceptance that samian was a desirable and recognisable item to own is clearly undeniable.

If the first large-scale users of samian in Britain were concentrated among the occupants of the cantonal capitals, what were they doing with it? The answer is that it is most likely by their own standards they were becoming 'civilised', in the sense that the rites of eating and drinking were an essential component of native society,[12] and aping Roman customs was attractive as a further distinction within tribal hierarchies.[13] However, it is unlikely that either in Britain or in other cultures which habitually used samian, that individual vessel forms were always used for the same purposes over long periods of time.[14]

Problems of terminology

The quest to find the correct Roman terminology for the forms of samian vessels as classified by modern scholars from the descriptions recorded by the scribes working at the samian kiln-sites is an intriguing one. It brings into sharp contrast the desire to synthesise the morphology of ceramics with the prime purpose of producing a type-series as an aid to archaeological dating on the one hand, with need to reconstruct the social and cultural milieux of the potters and their staffs, and also indeed their clienteles, for whom the vessels manufactured were objects of consumption. One cannot know at this stage whether the production of samian (and here I include also the output of the Italian factories)[15] was, to use the economist's terminology, a 'push' or a 'pull' model. To put it another way, were the shapes and sizes made at the whim of the potters, and then commercialised by *mercatores*, or did the market itself act to demand particular vessel types?[16] Certainly, styles changed over time and preferences can be observed. Innovative forms were created, and then waxed in popularity, before interest in them waned. Some were eliminated from the range, either absolutely,[17] or within individual markets.[18] Even colour mattered: the red-flecked 'marbled ware', for example, with its basically yellow slip, turns up more frequently in *Gallia Narbonensis* and the Mediterranean provinces than it does elsewhere.[19] Examples of discrete distribution suggest that, within a basic range of vessel types, consumer preference must have played some part in determining production strategies, as it filtered slowly back through the commercial chain to those who placed the orders with the kiln masters.

In recent years efforts have been made to try to understand the relationship between Dragendorff's catalogue of the shapes of samian vessels[20] (and of course, those that followed him in extending his series),[21] and what exactly was going on at the kiln sites. A notable advance for La Graufesenque has come with the study of the samian from Vechten.[22] An extensive statistical analysis of that material has produced evidence to suggest size-groups within shapes, traits which might lead to distinctions in chronology, how vessels might have been stacked in the kiln, and other practical matters.[23] Such studies help to explain *what* happened; but they do not attempt to explain *why* certain vessels were made, and what function they served their users.[24] They are studies of production, not consumption.[25]

Even at the time at which Dragendorff was writing, the first potters' accounts (*graffiti*) found at La Graufesenque had been published.[26] The inscriptions apparently recorded kiln loads for single firings, and gave the description of the various vessels fired, their sizes, the quantities, and the names of those who, it is presumed, had them fired in the kiln.[27] A large variety of vessels was described by the professional scribes, who used both the Latin and the Gaulish vocabularies; some terms appear to be explicit nouns, while others are more general and adjectival.[28] One of the principal difficulties is to try to align modern samian typology with the scribes' descriptions. A brief observation shows that it is rather like trying to squeeze the proverbial quart into a pint pot.

There are three vessels listed on the *graffiti* which have been interpreted by modern scholars as 'cups': *acetabula*, *licuiae* and *paropsides*,[29] with their various

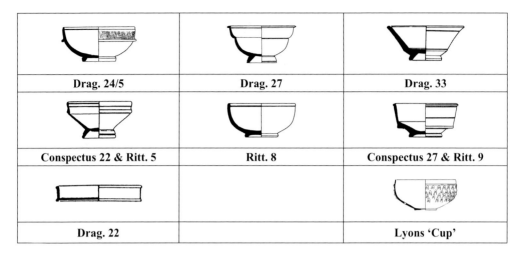

Fig. 6.1a Plain-ware 'cups' and 'bowls' (not to scale)

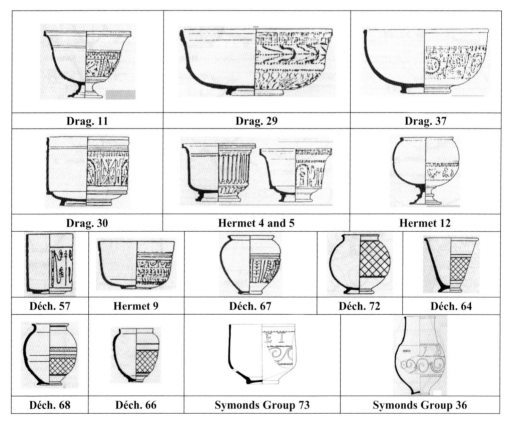

Fig. 6.1b Decorated mixing bowls and other vessels probably used for drinking (not to scale)

spellings and singulars.[30] The modern shapes which seem to suit are: Dragendorff forms 22, 24, and 24/5; Dragendorff form 27; Dragendorff form 33; and Ritterling forms 5, 8 and 9 (Fig. 6.1a and b). All these forms were being made in the earliest period of production both in Italy and at La Graufesenque.[31] They comprise considerable proportions of the totals.[32]

There are, however, far too many vessel shapes defined by modern terminology, and/or too little distinction made by the scribes, to obtain a satisfactory correlation between modern shape-name and ancient description.[33] Size, on the other hand, did seem to be important for the 'platters' and 'dishes', and there is an emphasis in the *graffiti* on kiln usage and capacity. The 'cups' did not generally have sizes attached to them, presumably because for the most part they nestled in piles on spare spaces between the larger vessels.[34]

'Cup' is a term which is automatically associated with drinking because of its association with modern custom and terminology. It naturally has no place in the records of the scribes at La Graufesenque. Thus, while the term 'cup' may be a useful shorthand as a modern descriptions of certain Roman vessels, much more work needs to be done on establishing the likely range of purposes for which cup-shaped vessels were actually produced.

Acetabula

Technically, the *acetabulum* was a measure of *c.* 0.068 cl in modern terms.[35] Marichal points out, usefully, that *acetabula* occur on *graffiti* of the second century AD, as well as at La Graufesenque. Thus, as he remarks: '. . . ils ont dû changer de forme'.[36] If the scribes had been describing single forms, this ought to limit the argument about correspondence between the *graffiti* and Dragendorff 27, or indeed to Dragendorff 33. Only those forms occur in both the first and the second centuries. Two qualifying adjectives, *duisom[* and *dupros[opi*, seem to indicate something related to duality (Marichal suggests for *duisom[* an archaism expressing 'à deux corps', i.e. with double body; *duprosopi* he translates as 'à deux visages' or ' à deux faces'. This description would suit Dragendorff 27 well. The word *strogia* is not clear, apart from the fact that some specialists see it as meaning 'hemispherical' (a reference to Ritterling 8?). Classical references to the word include the following – Apicius, where the *acetabulum* is related to the preparation of sauces;[37] Isidore, who related the term to vinegar;[38] and Seneca, who described the *acetabulum* as 'a vessel used by thimblemen'.[39] Pliny used the word in a general sense in both biological and botanical contexts.[40] It appears, admittedly from limited evidence, that the *acetabulum* is referred to on the *graffiti* in Pliny's terms: that is to say, an essentially semi-spherical vessel, which might therefore, in the case of Dragendorff 27, be said to have 'two aspects'. It is also clear that the term was used in a culinary context, and not necessarily in connection with drinking *per se*. The reference by Seneca can be seen in a similar way to those of Pliny, namely a suitable vessel for rattling dice, or playing the 'three-card trick'. Hilgers suggests the shapes of four vessels (Dragendorff forms 22, 24/5 27 and 33), which he thought might be suitable to fit the terminology *acetabulum*.[41]

Licuiae

Since all references to this vessel-form appearing on the *graffiti* are written in Gaulish,[42] there are no classical references. Marichal prefers the explanation of Thurneysen, deriving *licu(u)ia* from *liqui-*, and, if understood correctly, meaning a 'crucible' or 'melting-pot'. This in itself does not make a lot of sense, and may result from a confusion of translation in trying to match modern terminology with ancient usage. Samian is not known generally to have been used on the fire, but in the sense of a mixing vessel for warm contents it would stand examination. Again it was a popular vessel, representing *c.* 14% of the total output: that rules out Hermet's suggestion that it was an oil-jug, since suitable small jugs are very infrequently found.[43] Reference to *licuiae* appears on *graffiti* down to the later Flavian period.

The Roman habit of mixing their wine with water, however, may be relevant here. Discounting the use of snow to chill wines in this context, two other possibilities exist: water at room temperature, and hot water, for which the more sophisticated households might use an *authepsa* (see note 44).

Paropsides

For the *paropsis*, Marichal follows Hilgers (who opts for Dragendorff 24/5) and suggests, 'il s'agit de récipients creux pour le service du table'.[45] He notes that of those vessels mentioned in the *graffiti*, this one makes up 22% of the total, so it is a popular type(s). Of the adjectives associated, *aematini* would seem to refer to a colour; *bol[etari* to have a connection with mushrooms;[46] *brina, exan* and *uocaliati* are all unexplained. The *buxel* element is related to Fr. *boite*; *trocliati* is attributed to a characteristic of the vessel, and 'turned' has been suggested, rather than being a reference to form.[47] However Dr Susan Weingarten has made a very interesting suggestion that the root *troch-* (*tro – troximon*) might be more appropriate, relating the vessel in question to the service of raw vegetables.[48] Given the reference to *bessales* (with a rim diameter of *c.* 197 mm), Dragendorff 24/5 alone does not seem to suit. Classical sources relating to *paropsides* are very extensive.[49] Perhaps the key reference to them is in Athenaeus: the sympotic argument there revolved around whether the *paropsis* was a vessel, or the sauce or relish contained within it.[50]

Discussion

The varying dimensions of the 'cups' have been treated in detail by Polak, using the material from Vechten and elsewhere.[51] His fig. 6.40 shows that at the time of the *Fosse Gallicanus* (Gallicanus ii, in the Leeds Index of Potters' Stamps),[52] which is basically a Neronian deposit,[53] the overall diameters of rims and foot-rings of 'cups' fall into two groups, with a fair spread within each.[54] It is not easy to draw overall conclusions from Polak's diagrams in the absence of the raw data, particularly as he points out that there is considerable morphological development

Term	Weight Roman lbs.	Grains	Volume litres	Lesser Volumes cl.
coleus	1600.00	8080000	524.75	
quadrantal (*amphora*)	80.00	404000	26.24	
urna	40.00	202000	13.12	
congius	10.00	50500	3.28	
sextarius	1.67	8417	0.55	546.61
hemina	0.83	4208	0.27	273.31
quartarius	0.42	2104	0.14	136.65
sextans	0.28	1403	0.09	91.10
acetabulum	0.21	1052	0.07	68.33
cyathus	0.14	701	0.05	45.55
ligula	0.03	175	0.01	11.39

Fig. 6.2 Table of Roman liquid measures

in the ratios of rim to foot diameters for most forms over time. Fig. 6.2 shows known Roman liquid measures. Fig. 6.3 lists a range of forms from publications, sorted by ascending volume, with Roman measures marked for reference. Fig. 6.4 attempts to bring the two data-sets together in summary form, by estimating volumes for the average sizes of those forms with a sufficient vessel population, based on Polak's graphs. If one tries to establish relationships between recorded vessel-sizes and known Roman measures, the data turn out to be hopelessly inconsistent, suggesting that the potters were not concerned with mensuration (in its modern sense of 'Weights and Measures'). However, Polak's correlations do indicate size groups: four for Ritterling 8 and Dragendorff 33; two for the other cups. The difference between maxima and minima in each type is so large, however, and the variability of dimension within a grouping so marked, that the idea of standardisation, other than in Polak's very general terms of 'small', 'medium' and 'large', can be abandoned.[56] To match the requirements of the Apicius recipe, which seems to demand the measures 'big', 'regular' and 'small', the most likely candidate would be Dragendorff 27, since its popularity was established before that of Dragendorff 33. Neither of the references in Apicius suggests anything other than a measuring cup, which the cook's experience would judge for size and fill.[57]

The implications of the sizes and volumes shown in Fig. 6.3 are that the formers used to shape the external profiles of plain-ware vessels were cut to configure to a rough approximation of the size ranges. That is confirmed by finds of fused piles of vessels ('moutons') known from kiln sites, where accidents have led to disasters, and to the loss of entire kiln loads due to a failure of temperature control in the

Vessel Form	Volumes	Foot mm.	Height mm.	Rim	% Ratio of Rim:Height	Reference	Roman Measure
Ritt. 8	5.88	13.00	18.00	34.00	188.89	O&P 48.5	
Drag. 24 & 24/5	24.43	35.00	30.00	77.00	256.67	Cam Pl. 40.s15B	
Drag. 24 & 24/5	29.32	32.00	30.00	68.00	226.67	Polak 6.59l	
Drag. 24 & 24/5	31.87	30.00	30.00	66.00	220.00	Polak 6.59k	
Drag. 24 & 24/5	32.46	29.00	33.00	72.00	218.18	Polak 6.59j	
Ritt. 8	34.35	28.00	29.00	54.00	186.21	O&P 48.4	
Drag. 24 & 24/5	34.46	32.00	31.00	70.00	225.81	Cam Pl. 40.s15C	
Ritt. 9	34.81	23.00	52.00	59.00	113.46	O&P 39.8	
Drag. 27	34.82	33.00	33.00	75.00	227.27	O&P 49.10	
Ritt. 8	36.86	28.00	29.00	57.00	196.55	O&P 48.3	
Drag. 24 & 24/5	38.26	36.00	30.00	65.00	216.67	Polak 6.59i	
Drag. 27	39.05	34.00	38.00	79.00	207.89	O&P 49.7	
Drag. 27	40.19	35.00	41.00	77.00	187.80	Polak 6.61k	
Drag. 24 & 24/5	43.32	35.00	37.00	70.00	189.19	O&P 40.1	*cyathus*
Drag. 27	50.70	36.00	41.00	83.00	202.44	O&P 49.9	
Drag. 27	51.01	30.00	38.00	79.00	207.89	Cam Pl. 40.s14B'	
Drag. 27	51.27	36.00	46.00	80.00	173.91	Polak 6.61j	
Drag. 24 & 24/5	52.48	35.00	33.00	70.00	212.12	O&P 40.5	
Ritt. 9	54.78	31.00	38.00	67.00	176.32	O&P 39.9	
Ritt. 8	55.80	30.00	35.00	75.00	214.29	O&P 48.6	
Drag. 27	57.42	36.00	41.00	78.00	190.24	Polak 6.61i	
Drag. 24 & 24/5	57.91	30.00	29.00	68.00	234.48	O&P 40.9	
Drag. 24 & 24/5	58.80	34.00	31.00	75.00	241.94	O&P 40.11	
Ritt. 9	59.52	38.00	38.00	68.00	178.95	Klynne Pl. 26.406	
Drag. 27	60.82	37.00	38.00	90.00	236.84	O&P 49.17	
Drag. 24 & 24/5	61.23	39.00	43.00	80.00	186.05	Polak 6.59m	
Drag. 24 & 24/5	61.52	32.00	32.00	72.00	225.00	O&P 40.14	
Ritt. 9	61.93	32.00	37.00	76.00	205.41	O&P 39.3	
Drag. 33	68.00	32.00	41.00	87.00	212.20	Polak 6.64a	*acetabulum*
Drag. 24 & 24/5	69.67	33.00	34.00	69.00	202.94	O&P 40.10	
Ritt. 5	71.59	36.00	47.00	82.00	174.47	Polak 6.55e	
Ritt. 8	73.06	36.00	44.00	100.00	227.27	Polak 6.57a	
Drag. 27	73.11	38.00	46.00	84.00	182.61	O&P 49.8	
Ritt. 5	73.91	37.00	48.00	77.00	160.42	Polak 6.55d	
Ritt. 5	76.15	40.00	42.00	79.00	188.10	Cam Fig.43.s11B	
Ritt. 5	79.60	35.00	50.00	85.00	170.00	O&P 38.3	
Ritt. 9	80.75	38.00	40.00	80.00	200.00	Cam Pl. 40.s17C	
Drag. 24 & 24/5	86.75	5.50	37.00	103.00	278.38	Klynne Pl. 32.499	
Drag. 33	89.88	41.00	43.00	99.00	230.23	Polak 6.64b	*sextans*
Drag. 27	94.20	43.00	47.00	113.00	240.43	Polak 6.61l	
Drag. 27	94.72	40.00	44.00	96.00	218.18	Polak 6.61m	
Drag. 24 & 24/5	94.98	42.00	53.00	100.00	188.68	Polak 6.59h	
Drag. 27	95.52	42.00	49.00	89.00	181.63	Cam Pl. 40.s14A'	
Ritt. 5	100.65	41.00	48.00	85.00	177.08	Polak 6.55f	
Drag. 33	115.64	43.00	47.00	104.00	221.28	O&P 51.13	
Ritt. 8	116.32	58.00	47.00	114.00	242.55	Polak 6.57b	
Lyons Cup	122.26	32.00	44.00	95.00	215.91	Greene Fig. 12.2	
Drag. 24 & 24/5	124.18	4.30	47.00	103.00	219.15	Klynne Pl. 32.502	
Drag. 24 & 24/5	128.28	50.00	50.00	118.00	236.00	Polak 6.59c	
Drag. 24 & 24/5	129.01	4.50	46.00	95.00	206.52	Klynne Pl. 32.480	

Fig. 6.3 Dimensions and calculated volumes of samian and other 'cups' and beakers

Vessel Form	Volumes	Foot mm.	Height mm.	Rim	% Ratio of Rim:Height	Reference	Roman Measure
Ritt. 9	131.98	45.00	47.00	91.00	193.62	Polak 6.58a	
Drag. 33	135.16	39.00	55.00	108.00	196.36	O&P 51.12	
Ritt. 8	135.44	43.00	45.00	99.00	220.00	Cam Pl. 40.s16B	
Ritt. 9	136.36	32.00	45.00	90.00	200.00	O&P 39.5	*quartarius*
Conspectus 22	140.35	44.00	55.00	90.00	163.64	Klynne Pl. 21.313	
Drag. 27	146.73	50.00	60.00	115.00	191.67	O&P 49.5	
Conspectus 27	148.12	49.00	44.00	110.00	250.00	Klynne Pl. 26.398	
Drag. 33	150.27	40.00	52.00	113.00	217.31	O&P 51.14	
Drag. 24 & 24/5	150.64	50.00	50.00	106.00	212.00	Polak 6.59g	
Lyons Cup	154.71	35.00	50.00	103.00	206.00	Greene Fig. 11.9	
Drag. 24 & 24/5	154.71	5.10	55.00	107.00	194.55	Klynne Pl. 32.481	
Drag. 27	159.86	50.00	57.00	118.00	207.02	Polak 6.61f	
Conspectus 27	160.19	5.00	36.00	101.00	280.56	Klynne Pl. 26.399	
Lyons Cup	166.76	36.00	49.00	99.00	202.04	Greene Fig. 12.1	
Ritt. 9	174.02	45.00	57.00	101.00	177.19	O&P 39.10	
Drag. 24 & 24/5	176.80	60.00	53.00	119.00	224.53	Polak 6.59a	
Rhenish Mugs	177.65	34.00	83.00	72.00	86.75	Symonds 765	
Lyons Cup	184.30	36.00	49.00	100.00	204.08	Greene Fig. 11.10	
Drag. 24 & 24/5	184.31	53.00	54.00	119.00	220.37	Polak 6.59e	
Drag. 24 & 24/5	192.04	40.00	55.00	115.00	209.09	Polak 6.59f	
Drag. 27	195.44	52.00	61.00	124.00	203.28	Cam Pl. 40.s14B	
Drag. 24 & 24/5	199.50	50.00	54.00	119.00	220.37	Polak 6.59d	
Drag. 27	201.02	45.00	58.00	120.00	206.90	Polak 6.61h	
Drag. 27	207.51	50.00	58.00	125.00	215.52	O&P 49.14	
Drag. 24 & 24/5	214.47	42.00	49.00	98.00	200.00	O&P 40.4	
Ritt. 9	225.70	54.00	63.00	104.00	165.08	Polak 6.58b	
Drag. 24 & 24/5	230.10	61.00	54.00	125.00	231.48	Polak 6.59b	
Ritt. 5	232.57	58.00	70.00	117.00	167.14	Polak 6.55a	
Ritt. 5	236.23	47.00	50.00	110.00	220.00	O&P 38.2	
Drag. 27	242.19	58.00	68.00	126.00	185.29	Polak 6.61b	
Lyons Cup	245.31	41.00	52.00	118.00	226.92	Greene Fig. 11.8	
Drag. 27	247.78	55.00	67.00	126.00	188.06	Polak 6.61d	
Drag. 27	253.81	55.00	55.00	145.00	263.64	Klynne Pl. 31.474	
Ritt. 8	260.46	48.00	55.00	58.00	105.45	O&P 48.7	*hemina*
Drag. 24 & 24/5	284.84	46.00	51.00	116.00	227.45	O&P 40.3	
Drag. 27	289.09	55.00	57.00	139.00	243.86	Klynne Pl. 31.475	
Drag. 33	289.70	48.00	59.00	141.00	238.98	Polak 6.64c	
Ritt. 9	309.01	55.00	57.00	111.00	194.74	Klynne Pl. 26.395	
Drag. 33	309.13	57.00	61.00	144.00	236.07	O&P 51.8	
Ritt. 9	310.07	50.00	70.00	111.00	158.57	Cam Pl. 40.s17B	
Drag. 33	325.04	54.00	65.00	134.00	206.15	Polak 6.64d	
Drag. 33	326.59	50.00	81.00	129.00	159.26	O&P 51.17	
Ritt. 5	339.61	63.00	80.00	125.00	156.25	Polak 6.55b	
Ritt. 9	339.84	54.00	68.00	113.00	166.18	O&P 39.6	
Ritt. 9	340.02	48.00	65.00	119.00	183.08	Cam Pl. 40.s17A	
Drag. 33	345.86	60.00	72.00	151.00	209.72	O&P 51.4	
Ritt. 9	368.12	57.00	62.00	123.00	198.39	O&P 39.2	
Ritt. 5	371.56	59.00	77.00	125.00	162.34	Cam Pl. 40.s11A	
Conspectus 22	374.41	56.00	71.00	131.00	184.51	Klynne Pl. 21.304	
Drag. 33	378.58	53.00	78.00	139.00	178.21	O&P 51.11	

Fig. 6.3 (continued) Dimensions and calculated volumes of samian and other 'cups' and beakers

Vessel Form	Volumes	Foot mm.	Height mm.	Rim	% Ratio of Rim:Height	Reference	Roman Measure
Drag. 27	382.16	60.00	72.00	142.00	197.22	Cam Pl. 40.s14A	
Rhenish Mugs	391.03	40.00	97.00	86.00	88.66	Symonds 766	
Drag. 33	398.41	54.00	69.00	158.00	228.99	Polak 6.64g	
Ritt. 8	430.56	72.00	74.00	152.00	205.41	Polak 6.57c	
Ritt. 5	431.19	57.00	80.00	125.00	156.25	O&P 38.1	
Drag. 27	441.21	69.00	78.00	152.00	194.87	Klynne Pl. 30.462	
Conspectus 22	469.24	7.00	73.00	145.00	198.63	Klynne Pl. 21.303	
Drag. 30	473.02	67.00	96.00	114.00	118.75	O&P 8.5	
Rhenish Mugs	480.30	46.00	103.00	95.00	92.23	Symonds 764	
Ritt. 9	558.04	74.00	75.00	150.00	200.00	Polak 6.58c	sextarius
Drag. 30	716.60	80.00	110.00	134.00	121.82	O&P 7.5	
Drag. 33	728.28	73.00	85.00	175.00	205.88	Polak 6.64f	
Drag. 30	736.90	62.00	101.00	125.00	123.76	O&P 8.8	
Ritt. 9	820.15	80.00	90.00	162.00	180.00	Polak 6.58d	
Drag. 30	870.57	79.00	107.00	134.00	125.23	O&P 8.1	
Rhenish Mugs	913.54	60.00	114.00	129.00	113.16	Symonds 767	
Drag. 33	974.70	60.00	111.00	192.00	172.97	O&P 51.3	
Ritt. 8	1016.11	85.00	96.00	177.00	184.38	Polak 6.57d	
Drag. 30	1138.87	96.00	105.00	145.00	138.10	O&P 7.7	
Drag. 30	1186.70	93.00	120.00	150.00	125.00	O&P 7.1	
Drag. 30	1205.36	73.00	132.00	151.00	114.39	O&P 7.2	
Drag. 30	1226.85	77.00	119.00	146.00	122.69	O&P 8.3	
Drag. 30	1245.31	80.00	136.00	168.00	123.53	O&P 7.4	
Drag. 33	1316.50	85.00	90.00	211.00	234.44	Cam Pl. 40.s21A'	
Drag. 30	1351.31	75.00	122.00	150.00	122.95	O&P 8.4	
Drag. 30	1356.42	99.00	128.00	162.00	126.56	O&P 8.2	
Drag. 33	1416.82	97.00	100.00	203.00	203.00	Polak 6.64e	
Rhenish Mugs	1445.03	64.00	149.00	143.00	95.97	Symonds 768	
Drag. 30	1639.78	76.00	139.00	162.00	116.55	O&P 7.6	
Drag. 30	1683.00	85.00	142.00	152.00	107.04	O&P 8.6	
Drag. 30	2316.56	105.00	152.00	176.00	115.79	O&P 8.7	
Drag. 30	3141.30	87.00	196.00	208.00	106.12	O&P 7.3	congius

Fig.6.3 (continued) Dimensions and calculated volumes of samian and other 'cups' and beakers

firing process. Within these piles, the vessels show similar dimensions, and it seems likely that batches produced by the same workshop used similar formers. The problem is to know how long the formers, almost certainly made of wood, lasted, and therefore what consistency of profile might be expected over time.

The average foot-ring diameter for vessels of the 'small' class is *c.* 300/350 mm, but even smaller vessels exist, such as the Ritterling which has a foot-ring diameter of *c.* 240 mm,[58] or the tiny thimble-sized one from Strasbourg.[59] Such small vessels occur far more frequently in the southern Roman provinces than in the north.[60] This fact was confirmed by a recent examination of the samian stamps from Trion, where a significant (*c.* 10%) proportion of the foot-ring diameters of forms Ritterling 8 and 9, and 24/25, are between 225 mm and 300 mm in diameter.[61] If substantial regional differences in size-preferences were prevalent, some caution needs to be applied to statistics based on data which is weighted towards a particular part of

Polak Fig	Description	Rim Diameters mm.	Heights mm.	Estimated Volume cl.
6.42b	Ritt. 8 Small (All)	76	34	56
	Ritt. 8 Large (All)	116	59	115
6.42c	Ritt. 9 Small (All)	70	41	60
	Ritt. 9 Large (All)	112	63	310
6.42d	Drag. 24/5 Small (Vechten)	77	37	25
	Drag. 24/5 Large (Vechten)	128	58	230
6.42e	Drag. 27g Small (Vechten)	86	46	75
	Drag. 27g Large (Vechten)	112	62	145
6.42f	Drag. 33 Small (All)	93	46	85
	Drag. 33 Large(All)	154	69	360

Fig. 6.4 Rim diameters and overall heights of some 'cups' calculated from Polak 2000, averaged from his graphs

the samian distribution area. It is possible, where Polak shows two main size-groupings for a form, that a third, smaller one also exists – and this might satisfy the measuring vessels required for the Apicius recipe.

Nothing but approximate values can be claimed for the results.[62] To do the experiments conclusively would require the careful filling and recording of water poured into complete vessels, or perhaps sophisticated software, able to produce volumes from illustrations of vessel profiles. The internal measurements used as the maximum fill-height correspond to the level of the small internal grooves found on all of the 'cups' (except on Ritterling 9, where it is an inconsistent feature, as interestingly it is also on early versions of forms 24 and 24/5). The purpose of the groove is not known, but it may have provided a surface tension level for any liquid to assume, and thus reduce spillage.

The results also pose a fundamental question: while the individual *graffiti* at La Graufesenque (and elsewhere) give *acetabula*, *licuiae* and *paropsides* on the same lists, implying that the scribes were recording separate, recognizable features,[63] the general lack of associated dimensions suggests that in the case of 'cups', size was not an important feature for identification during the kiln operation itself. Against that, it is known that 'platters' and 'dishes' *were* made in size-related groupings from the evidence of the *graffiti*, so it is probable that the workers in the potteries used the vessel descriptions according to the most likely 'vernacular' applied to a particular vessel in a particular kiln-load being described at any one time. Certainly, there is little evidence to show that the classes of size described by Apicius, and the sizes confirmed in general by Polak's analyses of the Vechten material, are a reflection in any way of the records on the *graffiti*. Moreover, it is difficult to see how the function of a single vessel-shape might remain constant over the whole of its range of sizes. One might have expected that the orders for pots, and especially those for provisioning the army, would have demanded vessels of a certain dimension. Perhaps a piece is missing in the chain of evidence available?

Function

The large-scale production of samian vessels for exportation moved from sites in Southern Gaul in the first century, first to Central Gaul, then to East Gaul, while at the same time there was a scattering of local production sites elsewhere with limited geographical markets.[64] This geographical displacement was accompanied by a change in the range of vessels manufactured, especially the 'cups'. Broadly speaking, Ritterling 5 and 9 disappeared, as did Dragendorff 24/5. Ritterling 8 was apparently replaced by Dragendorff 40, which was however never a popular vessel.[65] Only Dragendorff 27 and 33 survived into the later second century, while Dragendorff 27 had faded considerably in significance by *c.* AD 160. The Ritterling forms, together with Dragendorff 24/5, are particularly associated with military sites, and those where 'Romanisation' might be expected to be embedded.[66] Dragendorff 27 and particularly Dragendorff 33 are more often found in larger dimensions, and more frequently occur on civilian sites.[67] This raises the possibility that the smallest-sized vessels of various forms may have been connected with food preparation and of accompanying food, in the context of Roman acculturation, in contrast to larger vessels, which were adopted increasingly into populations which did not have Hellenised or Romanised cultures. A similar tendency can be seen in the general decline of classical imagery on decorated samian vessels after the Flavian period.[68]

The association of samian vessels with wine is explicit; we have evidence from bowls for exactly that usage.[69] Potters at the production site of Banassac made Dragendorff 37s with mottos stamped into the moulds[70]. Many are wishes for 'good-luck' addressed to the tribes of *Gallia Belgica* (*Lingones, Remi, Sequani, Treveri*, plus the local *Gabali*). Some have vine-leaf decoration, but one has an explicit reference to beer.[71] Roman beer was frequently 'adultrated', both in the barrel and at the table.[72] If these bowls are for mixing drink – and it should be remembered that sometimes Dragendorff 11 was made at La Graufesenque with a pouring spout,[73] and that Dragendorff 37 was regularly made with both spout and strap handles[74] – then not only wine might be involved; by contrast, Dragendorff 29 was not generally a spouted or handled form. It is also worth noting that Dragendorff 27 has both an upper and a lower 'chamber'. Fig. 6.5 shows the ratio between the two for a limited number of vessels. It is not constant, but there is enough correspondence in the ratio, regardless of overall volume, to warrant further investigation as to whether Dragendorff 27 might not have been a 'mixer' vessel, in which wine was poured, to be topped up to the mark with water. Another matter which would be worth following up in detail concerns Dragendorff 30. It continued to be manufactured throughout the first and second centuries, at a rate of about a third to a quarter of that of the more popular decorated bowls, Dragendorff 29, and Dragendorff 37. Some of the larger Rhenish Tankards (Fig. 6.1.) are of similar size to Dragendorff 30 (as indeed are the smaller ones to Dragendorff 78). This suggests that Dragendorff 30 may well have been a drinking vessel, since later tankards are explicit in their association with wine.[75]

Wine was apparently drunk by the basic measure of the *cyathus*, which was the

Vessel Form	Volumes	Ratio of Upper/Lower zone	Rim	Height mm.	Foot mm.	Roman Measure
Drag. 27	39	174	126.00	67.00	55.00	Polak 6.61d
Drag. 27	40	200	90.00	38.00	37.00	O&P 49.17
Drag. 27	51	167	115.00	60.00	50.00	O&P 49.5
Drag. 27	51	188	113.00	47.00	43.00	Polak 6.61l
Drag. 27	51	175	83.00	41.00	36.00	O&P 49.9
Drag. 27	57	195	126.00	68.00	58.00	Polak 6.61b
Drag. 27	61	135	118.00	57.00	50.00	Polak 6.61f
Drag. 27	73	179	79.00	38.00	34.00	O&P 49.7
Drag. 27	94	163	84.00	46.00	38.00	O&P 49.8
Drag. 27	95	120	142.00	72.00	60.00	Cam Pl. 40.s14A
Drag. 27	96	187	124.00	61.00	52.00	Cam Pl. 40.s14B
Drag. 27	147	147	139.00	57.00	55.00	Klynne Pl. 31.475
Drag. 27	160	167	120.00	58.00	45.00	Polak 6.61h
Drag. 27	195	188	152.00	78.00	69.00	Klynne Pl. 30.462
Drag. 27	201	201	125.00	58.00	50.00	O&P 49.14
Drag. 27	208	208	145.00	55.00	55.00	Klynne Pl. 31.474
Drag. 27	242	167	77.00	41.00	35.00	Polak 6.61k
Drag. 27	248	125	78.00	41.00	36.00	Polak 6.61i
Drag. 27	254	253	79.00	38.00	30.00	Cam Pl. 40.s14B'
Drag. 27	289	199	80.00	46.00	36.00	Polak 6.61j
Drag. 27	382	187	89.00	49.00	42.00	Cam Pl. 40.s14A'
Drag. 27	441	206	96.00	44.00	40.00	Polak 6.61m

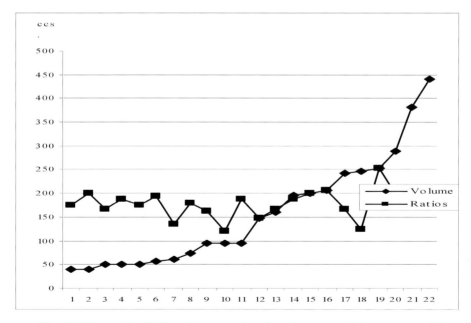

Fig. 6.5 Dragendorff 27, volumes and ratios of upper and lower concavities

name of the ladle used to serve from a *krater*.[76] The word was also used of vessels, and thus may the term be relevant to samian 'cups'. It is noticeable that there are quite a few vessels which fall well below the nominal volume of a *cyathus*, which in itself, as a basic wine measure, could not have provided a great 'kick' at one-third dilution.[77] There is little evidence to suggest that the *cyathus*, or other Roman liquid measure, was respected by the makers of the samian 'cup'.[78] The Roman, as opposed to the provincial, view of the use of pottery vessels for drinking was mixed.[79] Viticulture was a staple of the classical world,[80] and drinking wine very much an embedded ritual of the dinner table.[81] However, there is a great difference between the 'conspicuous consumption' of, say, Trimalchio's fictional feast, and everyday provincial practices.[82] The army, principal users of samian, were considerable consumers of wine, which formed part of their rations.[83] Most classical references to drinking refer to the use of a *calyx*, which is essentially a cup with a foot like Dragendorff 11, but it is possible that the development of samian 'cups' provided the option of a more safely transportable vessel, used for the same purpose.[84]

The *paropsis* is more difficult to identify as a 'cup'. While one might quibble about the exact nomenclature, the general sense of the discussion by Athenaeus implies a shallow dish, or, and more importantly, the possibility that the modern notion of 'cup' only as a drinking vessel is inaccurate.[85] This takes the discussion to dining, the table, and just those dishes and sauces which are mentioned as being associated with both the *acetabulum* and the *paropsis*.[86] It is clear from the literary evidence that the *hors d'oeuvres* course of the formal meal comprised a number of small items which were often accompanied by sauces,[87] and that the *paropsis* was numbered among the containers.[88]

How the *paropsis* was used may be explained from two Biblical sources: the first, from the Jewish Passover service; and the second, from the two accounts by John and Mark of the Last Supper,[89] which recount the identification of Judas through the dipping of 'a sop' during the Passover Meal.[90] Howsoever that may be, there is no doubting the reference in the original source:

שבכל-הלילות אין אנו מטבילין אפלו פעם אחתלילה הזה שתי פעמים

'On all other nights, we do not dip the herbs that we eat even once; why tonight, do we dip twice?'[91] The question reflects the fact that the order of service is seen by modern critics as having sympotic allusions.[92] Originally, the paschal lamb was eaten and a responsive discourse followed; the service adopted the customs of the Roman formal dinner.[93]

What was being dipped, and into what? The Jewish tradition was to dip lettuce (or a green vegetable) into a sweet sauce at the Passover table, and conforms closely to contemporary Roman dining habits.[94] Such 'dips' were prepared in the kitchen and served either hot or cold to diners.[95] The association of *acetabula* on the La Graufesenque *graffiti* with liquid measurement in the kitchen, and that of *paropsides* with sauces, suggests that while one of their purposes *may* have been as drinking vessels; they were also associated with food, and dipping at the table. Vessels in the samian services would have made eminently good containers for

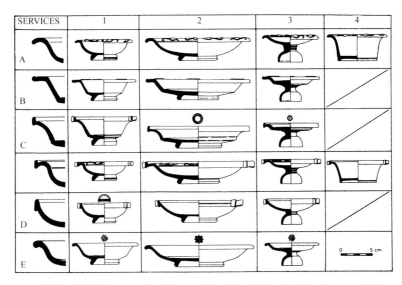

Fig. 6.6 New samian forms introduced in the Flavian period

this purpose. The very small-sized vessels would have been particularly suited to individual servings,[96] and any mixtures with contents of different gravities or viscosities would have needed to be 'refreshed' during the meal.[97] With this in mind, it is worth considering the Arretine series of *Conspectus* forms 33 and 34 (Dragendorff 24 and 24/5). The early examples almost all carry false handles, and are extremely squat; they also have rouletted rims, and have been described, subjectively, as 'bowls' elsewhere.[98] Not all Roman dining was in the *triclinium*, propped up on a couch, and eating 'one-handed'.[99] The chair, the stool or the bench also played its part, and this would have been especially relevant to the army, and probably in most domestic situations in the provinces.[100] The circumstances in which samian vessels were used did not make for easy handling, particularly when most food was eaten with the fingers.[101] A small vessel, therefore, which could be gripped easily, and in which sauces could also be served and stirred, would have been an attractive part of the service. This analogy might be extended to other forms (cf. *Conspectus* form 26). However, the markets into which Gaulish samian was sold were increasingly located away from the epicentres of luxurious meals, despite the efforts of Agricola. This means that continuity of the original purpose associated with a particular shape cannot be taken for granted. The terms *acetabula* and *paropsides* survive into late Classical sources, but may not carry the same meaning as in earlier times, and indeed the two terms tend to merge after the second century. The cup-shaped vessels were, after all, simply containers.

At approximately the same time as some of the small 'cups' disappeared, a new service was introduced: bowls fulfilling the description of both the *paropsis* and the *tryblion* more closely (see Fig. 6.6).[102] The vessels were made in varying sizes, were often decorated with barbotine ivy leaves,[103] and frequently appear in grave groups, presumably together with food offerings.[104] This raises the possibility that the potters rationalised their ranges, and eliminated some, which may have been more expensive to produce, or those for which demand was falling.[105] As prime consumers, it may be relevant that troops were increasingly recruited from areas away from Mediterranean influences, their own ethnicity asserting itself in both their cuisine and in the vessels they used.[106]

In this context other evidence from Britain can be addressed.[107] First, it is fairly certain that the culinary innovations of Roman food preparation survived, even though they may have changed over the 400 or so years of the Roman occupation: the *mortarium*, for example, continued to be made to the end of the fourth century.[108] While the production of wine for consumption in the northern provinces increasingly came from Gallic and German vineyards,[109] beer was also clearly in demand, and arguably was drunk in larger quantities than wine.[110]

There is much to suggest that beer, a grain-derived beverage, remained the indigenous staple throughout the Roman period,[111] as in all of the Gaulish provinces. As has been noted, wine was imported in significant quantities from the late Iron Age onwards, and remained (with the very limited evidence for domestic viticulture) a pervasive and perhaps more exotic import, particularly to military and urban sites.[112] Wine was relatively stable (a good Falernian might have a 25-year vintage) and most fine wines were white and sweet.[113] Beer on the other hand did not last, and was therefore prepared closer to the point of consumption. Perhaps the remaining samian 'cups' from the second century onwards (i.e. Dragendorff 27 and Dragendorff 33) served the two alcoholic beverages, and the survival of the two basic forms may reflect a drinking preference by that time.

Conclusions

In summary, it seems likely that as far as the workers on the pottery sites were concerned, *licuiae* were regarded as cups, and *paropsides* were bowls or dishes used on the side at the table, while the *acetabula* were somewhat more equivocal, given their apparently frequent overlap with *paropsides* in classical texts. We will never be sure of the forms involved, nor does there seem to be a great consistency in the sources, particularly when Greek terms are rendered in Latin. However, in a paper such as this, it is *de rigueur* for the author to give an opinion. For La Graufesenque this would be: *acetabula* = form 27; *licuiae* = Ritterling 5, Ritterling 9, and Dragendorff 33; and *paropsides* = Dragendorff 24/5, and perhaps Ritterling 8, both of which were succeeded by Dragendorff 35, and its 'friends and relations'.[114]

If further light can be thrown on this subject it will come, not from a further tilling of the classical sources,[115] but from data extracted from statistical distributions of vessel-types and their sizes, along the lines pioneered by Röttlander and Polak.[116] Large quantities of material are required, and on military sites it would be helpful to have GIS distributions by period to match to the observed structures, in an attempt to determine who was using which vessels.[117] Some practical 'drinking bouts' might be a useful (and enjoyable) form of experimental archaeology. How easy is it to drink out of the vessels discussed above? Bringing together real people with replicas of the artefacts actually used in antiquity should surely be one of the primary objectives of archaeological investigation.

Acknowledgements

Many people have helped with this paper, and thanks are particularly due to Sally Grainger and Susan Weingarten for their encyclopaedic knowledge of Roman food, to Dr Allard Mees for some references to beer, and to Dr John Peter Wild, for checking my limited Greek and Latin. The new edition of Apicius by Christopher Grocock and Sally Grainger appeared during the course of preparing this paper, and their translations have been used, whereas other translations of Latin texts are based upon the Loeb editions. Any remaining errors are entirely of my own making. Finally, of course, thanks to Sheppard himself, who has kept alive my interest in samian in a historical context.

Notes

1. However, his predilection for identifying newly-excavated coins with the aid of a six-inch nail horrified even his closest admirers.
2. E.g. Bagendon (Hull 1961), Hawkes and Hull 1947, Canterbury (Bird 1995), Chichester/Fishbourne (Dannell 1971; 1978), Silchester (Bird 2000), Skeleton Green (Dannell 1981) and Wheathampstead (Wheeler and Wheeler 1936).
3. Corder and Davies Pryce 1939.
4. Dannell 1979.
5. Manley and Rudkin 2005.
6. See, most recently, Cunliffe 2004.
7. The background is well covered in Frere 1999, 29–48.
8. Most indisputably at Skeleton Green, cf. Hartley 1981 (I am greatly indebted to Kay Hartley for sending me a copy of her address, 'Keeping up with the Romans' which she gave during a day organised by the Yorkshire Archaeological Society [Roman Antiquities Section] and the Yorkshire Philosophical Society, in which she added Sheepen to known sealed deposits, and mentioned other typologically early *mortaria*, from Heybridge, North Ferriby and Stanwick).
9. Is it pushing speculation too far to see, in perhaps the most favoured Roman to British Iron-Age relationships, the possible despatch of Roman or Romanised chefs, as status-enhancing gifts? In the nineteenth century, many of the nobility employed French chefs for status, as for example Monsieur Grill, who served the Earls Fitzwilliam of Milton at the time of E. T. Artis and J. Clare, and who was the highest paid of the domestic staff.
10. Dannell 2003.
11. Cf. Tacitus, *Agricola*, 21.2 . . . *conviviorum elegantiam*: '. . . the well-appointed dinner-table'.
12. The drinking habits of the Gauls shocked Roman sensibilities: cf. Appian IV.7, describing the Gauls' excessive eating and drinking: 'the Gauls filled themselves to

repletion with wine and other luxuries, being intemperate by nature and inhabiting a country which yielded only cereals, and was unfruitful and destitute of other produce. Thus their bodies, being large and delicate and full of flabby flesh, grew, by reason of their excessive eating and drinking, heavy and corpulent, and quite incapable of running or hard labour; and when exertion was required of them, they speedily became exhausted by perspiration and shortness of breath'. Cf. also Diodorus Siculus V.26.3: 'the Gauls are exceedingly addicted to the use of wine and fill themselves with the wine which is brought into their country by merchants, drinking it unmixed, and since they partake of this drink without moderation by reason of their craving for it, when they are drunken, they fall into a stupour or a state of madness. Consequently, many of the Italian merchants, induced by the love of money which characterises them, believe that the love of wine of these Gauls is their own godsend. For these transport the wine on navigable rivers by means of boats and through the level plains on wagons, and receive for it an incredible price; for in exchange for a jar of wine they receive a slave, getting a servant in return for the drink'. Cf. also Martial, *Epigrammata* I.106.8–10: *crebros ergo licet bibas trientes et durum iugules mero dolorem*: 'well then, you may drink bumper after bumper and kill harsh pain with neat liquor'.

13. Cf. Woolf 1998, 169–205, for Gaul, which must surely apply also to the case of Britain.
14. Form is used in this paper to denote a distinctive shape.
15. For a good summary of sources, cf. Klynne 2002.
16. Wells 1978.
17. E.g. Ritterling 9, which had gone by *c.* AD 70, if not before.
18. E.g. Dragendorff form 24/5, which was produced at La Graufesenque from the Tiberian period through to at least *c.* AD 80 (the end-date given by the finds in the wreck of Cala Culip IV: cf. Dickinson and Hartley 1989), which contrasts sharply with experience in the northern provinces, where the form disappeared a decade earlier.
19. At Ostia, possibly as much as 20% (pers. comm. from Dr. Allard Mees; information from Archer Martin).
20. Dragendorff 1895, criticised in Polak 2002 (65–8) as not being a typology. This comment is rather pernickity, since manifestly Dragendorff established a distinction between the major shapes. What he did *not* do, and what Polak 2002 has dealt with splendidly, is the morphology of each shape, and the resultant possibility of increasing dating accuracy.
21. Déchelette 1904, Hermet 1934, Ludovici 1912 and Ritterling 1912 are the principal 'inventors' of additional samian forms.
22. Cf. Polak 2002.
23. Polak 2002, 65–137.
24. Cf. Polak 2002, 69, where he discusses the proportions of classes of vessels, which he has created arbitrarily. So, because they are not stamped, Dragendorff forms 35 and 35/6 do not appear in his list; and Dragendorff 29 and 37 are lumped together with other bowls, which are not likely to have had the same function.
25. Cf. Greene 1979 for a pioneering approach, and a forthcoming paper by Webster for *Antiquaries Journal* ('Some smaller moulded samian forms from La Graufesenque'). New approaches can be seen in Willis 2004; and cf. also Monteuil 2005: 'I hope to have shown that by recording diameters and analysing samian assemblages with more detail, a fascinating set of insights into the usage of cups, plates and dishes can emerge. That dining was complex is not a surprise, but it is possible to understand it better by implementing this kind of methodology. I do believe that we need to pay particular attention to the sizes of vessels and the context in which they were used'; I

am indebted to Dr. Monteil for letting me see her conclusions in advance of publication.

26. Cérès 1886; cf. Marichal 1988, 18–19 for similar ones, together with Johnston 1985, for a *graffito* from Arezzo.

27. Cf., in general, Marichal, Bémont and Vernhet 1991, and Lambert 2002, chapter 2, for additions and further elucidation of readings. Marichal 1988, and Bémont and Lambert 1991, list other sites from which similar *graffiti* have been found.

28. Marichal, Bémont and Lambert 1991, 67–102.

29. Hilgers 1969, 33–4; Marichal 1988, 83–4, 88 and 90.

30. Hilgers 1969, 91 and 238. The spellings used here and in references are: *acetabulum, acetabula; licuia, licuiae; paropsis, paropsides;* but the potters of La Graufesenque used the forms *acitabli* (Celtic) or *acitabla* (Latin) in their texts, and instead of *licuiae* wrote *licuias*. See especially Adams 2003, 687–724, who notes (at 701): 'this last (*-as*) ending is common in certain *a*-stem nouns at La Graufesenque (*pannas, licuias*) and is probably to be interpreted not as a Latin accusative plural but as the Celtic nominative plural'.

31. Cf. *Conspectus*, and Genin, Hoffman and Vernhet 2002, 45–104.

32. Dannell 2002, Table 4: *acetabula* 141,050, *licuiae* 85,500, *paropsides* 92,900, out of a total for the more complete *graffiti* of 456,128 vessels – so altogether some 70% of that output. By comparison, Polak 2002, 6.5, when assessing only the stamped vessels from Vechten, has 2,748 'cups' out of a total vessel population of 4797, a proportion of 57%. Clearly some allowance has to be made for the unstamped vessels not studied by Polak, but the difference is rather large.

33. Marichal 1988, 81–2, where he discusses the measurement of vessels (see also note 115). The stamp-list from the contents of 'The Fosse *Cirratus*' (Genin and Vernhet, in a forthcoming paper) shows a large range of vessel types satisfying the criteria of 'cup', 'dish' and 'platter', apparently from the same kiln-load, so that the scribes' descriptions cannot possible apply to single shapes.

34. But cf. Marichal 1988, 81, where *licuiae* are described as *bessales* (197 mm), and *trientales* (98 mm).

35. See Fig. 6.2.

36. Marichal 1988, 84.

37. *De Re Coquinaria* 8.7.12: *Porcellum Celsinianum: ornas, infundes pipere, ruta, cepa, satureia, sub cute suo et ova infundes per auriculam, et ex pipere, liquamine, vino modico in acetabulum temperas, et sumes*: 'Celsinian Piglet: dress the piglet. Insert (a mixture of) pepper, rue, onion, savory, under its skin and pour eggs into the ear cavity. Blend a sauce of pepper, *liquamen*, a little wine in a cup and serve it up'; also 8.7.17: *in porcello lactante: piperis unc. I, vini heminam, olei optimi acetabulum maius, liquaminis acetabulum, aceti acetabulum minus*: 'sauce for suckling pig: 1 oz. pepper, 1 pt. wine, a generous cup of best-quality oil, a cup of *liquamen*, a smaller cup of vinegar'.

38. *Origines* 20.4.12: . . . *acitabulum quasi acetaforum quod acetum ferat*: '*acitabulum* as *acetaforum* because it bears vinegar (*acetum*)'.

39. Seneca, *Epist.* 45.8: *sic ista sine noxa decipiunt, quomodo praestigiatorum acetabula et calculi, in quibus me fallacia ipsa delectat*: 'such quibbles are just as harmlessly deceptive as the juggler's cup and dice, in which it is the very trickery that pleases me'.

40. *NH* XVIII.245: *cum folia pauca in cacumine acetabuli modo germinent, tunc maxime serendas ficus*: 'when a few leaves are sprouting from the top, like a vinegar-cup, that indicates that it is the best time for planting fig-trees'; cf. also XXI.92: *ex omnibus his generibus urtica maxime noscitur acetabulis in flore purpuream lanuginem fundentibus, saepe altior binis cubitis*: 'of all these kinds the best known is the nettle, often taller than two cubits, the cups of which pour out a purple down'; XXVI.58: *radix . . . acetabulis cavernosa ceu*

polyporum cirri: 'root . . . indented with cups like a polypus' tentacles'; XXVIII.179: *ossa quoque ex ungulis suum combusta eundem usum praebent, item ossa ex acetabulis pernarum circa quae coxendices vertuntur*: 'the bones also of pigs-feet, when burnt, have the same effect, as have the bones from the sockets round which the hip bones move'; XXX.87–8: *comitialibus morbis oesypum cum murrae momento et vini cyathis duobus . . . lichen mulei potus in oxymelite cyathis tribus*: 'for epilepsy, wool-grease with a morsel of myrrh, diluted with two *cyathi* of wine . . .: the excrescence on the leg of a she-mule taken in three *cyathi* of oxymel'.

41. Hilgers 1969, 34; for uses, 91.
42. Marichal 1988, 88.
43. Hermet 1934, 312, note 9.
44. Cf. Dunbabin 1993, who deals very fully with this subject.
45. Hilgers 1969, 238–9; Marichal 1988, 90–1.
46. Dr Susan Weingarten has two suggestions here: for *aematini*, she suggests the use as a container for blood-garum (*haimation*), and for *bol*[she suggests the possibility of bulbs, rather than mushrooms; but see note 86.
47. Marichal 1988, 91.
48. Cf. Suetonius, *Galba* 12.3, for *parobsidem leguminis* ('vegetable dishes'), and the remarks below about dipping and the Passover service (see note 90).
49. Hilgers 1969, 238–9.
50. *Deipnosophistae* IX.367: 'and now you should answer the question, in which author the word *paropsis* is used of the well-known vessel? For I know that Plato, in *Festivals*, uses the word of a specially prepared mixed dish, or some spice of that sort, thus: 'Whereas we might have a barley cake and side-dishes' . . . And in the next lines he goes on to describe these 'side-dishes' [*paropsides*] as if he were speaking of a relish at the table . . . 'Frivolous dallyings are like side-dishes; their delight is brief, and quickly are they spent' . . . Antiphanes uses the word *paropsis* of the vessel in the *Boeotian Woman* . . .: 'he called out, and served [it] in a saucer'.
51. Polak 2002, 99–123.
52. Hartley and Dickinson, in a forthcoming paper. For those who have waited so long for this publication, it is gratifying to be able to record thanks to Dr R. W. Brock and Professor M. G. Fulford in obtaining the generous support of the British Academy, which will enable final editing to commence during 2006. The full project is expected to take four years, and will be led by Brenda Dickinson.
53. Also to be published by Genin and Venhet (note 33).
54. Some caution is needed, because this graph includes the mass of rejected vessels from the *Fosse Gallicanus*, which has an unusually large component of Dragendorff form 33.
55. Polak 2002, Figs 6.50a–6.53d. There is another difficulty, in that understandably some of the quantities strain statistical significance (note the conflation of forms Ritterling 8 and 9 in Fig. 45a).
56. Polak 2002, 105–13.
57. For the Apicius recipe, see note 37. Obsessed as the modern world is with exact measurements, one forgets too easily that most of our grandparents would have measured in 'handfuls' and 'pinches', with a similar degree of variability as here.
58. Polak 2002, Fig. 6.57.
59. Oswald and Pryce 1920, Pl. 48.5.
60. Unfortunately, the Leeds Index of Potters' Stamps (note 52) does not record vessel dimensions, other than sometimes to make a comment such as 'very large' or 'unusually small' (pers. comm. from the late B. R. Hartley).

61. Musée de la Civilisation Gallo-romaine, with the active help and support of M. Hugues Savay-Guerraz and his staff, to whom many thanks. Note that in Fig. 6.3, the cluster of smallest vessels mostly comprises Ritterling form 8 and Dragendorff form 24/5.

62. There are considerable difficulties in making such estimations. The illustrated vessels were scanned and brought to a common scale of 1:1; all measurements were taken with a steel ruler. The volumes were calculated using the formulae given by S. D. Filip, Department of Agriculture and Biological Engineering, Mississippi State University (Website: http://grapevine.abe.msstate.edu/~ fto/calculator/index.html).

63. Marichal 1988, *graffitto* nos 1, 2 etc.

64. Bémont and Jacob 1986.

65. But it did continue in both red- and black-slipped forms from Central Gaul: Symonds 1992, Fig. 7.

66. Principally large urban sites: see for example the stamp-lists for London and Verulamium (for publications, cf. note 52).

67. For rare examples of earlier vessels being larger than later varieties, cf. Polak 2002, Fig. 6.64; Oswald and Pryce 1920, Pl. 51; and Romeuf 2001, Pl. 33.

68. This is a subject worthy of research in itself; cf., generally, the dating of mythological figures in Déchelette 1904 and Oswald 1937, where the extent to which Gallic and vernacular elements overtake classical figures can be traced.

69. Roman society considered it barbaric to drink wine undiluted, and this may bear on the numerous passages in classical texts about Gaulish drunkenness, e.g. Ammianus Marcellinus XV.12.4: *vini avidum genus, affectans ad vini similitudinem multiplices potus, et inter eos humiles quidam, obtunsis ebrietate continua sensibus, quam furoris voluntariam speciem esse Catoniana sententia definivit, raptantur discursibus vagis, ut verum illud videatur quod ait defendens Fonteium Tullius: Gallos post haec dilutius esse poturos quod illi venenum esse arbitrabantur*: 'it is a race greedy for wine, devising numerous drinks similar to wine, and some amongst them of the baser sort, with wits dulled by continual drunkenness (which in Cato's saying produced a voluntary kind of madness) rush about in aimless revel, so that those words seem true which Cicero spoke when defending Fonteius: 'the Gauls henceforth will drink wine mixed with water, which they once thought poison'. The normal Greek custom followed by polite Roman society was to mix three parts of water to one part of wine (thus, a *triton*). However, this was certainly not absolute, even in the classical world, and one suspects that dilution, or not, was both a matter of taste, both for the individual, and dependent on the wine itself. Cf. however Dunbabin 1993, 128–9, for a contrary view.

70. Déchelette 1904, Figs 80–81 (effected with movable letter-type poinçons, pre-dating that 'invention', attributed to the Chinese, by some 900 years!).

71. Hofmann 1988, Pl. 53.402:]CERVESA R[. Cf. Nelson 2003 for beer in the classical world.

72. With, for example, honey. Ale or beer was little known or appreciated in the classical world, but it was used very generally by the surrounding nations, whose soil and climate were less favourable to the growth of vines: cf. Pliny *NH* XIV.149: *est et occidentis populis sua ebrietas fruge madida, pluribus modis per Gallias Hispaniasque, nominibus aliis sed ratione eadem*: 'the nations of the west also have their own intoxicant made from grain soaked in water; there are a number of ways of making it in the various provinces of Gaul and Spain, under different names, but on the same principle'; and Tacitus, *Germania* 23: *potui humor ex hordeo aut frumento, in quandam similitudinem vini corruptus: proximi ripae et vinum mercantur. Cibi simplices, agrestia poma, recens fera aut lac concretum: sine apparatu, sine blandimentis expellunt famem. Adversus sitim non*

eadem temperantia. Si indulseris ebrietati suggerendo quantum concupiscunt, haud minus facile vitiis quam armis vincentur: 'for drink they use the liquid distilled from barley or wheat, after fermentation has given it a certain resemblance to wine. The tribes nearest the river also buy wine. Their diet is simple: wild fruit, fresh game, curdled milk. They banish hunger without great preparation or appetizing sauces, but there is not the same temperance in facing thirst: if you humour their drunkenness by supplying as much as they crave, they will be vanquished through their vices as easily as on the battlefield'. Is it mischievous to see a folk memory in Belgian lambic beers to which fruit has been added?

73. Depôt de Fouilles, inventory nos G79, G86, G81 G68, G81 and I35 (with mask).
74. Cf. Mees 1995, Taf. 17, for another bowl from the same mould as that from Fishbourne (cf. Dannell 1971, Fig. 130).
75. Cf. Fig. 6.1a and 6.1b for the decorated vessels most frequently found.
76. Cf. Horace, *Satires* I.6.116–18: . . . *et lapis albus pocula cum cyatho duo sustinet; adstat echinus vilis, cum patera gutus, Campana supellex*: '. . . and a white stone slab supports two cups with a ladle. By them stand a cheap salt-cellar, a jug and saucer of Campanian ware'. Cf. also *Odes* III.8.13: *sume, Maecenas, cyathos amici sospitis centum et vigiles lucernas perfer in lucem: procul omnis esto clamor et ira*: 'so quaff a hundred ladles, Maecenas, in honour of your friend's escape, and keep the lamp burning until daylight. Away with all shouting and quarrelling'. See Fig. 6.2 for the volume of the *cyathus*.
77. Cf. Athenaeus X.423d: 'but I will show you that the word *cyathos* is in good use'.
78. Nor necessarily the makers of the *cyathi*; the table setting depicted in a painting from the Tomb of Vestorius Priscus at Pompeii (cf. Dunbabin 1993, Fig. 3) shows four *cyathi* of clearly differing sizes, so perhaps it should not be surprising that there is little conformity in the 'cups'.
79. Cf. Martial, *Epigrammata* IV.46.15–16: *septenaria synthesis Sagunti, Hispanae luteum rotae toreuma*: 'a seven-piece set of crockery glazed at Saguntum, the muddy shaping of a Spanish wheel'; and I.53.6: . . . *sic Arretinae violant crystallina testae*: '. . . so crocks from Arretium dishonour crystal glasses'; XIV.98: *Arretina nimis ne spernas vasa monemus: lautus erat Tuscis Porsena fictilibus*; XIV.102: *accipe non vili calices de pulvere natos, sed Surrentinae leve toreuma rotae*: 'accept cups not born of common clay but smooth shapings of a Surrentine wheel'; VIII.6.1–2: *archetypis vetuli nihil est odiosius Aucti – ficta Saguntino cymbia malo luto*: 'Nothing is so boring as old Euctus' originals – I had rather have cups shaped from Saguntine clay'.
80. The best were for the most part whites like the Falernian. Virgil, *Georgics* II.408–09, for example, enjoins: *primus humum fodito, primus devecta cremato sarmenta, et vallos primus sub tecta referto; postremus metito* ('be the first to dig the ground, first to bear away and fire the prunings, first to carry the poles under cover; be the last to reap'), and the results must have satisfied a fairly sweet palate. Cf. also Athenaeus I.27c: 'the wine of Marseilles is good; but it is uncommon, rich, and full-bodied. The wine of Tarentum, and in fact all the wines of that latitude are soft, having no violent effect, and no strength. They are sweet and wholesome'. The author has a modern, unfortified red in his cellar, made at Jalon (*Carthaginensis*), with an alcohol content of 16%, which may be representative.
81. Cf. Dunbabin 1993, where illustrations of wine-drinking vessels and associated apparatus, taken from mosaics and wall-paintings, emphasise the importance of wine to the dining ritual.
82. Cf. Martial, *Epigrammata* XI.36.7–8, and his reference to the practice of toasting personal names 'by the measure': *quincunces et sex cyathos bessemque bibamus, 'Gaius' ut fiat*

'Iulius' et 'Proculus': 'let us drink five measures and six and eight to make up 'Gaius' and 'Julius' and 'Proculus'; and VIII.50(51).21: *det numerum cyathis Istanti littera Rufi*: 'let the letters of Istantius Rufus' name supply a number for our measures'. Cf. also Horace, *Satires* II.6.67–70: *prout cuique libido est, siccat inaequalis calices conviva, solutus legibus insanis, seu quis capit acria fortis pocula, seu modicis uvescit laetius*: 'each guest, as is his fancy, drains cups big or small, not bound by crazy laws, whether one can stand strong bumpers in gallant style, or with mild cups mellows more to his liking'. Also relevant is Petronius, *Satyricon*, and those meals discussed by Athenaeus of Naucratis in the *Deipnosophistae*. The reality of provincial dining, and that of the army in the western provinces, is more apposite to the use of samian vessels. However, as will be seen, well-heeled provincial households, and perhaps the officers' mess, kept up traditions and standards (cf. Tacitus, *Agricola* 21 [n. 11], talking of his father-in-law's encouragement to the British).

83. Davies 1971 for references to the wines consumed.

84. E.g. Bowman 1994, *Tab. Vindol.* ii.194. That the practice continued into the second and third centuries can be seen from the production of *calices* at Rheinzabern (Oswald and Pryce 1920, Pl. LXXX) and even in samian imitations made in Britain (Dannell 1973, Fig. 1.3). The vessels on *Tab. Vindol.* 194 are interesting, and since a number of the names are consonant with those on the *graffiti*, one wonders if it is just possible, in the context of Vindolanda, that some samian is described there?

85. Knorr and Sprater 1927, where a *graffito* mentions *paropsides*, with the adjective *golla[ti* (?=*colatæ*), which would imply some sort of strainer, although it is hard to see which form of those made at Blickweiler might be appropriate (cf. Taf. 101).

86. Cf. Grocock and Grainger 2006, 373–87.

87. Athenaeus IV.132: 'For the cook sets before you a large tray [*pinax*] on which are five small plates [*pinakiskoi*]. One of these holds garlic, another a pair of sea-urchins, another a sweet wine sop, another ten cockles, the last a small piece of sturgeon'; cf. Martial, *Epigrammata* XI.31.13–19: *. . . boletos imitatur et botellos, et caudam cybii brevesque maenas. Hinc cellarius experitur artes, ut condat vario vafer sapore in rutae folium Capelliana. Sic inplet gabatas paropsidesque, et leves scutulas cavasque lances:* 'he imitates mushrooms and sausages and a tunny's tail and little sprats. With them the confectioner tries out his skills, a master of complex flavours, to stuff Capelliana into a rue leaf. So he fills side-dishes and platters and polished saucers and hollow plates'; and, XIV.101: *boletaria. cum mihi boleti dederint tam nobile nomen prototomis – pudet heu! – servio coliculis*: 'although mushrooms gave me so noble a name, I cater (I am deeply ashamed to say) to early sprouts'; cf. also Athenaeus IX.366: 'in fact no sooner were some hams served to us . . . And who has called *napy* (mustard) *sinapy*? For I see that it is served in side-dishes [*paropsides*] along with the hams . . . Of the relishes that come from the sea we always have one, and that day in and day out I mean salt . . . With that to season it we manage to drink our poor wine – a speciality. Why it's the kind of thing that is expedient for the entire company to drink from the cruet, like a cup. And I see *garum* sauce beaten up with a mixture of vinegar. I know that in our day, some inhabitants of Pontus prepare a special kind which is called vinegar-*garum* . . . And Pherecrates in *Good-for Nothings* ... 'to make chick-peas tender on the spot''. This is in a [jokey] section on philology relating to the meaning of the word for mustard, and clearly indicates the story of sauces served in *paropsides* to accompany food, rather than be poured over it in advance. The mention of vinegar-*garum* is relevant to the remarkable list of silverware given in the Berlin Papyrus 8935 (cf. Oliver and Shelton 1979), which mentions various vinegar bowls; as the editors point out, they were also used for *garum*. *Oxybaphon*

(Greek) was the equivalent of *acetabulum* (Latin). Sally Grainger has provided the basis for the following: 'Fish sauce was fundamental to Roman cuisine and was used in the kitchen as we use salt to flavour food at the cooking stage. At some stage, a taste for a richer sauce was developed and it was made with blood, i.e. intestines, freshly drained in liquid form taken from the carcass, and fermented in the same way with salt. This is the Latin *garum*. It was used to finish off food at the table and also to make some of the *oenogarum* sauces for the table. This blood *garum* is the high-status sauce of satire and gourmet references and was invented by the Romans. The Greek fish sauce, made from anchovy or pieces of fish, continued to be called *garon*, and when this sauce was used in cooking in a Roman context it was renamed *liquamen* for the purpose of clarity. It was probably for marketing reasons that the Latinised *garum* was used for the more high-status product'.

88. Cf. Petronius, *Satyricon* 34: *ceterum inter tumultum cum forte paropsis excidisset et puer iacentem sustulisset, animadvertit Trimalchio, colaphisque obiurgari puerum ac proicere rursus pararopsidem iussit*: 'an entrée dish happened to fall in the rush, and a boy picked it up from the ground. Trimalchio saw him and directed that he should be punished by a box on the ear, and made to throw the dish down again'.

89. Cf. *Gospel according to St John*, Chapter 13, and *Gospel according to St Matthew* 4.26.23, both written in Greek. The dish described is the *tryblion*, which is translated both as an *acetabulum* and a *paropsis* in Latin versions of the New Testament. Epiphanius of Salamis in his *De mensuribus et ponderibus* gives the size of a *tryblion* as the equivalent of ½ *xeste*; of 2 *librae* of oil in Alexandria; of 8 *librae* in Pontus; of 22 *unciae* in Italy; of 20 *unciae* in Nicomedia, and 24 *unciae* in the *xestes castrensis*. The *xestes* is equivalent to the *sextarius* (see Fig. 6.2), and thus should be the same as a *hemina*, c. 273 cl. The *uncia* is a measure of dry weight, but is equal to ½ *sextans*, equivalent to a *cyathus*, so on this basis is c. 45.55 cl. There are clearly regional differences in the sizes associated with this dish.

90. It is difficult to reconcile this act with the *Seder* (Passover) service, since the two 'dippings' referred to in the question would have been have been communal events, and there is no point at which Judas alone should have been handed an individual portion.

91. This is third question that the youngest male present asks of the host at the traditional Passover meal (Seder). There are four questions, which went through various transformations as the service developed, until it came to its current formulation. King Josiah rediscovered 'The Book of Law', c. 622 BC, and ordered that the Passover be celebrated on an unprecedented scale (2 *Chronicles* 35). The modern order of service took its current shape at the time of the last days of the Second Temple, and it was in the century following that the now-traditional formulae were established in a Romanised context. The essential observances were set out in the Mishnah, redacted by Judah HaNasi (Judah the Prince, who lived AD 135–219).

92. Stein 1947, 8.

93. Goldschmidt 1947, who notes that the service contains four classical dining elements: 1. A ritual washing of hands; 2. An *hors d'oeuvres*; 3. Wine drunk before, during and after the meal; 4. The celebrants recline at the meal, emulating Graeco-Roman habit (a reference to the freedom from slavery associated with the Exodus from Egypt). Cf. Tabory 1999, who suggests that the earliest service comprised five elements, on the basis of the final chapter of *Tractate Pesachim*: 1. Recital of the blessing for the day and the first cup of wine was drunk; 2. The reception of bread, lettuce [to be dipped in] a fruit purée, and the paschal lamb; 3. The second cup of wine was taken, and followed

by the exposition of the passage 'My father was a wandering Aramaean . . .'; 4. The third cup of wine was taken before the recitation of Grace after Meals; 5. The fourth cup of wine was taken and the great hymn of praise, 'The Hallel,' was sung.

94. Cf. Martial, *Epigrammata* XI.52.5: *prima tibi dabitur ventri lactuca movendo utilis* ('first you'll be given lettuce (a good aperient)'). The Talmudic evidence is as follows: Mishnah Pesahim (ii.6) asks: 'with what vegetables can a person fulfil his obligations on Passover?' The Mishnah answers itself: 'With lettuce, chicory, tamkha, harhabina and bitter herb. The obligation is fulfilled if they are fresh or dry, but not pickled or soaked/cooked or cooked/boiled . . .' These are the vegetables to be dipped as in the Roman *hors d'oeuvres*. I am greatly indebted to Dr Susan Weingarten for this reference (cf. also Weingarten 2006, where she expands on the subject of chicory, and notes 'Greek names are given in the Jerusalem Talmud Kilayim (i) to help identify them, and by the way inform us that they are eaten raw: *entubin* from the Greek *entubon*, wild chicory or endive, is mentioned and identified by the Hebrew for chicory, *olshin*. *Olshin*, the JT continues, is also known as *troximon*, from the Greek general word for vegetables eaten raw . . .'. Cf. also note 93.

95. Cf. Apicius I.31.11 for condiment sauce; I.3.5 for citron sauce; and cf. Vinidarius, *Apici excerpta a Vinidario viri inlustri* for sweet cumin dressing for cold fish (X.6); onion dressing for cold sardines (IX); dressing for cold sardines (XI); cf. Columella XII.59, for purées.

96. Note the detail shown from the 'Mosaic of the House of the Buffet Supper' (Cimak 2000, 112), showing egg-cups ('little endians'!), finger bowls, the saucière, artichokes and pigs' trotters, and cf. Levi 1947, 134, who is quite definite about the sauce-dish, and followed by most commentators. At La Graufesenque (Marichal 1988, no. 165), there is the mention of *ouati*, and he suggests this was an ovoid shape. The writing is absolutely clear, but is there a possibility that what was meant were *ouaria*, as very small, cup-shaped vessels like egg-cups?

97. Cf. Biddulph 2005 for work concerning wear to samian vessels. He has an academic article in preparation (pers. comm.), where he discusses food preparation, and touches on the possibility of mixing spices and sauces in samian 'cups'.

98. Hawkes and Hull 1947, 187.

99. Cf. Dunbabin 1991.

100. The records from Vindolanda (Bowman 1994; *Tab. Vindol.* ii.190 (see note 109). These records indicate the extent of provisions for the formal *cenae* at which one might expect the full range of the samian services to have been used at table. For a discussion of celebratory meals themselves, cf. Donahue 2005.

101. Cf. Ovid, *Ars Amatoria* III.755: *carpe cibos digitis: est quiddam gestus edendi. Ora nec immunda tota perungue manu*: 'help yourself with your fingers: manners in eating count for something; and smear not all your face with a soiled hand'; cf. Martial, *Epigrammata* V.78.4–8: *viles Cappadocae gravesque porri, divisis cybium latebit ovis. Ponetur digitis tenendus ustis nigra coliculus virens patella, algentem modo qui reliquit hortum*: 'Cappadocian lettuces and smelly leeks, chopped tunny will lurk in halves of egg. A green cabbage-sprout fresh from the chilly garden will be served on a black plate for your oily fingers to handle'.

102. After Vernhet 1976.

103. Here, perhaps, used both as the symbol of Bacchus and/or death.

104. There are many examples: cf. Dannell and Hartley 1978, figs 39 and 40; Haalebos 1990, figs 49 and 54.

105. Part of the putative 'Flavian revolution': cf. Dannell, Dickinson and Vernhet 1998, 70

for other changes in forms, styles and organizational details around this time.

106. Swan 1992.
107. Cf. Dannell 1979, 177–84. Note too the continuing imitations of samian vessels (but not 'cups') at colour-coated kiln sites, well into the fourth century (cf. Symonds 1992 for a wide range of beakers, including the cylindrical forms, similar to Dragendorff form 30). Metallic slip-coated bulbous beakers decorated with vine-leaves or ivy leaves are less often copied in Britain: cf. Perrin 1999, figs 47.181, 60.141–50, and for a similarly-decorated jug, fig. 62.197, from the Nene Valley (and cf. Young 1977, fig. 55.27.1-3).
108. Cf. Hartley and Perrin 1999.
109. Cf. Fleming 2001, 13–20, and cf. Schallmayer 1992, who discusses the possibility of locally-produced amphorae being used to store beer; cf. also Künzl 1991 for a notable beer mug.
110. Cf. the references to beer from Vindolanda (Bowman 1994; *Tab. Vindol.* ii.190), particularly those which seem to be related to a celebratory meal (note 59); and cf. also *Tab. Vindol.* ii.182 for a brewer, Atrectus, with connections to the unit. Beer was clearly a *sine qua non*, to judge from Masclus' demands on behalf of his Batavians (*Tab. Vindol.* 1544).
111. However recent archaeological investigations in Northamptonshire have uncovered evidence to suggest that vineyards were established on a commercial scale during the Roman occupation: initial surveys at a 35-hectare Romano-British site at Wollaston in the Nene Valley (near Wellingborough) has revealed deposits of grape-vine pollen dating from this time (cf. Brown *et. al.* 2001).
112. Cf. Dragendorff form 37, which has been noted as having specific reference to wine consumption (see notes 70 and 71 above); it also had its imitations long after samian ceased to be available (cf. Young 1977, fig. 28.P30.1, for a fourth-century parchment-ware vessel, which seems to echo distant memories of decoration in zones).
113. Cf. Fleming 2001 for grape varieties and the wines made from them.
114. Stuart 1977, figs 3–35. In these earlier deposits, the contrast with the samian vessel-types recorded by Haalebos (note 103) is striking. Dragendorff form 35 and its associated forms are obviously missing from the production range. The deposit is dominated by platters and dishes: Dragendorff forms 24/5 and 27 and Ritterling forms 8 and 9. This suggests at least some of these cup-shaped vessels were serving the same function as Dragendorff form 35. The *Conspectus* has a plethora of forms, which might fit as *paropsides*. From La Graufesenque the claims of Dragendorff form 22 and small versions of Ritterling form 1 might also be advanced.
115. Prayers are offered weekly for a 'lucky strike' at Vindolanda!
116. Röttlander 1966 and Röttlander 1968 deal with important issues of standardisation. His vessel populations were too small to have the significance of those of Polak (2002), but his papers are too often overlooked. His remarks in the 1966 paper on the use of Roman standards of linear measurement predate the references quoted in Marichal 1988 (92–3), and, when combined with those on shrinkage, should be followed up more closely.
117. Robin Birley (to whom many thanks) observes that at Vindolanda he feels that the samian found in the area of the *praetorium*, and that from centurions' quarters, differs qualitatively from that found generally among the barracks.

References

Adams, J. N. 2003: *Bilingualism and the Latin language*, Cambridge

Bémont, C. and Jacob, J.-P. (eds) 1986: *La terre sigillée gallo-romaine. Lieux de production du Haut-Empire: implantations, produits, relations* [Documents d'Archéologie Française 6], Paris

Bémont, C. and Vernhet, A. 1991: 'Un nouveau compte de potiers de la Graufesenque portant mention de flamines', *Annales de Pegasus* 1990–91, 12–14

Biddulph, E. 2005: 'Samian wear', *Current Archaeology* 196, 191–3

Bird, J. 1995: 'The samian and other imported red-slipped finewares', in Blockley *et al.* 1995, 772–5 and 777–80

Bird, J. (ed.) 1998: *Form and fabric: studies in Rome's material past in honour of B. R. Hartley*, Oxford

Bird, J. 2000: 'The sigillata summary, and catalogue of decorated samian', in Fulford and Timby 2000, 183–7

Blockley, K., Blockley, M., Blockley, P., Frere, S. S. and Stowe, S. 1995: *Excavations in the Marlowe Car Park and surrounding areas. Part 2: The finds* [Archaeology of Canterbury 5], Canterbury

Bowman, A. K. 1994: *Life and letters on the Roman frontier*, London

Bradshaw, P. F. and Hoffman, L. A. (eds) 1999: *Passover and Easter: origin and history to modern times* [Two Liturgical Traditions 5], Notre Dame

Brown, A. G., Meadows, I., Turner, S. D. and Mattingly, D. J. 2001: 'Roman vineyards in Britain: stratigraphic and palynological data from Wollaston in the Nene Valley, England', *Antiquity* 75, 745–57

Burnham, B. C. and Johnson, B. J. (eds) 1979: *Invasion and response: the case of Roman Britain* [BAR British Series 73], Oxford

Cérès (Abbé) 1886: 'Fouilles à La Graufesenque et graffites', *Mémoires de la Société des Lettres, Sciences et Arts de l'Aveyron* 12, 198–203

Cimak, F. 2000: *A corpus of Antioch mosaics*, Istanbul

Clifford, E. M. 1961: *Bagendon, a Belgic oppidum: excavations 1954–1956*, Cambridge

Collis, J. 1978: *Winchester Excavations Volume 2: 1949–1960*, Winchester

Corder, P. and Davies Pryce, T. 1939: 'Note on an Arretine plate from North Ferriby, Yorkshire', *Antiquaries Journal* 19, 207

Cunliffe, B., 1971: *Excavations at Fishbourne, 1: The site* [Research Reports of the Society of Antiquaries 26], London

Cunliffe, B. 2004: 'Britain and the Continent: networks of interaction', in Todd 2004, 1–11

Dannell, G. B. 1971: 'The samian pottery', in Cunliffe 1971, 260–318

Dannell, G. B. 1973: 'The potter Indixivixus', in Detsicas 1973, 139–42

Dannell, G. B. 1978: 'The samian pottery', in Down 1978, 225–33

Dannell, G. B. 1979: 'Eating and drinking in pre-conquest Britain: the evidence of amphora and samian trading, and the effect of the invasion of Claudius', in Burnham and Johnson 1979, 177–86

Dannell, G. B. 1981: 'The Italian and Gaulish samian', in Partridge 1981, 152–4

Dannell, G. B. 2002: 'Law and practice: further thoughts on the organization of the potteries at La Graufesenque', in Genin and Vernhet 2002, 211–42

Dannell, G. B. 2003: 'Early decorated samian from London reassessed', in Wilson 2003, 54–8

Dannell, G. B., Dickinson, B. M. and Vernhet, A. 1998: 'Ovolos on Dragendorff form 30 from the collections of Frédéric Hermet and Dieudonné Rey', in Bird 1998, 69–109

Dannell, G. B. and Hartley, B. R. 1978: 'The samian', in Collis 1978, 98–102

Davies, R. W. 1971: 'The Roman military diet', *Britannia* 2, 122–42

174 *Geoffrey B. Dannell*

Déchelette, J. 1904: *Les vases céramiques ornés de la Gaule romaine*, Paris

Detsicas, A. (ed.) 1973: *Current research in Romano-British coarse pottery* [CBA Research Report 10], London

Dickinson, B. M. and Hartley, B. R. 1989: 'The evidence for the date of the potters' stamps from Culip IV', in Nieto et al. 1989, 21–32

Donahue, J. F. 2005: 'Towards a typology of Roman public feasting', in Gold and Donahue 2005, 95–114

Down, A. 1978: *Chichester Excavations 3*, Chichester

Dragendorff, H. 1895: 'Terra sigillata', *Bonner Jahrbücher* 96–7, 18–155

Dunbabin, K. M. D. 1991: '*Triclinium* and *stibadium*', in Slater 1991, 121–48

Dunbabin, K. M. D. 1993: 'Wine and water at the Roman *convivium*', *JRA* 6, 116–41

Ettlinger, E. *et al.* 1990: *Conspectus formarum terrae sigillatae Italico modo confectae* [Römisch-Germanische Kommission des Deutschen Archäologischen Instituts zu Frankfurt a.M.], Bonn

Fleming, S. J. 2001: *Vinum: the story of Roman wine*, Glen Mills

Frere, S. S. 1999: *Britannia*, fourth edition, London

Fulford, M. and Timby, J. 2000: *Late Iron Age and Roman Silchester: excavations on the site of the Forum-Basilica 1977, 1980–86* [*Britannia* Monograph 15], London

Genin, M., Hoffman, B. and Vernhet, A. 2002: 'Les productions anciennes de La Graufesenque', in Genin and Vernhet 2002, 45–104

Genin, M. and Vernhet, A. (eds) 2002: *Céramiques de La Graufesenque et autres productions d'époque romaine: nouvelles recherches*, Montagnac

Gold, B. K. and Donahue, J. E. (eds) 2005: *Roman dining*, Baltimore

Goldschnidt, D. 1947: *Seder Haggadah Shel Pesach*, Jerusalem

Greene, K. 1979: *The pre-Flavian fine wares* [Report on the Excavations at Usk, 1965–1976], Cardiff

Grocock, C. and Grainger, S. 2006: *Apicius: a critical edition with an introduction and English translation*, Totnes

Haalebos, J. K. 1990: *Het gravfeld van Nijmegen-Hatert: Eenbegraafplaats uit de eerste drie eeuwen na. Chr. Op het plaatland bij Noviomagus Batavorum* [Beschrijving van de verzamelingen in het Provincial Museum G. M. Kam te Nijmegen 11], Nijmegen

Hartley, K. 1981: 'The mortaria', in Partridge 1981, 196–9

Hartley, K. F. and Perrin, J. R. 1999: 'Mortaria', in Perrin 1999, 129–35

Hawkes, C. F. C. and Hull, M. R. 1947: *Camulodunum* [Research Reports of the Society of Antiquaries 14], Oxford

Hermet, F. 1934: *La Graufesenque*, Paris

Hilgers, W. 1969: *Lateinische Gefässename: Bezeichnungen, Funktion und Form römischer Gefässe nach den antiken Schriftquellen* [Beihefte der *Bonner Jahrbücher* 31], Düsseldorf

Hofmann, B. 1988: *L'Atelier de Banassac* [*Revue Archéologique*, Sites, Hors-série 33], Gonfaron

Hull, M. R. 1961: 'The red-glazed pottery found at Bagendon', in Clifford 1961, 202–11

Johnston, A. 1985: 'A Greek graffito from Arezzo', *Oxford Journal of Archaeology* 14, 119–24

Klynne, A. 2002: *Terra sigillata from the Villa of Livia, Rome: consumption and discard in the early Principate*, Uppsala

Knorr, R. and Sprater, F. 1927: *Die westpfälzischen Sigillata-Töpfereien von Blickweiler und Eschweiler Hof*, Speyer-am-Rhein

Künzl, S. 1991: 'Ein Biergefäss aus Mainz: Barbotinedekorierte Terra Sigillata mit Inschriften', *Mainzer Zeitschrift* 86, 171–85

Lambert, P.-Y. 2002: *Receuil des inscriptions gauloises: textes Gallo-Latins sur Instrumentum. Vol. 2, Fasc. 2* [*Gallia*, Supplément 45], Paris

Laubenheimer, F. (ed.) 1992: *Les amphores en Gaule. Production et circulation* [Centre de Recherches d'Histoire Ancienne, 116]

Levy, D. 1947: *Antioch mosaic pavements*, Princeton

Ludovici, W. 1912: *Römische Ziegel-Graber in Rheinzabern* [Katalog 4], Munich

Manley, J. and Rudkin, D. 2005: 'A pre-A.D. 43 ditch at Fishbourne Roman Palace, Chichester', *Britannia* 36, 55–99

Marichal, R. 1988: *Les graffites de La Graufesenque* [*Gallia*, Supplément 47], Paris

Mees, A. M. 1995: *Modelsignierte Dekorationen auf südgallischer Terra Sigillata*, Stuttgart

Monteil, G. 2005: *Samian ware in Roman London* [unpublished PhD thesis, University of London]

Nelson, M. 2003: 'The cultural construction of beer among Greeks and Romans', *Syllecta Classica* 14, 101–20

Nieto, X. and Puig, A.-M. 1989: *Culip IV: la Terra Sigillata decorada de La Graufesenque* [Excavaciones Arqueològiques Subaquàtiques a Cala Culip 3], Girona

Oliver, A. and Shelton, J.: 'Silver on papyrus', *Archaeology* 32, 22–8

Oswald, F. and Pryce, T. D. 1920: *An introduction to the study of Terra Sigillata*, London

Oswald, F. 1937: *Index of figure-types on Terra Sigillata ('Samian Ware')*, Liverpool

Partridge, C. 1981: *Skeleton Green: a Late Iron Age and Romano-British site* [*Britannia* Monograph 2], London

Perrin, J. R. 1999: *Roman Pottery from excavations at and near to the Roman Small Town of Durobrivae, Water Newton, Cambridgeshire, 1956–58* [Journal of Roman Pottery Studies 8], Oxford

Polak, M. 2002: *South Gaulish Terra Sigillata with potters' stamps from Vechten* [Rei Cretariæ Romanæ Fautorum Acta, Supplementum 9], Nijmegen

Ritterling, E. 1912: *Das frührömische Lager bei Hofheim im Taunus* [Annalen des Vereins für Nassauische Altertumskunde und Geschichtsforschung 40], Wiesbaden

Romeuf, A.-M. 2001: *Le quartier artisanal Gallo-Romain des Martres-de-Veyre* [*Revue Archéologique* Sites, Hors-série 41], Lezoux

Röttlander, B. C. A. 1966: 'Is provincial Roman pottery standardised?', *Archaeometry* 9, 76–91

Röttlander, B. C. A. 1968: 'Standardization of Roman provincial pottery, 3: the average shrinking rate and the bills of La Graufesenque', *Archaeometry* 11, 76–91

Schallmayer, E. 1992: 'Production d'amphores en Germanie Supérieure', in Laubenheimer 1992, 179–83

Slater, W. J. (ed.) 1991: *Dining in a classical context*, Ann Arbor

Stein, S. 1947: 'The influence of symposia literature on the literary form of the Pesach Haggadah', *Journal of Jewish Studies* 8, 13–44

Stuart, P. 1977: *Een Romeins grafveld uit de eerste eeuw te Nijmegen: Onversierde terra sigillata en gewoon aardewerk* [Beschrijving van de verzamelingen in het Provincial Museum G. M. Kam te Nijmegen 8], Nijmegen

Swan, V. G. 1992: '*Legio VI* and its men: African legionaries in Britain', *Journal of Roman Pottery Studies* 5, 1–34

Symonds, R. P. 1992: *Rhenish wares: fine dark coloured pottery from Gaul and Germany* [Oxford University Committee for Archaeology Monograph 23], Oxford

Tabory, J. 1999: 'Towards a history of the Paschal meal', in Bradshaw and Hoffmann 1999, 62–80

Todd, M. (ed.) 2004: *A companion to Roman Britain*, Oxford

Vernhet, A. 1976: 'Création flavienne de six services de vaisselle à la Graufesenque', *Figlina* 1, 13–27

Wells, C. M. 1978: 'L'implantation des ateliers de céramique sigillée en Gaule. Problématique de la recherche', *Figlina* 3, 1–11

Weingarten, S. 2006: 'Wild foods in the Talmud: the influence of religious restriction on consumption', in *Wild foods: proceedings of the Oxford Symposium on food and cookery, 2004*, Totnes, 324–5

Wheeler, R. E. M. and Wheeler, T. V. 1936: *Verulamium: a Belgic and two Roman Cities* [Research Reports of the Society of Antiquaries 11], Oxford

Willis, S. 2004: *Samian pottery, a resource for the study of Roman Britain and beyond: the results of the English Heritage funded Samian Project. An e-monograph* [Supplement to *Internet Archaeology* 17]: http://intarch.ac.uk/journal/issue17/willis_index.html

Wilson, P. (ed.) 2003: *The archaeology of Roman towns: studies in honour of John S. Wacher*, Oxford

Woolf, G. 1998: *Becoming Roman: the origins of provincial civilization in Gaul*, Cambridge

Young, C. J. 1977: *The Roman pottery industry of the Oxford Region* [BAR British Series 43], Oxford

Chapter 7

AN ANONYMOUS TRAVELLER
ON THE ANTONINE WALL IN 1697

Lawrence Keppie

Sheppard Frere has been my mentor throughout my academic career, from the time when as my tutor in the Institute of Archaeology, Oxford, he encouraged me to work-up a short paper for inclusion in an early volume of **Britannia**, *of which he was then Editor. The present paper is offered as a tribute to Sheppard on his 90th birthday, in the hope that it may appeal to his love of detective thrillers. Here certainly is a puzzle, a number of suspects, and a dénouement. There is also a strong Oxford connection.*

Introduction

In July 1697, an unnamed gentleman rode on horseback from Edinburgh westwards along the line of the Antonine Wall. A much later manuscript copy of his account of the first part of that journey survives in the British Library, London.[1] The document, a seven-page letter, came into the public domain in 1893, on the publication of manuscripts then in the collection of the 6th Duke of Portland at Welbeck Abbey, Nottinghamshire.[2] There is no addressee given.

The letter, as we have it now, was known to the authors of reports on early excavations of Roman fort-sites undertaken by the Society of Antiquaries of Scotland, on and adjacent to the Antonine Wall at Camelon,[3] Castlecary[4] and Rough Castle,[5] and was deployed by Dr (later Sir) George Macdonald in his *Roman Wall in Scotland* (1911 and 1934).[6] Thereafter it has received scant attention. This paper re-publishes the manuscript, now held by the British Library, and aims to place the traveller's visit in a historical and cultural context, to comment on the information he imparts about the Wall at a fixed date, and to consider his identity.

The antiquarian context

The period following the 'Glorious Revolution' of 1688–89 saw a flourishing of British interest in classical antiquities.[7] The aristocracy began to see the Romans as their natural predecessors and, with increased opportunities of travel abroad, were able to place Roman Britain in its wider European context. The decade witnessed the publication in 1695 of a much revised edition,[8] in English, of William Camden's hugely influential *Britannia*, originally published in 1586,[9] but with successive enlargements by its author. The editor of the 1695 edition was the young Edmund Gibson, newly graduated from Queen's College, Oxford, soon to be librarian to the Archibishop of Canterbury at Lambeth Palace, afterwards Bishop of Lincoln, and then of London.[10] Gibson sought the help of many respected antiquaries, for example Edward Lhwyd for Wales, Sir Robert Sibbald for Scotland, Archdeacon Nicolson of Carlisle for Cumbria, Thomas Tanner of Queen's College, Oxford, for Wiltshire, and others, listed in his 'Preface to the Reader'.[11] The publication of Gibson's edition sparked off antiquarian activity in many parts of Britain.[12]

There was a flurry of activity on the Antonine Wall (Fig. 7.1), which was visited by two Oxford-based scholars: John Urry, Student (i.e. Fellow) of Christ Church,[13] and Edward Lhwyd, Keeper of the Ashmolean Museum,[14] who had received from Sir Robert Sibbald, in advance of his visit in December 1699, 'Directions how to trace and remarke the vestiges of the Roman wall betwixt Forth and Clyde'.[15] Within Scotland the polymathic Sibbald, 'Geographer for the Kingdom of Scotland', President of the Edinburgh Royal College of Physicians from 1684, and Professor of Medicine at Edinburgh from 1685, was the doyen of antiquarian studies.[16] The cartographer John Adair, at times working in association with Sibbald, may have been the first to seek out and record stones along the Wall in this decade; his drawings of them were much praised and widely copied.[17]

At Glasgow University (more usually at this time known as Glasgow College), the Principal, William Dunlop, a collector of ancient coins,[18] who had recently argued for a Roman fort in his home town, nearby Paisley,[19] provided, it may be suspected, the stimulus for the acquisition by the College in 1694–1700 of several inscribed and sculptured stones from the line of the Antonine Wall.[20] They came under the care of Robert Wodrow, youthful Librarian of the College (1698–1703), and later an eminent historian of the Church of Scotland, who maintained a vigorous correspondence with established scholars and with fellow Glasgow graduates of antiquarian bent.[21] For archaeological information Wodrow relied on the learning and knowledge of William Nicolson, Archdeacon and later Bishop of Carlisle, who in 1699 made a 'ramble into Scotland,' visiting both Glasgow and Edinburgh during preparation of a bibliographical *magnum opus*, *The Scottish Historical Library*.[22] This was a period when there was among antiquaries still an emphasis on the recording of inscribed texts, but there were the beginnings too of an awareness of the standing remains.

The text[23]

"I Send you, not knowing when I may have the Good fortune to see you, an account of a Progress I made in July last ye 20th, Anno 1697. I left Edingborough and came to the S. side of the Queens Ferry: this is a pretty village, just upon the side of a Bank. The Streets are all Substantial Stone, and the Tide comes up to the very houses in high Spring Tides. On the 21 [July] I rode at length by the River Forth Side, designing to trace the Roman Wall which runs

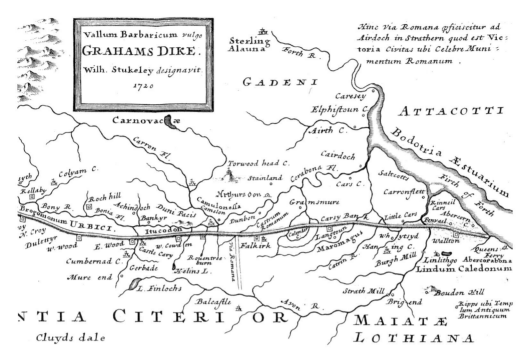

Fig. 7.1 Detail from the map of the Antonine Wall, drawn by William Stukeley (An Account of a Roman Temple, 1720), showing central Scotland between Kilsyth and Queensferry

between Forth and Clyd, our two most considerable Rivers, like your Thames and Severne. Near to the Queens Ferry are Several Quarrys of very fine white Free Stone just upon the Shore, so that they [are] easily transportable. A little farther West of these were some people at work upon the Side of a Bank for an Alum stone, intending there to set up an Alum Work about Abercorn, which is an Old ruin'd Square Tower Castle.[24] The[y] were emparking a great parcel of Ground with a handsome Wall having stone and Lime in great plenty thereabouts. Here the shore is paved with broken Cockle and muscle Shells for a great way together, and to a Considerable depth, the best of these kinds of Fish being taken hereabouts. You leave the house that belong'd to old Generall Dalzel, now his son S[i]r Thomases.[25] It stands on a riseing ground in a good Soyle good Gardens about it, and much planting; tis farenough from the River [not] to be annoy'd with the Steams and Fogs that rise thence, and near enough to have a full prospect of it for Several Miles. Not far from this is Blackness, a Fortress upon the very Brink of the River Standing on a Rock.[26] Tis a large pile of Building, for the most part after the old manner of Fortifications, whose chiefest Strength consisted in the thickness of their Walls. Here are some additions of a newer Work to the Campain; but the two little hills just before the Entry make it of no use against an Enemy, so that the only use it can be put to, is that which is made of it, vizt., A Prison to hold state prisoners. One Mr. Rolle of Wood Sydes is Governor of it.[27] I did not go in, so can say no more of it. Hence I came to Carvin,[28] a pleasantly well built new house with Good Gardens. It belongs to Collonell Aereskin.[29] Hence having some business I went to Linlithgow [Fig. 7.2]. This is a Sweet, pleasant Town as any I have seen in Scotland. The streets are broad and well paved.[30]

In the middle of the market place Stands a fine Fountain near twenty feet high of Stone. The Water being Conveyed up to the top by pipes fall[s] from the very Top of it *encascade* into a Cistern which is Supported by Grotesque Figures.[31] This emptys itself again thro' antique Spouts into a larger Bason, which letts the water into the streets thro' eight Spouts. In this part of the [Town is the] Town house, which is a large well-built Fabrick.[32] Few towns in Britain have a better. In it is kept by Statute, the Standard measure for dry things. Above this part of the Town upon an Eminence Stands a palace built by King James the 5th.[33] It has upon the outward Gate, as you enter into it, the Armes of Scotland done four times with different ornaments vizt. that of ye Garter, the Order of France, that of the *Toison d'Or*,[34] and that of the Thistle, he being a Knight Companion of the first three orders, and Severain of the Latter.[35] It is a very Sumptuous Edifice of a Square Figure uniforme, and Contains a large Court within, in the middle of which Stands a Curious Fountain, embellsht with much carveing and Imagery, but now Somewhat out of order.[36] At the foot of this eminence, on which the palace Stands, is a pleasant Lake of half a mile in Length and a quarter in Breadth, in which is Store of good Fishes. What added to the beauty of the place, this day, was a great concourse of Strangers, it being one of their Fair days for Linnen and Woollen Cloath, as the next day was to be one for Horses and meat.[37]

A little above Bostrostowness (which is a rich thriveing Town of Trade, of which D[uke] Hamilton[38] is Superiour, and has Several good Ships that sail to all ports of Europe),[39] you meet with the first vestiges of the Roman Wall, which runs within a Bow shoott of Kinniel, a house belonging to the Dukes of Hamilton, now in the possession of the Earl of Arran.[40] This is a very fine house indeed, here are Excellent Gardens kept in very good order and as much Wall Fruit as anywhere benorth Trent I daresay; here is a large Park with a Wood in it inclosed with a high Stone Wall. The house of Kinniel stands on the Northside of the Roman Wall which is here made of Stone and Turff and a Ditch behind it.[41] Thus it continues, tho' the vestiges are somewhat faint till you come to Inveravon. This is a Strong antient Building of Square Stone, and round Towers on the Corners.[42] Here the Roman Wall begins to disappear, and the Cause of its not being so visible may be from the Sandiness and Inequallity of the Ground thereabouts: the former by reason 'tis easily driven with Stormy winds, as easily fills up the Ditch, and by time Growing to the Wall, make it now undistinguishable from the rest of the Ground, and the many inequallitys makes it hard to conjecture upon which the Wall stood. This Wall nowhere Runs Streight but keeps the riseing Ground exactly. The trace then of the Wall remains dubious, till you come near to the house of Calender, where it appears very visibly. This is the Chief house of the E[arl] of Calender.[43] This is a noble Fabrick: the visto to it is cut thro' ye Roman Wall, thro' which you have a pleasant prospect of this house and a tall shady wood, which standing at a little distance from it, overtops it, and set it of[f] very much.[44] Not far from this house is another very handsom house belonging to Mr Levinston of West quarter,[45] married to the Dowager of Calender. When you have gon a little way from this, you loose Sight of the Roman Wall, nor do you recover it againe till you come to Fallkirk which some think should be Spelled Vallkirk, *quale Fanum ad vallum*.[46] This is a pretty market Town, as big but not so neat as Lithgow. They are building many new Tennements, so that in a few years more it will make a better figure than it does at present. They intend to make a good Town house with a Steeple to it.[47] The Church is of a good age. The Isles that form the Cross, Standing North and South, are covered with flag Stones. On the North side on these Isles are Coats of Armes, not very visible what they are, but said to be the Coats of the Levingstones.[48] Here are severall Grave Stones that are Antient, but none more remarkable than that of S[i]r John the Greme.[49] It stands in the open Church-Yard and is much injured by the Weathers so that with much poaring I got the Inscription read, which goes round the Edge of a Flat Stone Supported by four Small pillars, each marked S.J.G.

Fig. 7.2 The palace and town of Linlithgow, drawn by John Slezer (John Slezer, Theatrum Scotiae, *1693)*

The Inscription is
      Here Lyes Sir John the Greme baith wight and wise,
      Ane of the Chief rescuit Scotland thrice.
      An better Knight not to the world was lent
      Nor was Gude Greme: of Trueth and hardiment.
                              Anno 1298.[50]

At the top of the Stone is the Coat Armorical with Supporters as his Descendent the Marq[uis] of Montrosse Carrys them; on the Middle of this Stone is this Inscribed –
      Mente, manuque, potens, et vallae fidus Achates
      Conditur hic Gremius, bello interfectus ab Anglis Jul: 22[51]

A little beneath this toward the bottom of the Stone is a knot with S.J.G. cast in it, and round it, *vivit post funera virtus*.[52] Under this Square Stone lyes the figure of a Knight Supine in Freestone. You may enquire who this *Walla* was, to whom he was Achates: a famous Champion, one Sir Wm. Wallace who stood up for the rights of his Countrey and being taken by the English was burnt in Smithfield. Such was their despite to him.[53] We have a famous legend of him, which, if I can get, you shall in good time see. Beyond this Town a little on the Southside of the Highway is the Ditch of the Wall very visible all along till you come to Bantaskin, where are some rows of Stone on the Inside of the Ditch probably the remains of some Castellum.[54] Leaving the Wall, we went over the River Carron to the *Templum Victoriae ad Ripam Carronis*, as Ninnius calls it,[55] tho' Commonly, and by our careless Enlarger of Camdens *Britannia* called Arthurs Oven [Fig. 7.3].[56] This makes a part of Sir [*vacat*] Bruce of Stenhouse Parkwall.[57] I did not take the dimensions of it, being promised an exact Draught of it.[58] It is of no great Bulk. I have seen a round Dove-cot almost as big; and it look't more like such than an Oven. It is of great hewn Stones without any sort of morter, or any sort of binding, but what one Stone gives another. It is very Open atop which I presume was never closed being built like the Tonda in Rome.[59] It hath the Door to the East which had an Iron Gate upon it, within the memory of man. Above the Door about a yard and half stands a Square Window. It is a very pretty building, and very particular, there not being another like this in Britain, that I know of. There is no Inscription nor Carving save, upon one Stone above the Door, there seems to be a Mans head, a Tree and a victory upon the end of one of the Stones,[60] but this is but my Fancy; another that sees it may Fancy it something else. For really it is not any thing determinately. Within, it is Smooth tho' the weather has Split the outside and made it rugged. Thence I came to Cabor,[61] a small village where on the road is a pretty dunan,[62] i.e. a green artificial hill. Of these kind of hills or Mounts there are severall in this Country, and in the highlands in this place they say, the Baron used to keep his Court upon them, and do justice upon or to his Tennants and Vassals, and at this place they meet to do all their peculiar business.[63] The like Mr Spencer the Poet observes of the Irish in his discourse upon Ireland.[64] Hence he [*sic*] went to Halbertshire. This is a Strong, high Tower house built by the Laird of Roslin in K[ing] J[ames] the 5th time.[65] The Laird[s] of Roslin have been great Architects and Patrons of Building for these many Generations.[66] They are oblidged to receive the Masons word, which is a Secret Signall Masons have thro'out the world to know one another by.[67] They Alledge 'tis as old as since Babel. When they could not understand one another they conversed by signs, others would have it no older than Solomon. However it is, he that hath it, will bring his brother mason to him, without calling to him or your perceiveing of the Signe.[68] This house Stands pleasantly in a woody Corn Country, a pleasant River running just under the park wall along a Cistern of Solid rock for more than a hundred Yards, so that you may see the Trouts and other fish as they play themselves there.[69] Hence I came back by Dunipeace an old house, that has been formerly a Religious house.[70] It stands Conveniently towards the Bottom of a Sloping hill from South to North. Here hard by are *Duni Pacis*, which tho' they are said to be an Artificial, and thrown up by the Inhabitants the Scots Picts &c when they made peace with the Romans.[71] Yet doubtless they are natural, and form'd so round by the impetuosity of the River, which changing current, has from peninsulas worn them in Islands, and by time taking new courses has left them Standing on Dry land. The top of the Southermost seems to be formed by art.[72] From this I came to view the ancient City of Camelon, where are the vestiges of two larg[e] Squares of 600 feet each, in Both of which are Several Steads or ruines of Stone buildings; and a Ditch and Rempart round each Square.[73] Rom[an] Coyns have been dug up here,[74] but I could not get the people to own they had any. To the N. of this the River Carron has made a large bay to which the people reports the Sea came up, and affirm that Anchors and such Sea Tackle have been found in the Moss there,[75] as they have been digging for Peats (which is a Sort of fewel they use here where they are Scarce of Coal or Wood and are called so from the pitts out of which they are dugg). Between the Squares above said is a paved way of half a mile long[76] which lead up to the Roman Wall at the end of which stood a great Castle called by the Country folks the Maiden Castle but now little is to be seen of it.[77] They have a famous Legend of the Maiden and K[ing] Arthur, which I did not much mind.[78] But here and all along from Bantaskin the wall is very visible; the Ditch is 16:18:20 and some places 30 feet broad, 10 or 12 deep and, at 60 or a 100 feet distance from the Ditch, runs upon a parallel to it a paved way winding with the Rempart. This is pretty entire in many places, especially in the Morelands where the Ground has not been manured. About 2 Miles from the Maiden Castle on the Inside of the Ditch is a large Square work of Stone with a double Ditch about it. The common people thereabouts call it Castle Ruff.[79] Here are the Ruins of Several Stone buildings. About the middle of the Square is an overture thro' which Shepherd

Fig. 7.3 Arthur's O'On, drawn by William Stukeley (An Account of a Roman Temple, 1720)

boys creep into a vault under Ground.[80] From this the Roman Wall runs to a little height called Elf Hill,[81] so on by the northside of Seabeggs Garden Wall. As you come to this Seabeggs, there is an heap of earth on the outside of the Ditch of a Square figure, about 60 feet long 40 broad and 20 high flat on the top.[82] Tis very entire and has had a ditch round. From Seabeggs as you go thro' the wood you see the Wall very plainly, and after as you ride over some Rockey ground, on the Edge of which stands Several Cottages, it continues plain enough till you come to the Castle Cary. This is another large Square Castellum of hewn Stone with a double fossa. The ruins of many Stone Buildings are to be seen in it.[83] Some Stones with Inscriptions have been dug up here but I saw none but a broken one, which is in the side of the outward gate, as you enter to Mr. Baylys house of Castle Cary.[84] On it are only H. BAT - may be *Batavorum Cohors*.[85] Tis an old Square Tower. The master is a hearty old Man.[86] He shew'd a missal that belonged to Koha Kill[87] with a Book of heraldry with many English Coates, particularly some of Glamorganshire. He has a Roman Lamp and two Coyns which were dug up here.[88] From this the Wall Continues visible, but makes several turnings as it runs over some rocky heights till it comes to the Castle hill about 1/3 Mile from Kilsyth.[89] This [is] a pretty good Countrey Town, but inferior to Fallkirk or Linlithgow; but this I say for it, there is better entertainment for Man and horse and more reasonable than anywhere upon the Road. Out of a Moss rise two Rivers, [*vacat*] which runs East and falls into Carron,[90] and Kelvin, which runs West and falls into Clyd over against Govan below Glassgow. When I am at leasure I will give you the rest of this.

My Correspondent never sent me the remaining part of this Account".[91]

The itinerary

The document records the observations of a traveller who left Edinburgh on 20th July 1697, with the stated intention of viewing the remains of the Antonine Wall. His itinerary was similar to that followed by many antiquaries before and since. This was the natural route across the Forth–Clyde isthmus, used by the Forth & Clyde Canal in the later eighteenth and the railways in the mid-nineteenth century. After Kilsyth he would have headed towards Kirkintilloch and then Old Kilpatrick, with a diversion during or after the journey to Glasgow College. He seems to have taken several days over the journey, though no overnight stops are specifically indicated: one at Queensferry can be inferred, and others at Linlithgow, Falkirk and especially Kilsyth are likely. He appears to have travelled alone,[92] though we might wonder whether he had a servant or other companion, as had Edward Lhwyd in 1699 and John Horsley in 1729.[93] Sir Robert Sibbald, advising Lhwyd in 1699 on the best route along the Wall, supposed that he would need local guides.[94]

The traveller

For his time, the traveller shows commendable powers of observation of the Wall as a standing monument and good judgement in interpreting what he saw. He correctly identified most of the constituent elements of the Roman frontier: the rampart, the broad defensive Ditch, and the Military Way, together with two forts on its line, Castlecary and Rough Castle, and suggested a 'castellum' at Bantaskin. The fort at Camelon a little to the north was also accurately described.[95] He does not claim as Roman forts, as did other antiquaries, some structures of much later date, e.g. Inveravon Tower.[96] He seems to be the first modern visitor who noted correctly from personal inspection, perhaps from a section cut through it, that the Wall was made of stone and turf.[97] He had read, but was evidently unimpressed by, Edmund Gibson's revised 1695 edition of Camden's *Britannia*.[98] The Wall was not his only object of interest. Barely a quarter of his account is devoted to it. He wrote too about the towns he passed through and the country seats of the gentry. He made a number of diversions, for example, to Linlithgow, in order to undertake some unspecified 'business', and to see celebrated antiquities (e.g. Arthur's O'on and the Hills of Dunipace). He shows an awareness of Scottish history, which he did not expect in his correspondent, and of Latin and English literature, which we would readily look for in an educated gentleman of the time.

Exactly when the letter was written is not clear. It was not necessarily penned in Edinburgh. Some time may have elapsed after the traveller's return home (see also below, p. 188).[99] The document as we have it now is not his original epistle. The final two sentences, in my view, did not form part of the original letter. I conjecture that the penultimate sentence (above, p. 184) was penned by the letter's immediate recipient, and the final sentence by someone to whom the recipient had sent on a copy.[100] For the modern reader there is a danger of mistaking these added comments for the testimony of the traveller himself. At some uncertain date, in the mid-eighteenth century or later, presumably when already in the Harley Collection (see below) and perhaps due to deterioration of the original, the document was copied, hurriedly and rather carelessly.[101] When transcribed again for publication in 1893, it was slightly edited and further spelling errors crept in.[102]

Sir George Macdonald, in drawing attention to our document, described the traveller as a 'casual but observant visitor to Scotland.'[103] Nevertheless the text identifies him as Scottish, at least in origin, rather than English,[104] and perhaps then living in Edinburgh.

The manuscript, as we have it now, was first reported in the collection of Robert Harley, from 1711 Lord High Treasurer and 1st Earl of Oxford, a prodigious collector of manuscripts.[105] Thereafter it passed by inheritance into the hands of the Dukes of Portland, and in 1893 was preserved at their country seat, Welbeck Abbey in Nottinghamshire.

We can however identify someone who saw the letter at a much earlier date, the antiquary William Stukeley, in whose own working copy of his monograph on Arthur's O'on, *An Account of a Roman Temple, and other Antiquities, near Graham's Dyke in Scotland*, published in 1720, are numerous notes in the margins and on the reverse sheets, including substantial excerpts from our manuscript.[106] Stukeley himself was too young to have been its immediate recipient in 1697, and it was obviously not in his hands in 1720 when compiling the *Account*. As Stukeley had access to Harley's library at his town-house in London,[107] one possibility could be that he saw our document (or a version of it) there.[108]

Stukeley incorporated substantial elements of the traveller's text, all but verbatim, perhaps intending a revised edition of his own monograph, along with opinions of the controversial William Baxter on place-name evidence,[109] and information deriving from the Somerset antiquary and geologist John Strachey, who visited Scotland in 1721 in the aftermath of the First Jacobite Rebellion.[110] Stukeley's extracts help to confirm and at times correct the text of the document as we now have it.[111]

The identity of the traveller

From the document itself we can say only that he was Scottish, and not English (see above). If we are to proceed to an identification, a number of possible names come to mind, several of them among correspondents of the young librarian, Robert Wodrow, at Glasgow College, and known also to Sibbald in Edinburgh: for example, a lawyer, William Strahan (or Strachan), student of Balliol College, Oxford, 1689–90, later 'king's advocate in the concerns of the admiralty';[112] James Paterson, Keeper of the College Museum at Edinburgh University, 1699–1702;[113] Lachlan Campbell, minister at Cambeltown 1703–1707;[114] and Alexander Edward, architect, garden designer and deposed episcopalian minister.[115] Attention could be directed also at the cartographer John Adair (above, p. 178).

However, by far the strongest candidate must be John Urry of Christ Church, Oxford (above, p. 178), who is known to have been travelling in Scotland in 1697, and who reported to his Oxford colleagues the texts of inscriptions preserved at country houses and farms on and near the line of the Wall and at Glasgow College (Fig. 7.4).[116] Born in 1666, the son of Colonel William Urry of Pitfichie in Aberdeenshire,[117] John Urry matriculated at Christ Church, Oxford in 1682.[118]

John Urry is remembered now for his controversial edition of Chaucer's *Canterbury Tales*, published posthumously.[119] In a scheme devised by Francis Atterbury, then Dean of Christ Church, to produce new, authoritative editions of major literary texts,[120] John Urry unexpectedly found himself, as an antiquary, assigned in 1711 the role of editing a new edition of Chaucer, which both contemporary and later scholars felt he had been ill-qualified to undertake.[121] Yet he applied himself with enthusiasm and conviction. He perceived his Scottish antecedents as an advantage: 'his skill in the Northern Language spoken in the Lowlands of *Scotland* qualified him to read this Poet with more ease and pleasure than one altogether bred be-South *Trent*.'[122] Urry is warmly depicted in the *Remarks and Collections* of his friend Thomas Hearne, 'second librarian' of the Bodleian,[123] who notes Urry's familiarity with Anglo-Saxon.[124] Urry's antiquarian approach is illustrated by his wide-ranging consultation of Chaucerian manuscripts.[125] When Urry died, in his 50th year, his literary task was incomplete. 'Yesterday about 3 Clock in the Afternoon,' wrote Hearne on 19th March 1715, 'died of a Feaver my great and good Friend, Mr John Urry, Student of Christ-Church. This Gentleman was Bachelor of Arts, & bore Arms against Monmouth in the Rebellion called Monmouth's Rebellion [1685], as several other Oxford Scholars did.[126] He was a stout, lusty Man, & of admirable Principles. His Integrity & Honesty & Loyalty gain'd him great Honour and Respect. He refused the Oaths, & died a Non-Juror'.[127] William Brome, fellow undergraduate at Christ Church in the 1680s,[128] and a long-time friend,[129] was named in Urry's Will (for which see below, p. 187) as his executor.[130]

John Urry had corresponded with Robert Harley, 1st Earl of Oxford, on his Chaucerian endeavours,[131] spent time working in Harley's library,[132] and borrowed manuscripts from his collection, which after his untimely death the Earl was anxious to recover.[133] Urry's life is generally assessed in the context of Chaucerian scholarship, with his antiquarian interests forgotten.[134] However, from Hearne's *Remarks and Collections* we learn of Urry's collection of coins and medals, of rare books and manuscripts, and of epitaphs in country churches.[135] In February 1712 he wrote to Lord Harley about finds made at a Roman villa, with extensive mosaics, recently discovered at Stonesfield, near Woodstock, Oxfordshire.[136]

While John Urry has long been known as a traveller along the Antonine Wall in 1697,[137] a recently published document shows that he had been in Scotland several times over a three-year period, 1696–98.[138] On 25th September 1696, 'being about to take a long winter journey', its course or destination unspecified but part of it likely to have been by sea, he prepared a Will.[139] In April 1698, after (it may be supposed) his return to Oxford, he passed to his colleagues, Thomas Tanner, Fellow of All Souls, later Bishop of St Asaph's (1732–35),[140] and David Gregory, Fellow of Balliol and Savilian Professor of Astronomy (1691–1708),[141] the texts of various Latin inscriptions from the Antonine Wall, some of which Urry was the first to make known to the wider scholarly community (Figs 7.5–6).[142] Tanner sent on copies to Edmund Gibson, recently the editor of Camden's *Britannia* (above, p. 178), categorizing Urry as a 'very curious Gentleman', on whose drawings Gibson could therefore rely.[143] The texts included the *cohors Batavorum* stone at Castlecary (above, p. 183). Gregory notes that Urry 'saw them all in Scotland, when he was there in 1696, 1697 and 1698, and these draughts were given him by Mr John Adair' (see Fig. 7.6). Assuming the identification, it may therefore have been Adair who promised the traveller a drawing of Arthur's O'on (above, p. 181).[144]

Though born in Dublin, Urry's Scottish ancestry is assured.[145] In 1709 we know he was again in Edinburgh.[146] We could suspect he had surviving relatives there.[147] In April 1715, after his death, Humphrey Wanley, Librarian to Lord Harley, observed: 'Mr Urry of Christ-

Fig. 7.4 John Urry, engraved by N. Pigné (J. Urry, The Works of Geoffrey Chaucer, *compared with the former Editions, 1721, frontispiece)*

churches Closet is sealed up; & will continue so until the arrival of his Relations from Scotland.'[148] William Brome, his executor (above, p. 186) feared that 'there may be trouble from Scotland about the Will', presumably since it favoured Brome himself.[149] Urry nevertheless remains a somewhat shadowy figure, 'curious' in the modern as well as antiquarian sense.

The identity of the recipient

Equally puzzling is the identity of the recipient. The letter's text itself offers few clues, except that he was probably English, and not Scottish (above, p. 184). As the traveller wrote out his account 'not knowing when I may have the Good fortune to see you', the recipient cannot have been an immediate colleague. It is perhaps easier to say who he was not. The young Robert Wodrow, Sir Robert Sibbald and Professor David Gregory can be ruled out as Scottish, as can the Welshman Edward Lhwyd. Given the derogatory comment about the 1695 edition of Camden's *Britannia*, we can safely exclude Edmund Gibson![150]

In another of the many annotations to his own copy of the *Account of a Roman Temple*, Stukeley reports: 'I have met with another inscription in a letter from an anonymous gentleman in Edinburgh to Mr William Brome of Herefordshire dated 13 Oct. 1697.'[151] In Stukeley's gloss, there is a drawing of the inscription, allowing it to be identified as a distance slab of the Second Legion.[152] Though long known (since *c.* 1600), this inscription is absent from the main body of Stukeley's *Account*, as a result of confusion with other stones recording identical lengths.

William Brome (above, p. 186) was a landowner, interested in the antiquities of his county, who lived at Withington near Hereford.[153] He too features regularly in Thomas Hearne's *Remarks and Collections.* Brome is in my view the likely recipient not just of the document as we have it now, but an account of the complete visit, and I conclude that it was Brome who subsequently sent on the first part to an unknown third party, perhaps Lord Harley himself, but never in the end found enough 'leasure' to send the rest.

It is not clear whether Urry wrote full accounts of his journey also to Tanner and Gregory, or merely sent the sketches of the inscribed texts, with brief captions, on his return to Oxford. Gregory copied out the texts he had received, and may have returned the original sketches to Urry.

Some of Urry's papers also reached the collection of John Anstis, Garter King of Arms (1714–44),[154] perhaps given to him by Brome, since the latter was presumably free to dispose of them as he saw fit.[155] These included texts of stones,[156] a sketch of diamond-broached stonework at Kirkintilloch,[157] a rough drawing of Arthur's O'on,[158] and the text of a well-known inscription from Rome, which commemorated the emperor Claudius' conquest of Britain in AD 43.[159] A widespread network of scholarly exchange existed at this time, though we often lack the evidence to document every connection.[160]

Conclusion

The links between John Urry and William Brome of Herefordshire surely indicate that the 'anonymous gentleman in Edinburgh' who wrote to Brome on 13th October 1697 was his lifelong friend, the later Editor of Chaucer. However, although there is no definitive proof that Urry was also the author of the longer account, it seems very likely.[161] Again, although I have detected no conclusive stylistic link between our document and the somewhat limited corpus of known writings in Urry's own hand,[162] some matching phraseology can be observed between our document and David Gregory's notes on the inscriptions sent him by Urry, and between Gregory's notes and folios in MS Stowe 1024, some of which are stated to be 'out of Mr Urry's papers'.[163]

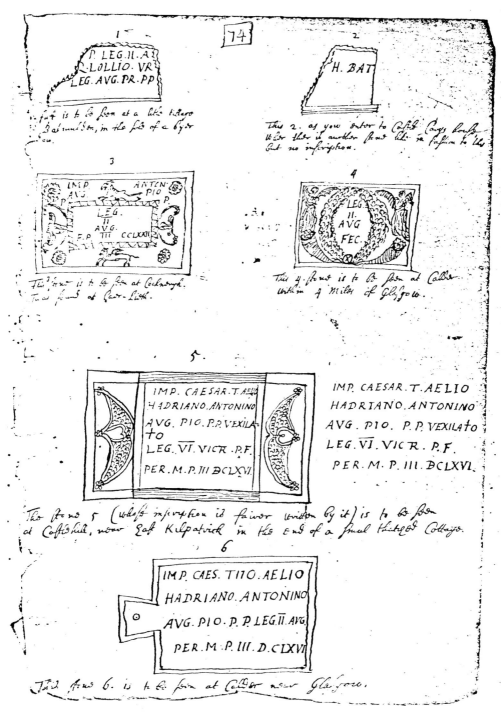

Fig. 7.5 *Roman Inscriptions seen by John Urry, and copied by Professor David Gregory, 1698 (Edinburgh University Library)*

Assuming the identity of the traveller as John Urry, we can go some way towards reconstructing the rest of his itinerary along the Wall, westwards from Kilsyth, from the locations of the other inscriptions he communicated to Thomas Tanner and David Gregory (and perhaps, of course, to others unknown), at Cadder, Balmuildy, Dougalston, Bearsden (Castlehill), Carleith, all on the line of the Wall,[164] and at Erskine (near Old Kilpatrick, but on the opposite bank of the Clyde) and Glasgow College.[165] At the last he could have met the librarian Robert Wodrow (above, p. 178), if the latter was already in post; but Wodrow's surviving correspondence, which begins in December 1698, lacks any reference to him. It is a great pity that an account of the remaining part of this most interesting journey has not survived.

Acknowledgements

I should like to thank the following for their help during the preparation of this paper: Elizabeth Bell, Roger Goodburn, Dr Lynn Pitts, Margaret Robb, Sue Hubbard (Record Office Manager, Herefordshire Council), Michael J. Boggan (British Library), Dr Costas Panayotakis (University of Glasgow), Dr Iain Gordon Brown and colleagues (National Library of Scotland, Edinburgh), Geoff Bailey (Falkirk Museums), Dr Will Stenhouse (Yeshiva University, New York), Sheila Noble and colleagues (Edinburgh University Library), Dr Graham Piddock and colleagues (Sackler Library, Oxford), Mrs Judith Curthoys (Archivist, Christ Church, Oxford), Anna Sander (Curator of Archives and Manuscripts, Balliol College, Oxford), and Professor Hew Strachan (All Souls College, Oxford). For permission to republish the text, I am grateful to the British Library. David Gregory's drawings of inscriptions sent to him in 1698 by John Urry are reproduced by kind permission of Edinburgh University Library. Dr Brown and Mr Bailey kindly commented on a draft of this paper, to my advantage.

Notes

1. British Library Add. Mss. 70518, fols 290–93.
2. HMC 1893, 54–57.
3. Christison, Buchanan and Anderson 1901, 331.
4. Christison, Buchanan and Anderson 1903, 273.
5. Buchanan, Christison and Anderson 1905, 443.
6. Macdonald 1911, 87, 146, 220, 247; 1934, 75, 105, 215, 217 and 344.
7. Ayres 1997, 84ff.; Sweet 2004.
8. Gibson 1695.
9. Camden 1586.
10. Sykes 1926; Taylor 2004.
11. Gibson 1695, Preface; Sykes 1926, 16–17; Mendyk 1989, 213ff.; Parry 1995, 331ff.
12. Sweet 2004, 160.
13. Edwards 2004.

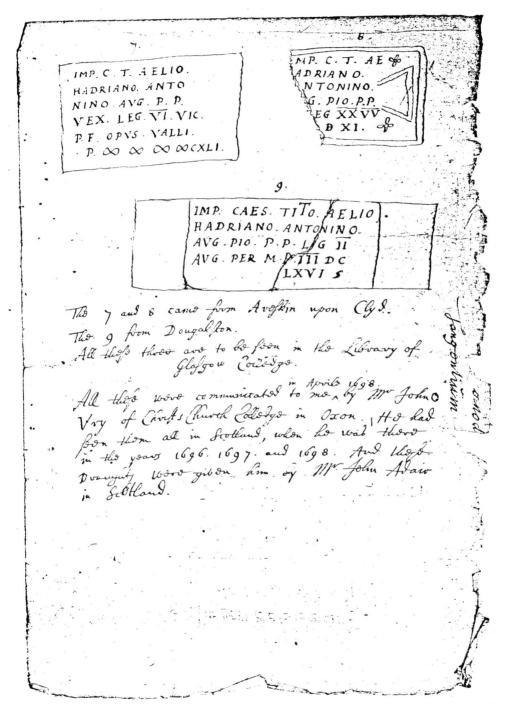

Fig. 7.6 Roman Inscriptions seen by John Urry, and copied by Professor David Gregory, 1698 (Edinburgh University Library)

14. Gunther 1945; Roberts 2004.
15. Haverfield 1910. The route Sibbald proposed is generally similar to that followed by our traveller, but the latter does not seem to have halted at Cramond west of Edinburgh. Perhaps he had been there before (see also below, p. 197, note 156).
16. Emerson 1988; Withers 2004b.
17. Brown and Vasey 1989; Vasey 1993; Keppie 1998, 8–9; Withers 2004a.
18. Bodleian Library MSS Rawlinson D 377, fol. 25.
19. Hamilton 1831, 142–5.
20. Keppie 1998, 6.
21. Sharp 1937; Durkan 1977; Keppie 1998, 7–8 and 10–13.; Yeoman 2004.
22. Bodleian Library MSS Rawlinson D 377, fols 25, 46; Nicolson 1702, Preface, pp. xxxviii–xxxix; James 1956; Sharp 1937, 10; Keppie 1998, 8–12.
23. The text offered is here based on a personal reading of the document as preserved in the British Library (Add. Mss. 70518, fols 290–3), and of the text on microfilm. A few errors of place-names have been corrected and some punctuation added or adjusted, to ease comprehension. Otherwise I have, with a few exceptions, retained the original spellings.
24. Early antiquaries argued that the Antonine Wall began at Abercorn (e.g. Stukeley 1720, 5), and some placed a Roman fort there. Many of the towns and monuments visited by our traveller are described also in Sibbald 1710.
25. The Binns, for which see Salmon 1913, 197–8; RCAHMS 1929, 182ff., no. 276; Hendrie 1986, 98; Jaques and McKean 1994, 35–6.
26. Blackness Castle, for which see RCAHMS 1929, 192ff., no. 303; Hendrie 1986, 90ff.; Jaques and McKean 1994, 33–4.
27. (Sir) Henry Rollo of Woodside, near Larbert, for whom see Gibson 1908, 64ff.
28. Carriden.
29. Salmon 1913, 165; RCAHMS 1929, 192, no. 302; Jaques 2001, 151–2.
30. RCAHMS 1929, 213ff.; Jaques and McKean 1994, 1ff.
31. The Cross Well', for which see Hendrie 1989, 31ff.
32. RCAHMS 1929, 232, no. 360; Jaques and McKean 1994, 8.
33. RCAHMS 1929, 219ff., no. 356; Jaques and McKean 1994, 2ff.
34. 'Order of the Golden Fleece'. The Knights at this time were chosen by the Holy Roman Emperor.
35. For the gate, see RCAHMS 1929, fig. 264; Hendrie 1989, 38–9 with figs.
36. Believed to be the oldest in Britain, it was commissioned by King James V in 1537 (RCAHMS 1929, fig. 266). The fountain has recently been restored to working order by Historic Scotland.
37. Hendrie 1989, 42.
38. The 4th Duke of Hamilton, who succeeded in 1694.
39. On Borrowstounness (Bo'ness) as a flourishing seaport, see Salmon 1913; Hendrie 1986, 3ff.
40. Salmon 1913, 43ff.; RCAHMS 1929, 190ff., no. 300; Jaques 2001, 126–7.
41. A recent excavation has confirmed the line of the Wall just south of Kinneil House (Glendinning 2000).
42. Inveravon Tower, a fifteenth-century castle, for which see RCAHMS 1929, 190, no. 299.
43. Callendar House, for which see RCAHMS 1963, 348ff., no. 311; Jaques 2001, 31–2.
44. The cut, which allowed travellers on the public road to view the house to advantage, was made by the 2nd Earl of Callendar, before *c.* 1680 (Livingstone 1682, stanzas 133,

135). Begun as a tower house, the building was progressively enlarged to the present-day grandiose structure.

45. RCAHMS 1963, 397, no. 396; Jaques 2001, 98.
46. 'That is, the church on the wall'. The meaning of the place-name name is still disputed.
47. RCAHMS 1963, 310–11, nos 252–3; Jaques 2001, 7ff.
48. For the Livingstones of Callender, see Livingston 1920.
49. Sir John (de) Graham, for whom see Scott 1994, 24ff. Summerson 2004, 212 doubts his existence as a historical figure.
50. The text is reliably reported by Nimmo 1777, 177. The date (*Anno* 1298) has, in the traveller's version, been transferred from the following Latin inscription. For a description of the tomb, much remarked on by travellers through the centuries, see RCAHMS 1963, 152–3. It was restored shortly after our traveller's visit, and subsequently, and so does not now match what he saw.
51. 'Strong in mind and in physical prowess, and Wallace's faithful Achates, Graham lies here, slain in war by the English, 22nd July'. Achates was the loyal lieutenant of Aeneas in Vergil's *Aeneid.*
52. 'Virtue outlasts the grave' or 'Honour triumphs over death', a popular motto for towns and schools through the ages.
53. Sir William Wallace's intestines were burnt at Smithfield in 1305. He was hanged, drawn and quartered, the quarters being put on view at Newcastle, Berwick, Stirling and Perth, and his head displayed on London Bridge.
54. Presumably an otherwise unknown milefortlet, unless he saw here merely the east-west kerbs edging the stone foundation-course of the Wall.
55. 'Victory's Temple on Carron's bank.' The traveller is here paraphrasing rather than quoting Nennius (*Historia Brittonum*, ch. 23) verbatim: . . . *domumque rotundam politis lapidibus super ripam fluminis Carun quod a suo nomine nomen accepit fornicem triumphalem in victoriae memoriam erigens construxit* – 'and he [Carausius] built a circular house in smooth stone blocks on the bank of the River Carun, which took its name from his own, putting up a triumphal arch in memory of his victory' (Stevenson 1838). On this gloss, see Macdonald 1934, 31.
56. The reference is to Edmund Gibson. On Arthur's O'on (= Oven), much remarked on, and often drawn by the early antiquaries, e.g. by Robert Gordon of Straloch, copying a sketch by Timothy Pont *c.* 1580 ('Temply', as illustrated in Maxwell 1989, 5, fig. 1.1), see Camden 1607, 700; Gibson 1695, 922, 1104 (with a sketch by Sibbald; see also Haverfield 1910, 326); Sibbald 1707, 44ff.; Sibbald 1710, 5; Stukeley 1720, 12ff.; Gordon 1726, 24ff. with fig.; Nimmo 1777, 64ff. For recent scholarship on the O'on, see Steer 1958; RCAHMS 1963, 118, no. 126; Keppie and Arnold 1984, 62, no. 165; Coulston and Phillips 1988, 105, no. 265; Brown and Vasey 1989.
57. Sir William Bruce, 4th Baronet, of Stenhouse (i.e. 'stone house', the estate's name commemorating the Roman structure; hence the modern place-name Stenhousemuir, and the resulting football club). On the house, now demolished, see RCAHMS 1963, 237ff., no. 200 with plate 102, illustrating a date-stone of 1698. Sir Michael Bruce, 6th Baronet, had the O'on demolished in 1743, attracting the opprobrium of antiquaries then and since (Brown 1974). The park-wall itself is depicted by Stukeley (1720, end map; Steer 1958, fig. 2). A full-size replica of the O'on was constructed in 1763, as a dovecot at Penicuik House, Midlothian, by Sir James Clerk of Penicuik.
58. See below, p. 187.
59. The traveller refers here to the Pantheon, known also as La Rotonda, with which the

circular and domed O'on was sometimes compared: see Sibbald 1707, 46; Stukeley 1720, 15ff.; Horsley 1732, 174. General William Roy (1793, pl. xxxvi) calls it 'The Little Pantheon'.

60. See Steer 1958.
61. Larbert (see below, p. 195, note 101). A variety of spellings is attested at this time, including Larbor, Lairbar and Lerbeirt.
62. Now destroyed, but likely to have been a motte. See Nimmo 1777, 15–16; RCAHMS 1963, 450, no. 592.
63. In early medieval times people came to the houses of their landlords to have land-transfers legalised, a connection drawn to my attention by Geoff Bailey.
64. Hadfield and Maley 1997, 79.
65. Herbertshire. See Gillespie 1879, 99–100; Gibson 1908, 167–86; RCAHMS 1963, 268, no. 216; Jaques 2001, 77. In 1697 it was in the hands of the Stirlings of Herbertshire. The house, which later became a school, was destroyed by fire in 1914.
66. On the enigmatic Roslin (or Rosslyn) Chapel, Midlothian, see RCAHMS 1929, 98, no.138.
67. The St. Clairs (Sinclairs) of Roslyn claimed to be hereditary Grand Masters of the Masonic Order in Scotland. On their various properties, see Hay 1835.
68. I suppose here, from the necessity of giving this extended account, that the recipient wasnot himself a mason.
69. The River Carron. The estate is now swallowed up in the modern town of Denny.
70. Dunipace House, now demolished, for which see Gillespie 1879, 92; RCAHMS 1963, 397–8, no. 397.
71. The 'Hills of Peace', a supposed explanation of the place-name Dunipace. These natural hillocks, formed by geological action, were widely believed by older antiquaries to be man-made (so Camden 1607, 700, hence Gibson 1695, 921; Sibbald 1710, 51; Stukeley 1720, 7; Nimmo 1777, 58ff.); cf. Gillespie 1878, 91–2; RCAHMS 1963, 446, no. 575.
72. The more easterly was utilized as a motte in medieval times, so the traveller was correct in his observation. Robert Gordon of Straloch, copying Timothy Pont, *c.* 1580, shows two hillocks, one triangular in section, the other rectangular with a flattish top (Maxwell 1989, 5, fig. 1.1).
73. Sibbald 1707, 33–4. The traveller is here referring to the 'North' and 'South' camps at Camelon, for which see Nimmo 1777, 10ff.; Christison, Buchanan and Anderson 1901, 329ff.; RCAHMS 1963, 107ff., n. 122.
74. Sibbald 1707, 31; Stukeley 1720, 7.
75. Gibson 1695, 958; Sibbald 1707, 33–4; Stukeley 1720, 7; Gillespie 1879, 68ff.; Christison, Buchanan and Anderson 1901, 331; Tatton-Brown 1980.
76. The road exited from the south gate of the south camp (Roy 1793, pl. xxxv; simplified version in Christison, Buchanan and Anderson 1901, 333 as fig. 1).
77. A medieval motte, removed in 1894, for which see Christison, Buchanan and Anderson 1901, 336; Macdonald 1934, 344–7, with plate 58.1; RCAHMS 1963, 178, no. 188. For the adjacent Roman milefortlet now known as Watling Lodge, which guarded the passage of the road through the Antonine Wall, see RCAHMS 1963, 100, no. 114; Breeze 1974; Bailey 1995, 664–5.
78. The name 'Maiden Castle' was regularly given to prehistoric, Roman, and medieval fortifications throughout Britain.
79. Rough Castle fort, for which see Buchanan, Christison and Anderson 1905; Macdonald 1934, 217–38; MacIvor, Thomas and Breeze 1980.
80. Perhaps the hypocaust system of the annexe bath-house: see Gordon 1726, pl. 25.

81. A natural hillock for which see Horsley 1732, 171; Nimmo 1777, 42; Macdonald 1934, 130 and 352. It was here that Graham or Graeme, a legendary king of Scotland, broke through the Wall, which henceforth, in local tradition, bore his name as 'Grahamsdyke'.
82. Seabegs Motte was, like the Maiden Castle at Watling Lodge, constructed atop the upcast mound north of the Antonine Wall, with the broad ditch as its southern defence (Smith 1934; 1936; RCAHMS 1963, 173, no. 180).
83. Castlecary fort, for which see Christison, Buchanan and Anderson 1903; Macdonald 1934, 241–52; RCAHMS 1963, 103, no. 117.
84. For Castle Cary, see RCAHMS 1963, 243ff., no. 203.
85. *RIB* 2154, now lost. See Stukeley 1720, 12; Gordon 1726, 57 with pl. xv.4; Horsley 1732, 202, with pl. (Scotland), no. xxii.
86. Alexander Baillie, 'a learned Gentleman well seen in the Antiquities' (Sibbald 1710, 49).
87. St. Columba, 'Colum Cille' in Old Irish.
88. When Edward Lhwyd visited Castle Cary in December 1699, Alexander Baillie gave him two brooches, presumably picked up at the nearby fort (Sharp 1937, 36, no. 19; cf. Keppie 1998, 11).
89. Castle Hill, just to the east of the fort of Bar Hill, above Twechar. The traveller seems not to have found anything worthy of report in the 8 km stretch between Castlecary (via Westerwood and the 'rocky heights' over Croy Hill) and Castlehill, unless he had diverted from the line in search of accommodation.
90. The Bonny Water, which flows into the Carron near Dunipace.
91. This sentence was omitted when the document was first published (HMC 1893, 57).
92. At one point 'we' is used ('we went over the Carron').
93. Edward Lhwyd in 1699 was accompanied by his assistant David Parry, and John Horsley in 1729 by his draughtsman George Mark. Alexander Gordon travelled in 1723–5 with an acquaintance, James Glen of Linlithgow (Keppie 1998, 14).
94. Haverfield 1910, 324.
95. The traveller's reference (here at p. 180) to the Wall having 'a Ditch behind it' might on first reading indicate confusion between the rampart and the substantial 'upcast mound' on north side of the Ditch (cf. Gordon 1726, 58); but it seems clear elsewhere from the account that he did correctly place the Wall itself on the south side of the Ditch.
96. On the history of antiquarian observation of the Wall, see Glasgow Archaeological Society 1899, 35ff.; Macdonald 1934, 74–80.
97. The traveller does not specifically state that the Wall was of turf on a stone base. Sibbald believed the Wall to be built of turf westwards from Kirkintilloch, as no stonework had ever been found (1707, 8). East of Watling Lodge the Wall was, as we now know, built of earth revetted by clay or turf cheeks. For the rampart at Kinneil, where the traveller comments on its make-up, see Keppie and Walker 1981, 151; Bailey and Cannel 1996, 304ff.
98. The Oxford librarian Thomas Hearne had a similarly negative view (Hearne 1898, 161).
99. Conceivably 'Anno 1797', near the beginning of the document, was inserted later, in order to clarify the date.
100. Less probably, in my view, only the final sentence is a later addition. It seems more natural to suppose from the phraseology that 'the rest of this' means the remainder of the account his correspondent had in front of him, rather than the rest of the traveller's account of his own journeyings.
101. Certainly the handwriting is neither that of Urry nor of Brome, which can both be

checked in surviving documents. It was perhaps at this time that mis-spellings such as 'Rolle' for 'Rollo', 'Cabor' for 'Larbor', 'Koha Kill' for 'Colum Cille', appeared, and the forename of Sir Michael Bruce of Stenhouse was omitted.

102. 'Nimius' for 'Ninnius' and **'Dumpeace'** for 'Dunipace'.
103. Macdonald 1911, 87; 1934, 75.
104. He refers (above, p. 179) to the Rivers Forth and Clyde as 'our two most considerable Rivers, like your Thames and Severne.' Cf. 'We [*sc.* in Scotland] have a famous legend'.
105. Speck 2004.
106. This copy is now in the Sackler Library, Oxford (533.7. G.42). How it was acquired is not known.
107. A note in Stukeley's diary for 21st April 1720 reports: 'With Ld Harley in his Library, Dover Street' (Lukis 1882, 59).
108. But see further below, p. 188.
109. Baxter 1719.
110. Fuller 2004. Strachey's journal of his Scottish travels survives in the Somerset Record Office, Taunton (DD/SH 382 c/202).
111. For example, his spelling of 'Herbertshire' as 'Halbertshire' shows that the latter was the version of the name recorded by the traveller himself rather than a later mis-transcription.
112. Foster 1891–92, 1433; Coote 1804, 110. A text of *RIB* 2205, 'communicated by Mr Strachan of Baliol College', is among papers surviving in the British Library (MS Stowe 1024, fol. 87).
113. Sharp 1937, 34.
114. Scott 1923, 50.
115. Scott 1925, 206; Colvin 1995, 332–3; Keppie 1998, 10 with National Archives of Scotland GD 45/26/140.
116. Keppie 1998, 9.
117. Dalton 1909 (Part 2), 13, 15, 17, 185.
118. Edwards 2004.
119. Urry 1721.
120. Beeching 1909, 176ff.; Alderson and Henderson 1970, 69ff., 85ff.
121. Beeching 1904, 177–8; Spurgeon 1914, 353f; Alderson and Henderson 1970, 92–3.
122. Urry 1721, Preface by Timothy Thomas, Student of Christ Church, based on a note found by him among Urry's own papers.
123. Harmsen 2004. Cf. Hearne 1898, 113.
124. Hearne 1889, 264; Spurgeon 1914, 317.
125. Urry 1721, Preface; Spurgeon 1914, 315ff.
126. Thus he maintained the military tradition of his family. Having served in the Oxford regiment as a Corporal, John Urry afterwards proudly retained (and displayed in his rooms at Christ Church) his halberd, the symbol of his rank. For a list of those who served, including Edward Lhwyd of Jesus College, see Hearne 1901, 248.
127. Hearne 1901, 33ff.; Spurgeon 1914, 332–3. Non-Jurors had declined to take an oath of allegiance to the Protestant monarchs, William and Mary, and their successors. For Non-Jurors at Christ Church, see Bill 1988, 144.
128. Foster 1891–92, 186, 1531. Urry matriculated on 30 June 1682 and graduated in 1686, Brome on 18 March, 1684 and graduated in 1687.
129. Urry 1721, Preface.
130. Hearne 1901, 58; Spurgeon 1914, 333ff.; Alderson and Henderson 1970, 95ff. Writing in

April 1702, soon after the death of King William, Urry asked that Brome pick up his belongings from Christ Church, should he be evicted as a Non-Juror on Queen Anne's succession (Bodleian Library MSS Rawlinson D 377, fol. 23).

131. HMC 1899, 247–8.
132. Spurgeon 1914, 316.
133. Wanley 1966, 5–6.
134. So Edwards 2004. The epitaph Urry composed for himself, and which was 'found in his Pockett after his Death' (Spurgeon 1914, 332), lauds his steadfastness in civil and religious duties, and observes that editing Chaucer was a task beyond his strength (Nichols 1812, 196; Hearne 1901, 36).
135. Hearne 1889, 299; 1898, 305.
136. HMC 1893, 142, 144–5. On the discovery of the villa, see Taylor 1939, 315–6 with plate xxiv.
137. Edinburgh University Library MS La.II.644/7.
138. Edinburgh University Library Dk.1.2, A74a-b (on two sides of a quarto sheet); Vasey 1993.
139. National Archives (London) PROB 11/547.
140. Sharp 2004.
141. Guerrini 2004.
142. Keppie 1998, 9.
143. 'Two of [the drawings] have a great deal of carv'd work about them, which I would not pretend to delineate. Neither was it drawn very well in Mr Urry's papers' (Edinburgh University Library MS La.II.644/7). However, we know that the drawings themselves were copied from John Adair, an example of whose work, preserved in the collection of Adair's patron, Sir John Clerk of Penicuik, allows us to gauge their high quality (Vasey 1993). See also British Library MS Stowe 1024, fol. 89 (on *RIB* 2203 from Carleith), 'Out of Mr Wry's [sic] papers. Who had them from Mr Adair's collections'.
144. Steer 1958; Brown and Vasey 1989.
145. Nichols 1812, 196.
146. Maidment 1837, 149, no. 14; Keppie 1998, 9.
147. His uncle, Major-General Sir John Urry, a soldier as remarkable for his frequent changings of side in the English Civil War period of the mid-seventeenth century as for his military competence, was beheaded at Edinburgh in 1650. Sir John Urry left five children (Furgol 2004). Watson 1929; 1930 lists a number of burgesses of Edinburgh at this time with the surname Urie or Urrye, but none who can securely be linked to this family. Urry's Will of September 1696 names as his heirs William Brome, a friend Mr Michael Bold (also a Student of Christ Church), a cousin John Urry (presumably a son of Major-General Sir John Urry), and other cousins named as James and Charles Chalmers, children born to James Chalmers, one-time Minister at Paisley (Scott 1920, 164). His books and silverware went to Brome.
148. Wanley 1966, 8.
149. Hearne 1901, 72.
150. Tanner's letter of April 1699 to Gibson (Edinburgh University Library MS La.II. 644/7) implies that the latter did not know Urry.
151. Stukeley 1720, opposite p. 10.
152. *RIB* 2186.
153. Robinson 1872, 307.
154. Handley 2004.

Harmsen, T. 2004: 'Thomas Hearne', *Oxford Dictionary of National Biography*, vol. 26, Oxford, 156–9

Haverfield, F. 1910: 'Sir Robert Sibbald's "Directions for his honoured friend Mr. Llwyd how to trace and remarke the vestiges of the Roman wall betwixt Forth and Clyde"', *PSAS* 44 (1909–10), 319–27

Hay, R. A. 1835: *Genealogie of the Sainteclaires of Rosslyn*, Edinburgh

Hearne, T. 1889: *Remarks and Collections of Thomas Hearne*, vol. 3, ed. by C. E. Doble, Oxford

Hearne, T. 1898: *Remarks and Collections of Thomas Hearne*, vol. 4, ed. by D. W. Rannie, Oxford

Hearne, T. 1901: *Remarks and Collections of Thomas Hearne*, vol. 5, ed. by D. W. Rannie, Oxford

Hendrie, W. F. 1986: *Discovering West Lothian*, Edinburgh

Hendrie, W. F. 1989: *Linlithgow, six hundred years a Royal Burgh*, Edinburgh

HMC 1893: *The manuscripts of His Grace the Duke of Portland preserved at Welbeck Abbey*, vol. 2, Historical Manuscripts Commission, London

HMC 1899: *The manuscripts of His Grace the Duke of Portland preserved at Welbeck Abbey*, vol. 5, Historical Manuscripts Commission, London

Horsley, J. 1732: *Britannia Romana*, London

James, F. G. 1956: *North Country Bishop: a biography of William Nicolson*, New Haven, London and Oxford

Jaques, R. 2001: *Falkirk and District: an illustrated architectural guide*, Edinburgh

Jaques, R. and McKean, C. 1994: *West Lothian: an illustrated architectural guide*, Edinburgh

Keppie, L. J. F. 1998: *Roman inscribed and sculptured stones in the Hunterian Museum, University of Glasgow* [*Britannia* Monograph 13], London

Keppie, L. J. F. and Arnold, B. J. 1984: *Corpus Signorum Imperii Romani, Great Britain, vol. 1, fasc. 4, Scotland*, London

Keppie, L. J. F. and Walker, J. J. 1981: 'Fortlets on the Antonine Wall at Seabegs Wood, Kinneil and Cleddans', *Britannia* 12, 143–62

Livingston, E. B. 1920: *The Livingstons of Callendar and their principal Cadets: the history of an old Stirlingshire Family*, Edinburgh

Livingstone, M. 1682: *Patronus Redux: or our Protectour is return'd safe again*, Edinburgh

Lukis, W. 1882: *The family memoirs of the Rev. William Stukeley, M.D.*, vol. 1 [Surtees Society 73], Durham, London and Edinburgh

Macdonald, G. 1911: *The Roman Wall in Scotland*, Glasgow

Macdonald, G. 1934: *The Roman Wall in Scotland*, second edition, Oxford

MacIvor, I., Thomas, M. C. and Breeze, D. J. 1980: 'Excavations on the Antonine Wall fort of Rough Castle, Stirlingshire, 1957–61', *PSAS* 110 (1978–80), 230–85

Maidment, J. 1837: *Analecta Scotica*, vol. 2, Edinburgh

Maxwell, G. S. 1989: *The Romans in Scotland*, Edinburgh

Mendyk, S. A. E. 1989: *"Speculum Britanniae": regional study, antiquarianism, and science in Britain to 1700*, Toronto, Buffalo and London

Murray, D. 1927: *Memories of the Old College of Glasgow*, Glasgow

Nichols, J. 1812: *Literary anecdotes of the eighteenth century*, vol. 1, London

Nimmo, W. 1777: *A general history of Stirlingshire*, Edinburgh

Parry, G. 1995: *The trophies of time: English antiquarians of the seventeenth century*, Oxford and New York

RCAHMS 1929: *Inventory of monuments and constructions in Midlothian and West Lothian*, Edinburgh

RCAHMS 1963: *Stirlingshire: an inventory of monuments in Stirlingshire*, Edinburgh

Roberts, B. F. 2004: 'Edward Lhuyd', *Oxford Dictionary of National Biography*, vol. 33, Oxford, 710–12

Robinson, C. J. 1872: *The mansions of Herefordshire and their memories*, London and Hereford

Salmon, T. J. 1913: *Borrowstounness and district, being historical sketches of Kinneil, Carriden, and Bo'ness*, Edinburgh

Salzman, L. F. (ed.) 1939: *Victoria County History. Oxfordshire*, vol. 1, London

Scott, H. (ed.) 1920: *Fasti Ecclesiae Scoticanae*, vol. 3, Edinburgh

Scott, H. (ed.) 1923: *Fasti Ecclesiae Scoticanae*, vol. 4, Edinburgh

Scott, H. (ed.) 1925: *Fasti Ecclesiae Scoticanae*, vol. 5, Edinburgh

Scott, I. 1994: *The life and times of Falkirk*, Edinburgh

Sharp, L. W. 1937: *Early letters of Robert Wodrow, 1698–1709* [Scottish History Society, series 3, 24], Edinburgh

Sharp, R. 2004: 'Thomas Tanner', *Oxford Dictionary of National Biography*, vol. 53, Oxford, 775–7

Sibbald, R. 1707: *Historical Inquiries*, Edinburgh

Sibbald, R. 1710: *The history ancient and modern, of the Sheriffdoms of Linlithgow and Stirling*, Edinburgh

Smith, S. 1934: 'Notes on an artificial mound at Bonnybridge', *PSAS* 68 (1933–34), 59–68

Smith, S. 1936: 'Note on the Antonine Wall and Ditch near Bonnybridge', *PSAS* 70 (1935–36), 146–7

Speck, W. A. 2004: 'Robert Harley', *Oxford Dictionary of National Biography*, vol. 25, Oxford, 317–26

Spurgeon, C. F. E. 1914: *Five hundred years of Chaucer criticism and allusion, 1357–1900*, London, Part 1

Steer, K. A. 1958: 'Arthur's O'on: a lost shrine of Roman Britain', *Archaeological Journal* 115, 99–110

Stenhouse, W. 2000: 'Classical inscriptions and antiquarian scholarship in Italy, 1600–1650', in Cooley 2000, 77–89

Stevenson, J. 1838: *Nennii Historia Britonum*, London

Stukeley, W. 1720: *An Account of a Roman Temple, and other Antiquities, near* Graham's Dyke *in Scotland*, London

Summerson, H. 2004: 'Sir John Graham', in *Oxford Dictionary of National Biography*, vol. 23, Oxford, 212

Sweet, R. 2004: *Antiquaries: the discovery of the past in eighteenth-century Britain*, London and New York

Sykes, N. 1926: *Edmund Gibson, Bishop of London, 1669–1748*, Oxford

Tatton-Brown, T. W. T. 1980: 'Camelon, Arthur's O'on and the main supply base for the Antonine Wall', *Britannia* 11, 340–3

Taylor, M. V. 1939: 'Stonesfield (2): Chesthill Acres', in Salzman 1939, 315–16

Taylor, S. 2004: 'Edmund Gibson', *Oxford Dictionary of National Biography*, vol. 22, Oxford, 68–75

Urry, J. 1721: *The Works of Geoffrey Chaucer, compared with the former Editions*, London

Vasey, P. G. 1993: 'Roman distance slabs: two 17th century drawings based on fieldwork by John Adair FRS and their inter-relationship and context', *Glasgow Archaeological Journal* 18, 65–72

Wanley, H. 1966: *The Diary of Humphrey Wanley, 1715–1726* (edited by C. E. and R. C. Wright), London

Watson, C. B. B. 1929: *Roll of Edinburgh Burgesses and Guild-Brethren, 1406–1700* [Scottish Record Society 59], Edinburgh

Watson, C. B. B. 1930: *Roll of Edinburgh Burgesses and Guild-Brethren, 1701–1760* [Scottish Record Society 62], Edinburgh

Withers, C. W. J. 2004a: 'John Adair', *Oxford Dictionary of National Biography*, vol. 1, Oxford, 186–8

Withers, C. W. J. 2004b: 'Sir Robert Sibbald', *Oxford Dictionary of National Biography*, vol. 50, Oxford, 483–5

Yeoman, L. A. 2004: 'Robert Wodrow', *Oxford Dictionary of National Biography*, vol. 59, Oxford, 938–9

Chapter 8

HADRIAN'S WALL
CONSERVATION AND ARCHAEOLOGY
THROUGH TWO CENTURIES

C. J. Young

Sheppard Frere's career and achievements illustrate with brilliant clarity one of the principal themes of this paper, the close links between conservation and research. A distinguished academic and teacher, who has done so much to shape our view of Roman Britain through his magisterial **Britannia**,[1] *and his major excavations at Canterbury, Verulamium and Dorchester-on-Thames, which in their day helped to develop the concept of rescue archaeology, he has also made a distinguished and very significant contribution to the conservation of archaeological sites as the basic resource of future study and education, through his service for many years on bodies such as the Ancient Monuments Board of England. In doing so he has helped to shape many of the seminal sites to which we continually return in our study of the past through man's material remains. The brief sketch below of Hadrian's Wall as an example of the frequently changing and always complicated inter-relationship between research, conservation and display is offered as a small tribute to Sheppard Frere's distinguished contribution to the display and study of the raw material of our subject. In particular it is hoped that it will reflect the time and effort he put into the work of public bodies, advising on the conservation of sites and the moulding of the system of monument protection and research within which we work.*

Introduction[2]

Archaeology is the study of humanity's past through its material remains, whether above or below ground, or in a museum. To inform our understanding of the past, they have first to be discovered and then studied. Much of this material can be preserved, stored or displayed either in a museum or *in situ*, so that it is available for inspiration, for education, interpretation and display and, not least, for future re-examination and study. Curation of significant archaeological material is vital to future study, and also essential to telling the story of humanity's past.

In the early days of archaeology, those who researched and studied were often the same as those who owned and displayed sites and museums. Pitt-Rivers dug sites on his estate in Cranborne Chase. Alexander Keiller bought Avebury in order to excavate it and reshape it in accordance with his interpretation of the evidence. John Clayton spent much of his lifetime acquiring, excavating and conserving Hadrian's Wall. Then as now, there were many museum curators who were also leading experts in their field.

In the field of archaeological field monuments, however, the phase in which sites tended to be owned by those who dug them or by their friends and peers was replaced by one dominated by specialist university archaeologists. More recently we have had the apparent distinction between university-based scholars, who do research, on the one hand, and on the other the state agencies, local authorities and charitable trusts who conserve and maintain sites. It is now a common complaint that there are insufficient links between academic archaeologists who study the material evidence of humanity's past on the one hand, and those responsible for site management on the other.

Of course, research is not confined to universities. Neither is expertise in site management located only in government agencies. For example, one of the leading experts on Hadrian's Wall was until recently Chief Inspector of Historic Scotland,[3] while university-based archaeologists have been responsible over many decades for the excavation and research which has underpinned conservation and display at Silchester and Wroxeter. Hadrian's Wall is one of the most studied monuments of Roman Britain over a period of over 400 years. As such, it is particularly well-suited for a study of this sort.

Hadrian's Wall to 1914

Hadrian's Wall is possibly the British monument with the longest history of antiquarian interest. Noted first by Bede around thirteen centuries ago, it has been the subject of regular comment from the time of Camden in the late sixteenth century. It also has one of the longest traditions of efforts to conserve it. This began two centuries ago with William Hutton in 1801. Possibly also the first person to walk the Wall from one end almost to the other (at the age of 78), he persuaded the then owner of Planetrees not to demolish the small length of Hadrian's Wall (now in the care of English Heritage) on the hill down to the North Tyne.[4] As far as is known, this was the first successful effort to preserve the Wall from what we would now call development pressures, although Stukeley in the previous century had protested in vain at its wholesale destruction to allow the creation of the Military Road between Newcastle and Sewingshields.[5]

This early notice of the Wall led also to early and continuing description and research on it. Camden wrote an account of the Wall, subsequently improved after he had visited parts of it. Stukeley visited it in 1725. The first attempt to map the Wall in detail came in 1716. Horsley's *Britannia Romana* in 1733 contained the first detailed plan of the Wall along with engravings of finds from it.

During the nineteenth century, a number of strands emerged and mingled, all reflecting an increasing interest in the Wall, its history and its conservation. The Society of Antiquaries of Newcastle upon Tyne was founded in 1813, followed by the Cumberland and Westmoreland Antiquarian and Archaeological Society in 1866. John Hodgson published the *History of Northumberland* between 1828 and 1840. He began excavations at Housesteads in 1822. Excavation started at Birdoswald before 1830. Hodgson was the first to suggest that all the elements of the frontier – Wall, Vallum, forts and so on – could all have been part of one concept for a barrier.[6]

Collingwood Bruce came on the scene in 1848, with his first visit leading directly to the first Pilgrimage in 1849 and the publication of the first edition of *The Roman Wall* in 1851. By the end of the nineteenth century a recognisable pattern of interest had emerged, with the two local antiquarian societies taking a strong interest, Pilgrimages at irregular intervals, and an increasing number of excavations and descriptions of the Wall.[7] This academic and antiquarian interest has to be set in a wider context.

Hadrian's Wall passed through a transect of Northern England which throughout the late eighteenth and nineteenth centuries was developing at a fantastic rate. The North-East in particular was a centre of technological and industrial innovation. Coal-mining, steel-manufacture, ship-building and other industries led to an explosive urban development on Tyneside, while in the countryside the increased demand of the urban areas for food led to rapid advances in agriculture. These included improvements of the land through liming (requiring a sizeable quantity of lime kilns, many of them still visible), land enclosure with stone boundary walls, and the establishment of large numbers of new and expanded farm houses (and their associated buildings) throughout the Wall area. For both field walls and farm buildings the Wall was an obvious source of raw material. There was also considerable industrial impact on the countryside, in particular for extractive industries such as coal-mining and stone-quarrying, some of the latter on the line of the Wall itself.

By the mid-nineteenth century, the Wall was therefore under enormous pressure in both urban and rural areas. While this could lead to new discoveries (as, for example, at Wallsend), it also led to enormous destruction on a scale not previously seen. The nineteenth century therefore saw the first concerted moves towards protection of the Wall, many decades before the United Kingdom's first Ancient Monuments Act in 1882. Before legal protection through designation was available, the only way to protect the Wall was for it to be acquired by a sympathetic owner.

In this area, one figure towers above all others. This was John Clayton (1792–1890). Clayton inherited the Chesters estate from his father, as well as being a major figure in the development of Newcastle. Starting with one Roman fort in his park, if not his garden, he moved on in the 1830s systematically to buy up farms along the line of Hadrian's Wall in its central sector. At his death his estate stretched from Acomb in the east to Cawfields, including five forts, larger than any part of the Wall now in public or private ownership.[8] Ownership led naturally to excavation and curation. From 1843, he began digging, first at Chesters fort itself and then further west along the line of the Wall. As well as working at Housesteads and at three milecastles, he was also responsible for clearing much of the line of the Wall on his estate. After he had cleared it, he restored it by building a dry-stone wall over the surviving Roman material from the fallen stones.[9] Built to a height just too great for a sheep to climb over, the 'Clayton Wall' was then capped with turf. It is now one of the most distinctive features of the landscape of the central section of the Wall.

It is important to remember that Clayton was not alone in acquiring parts of the frontier in order to conserve them. Beyond the eastern end of the Wall, the South Shields Urban District Council in 1875 acquired part of the fort of Arbeia and laid it out for public display as the Roman Remains Park. One of the first municipal ventures into the area of monument protection, this demonstrates the potential for survival of the Wall and its component parts even in an urban environment.

The turn of the century and the Edwardian period saw major excavations at both Housesteads and Corbridge, sponsored in each case by a learned society, followed by work at Haltwistle Burn which began F. Gerald Simpson's long association with Hadrian's Wall studies. Significantly, Simpson's work also included investigation and conservation of stretches of the Clayton Wall and of Milecastle 39, both by now falling into disrepair fifty or more years after their first exposure and consolidation by Clayton.[10]

By the outbreak of the First World War, therefore, a clear pattern had emerged of the linking of excavation and research to the interest of owners of stretches of the Wall, and the conservation of what they owned. There was also conservation resulting from excavation carried out for research purposes, while excavators were drawn both from local antiquarians and from the emerging profession of archaeology. As yet there was comparatively little interest from universities, with the exception of Francis Haverfield, Camden Professor of Ancient History at Oxford from 1907, although at the time of his first involvement on the Wall he was still a master at Lancing College (where many years later Sheppard Frere was to follow him), and of R. G. Collingwood. Work was funded from private and voluntary sources and state involvement was totally absent.[11]

Between the Wars

Following the inevitable hiatus caused by the First World War, research began again in the late 1920s. F. Gerald Simpson remained active but there were a number of other players in the field. The University of Durham Excavation Committee and the Cumberland Excavation Committee were both active, and there were extensive excavations at a number of sites including Birdoswald, Housesteads and Corbridge.[12] This was a period when the University of Durham and its offshoot at Newcastle were very active, with figures such as Eric Birley and Ian Richmond being very prominent. Much of this excavation was research-led, but there were also strong links to display and conservation at both Corbridge and at Housesteads.

There were two very significant trends during this period. The first was the development of state protection of archaeological sites through the application of successive Ancient Monuments Acts. State protection generally was given a major impetus by events on Hadrian's Wall. As noted above, quarries had been active in the Wall area for many generations. The threat of major new quarries following the break-up of the Chesters Estate led to a new Ancient Monuments Act in 1931, with the power to create Preservation Schemes which would protect the landscape setting of Ancient Monuments as well as the site itself. This was sufficient to stop the threat of new quarrying on a massive scale. It was not until 1943 that the Hadrian's Wall and Vallum Preservation Scheme was finally confirmed, and the Northumberland Whinstone Company was paid substantial compensation to cease expanding the Walltown Quarry outwards.[13]

Alongside increased government powers to protect the Wall through legislation, the second trend was the acquisition of parts of the Wall and its associated sites by public bodies. At this stage, there were two – the Office of Works and the National Trust, the latter strictly a private charitable trust – with the power to acquire land and hold it in perpetuity. The Office of Works acquired Corbridge in 1932. It and its successors, most recently English Heritage, have acquired lengths of the Wall, forts and other features along most of the Wall's length ever since.

The National Trust has focused on building up its estate in the central sector, beginning with Housesteads Fort in 1930, so that it now owns several miles of the most spectacular part of the Roman frontier. The ability of the Trust to acquire land rather than monuments has meant that they have been able to own not just the monument but also its surrounding landscape and context.

Post-1945

Since 1945 there have been a number of changes, particularly in the last 30 years. For the first few decades things continued much as before. The Ministry of Works administered its ancient monuments legislation and managed the sites in its care, acquiring further significant stretches of the Wall in the process. The National Trust continued to acquire land to consolidate and extend its estate. The Universities of Durham and Newcastle continued major excavations at Corbridge and elsewhere, although these were often linked to conservation and display, as at South Shields in the 1950's. Apart from academic studies and the decennial Pilgrimages (resumed in 1949), there was little attempt to visualise the Wall as an entity, and to manage it as such. The Universities were also significantly involved in rescue excavations, for example at Wallsend and at Corbridge Red House.

From the early 1970s things have changed. The range of public and charitable ownership has expanded. This began with the creation of the Vindolanda Trust in 1972. They have gradually expanded their holding at Vindolanda itself to which they have added the fort of Carvoran. The results of their excavation have transformed the appearance of Vindolanda, and revolutionised our understanding of many aspects of Hadrian's Wall and the frontier. In 1981, Cumbria County Council acquired Birdoswald in lieu of death duties,[14] followed shortly thereafter by Northumberland County Council's purchase of Rudchester. On Tyneside, South Tyneside have extended their holding at South Shields, and North Tyneside purchased the fort at Wallsend, first to clear Victorian housing and then replace it with new housing, subsequently deciding, in the light of the survival of the fort as revealed by rescue excavations, to maintain the site as an ancient monument.

Development pressures have increased both in urban and rural areas, although so far all major threats to the integrity of the Wall have been thwarted. A new pressure in the 1970s was recognised to be tourism. Managed positively, this can improve access to sites of interest and generate employment and wealth in the local economy. There were grave concerns, however, that tourism was leading to damage through over-visiting and consequent erosion. This led to the Dart Report of 1976, and the Report of the Hadrian's Wall Consultative Committee in 1984, both of which addressed much of their attention to the sustainable management of tourism. One result of these reports was the decision to create a National Trail along Hadrian's Wall, which was finally opened in 2004.

These changes have not ended excavation and research on Hadrian's Wall, although the protagonists and the reasons for the work have changed. The last major University excavation on Hadrian's Wall finished in 1984. From 1982 to 1988, the National Trust, with considerable support from English Heritage, excavated considerable stretches of Hadrian's Wall to deal with the problems of erosion by visitors and stock.[15] The Vindolanda Trust has continued excavations throughout this period, while at Birdoswald English Heritage carried out major excavations from 1987 to 1992.[16] On Tyneside, Tyne and Wear Museums, who manage South Shields and Wallsend on behalf of the site owners, have excavated extensively at both forts. At Wallsend, first excavated under rescue conditions by the University of Newcastle between 1975 and 1984, the Museum has now totally cleared and displayed the site.

Apart from these excavations, there have been numerous other investigations and surveys. Some, such as the excavations at Denton in advance of the construction of the A1 in 1987–9, or the work by English Heritage in 1988 which established the plan of the fort at Bowness on Solway for the first time, were in advance of development. Others have been to improve our understanding of the site in order to manage it better. An example of this was the work of English Heritage at Blackcarts in 1998. Other work has been to improve access and interpretation. As well as excavation there have been significant surveys. The Royal Commission for Historic Monuments (England) surveyed the whole earthwork remains of Hadrian's Wall from 1989 to 1993, while English Heritage has created a drawn record of upstanding masonry of the Wall.

The overall management of the Wall has also changed. Created a World Heritage Site under the UNESCO World Heritage Convention in 1987, this was at first thought to be a largely honorific distinction. A series of planning cases, two of them on Hadrian's Wall, showed that World Heritage status was a key factor in planning terms, leading in 1994 to government advice that integrated World Heritage Sites into the planning system, as well as recommending the creation of World Heritage Management Plans for each of the United Kingdom's World Heritage Sites (now 27 in all). Work on the first Hadrian's Wall Management Plan, completed in 1996, in fact began in 1993. The second iteration was published in 2002.[17]

The Plan, now about to be revised for the second time, is not a statutory document. It does provide an overall framework for the coordination of all activities to do with Hadrian's Wall, and it works because it is supported by a consensus among the key stakeholders, be they the principal owners, local authorities or regional and national agencies. The Plan has thus created a more holistic approach to the management of the World Heritage Site as a whole. It has stimulated considerable investment, primarily related to access and sustainable tourism. These have in their turn prompted archaeological work, for example on the line of the National Trail and at Wallsend. It has not yet led to a unified research strategy for Hadrian's Wall, although this remains a priority.[18]

Conclusion

Over the last two hundred years, much has changed on Hadrian's Wall. The Wall has been formally recognised as being of outstanding universal value to all humanity. There have been numerous losses of fabric and considerable development in the wider setting of the Wall, although its essential character remains much the same. The area has passed from pre-industrial through industrial to a post-industrial society, increasingly dependent on tourism and service industries. Much of the Wall has passed into public or charitable ownership, and what can be done to it is much more regulated by legislation than was the case two centuries ago. The players who influence what happens and who study and interpret the Wall have changed considerably. We have passed from an age of gentleman antiquarians through several generations of university-based archaeologists to an era in which most archaeology is carried out by or for the bodies who own and regulate the site, often in response to development pressures, or the need to improve interpretation for visitors.

While the players may have changed, other things remain remarkably the same. From the outset of modern interest in Hadrian's Wall, archaeological investigation and the management of the site have been closely intertwined. From Clayton's excavation of the fort at Chesters down to the current work at Vindolanda and elsewhere, this has remained the same. What also remains the same is the vast amount of new knowledge provided by every investigation of Hadrian's Wall, and how much still remains to be discovered. On Hadrian's Wall, new archaeological work continues as an integral part of the management of the site and the development of access to it. Whatever the reasons for the work may be, the results are still substantial and worthwhile. While it is sad that some past players, such as the two local universities, are no longer active in the field, there are still substantial numbers of scholars in the agencies and other bodies working on Hadrian's Wall. Here at least, the links between conservation (even as the recording of evidence in advance of development) and research, which has so typified Sheppard Frere's work, survive well, and so provide new insights into our understanding of this most important of sites, as well as helping us to conserve the evidence for future re-examination.

Notes

1. Originally published in 1967, it is now in its fourth edition: Frere 1999.
2. This paper is based on my experiences of dealing with the management of Hadrian's Wall in a variety of roles for over 25 years, five of which I spent as co-ordinator for the Hadrian's Wall World Heritage Site Management Plan. The debt I owe to present and former colleagues on Hadrian's Wall and elsewhere will be obvious. The opinions expressed, together with any errors, are entirely my own.
3. Cf. Breeze and Dobson 2000; Breeze 2000.
4. Wilmott 2001, 155.
5. Woodside and Crow 1999, 96.
6. Woodside and Crow 1999, 96–102.
7. Bidwell 1999a.
8. Woodside and Crow 1999, 84–6.
9. Woodside and Crow 1999, 102–04.
10. Woodside and Crow 1999, 108–10.
11. Wilmott 2001, 163.
12. Woodside and Crow 1999, 110 – 111.
13. Woodside and Crow 1999, 93; Charlton 2004.
14. Wilmott 2001, 172.
15. Woodside and Crow 1999, 112.
16. Wilmott 1997.
17. English Heritage 1996; Austen and Young 2002.
18. Cf. Young 1999 for a fuller discussion of the development of the Management Plan.

References

Austen P. and Young C. 2002: *Hadrian's Wall World Heritage Site Management Plan 2002–2007*, Hexham

Bidwell, P. 1999a: 'The pilgrimages of Hadrian's Wall', in Bidwell 1999b, 1–6

Bidwell, P. (ed.) 1999b: *Hadrian's Wall 1989–1999: a summary of recent excavations and research*, Newcastle

Breeze, D. J. 2000: *Hadrian's Wall: a souvenir guide to the Roman Wall*, London

Breeze, D. J. and Dobson, B. 2000: *Hadrian's Wall*, fourth edition, London

Charlton, J. 2004: 'Saving the Wall: quarries and conservation', *Archaeologia Aeliana*, Fifth Series, 33, 5–8

English Heritage 1996: *Hadrian's Wall World Heritage Site Management Plan 1996*, London

Frere, S. S. 1999: *Britannia: a history of Roman Britain*, fourth edition, London

Wilmott, T. 1997: *Birdoswald: excavations of a Roman fort on Hadrian's Wall and its successor settlements* [English Heritage Archaeological Report 14], London

Wilmott, T. 2001: *Birdoswald Roman fort: 1800 years on Hadrian's Wall*, Stroud

Woodside, R. and Crow, J. 1999: *Hadrian's Wall: an historic landscape*, London

Young C. 1999: 'The management of Hadrian's Wall', in Bidwell 1999b, 65–72

LATE ROMAN AFRICAN RED SLIP WARE FROM THE FRONTIER REGION IN THE PROVINCE OF *THEBAÏS* (UPPER EGYPT)

Michael Mackensen

I first met Professor Sheppard Frere in 1972/73 when I came to Oxford as a young student to study with him for two terms the archaeology of Roman Britain and the Celtic coinage of Britain. I was surprised not only by the excellent study conditions in Oxford, but also in particular by the very personal one-to-one tuition that I received on these topics by the famous Professor himself. In addition he kindly took me to various important Roman sites in England, and also showed me some slides of impressive Roman towns in North Africa, such as Cuicul (Djemila), which he had taken during a recent trip to Algeria. I was deeply fascinated, and some years later I got the chance to travel myself for six months in Roman Africa, a region where I have conducted many archaeological field projects during my career (mostly in Tunisia and now in Upper Egypt). Over the past thirty years I have been able on numerous occasions to ask Sheppard Frere for his advice, always freely given and always highly appreciated by me; and in addition I have to thank him for his kindness and incredible patience whenever I sent him contributions by me in English in urgent need of final polishing, which he invariably did with speed, tact and good humour.

Introduction

The wide distribution of mid- and late Roman African red slip (hereafter ARS) ware, even to the eastern provinces of the Roman Empire, is well known. Plain dishes, plates and bowls, partly decorated with bands of fine feather-rouletting and produced in so-called C^1 and C^2 fabrics – according to the terminology of the fabrics introduced by A. Carandini in 1968 and then elaborated in the *Atlante delle forme ceramiche* I^1 – were much appreciated because of their unrivalled high quality, such as the thin-walled forms Hayes 45A and B, 48A and B, 49 and 50A with a slip of lustrous (C^1), or slightly glossy, but mostly matt (C^2) appearance on both sides of the vessel. From the fourth century to the sixth and early seventh century also, plain, stamped, appliqué- and mould-made relief-decorated ARS ware was produced with a wide range of forms in various fabrics (north Tunisia: D^1 and D^2; central Tunisia: C^3–C^5).[2] It was traded in remarkable quantities from the north African provinces, *Africa Proconsularis* and *Byzacena*, to the western provinces, and on a slightly reduced level also to the eastern provinces.

J. W. Hayes noticed that, in Egypt, ARS ware of the third century was mostly limited to sites along the Mediterranean coast and the main consumer city of Alexandria,[3] whereas the distribution of late Roman ARS ware included in addition various inland sites in Lower and even in Middle and Upper Egypt.[4] Third-century ARS ware in C^1 and C^2 high-quality fabrics seems to be so far unknown from important mid-Roman urban centres south of Cairo, such as Karanis in the Fayum, Hermopolis (el-Ashmunein) and Antinoopolis, or even Upper Egyptian cities such as Coptos (Qift), Thebas (Luxor) and Syene (Aswan), or the quarry settlements of Mons Claudianus and Mons Porphyrites. Although the ARS forms noted above (Hayes forms 45, 48, 49 and 50) in their characteristic fabrics should be easily recognisable amongst the other imported and local/regional red-slipped fine wares, and classified according to the typology of Hayes, no fragments of these C^1 and C^2 forms seem to be known from Middle and Upper Egyptian sites.[5] In this context, therefore, a rim-fragment of a dish of form Hayes 48B in C^2 fabric should be mentioned from Dionysias (Qasr Qarun) at the western edge of the Fayum, which I found during a visit to the site in the spring of 2005, lying on the surface inside the Roman town, just north of the restored temple.[6]

The apparent absence of central Tunisian ARS forms in C^1 and C^2 fabric from the Middle and Upper Egyptian cities – not to mention rural villages – might be caused simply by a lack of closed deposits and levels of third-century date from stratigraphical excavations – for instance, at the Roman towns of Coptos (Qift) and Syene (Aswan), as well as at the village on the Nile island of Elephantine. Perhaps it is also the result of a lack of interest in evaluating both stratified and unstratified Roman pottery, and even fine wares, during excavations carried out more than half a century ago. More significantly, it might be the result of a different methodological approach adopted by archaeologists in the past: if they had realized the significance of pottery fine wares for understanding aspects of everyday life, commerce and long-distance trade, our present knowledge of pottery distribution might have been different. It seems remarkable that there is only a handful of reports by specialists on (imported) Roman red slip wares from Egypt before the 1970s.

Very similar is the situation for plain ARS forms of the late third and the first half of the fourth century in C^3 fabric: the latter has a smooth, mostly matt slip which covers the inside, the rim and the upper part of the outside of the vessel only. For the characteristic forms Hayes 45B and C, 48B, 50A and 52A, as well as appliqué-decorated forms Hayes 48B (variant), 52B and 53A, there is no evidence for their presence in the urban centres of Middle and Upper Egypt listed above (and that includes the more southerly region beyond Syene called *Dodekaschoinos*).[7] Nor do the forts constructed under Diocletian in the late third and early fourth century, such as Sile (Tell Abu Sayfi) and Magdolum (Tell el-Herr), both in the eastern Nile delta, Dionysias (Qasr Qarun) in the Fayum, Abu Sha'ar (which lies north of Hurghada on the Red Sea coast), Thebas (Luxor) and probably Praesentia (?) (Nag el-Hagar near Kom Ombo),[8] provide us with ARS forms in C^3 fabric – not least because, from some of these military sites, comprehensive pottery reports are not yet available.

According to the current state of research on imported late Roman fine wares from Egypt, the situation changed in either the mid-fourth century or, more broadly, during the second half of the fourth century and in the fifth century. Then stamped and even moulded relief-decorated ARS forms in different fabrics (D^1 and D^2 as well as C^5) are known from many sites and from important cities in the area of the Nile Delta and in Lower Egypt: examples include the pilgrimage centre at Abu Mina, the monastic settlements in the Kellia and the towns in the Fayum, as well as cities in the Nile valley in Middle and Upper Egypt.[9] The distribution of these late Roman ARS fabrics from the fourth to the sixth century was recently plotted on a map prepared by M. Bonifay (Fig. 9.1),[10] to which the site of Nag el-Hagar has been added (see below). Obviously the ARS dishes, plates and bowls, partly with elaborate stamped decoration of different styles (north Tunisian: A[II]–[III], A[III]/ E[I], E[I]–[II]; central Tunisian: B, C and D [after Hayes]), and partly with feather-rouletting, were table-wares much in demand in Egypt. They were distributed upstream almost as far as the first cataract of the Nile, i.e. to the region around the urban centre of Syene (Aswan)[11] – since the early second century AD, also the military headquarters for the southern frontier[12] – and the islands of Elephantine and Philae. This area in the vicinity of the first cataract became the new late Roman frontier district when Diocletian decided in AD 298 to give up the more southerly Nubian Nile valley (the region of *Dodekaschoinos*), with its cost-intensive outposts: above all this decision was prompted by the continuous menace caused by raids of the *Blemmyes* tribe.[13] The Roman garrisons were withdrawn from *Nubia*, and the land was eventually handed over to the *Nobades* tribe, allied to Rome.[14]

From the Upper Egyptian Nile valley south of the area of Thebas (Luxor), however, as far as the first cataract, late Roman and early Byzantine pottery has been published from Gurna, Deir el-Bachit, Hermonthis (Armant), Tôd and Elephantine.[15] Besides the huge quantities of Egyptian red slip wares of different fabrics – the vast majority being Egyptian Red Slip (hereafter ERS) ware A – there are mostly only small quantities of ARS fragments in D^1, D^2 and C^5 fabric which have been identified and published.[16] However, ongoing research on late Roman pottery from the current excavations at Syene (Aswan) and Elephantine, conducted by C. von Pilgrim of the Swiss Institute of Architectural and Archaeological Research on Ancient Egypt (Cairo), is likely to expand the range of forms and stamp-types present, and in general improve our knowledge of imported ARS ware in the region.

At the moment it is still rather difficult to draw a reliable picture of the supply of ARS wares to Middle and Upper Egypt by long-distance and then inter-provincial trade, because of an absence of the necessary specialists' reports before the mid-1970s. Apart from the publications by B. Johnson on the late Roman pottery from Karanis,[17] by R. D. Gempeler on the Roman and early Islamic pottery from El-ephantine,[18] and by D. M. Bailey on pottery of the late Roman and early Arab period at Hermopolis (el-Ashmunein)[19] – without a doubt a key site for pottery studies of these periods in Egypt – no substantial quantities of late Roman ARS wares from anywhere in this region have been published.

For a better insight into the market of red-slipped fine wares, and for a

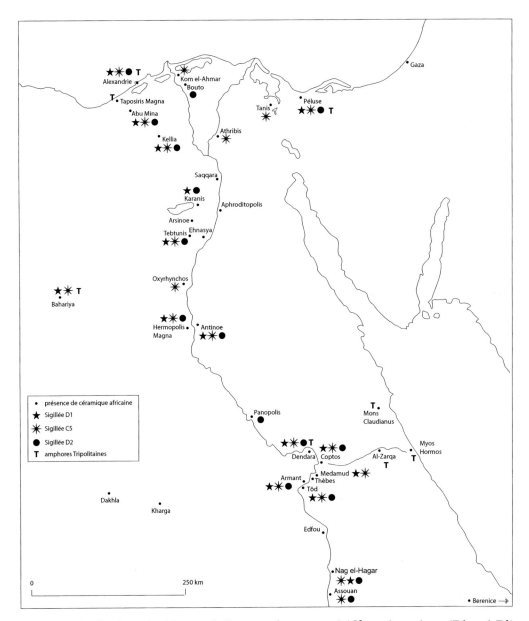

Fig. 9.1 Distribution of African red slip ware from central (C⁵) and northern (D¹ and D²) Tunisia in Egypt

comparison with that of Egyptian red slip ware A – the latter a pottery which dominated the Upper Egyptian market (and which was produced at Aswan [on the Nile island of Elephantine], and at other Upper Egyptian centres of minor importance, such as Nag el-Hagar[20]) – more work on the ARS ware (not least in view of its importance as a reasonably accurate dating tool) needs to be done in the near future. In particular we need comparable quantified data of ARS wares from sites of different size, character and significance for the region – both urban and military settlements, as well as rural villages and monastic sites in the Nile valley and the oases of the western desert. This would allow us to assess both the continuity and the differences of demand and supply to individual local populations and/or military garrisons, contrasting the volumes of ERS with imported ARS ware from the late third/early fourth century to the second half of the sixth century and to the early or mid-seventh century.

Nag el-Hagar

One of the more important military sites in the Upper Egyptian frontier region is the late Roman fort at Nag el-Hagar, which is situated right on the east bank of the Nile, surrounded by an expanding small village and fertile palm gardens, about 30 km north of Aswan and 17 km south of Kom Ombo respectively (for its location, see Fig. 9.1). The curtain wall of the fort is partly preserved up to a height of *c.* 1.5 m, but, tragically, the mudbrick structures and buildings in the interior of the fort have been severely damaged, and in some cases even almost entirely destroyed, by clandestine digging for re-usable building material, such as sandstone blocks and mudbrick (*sebakh*).

Several seasons of excavation work were conducted here by the Inspectorate of Aswan of the Supreme Council of Antiquities (SCA) from 1984 to 1989. The Swiss Institute at Cairo was invited to participate in the rescue project, and two architects, H. Jaritz and P. Zignani, prepared ground plans of the structures excavated in the western half of the fort; two preliminary reports were published.[21] After my first visit to Nag el-Hagar in 2001, which is an impressive site both because of its archaeological remains and for the beauty of its landscape setting, the project was finally resumed by an Egyptian-Swiss joint mission (SCA Aswan and Swiss Institute). Two seasons of documentation and fieldwork have been carried out in 2005 and 2006, which were co-directed by M. El-Bialy and the author.[22]

The fortification, with a square layout measuring 142 m by 142 m (2.0 ha), shows the characteristic features of late Roman fortresses and forts (Fig. 9.2): all the towers are of the projecting type, those flanking the three gates as well as the intermediate towers being U-shaped, while the corner towers are square-shaped. The main gate on the western side and the western curtain wall with its intermediate and corner towers were constructed of rectangular stone blocks, whereas the northern, eastern and southern curtain wall were built of mud-bricks. Opposite the west gate, in the central axis of the eastern curtain wall, the remains of a third intermediate tower were traced instead of an expected gate. A dozen column shafts and two bases of red granite (from Aswan) were located on the surface of the eastern half of the fort, close to the enclosure wall. They indicate a structure of architectural importance, probably the headquarters building (*principia cum praetorio*). Most spectacular, however, is the palace complex (*palatium*) in the south-

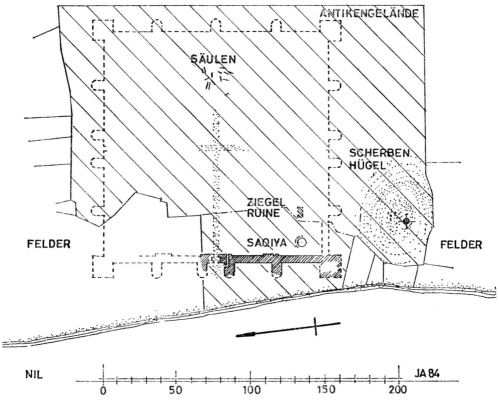

Fig. 9.2 Nag el-Hagar, provisional schematic plan of the late Roman fort

western quarter of the fort (Fig. 9.3), excavated in 1984–89. The residential area shows an elaborate sequence of various official rooms with apses, and a central courtyard with portico and a two-phased, elevated reception-room with an apse (*aula*), connected with two lateral groups of four rooms each. The presence of this palace complex appears to be highly unusual for a fort which is approximately half the size of a legionary fortress. The palace, which covers an area of *c*. 50 m by 35 m (0.18 ha), must be seen in connection with the presence in this part of Egypt of high-ranking officials and dignitaries of the late Roman administration. One of its purposes might have been the reception of foreign embassies from tribes such as the *Blemmyes*, which might have been welcomed here by the governor or the military commander of the Thebaid.[23]

Zignani dated the fort to the period of the emperor Diocletian, i.e. around AD 300, based on arguments of a fairly general character (such as comparisons with other late Roman fortifications in Egypt, or supposed links with historical or papyrological records) rather than on specific dating evidence.[24] Stratified and coin-dated pottery deposits (for instance, from underneath the limestone pavements of the first period in the palace), however, were missing from his reports; nor was

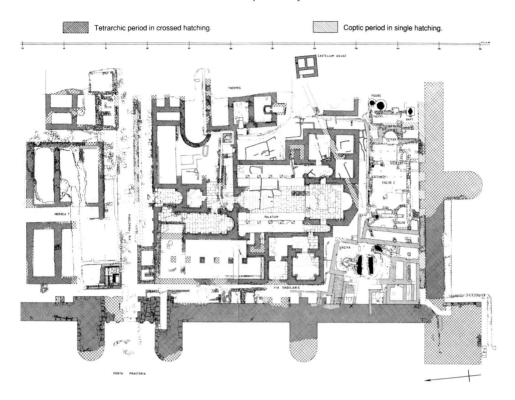

Fig. 9.3 Nag el-Hagar, south-west area with enclosure wall and palace (after Wareth and Zignani 1992, pl. 22)

any systematic work done on the unstratified red-slipped table-ware from the excavations of 1984–89. The identification of Nag el-Hagar with a fort called Praesentia, noted in the *Notitia Dignitatum* (Or. 31.33), is still uncertain.[25] There is no reliable numismatic evidence, or even direct papyrological or epigraphic evidence, for an assumed visit and a temporary stay of Diocletian at Nag el-Hagar – in connection with the re-organisation of the late Roman frontier and the evacuation of the *Dodekaschoinos* in the summer of AD 298 – or even of the building of the fort and its architecturally ambitious palace by and for this emperor.

As a result, before we started on our new project in 2005, there was no chronological information available (neither coins nor imported fine ware) to justify the assumption that the fort was continuously garrisoned by a (still-unknown) unit from the early fourth until the first third or the middle of the fifth century (and perhaps later); nor did we know when the end of the military occupation occurred, and when the later, supposedly civilian, settlement of the early Byzantine/Coptic period was established.

In particular, archaeological evidence was urgently needed for dating the construction of the fort at Nag el-Hagar, and for defining the period of its military use. In this paper I shall deal only with some chronological aspects of the fort, as

Michael Mackensen

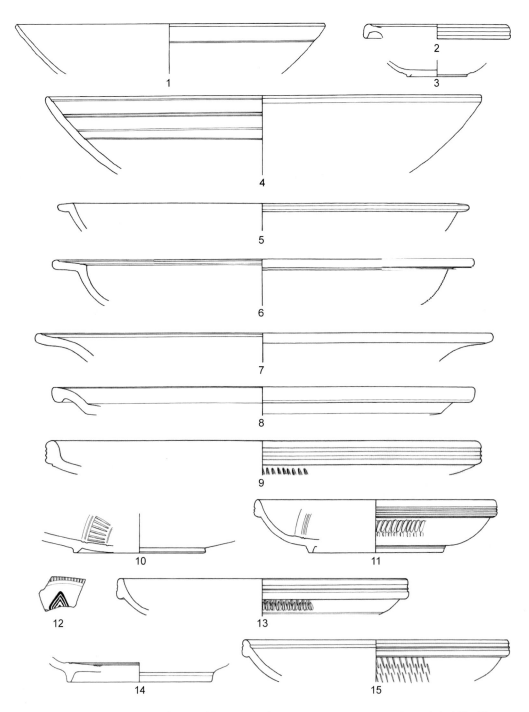

Fig. 9.4 Nag el-Hagar (2005/06), African red slip ware. 1–4, 9–15 central Tunisia (C^3–C^5), 5–8 northern Tunisia (D^1 and D^2). Scale 1:3

well as with the first results of the study of ARS ware from the pottery survey of the fort itself and of the directly adjacent areas to the east and to the south; the results of a geophysical survey and a topographical survey, as well as the findings of the four trial trenches carried out during the second season of our Egyptian-Swiss joint mission in spring 2006, will be discussed elsewhere.[26]

Dating evidence: coins and pottery

Of only nine (unstratified) late Roman bronze coins, classified by H.-C. Noeske, which were found as single items during the excavations in 1987/88 in the residential area, eight can be attributed to the Tetrarchic period. Six of these are so-called radiate fractions (*antoniniani*), minted at Alexandria in AD 296/297, and two are *folles* (*nummi*), one of them dated to AD 304/305. This modest numismatic evidence, unfortunately without any stratigraphical context, seems to provide us with a good argument for building-activity and a possible fort construction-date in the late 90s of the third century, i.e. around AD 300,[27] or maybe in the early fourth century (see below, with note 35).

Very astonishing and totally unexpected were the huge quantities of late Roman fine wares (especially by comparison with the published, limited range of ARS ware from Elephantine) – not only the dominant (Upper) Egyptian red slip ware A, which makes up the lion's share of the fine wares, but also 162 fragments of African red slip ware. The latter comprised 107 rims, 42 base- and foot-sherds (of separate vessels) as well as 13 wall-fragments, scattered on the surface in the interior of the fort (almost all of them were found to the east of the excavated areas), and in the areas adjoining the eastern and southern enclosure wall (up to a distance of *c.* 20 metres). No ARS sherds were found in the area of a huge, late Roman and early Byzantine/Coptic rubbish heap near the south-western corner tower of the fort (cf. Fig. 9.2).[28] Table 1 lists the fragments of ARS ware from the surface collection and the substantial layers (0.2 m–0.5 m thick) of demolition debris in trenches 1 and 3.

Various forms of ARS ware, dating between the early fourth century and the late sixth and first half of the seventh centuries, from important production centres in *Africa Proconsularis* and *Byzacena*, were classified. It was possible to identify and differentiate the north Tunisian fabrics D¹ (el-Mahrine, Bordj el-Djerbi) and D² (from an unlocated production centre [= Bonifay 2004, 49: so-called 'atelier X'], and Oudhna) as well as the central Tunisian fabrics C³, C⁴ and C⁵ (Sidi Marzouk Tounsi). Missing were the characteristic forms (Hayes 87 and 88) of the north-eastern Tunisian production centre of Sidi Khalifa (D²), and the forms and fabrics of the central Tunisian production sites at Henchir el-Guellal near Djilma (A/D, C¹–C⁴) and Henchir es-Srira (similar to C²–C⁴).[29]

The documented range of forms comprises the following standard forms (see Table 1): during the fourth and the first half of the fifth century, flat plates (Hayes 58B, 59B, 61B) and bowls (Hayes 67), in north Tunisian D¹ and D² fabric, represent the major part of the available ARS forms, apart from a few dishes of Hayes 50A and B as well as a small bowl of Hayes 52 (A?) in central Tunisian C³ and C⁴ fabric.

There are no fragments of appliqué- or mould-made relief-decorated forms, such as the small bowls of Hayes form 52B or the rectangular plates (Hayes 56). From the mid-fifth century until the mid-sixth century, dishes and large plates of various sizes (mostly Hayes 84 and some Hayes 82), with broad bands of fine feather-rouletting, as well as large plates with a high pedestal foot (Hayes 89B and 90) in C^5 fabric, are the dominant forms numerically, and were evidently highly appreciated; the latter were manufactured in the central Tunisian production centre of Sidi Marzouk Tounsi. Smaller deep bowls of several forms (Hayes 94B, 96, 99A–C) and flanged bowls (Hayes 91A/B, C and D) occur in D^1 and D^2 fabrics, which all originate from north Tunisian production centres. It seems remarkable that no large north Tunisian dishes in D^1 and D^2 fabric, such as the stamped forms Hayes 103A–B, 104A–C and the undecorated form Hayes 105, as well as the large bowls Hayes 107, were found, except for a single rim-sherd of form Hayes 104B variant, no. 22.

Mid-Roman ARS forms in fabrics A^1 and A^2, A/D and C^1–C^2, of the late second and the first half of the third century, are definitely absent at Nag el-Hagar. The earliest ARS forms from the fort site, which probably belong to the late third and the early fourth centuries, are fairly rare, in contrast to ARS forms of the second half of the fifth and the first half of the sixth century: they include a rim fragment of a C^3 dish of Hayes form 50A (Fig. 9.4, 1), and a floor fragment of a small C^3 bowl, probably of Hayes form 52(A?) (Fig. 9.4, 3), both dating from *c.* AD (280)/300 until the middle or third quarter of the fourth century.[30] To the same period belongs the rim of a dish Hayes 58B (Fig. 9.4, 5) in D^2 fabric,[31] whereas six rim fragments of forms Hayes 59 and 59B (Fig. 9.4, 6) in D^1 and D^2 fabric, are dated from *c.* AD 320/330 until the late fourth century.[32] Typical ARS forms of the second half of the fourth and the first half of the fifth century are north Tunisian dishes Hayes 60 (Fig. 9.4, 7) and 61B, large bowls of Hayes 67 (Fig. 9.4, 8) and probably a small bowl of Hayes 73, all in D^1 and D^2 fabric,[33] as well as a central Tunisian dish of Hayes form 50B (Fig. 9.4, 4) in $C^{3/4}$ fabric;[34] each of these forms is represented by one or two specimens only (Table 1). All of these ARS fragments can probably be related to the military garrison at Nag el-Hagar. As for the construction of the fort, some of them point to the first half or the first third of the fourth century; but the paucity of ARS forms Hayes 50A, 52(A?) and 58B – particularly so because they are only surface finds without an archaeological context – suggests that there is not sufficient evidence for us to fix with any confidence the building activity of the fort to around AD 300 or in the first decade of the fourth century.[35]

A typical fifth-century pot-type is the flanged bowl of Hayes form 91A/B in D^1 (5 rims) and D^2 fabric (15 rims) with feather-rouletting on the inside (Fig. 9.5, 4–6). They were manufactured for more than a century in different north Tunisian production centres, probably from the late (or very end of the) fourth century (Hayes 91A), but certainly from the early fifth century until the late fifth or early sixth century.[36] A reliable chronological distinction between different versions of the broad flange and the various different profiles of the hanging lip of forms Hayes 91B seems to be difficult, if not impossible, to establish; Bonifay has suggested a rather late date for the smaller specimens of form Hayes 91B (his Bonifay form 51),[37] similar to Fig. 9.5, 6. Large variants of flanged bowls Hayes 91 (variant) no. 28

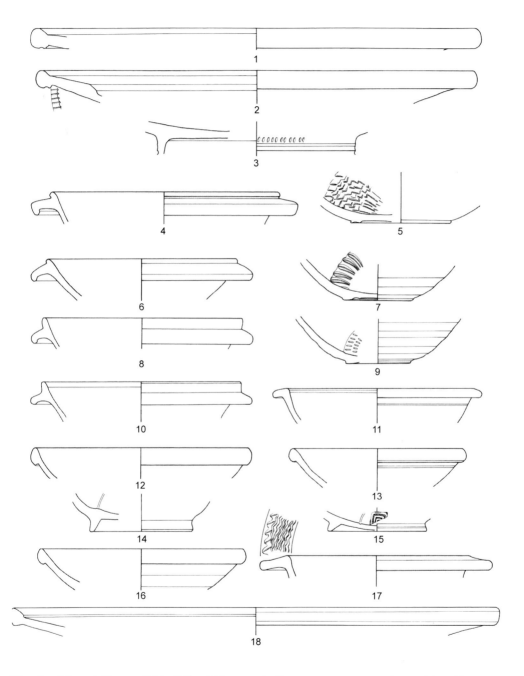

Fig. 9.5 Nag el-Hagar (2005/06), African red slip ware. 1–3 central Tunisia (C^5), 4–18 northern Tunisia (D^1 and D^2). Scale 1:3

(= el-Mahrine form 53/54) in D^1 fabric[38] were not found at Nag el-Hagar.

A small central Tunisian bowl Hayes 74 (Fig. 9.4, 2) in C^4 fabric can probably be dated to the second third and certainly the second half of the fifth century.[39] Further typical forms of the late fifth century are the large plates of Hayes 82A in C^5 fabric (2 rims), with bands of feather-rouletting on the outside (Fig. 9.4, 9–10), which are normally dated $c.$ AD 430/475.[40] Because of a rare figured stamp-type of a Silenus with grape (style D) on a plate of Hayes 82A, which was recently recognized on a dish from Ballana, tomb 3 (*Nubia*), in the Egyptian Museum at Cairo,[41] the dating of this form should be revised: a production at the central Tunisian centre of Sidi Marzouk Tounsi down to $c.$ AD 520/530 now seems probable.[42] The dishes of Hayes form 84, also in C^5 fabric with the same decoration of bands of fine feather-rouletting (Fig. 9.4, 11–15), which has been dated $c.$ AD 440–500,[43] are numerous at Nag el-Hagar – 25 rims and 20 base fragments, one of them with stamped decoration in style D (Fig. 9.4, 12). For this form a dating until $c.$ AD 520/530 or even until the mid-sixth century has been suggested.[44] It has to be mentioned that small bowls of Hayes form 85 with feather-rouletting, corresponding to forms Hayes 82 and 84, were not found during the pottery survey. Also of central Tunisian provenance are four rim- and two foot-fragments of the very large C^5 plates of form Hayes 89/90, with heavy knobbed rim (Fig. 9.5, 1) and high pedestal foot (both with and without feather-rouletting) (Fig. 9.5, 3), as well as two rims of form Hayes 90A with a type-specific low ledge (Fig. 9.5, 2), which can be dated to the (mid-) fifth and to at least the early part, and probably the whole of, the first half of the sixth century.[45]

A series of north Tunisian dishes of Hayes form 93B (1 rim) and bowls of form Hayes 94B (Fig. 9.5, 11) (6 rims), as well as the rare form Hayes 96 with feather-rouletting on the horizontal rim (Fig. 9.5, 17) (3 rims), can all be dated to the late fifth and the first half of the sixth century.[46] The dominant bowl-form of this period, however, is form Hayes 99A (Fig. 9.5, 12,14) and 99B (Fig. 9.5, 15–16) (17 rims and 9 floor fragments), both types[47] being represented in D^1 and D^2 fabric with similar numbers (Table 1); only one rim fragment (D^2) was classified as Hayes 99C (Fig. 9.5, 13), dated $c.$ AD 560/580–620.[48] Whereas the D^1 fabric can be attributed to the production centre at el-Mahrine, the thick lustrous slip of the D^2 vessel-forms Hayes 96 and 99A–C is typical of the production of the Oudhna potteries. To this period belong also three rims of flanged bowls Hayes 91C with plain rim (Fig. 9.5, 8), dated to $c.$ AD 530–580,[49] two rims of flanged bowls of Hayes form 91D with a short rudimentary flange (Fig. 9.5, 10), dated $c.$ AD 600/650,[50] and two floor-fragments of Hayes 91C (Fig. 9.5, 7) and 91D (Fig. 9.5, 9), with bands of rouletting. A sherd of a large dish was classified as form Hayes 104B (variant), no. 22, with sloping floor and heavy knobbed rim (Fig. 9.5, 18), a form which was recognized by Hayes as the final stage of the series of his form 104A and B;[51] its variant marks the late development of Hayes 104B and the typological transition to form Hayes 105, and may be dated to the very end of the sixth and to the first half of the seventh century.[52] All of these late ARS fragments are in D^2 fabric.

Form (Hayes 1972)	Fabric (Atlante 1981)	Rim	Base/foot	Wall	Sum (Σ)
50 A	C³	1			1
50 B	C³/⁴	1			1
52 (A?)	C³		1		1
58 B	D²	1			1
59	D¹	2			2
	D²	3			3
59 B	D²	1			1
60	D²	1			1
61 B	D²	1			1
62 (?)	D²	1			1
67	D¹	1			1
	D²	1			1
59, 61 or 67	D¹			2	2
	D²			2	2
73 (?)	D¹		1		1
74	C⁴	1			1
82 A	C⁵	2	1	3	6
84	C⁵	25	20	4	49
82 or 84	C⁵		1		1
89/90	C⁵	4	2		6
90 A	C⁵	2			2
91 A/B	D¹	5	1	1	7
	D²	15	1		16
91 C	D²	3	1		4
91 D	D²	2	1		3
91	D²	1		1	2
93 B	D¹	1			1
93 B/94 B	D¹	1			1
94 B	D²	6			6
96	D²	3			3
99 A	D¹	5	2		7
	D²	7	2		9
99 A/B	D¹	1	3		4
	D²	4	2		6
99 C	D²	1			1
99 B/C	D¹	1	1		2
	D²	2	2		4
104 B (Var.) no. 22	D²	1			1
Sum (Σ)		107	42	13	162

Table 1 Nag el-Hagar (2005/06), quantities of African red slip forms and fabrics (C³–C⁵, D¹ and D²)

Chronological conclusions

The extraordinarily great number of 162 classified late Roman/early Byzantine ARS sherds from the surface collection and the demolition debris of trenches 1 and 3 at Nag el-Hagar results in a clear chronological distribution:

Period 1 (military garrison: early or first third of the fourth century AD to the first half or middle of the fifth century) is represented by three ARS fragments of central Tunisian production (Hayes 50A, 50B and 52[A?]) in C³ and C³/⁴ fabric and about twenty ARS fragments of the north Tunisian production centres (Hayes 58B, 59, 59B, 60, 61B, 67, probably 62 and 73, as well as a few flanged bowls Hayes 91A) in D¹ and D² fabric. Some of these forms might be connected with a supply to the military unit already garrisoned here in the Tetrachic/Constantinian period.

Period 2 (civilian settlement, probably second half of the fifth century to the first half of the seventh century) is represented by 65 ARS fragments of central Tunisian production (Hayes 74, 82A, 84, 89/90 and 90) in C⁵ fabric and about 75 ARS fragments of the north Tunisian production centres (Hayes 91B–D, 93B, 94B, 96, 99A–C and 104B [variant] no. 22) in D¹ and D² fabric. Most of these forms can be attributed to the second half of the fifth and the first half of the sixth century.

If we consider the imported pottery from *Africa Proconsularis* and *Byzacena* on its own, the available evidence suggests a rather prosperous period (with a time-span of at least some decades, and probably half a century or more) when there was an unbroken supply to the Thebaid (Upper Egypt) of ARS ware, even if only a limited range of forms was supplied. But these ARS forms were obviously much in demand, as most of them were copied in local fine-ware (ERS A) by the Upper Egyptian potteries at Elephantine and Nag el-Hagar.[53] After the middle of the sixth century, the hitherto dominant form Hayes 84 (Fig. 9.4, 11–15)[54] was no longer produced, because of the decline, or even the end, of ARS production at the most important and prolific central Tunisian fine-ware pottery, that of Sidi Marzouk Tounsi; its demise may have been caused by raiding by local nomadic tribes.[55] Judging from the quantities of the ARS forms at Nag el-Hagar later than the mid-sixth century, one notes a sharp decline in supply: just a few bowl-forms such as Hayes 91C, 91D and 99C, as well as a large dish of Hayes 104B (variant) no. 22 (Fig. 9.5, 7–10, 13 and 18), can be dated to the second half or the late sixth century, and/or to the first third or even the first half of the seventh century[56] – but most probably no later than the invasion of Egypt by the Arabs in 639/641.

For the time being a comparison with other sites – either of military or civilian character – in particular in the Upper Egyptian frontier region of the Thebaid[57] seems to be premature, because of the small numbers of ARS vessels which have been published. With regard to Elephantine with its modest but similar range of ARS forms (Hayes 52B, 67, 72B, 84, 91B and C, 93B, 99B and C), two cross-monogram stamps of style D on Hayes form 84, one small figural stamp of the north Tunisian style E(I), and two stamps of the north Tunisian style E(II), with large jewelled, central crosses and subsidiary motifs on two floor fragments (they probably belong to form Hayes 103 or 104A/B),[58] we have to await further stratified evidence from recent excavations on the Nile island in the areas adjoining the famous Chnum temple.[59] In or near the Roman urban centre of Syene (Aswan), the late Roman fortification of the *milites Miliarenses*, mentioned in *Notitia Dignitatum* (Or. 31.35), has not yet been located underneath the modern town.[60] Furthermore, no imported fine ware – or any late Roman pottery at all, for that matter – is known from the supposed late Roman fortress of *legio prima Maximiana* at Filas (Philae),[61] also mentioned in *Notitia Dignitatum* (Or. 31.37).

The surface collection of the fort-site at Nag el-Hagar, carried out in 2005/06, has yielded an outstanding quantity and range of late Roman ARS forms (Table 1 and Figs 9.4–5),[62] which for the first time allows an insight into the distribution and supply of a military and civilian settlement site of the early fourth to the mid-seventh century in the Upper Egyptian frontier region, with imported red-slipped fine wares from various production centres in central and northern Tunisia.

Acknowledgements

I am indebted to M. el-Bialy and C. von Pilgrim for their continuous and efficient support of the first two campaigns of the Egyptian-Swiss Joint Mission at Nag el-Hagar; to the Gesellschaft von Freunden und Förderern der Universität München and to the Gerda Henkel Stiftung (Düsseldorf) for generously funding the project; to F. Schimmer and C. Soraya for drawings of the pottery, and to S. Peisker for preparing the illustrations. I am also grateful to the Editor of this volume for kindly polishing the final version of my English text and for removing stylistic infelicities.

Notes

1. Carandini 1968, 28–37; Atlante 1981, 58–60. The fabrics were already differentiated and described by Hayes 1972, 289–92.
2. Cf. Mackensen 1993, 441–57; 1998a; 1998b; 2004. For the attribution of some fabrics not only to regions such as northern or central Tunisia, but to specific important pottery-production centres, cf. Mackensen and Schneider 2002; Bonifay 2004, 45–58.
3. Hayes 1972, 420, 442–3, 455, map 6, 462, map 24; cf. also Rodziewicz 1976, 26–30 pl. 1.
4. Hayes 1972, 463, map 25.
5. Cf. Bonifay 2004, 454–6 with fig. 256 (= here Fig. 9.1).
6. Cf. Schwartz 1969, Plan 1, H.
7. Cf. Hayes 1972, 455–6, maps 6–7; Bonifay 2004, 454, fig. 356. An exception seems to be an appliqué-decorated rim-sherd of Hayes 52B at Elephantine: Gempeler 1992, pl. 1.5.
8. El-Maqsoud *et al.* 1997; Valbelle and Carrez-Maratray 2000; Schwartz 1969; Sidebotham 1994 and R. Tomber (pers. comm.) for the absence of ARS ware at Abu Sha'ar; El-Saghir *et al.* 1986; Wareth and Zignani 1992, 207. Cf. Mackensen 2003a for a Tetrarchic building programme of forts in Egypt.
9. Hayes 1972, 420–1, 442–3, 456–7, with maps 8–10.
10. Cf. note 5; for the distribution of stamp-decorated ARS ware in D^1 fabric from the production centre of el-Mahrine and the different decoration (el-Mahrine I.2 and I.3, II, III.1 and III.2 as well as IV.3) in Egypt, cf. Mackensen 1993, 651–9, esp. 656–7, fig. 128, 659, fig. 129; see also below, note 44.
11. Cf. von Pilgrim, Bruhn and Kelany 2004.
12. Speidel 1988, 773–5, fig. 2.
13. Cf. Speidel 1988, 775; Bowman 1978, 30.
14. Cf. Speidel 1988, 775.
15. Mysliwiec 1987, 98–179; Burkard, Mackensen and Polz 2003, 56–60, with figs 4–6 (no ARS ware); Pierrat 1996; Gempeler 1992.
16. Mysliwiec 1987, 98, cat. no. 988, 1042, 1171, 1180, 1192 with figs, pl. 20.988.1042; Pierrat 1996, 199, 204 pl. 6.85–87; 8.121; Gempeler 1992, 41–2, 60, fig. 2.1.5–12, pl. 1.5; 2.1–5.
17. Johnson 1981; on ARS ware, ibid. 46–50, nos 213–254, pl. 33–40.
18. Gempeler 1992; on ARS ware, ibid. 41–2, 60, fig. 2.1.5–12, pl. 1.5; 2.1–5.
19. Bailey 1998; on ARS ware, ibid. 1–7, nos A1–196, pl. 2–5; cf. Bailey 1996, 54–5.
20. Ballet 1991, 140–3; cf. Bailey 1998, 8–9.
21. Mustafa and Jaritz 1985; Wareth and Zignani 1992.
22. El-Bialy and Mackensen, in press; Mackensen, in press.
23. Wareth and Zignani 1992, 207–10; Mackensen, in press.
24. Wareth and Zignani 1992, 205–7.
25. Wareth and Zignani 1992, 208–10.
26. El-Bialy and Mackensen, in press.
27. H.-C. Noeske, in Mackensen, in press.
28. No ARS sherds could be identified in pottery assemblages, probably deriving from the 1984–89 excavations, in the storerooms of the SCA at Kom Ombo.
29. Cf. Mackensen and Schneider 2002, 125–34; Mackensen and Schneider, in press.
30. Hayes 1972, 72–3, 78.
31. Hayes 1972, 95–6 (*c.* AD 290/300–375); cf. Mackensen 1993, 398 (*c.* AD 300/310–340/350).

32. Hayes 1972, 100–01 (59B: *c.* AD 320–420); cf. Mackensen 1993, 400–01 (*c.* AD 320/330–380/400).
33. For a detailed discussion of these forms, cf. Hayes 1972, 106–7, 115–16, 123–4; Hayes 1980, 515–16; Mackensen 1993, 401–07; Bonifay 2004, 167–73.
34. Hayes 1972, 73.
35. Also the above-mentioned Tetrarchic coins from the residential area are unstratified (cf. note 27) and cannot be linked with certainty to building activities around AD 300, as long as the earlier mudbrick buildings underneath the palace cannot be dated by archaeological material; cf. Wareth and Zignani 1992, 196.
36. Hayes 1972, 140–145 (91B, *c.* AD 450–530); Hayes 1980, 516; Mackensen 1993, 430–2.
37. Bonifay 2004, 179 (Hayes 91B, late variant).
38. Cf. Mackensen 1993, 432.
39. Hayes 1972, 124; Bonifay 2004, 165.
40. Hayes 1972, 131; cf. Bonifay 2004, 165.
41. Hayes 1972, 129 (form 82A, no. 3); for the stamp-type, cf. Mackensen 2003b, 107, fig. 2.3, pl. 7.
42. Mackensen, in press.
43. Hayes 1972, 132–3; Bonifay 2004, 165. Cf. Hayes 1980, 517 and Bailey 1998, 2 for the large-scale export of forms 82–85 to the East.
44. Mackensen and Schneider 2002, 132–4; Mackensen 2003b, 106–08. Cf. Bailey 1998, 2 for the availability of form Hayes 84 at el-Ashmunein from *c.* AD 450/460 onwards; Bailey 1998, 2, 6, no. A169, pl. 4, is not a central Tunisian stamp-type on a base-fragment of a C^5 dish Hayes 84, but a north Tunisian stamp-type el-Mahrine 217–219 of stamped decoration el-Mahrine II (= A[III]/E[I]), probably on a D^1 dish el-Mahrine 18; cf. Mackensen 1993, 254–69, 576 (type 217–219) pl. 19.1–6.
45. Hayes 1972, 139–40; Bonifay 2004, 166; Mackensen, in press.
46. Hayes 1972, 147–8, 150; Hayes 1980, 516; Mackensen 1993, 414–15.
47. Hayes 1972, 155 (99A, *c.* AD 510–540; 99B, *c.* AD 530–580); Mackensen 1993, 415–17 (99A, *c.* AD 480 – mid-sixth century; 99B/C: 2nd quarter of the sixth century – *c.* AD 580); Bonifay 2004, 181 (99A, *c.* late fifth/mid-sixth century; 99B: second quarter of the sixth century/early 7th century).
48. Hayes 1972, 155; Bonifay 2004, 181 (late sixth/seventh centuries).
49. Hayes 1972, 144 (*c.* AD 530–600+); Mackensen 1993, 431–2 (*c.* AD 520/530–580); Bonifay 2004, 179.
50. Hayes 1972, 144; Bonifay 2004, 179 (seventh century).
51. Hayes 1972, 165, fig. 31.
52. Hayes 1972, 166 (104B: *c.* AD 570–600, with late variants to 625+); Mackensen 1993, 429; Bonifay 2004, 181–83. For form 105, cf. Hayes 1972, 166–9 (*c.* AD 580/600–660+).
53. Hayes 1972, 421; recently Bonifay 2005, 577–8; B. Seeberger and M. Sieler, in Mackensen, in press; for the ERS A production at Nag el-Hagar, a study by M. Sieler is in preparation.
54. For the predominance of forms Hayes 82–84 in Egypt, cf. Hayes 1972, 421; Bonifay 2005, 568–9.
55. Mackensen 1998a, 370 with note 77; Mackensen 2003b, 108; Mackensen and Schneider 2005, 376–7.
56. Cf. Bailey 1998, 2, with rare ARS vessel-forms of the late sixth/early seventh century at el-Ashmunein.
57. Cf. Speidel 1988, 770–83; Grossmann 1980, 26–9.
58. Cf. note 18; the bowls classified by R. D. Gempeler as Hayes 68 (Gempeler 1992, 42,

fig. 2.2.3) show very unusual profiles, similar to ERS A forms, and were not considered as ARS ware. For the destroyed stratigraphy of the late Roman buildings in the courtyard of the Chnum temple, which were interpreted as being for the military garrison of the second quarter of the fifth century, and the lack of datable pottery deposits, cf. Grossmann 1980, 7; 9–10; 21–6.

59. For the recent excavations of late Roman/Coptic houses south and west of the Chnum temple at Elephantine, cf. Arnold 2003.

60. Neither the early- and mid-Roman fort for three auxiliary cohorts, nor the late Roman fort is known; cf. Speidel 1988, 770–5. Research on the late Roman pottery from different excavations at Aswan, conducted by the Swiss Institute Cairo (cf. note 11), is ongoing, directed by S. Martin-Kilcher (Bern).

61. Cf. Grossmann 1980, 11, fig. 1, and 27 with note 156.

62. Cf. the total amount of 196 separate ARS-ware vessels at el-Ashmunein: Bailey 1998, 2–7, pl. 2–5.

References

Arnold, F. 2003: *Elephantine XXX. Die Nachnutzung des Chnumtempelbezirks. Wohnbebauung der Spätantike und des Frühmittelalters* [Archäologische Veröffentlichungen des Deutschen Archäologischen Instituts Kairo 116], Mainz-am-Rhein

Atlante 1981: A. Carandini *et al.*, *Atlante delle forme ceramiche, I. Ceramica fine romana nel bacino mediterraneo (medio e tardo impero)* [Enciclopedia dell'Arte Antica, Classica ed Orientale], Roma

Bailey, D. M. 1996: 'The pottery from the South Church at El-Ashmunein', *Cahiers de la Céramique Égyptienne* 4, 47–86

Bailey, D. M. 1998: *Excavations at El-Ashmunein, V. Pottery, lamps and glass of the Late Roman and Early Arab periods*, London

Ballet, P. *et al.* 1991: 'Artisanat de la céramique dans l'Égypte romaine tardive et byzantine. Prospections d'ateliers de potiers de Minia à Assouan', *Cahiers de la Céramique Égyptienne* 2, 129–43

Bonifay, M. 2004: *Etudes sur la céramique romaine tardive d'Afrique* [BAR International Series 1301], Oxford

Bonifay, M. 2005: 'Observations sur la diffusion des céramiques africaines en Méditerranée orientale durant l'antiquité tardive', in *Mélanges J.-P. Sodini* [Travaux et Mémoires 15], Paris, 565–81

Bowman, A. K. 1978: 'The military occupation of Upper Egypt in the reign of Diocletian', *Bulletin of the American Society of Papyrologists* 15, 25–38

Burkard, G., Mackensen, M. and Polz, D. 2003: 'Die spätantike/koptische Klosteranlage Deir el-Bachit in Dra Abu el-Naga (Oberägypten)', *Mitteilungen des Deutschen Archäologischen Instituts Kairo* 59, 41–65

Carandini, A. (ed.) 1968: *Ostia I. Le Terme del Nuotatore* [Studi Miscellanei 13], Rome

De Vos, M. (ed.) 2004: *Archeologia del territorio. Metodi, meteriali, prospettive, Medjerda e Adige: territori a confronto* [Labirinti 73], Trento

El-Bialy, M. and Mackensen, M., in press: 'Second report of the Egyptian-Swiss Joint Mission at the late Roman Fort at Nag el-Hagar', *Annales du Service des Antiquités de l'Égypte*, forthcoming

El-Maqsoud, M. A. *et al.* 1997: 'The Roman castrum of Tell Abu Sayfi at Qantara', *Mitteilungen des Deutschen Archäologischen Instituts Kairo* 53, 221–6

El-Saghir, M. *et al*. 1986: *Le camp romain de Louqsor* [*Mémoires de l'Institut Français d'Archéologie Orientale* 83], Cairo

Gempeler, R. D. 1992: *Elephantine X. Die Keramik, römischer bis früharabischer Zeit* [Archäologische Veröffentlichungen des Deutschen Archäologischen Instituts Kairo 43], Mainz-am-Rhein

Grossmann, P. 1980: *Elephantine II. Kirche und spätantike Hausanlagen im Chnumtempelhof* [Archäologische Veröffentlichungen des Deutschen Archäologischen Instituts Kairo 25], Mainz-am-Rhein

Hayes, J. W. 1972: *Late Roman Pottery*, London

Hayes, J. W. 1980: *A Supplement to Late Roman Pottery*, London

Johnson, B. 1981: *Pottery from Karanis. Excavations of the University of Michigan* [Kelsey Museum of Archaeology Studies 7], Ann Arbor

Mackensen, M. 1993: *Die spätantiken Sigillata- und Lampentöpfereien von El Mahrine (Nordtunesien). Studien zur nordafrikanischen Feinkeramik des 4. bis 7. Jahrhunderts* [Münchner Beiträge zur Vor- und Frühgeschichte 50], Munich

Mackensen, M. 1998a: 'New evidence for Central Tunisian red slip ware with stamped decoration (ARS style D)', *JRA* 11, 355–70

Mackensen, M. 1998b: 'Centres of African red slip ware production in Tunisia from the late 5th to the 7th century', in Saguì 1998, 23–39

Mackensen, M. 2003a: 'Das diokletianische Kastell *Magdolum*/Tell el-Herr am Ostrand des Nildeltas und andere spätrömische Kastelle in Ägypten', *JRA* 16, 725–33

Mackensen, M. 2003b: 'Datierung und Provenienz einer spätantiken figürlichen Punze für nordafrikanische Sigillata. Zur Spätphase der Feinkeramikproduktion in Sidi Marzouk Tounsi (Zentraltunesien), *Bayerische Vorgeschichtsblätter* 68, 101–08

Mackensen, M. 2004: 'Produzione e diffusione della ceramica sigillata africana nella Tunisia centrale e settentrionale dalla metà del III secolo alla metà del V secolo d.C.', in De Vos 2004, 131–60

Mackensen, M., in press: 'The Late Roman fort at Nag el-Hagar near Kom Ombo in the province of Thebaïs. Report on the first season of the Egyptian-Swiss Joint Mission', *Mitteilungen des Deutschen Archäologischen Instituts Kairo* 62, forthcoming

Mackensen, M., and Schneider, G. 2002: 'Production centres of African red slip ware (3rd–7th c.) in northern and central Tunisia: archaeological provenance and reference groups based on chemical analysis', *JRA* 15, 121–58

Mackensen, M. and Schneider, G. 2005: 'Chemical analyses of red-slipped roof-tiles from Bir Ftouha', in Stevens 2005, 371–8

Mackensen, M., and Schneider, G., in press: 'Production centres of African red slip ware (2nd–3rd c.) in northern and central Tunisia: archaeological provenance and reference groups based on chemical analysis', *JRA* 19, forthcoming

Mustafa, M. ed-D. and Jaritz, H. 1985: 'A Roman fortress at Nag el-Hagar. First preliminary report', *Annales du Service des Antiquités de l'Égypte* 70, 21–31

Mysliwiec, K. 1987: *Keramik und Kleinfunde aus der Grabung im Tempel Sethos' I. in Gurna* [Archäologische Veröffentlichungen des Deutschen Archäologischen Instituts Kairo 57], Mainz-am-Rhein

Peacock, D. P. S., Bejaoui, F. and Ben Lazreg, N. 1990: 'Roman pottery production in central Tunisia', *JRA* 3, 59–84

Pierrat, G. 1996: 'Évolution de la céramique de Tôd de IIe au VIIe siècle apr. J.-C.', *Cahiers de la Céramique Égyptienne* 4, 189–214

Rodziewicz, M. 1976: *Alexandrie I. La céramique romaine tardive d'Alexandrie*, Warsaw

Saguì, L. (ed.) 1998: *Ceramica in Italia: VI–VII secolo. Atti del Convegno in onore di John W.*

Hayes, *Roma 1995* [Biblioteca di Archeologia Medievale 14], Florence

Schwartz, J. 1969: *Qasr Qarun/Dionysias 1950. Fouilles franco-suisses. Rapports II* [Publications de l'Institut Français de l'Archéologie Orientale], Cairo

Sidebotham, S. E. 1994: 'University of Delaware fieldwork in the Eastern Desert of Egypt, 1993', *Dumbarton Oaks Papers* 48, 263–75

Speidel, M. P. 1988: 'Nubia's Roman garrison', *Aufstieg und Niedergang der römischen Welt* II 10.1, Berlin and New York, 767–98

Stevens, S. T., Kalinowski, A. V. and vanderLeest, H. 2005: *Bir Ftouha: a pilgrimage church complex at Carthage* [*JRA* Supplementary Series 59], Portsmouth, Rhode Island

Valbelle, D. and Carrez-Maratray, J.-Y. 2000, *Le camp romain du Bas Empire à Tell el-Herr. Mission Franco-Égyptienne de Tell el-Herr (Nord-Sinaï)*, Paris

Von Pilgrim, C., Bruhn, K.-C. and Kelany, A. 2004: 'The town of Syene. Preliminary report on the 1st and 2nd season in Aswan', *Mitteilungen des Deutschen Archäologischen Instituts Kairo* 60, 119–48

Wareth, U. A. and Zignani, P. 1992: 'Nag al-Hagar, a fortress with a palace of the late Roman Empire. Second preliminary report', *Bulletin de l'Institut Français d'Archéologie Orientale* 92, 185–210

INDEX

The notes are not indexed except where they contain substantial new material for which no obvious signpost exists in the text. Places are indexed by their modern, not their ancient names (although for towns the Latin names are included in parentheses), except for some, especially in Egypt, which are more familiarly known by their ancient names. Persons are indexed if they lived at any period down to, and including, the eighteenth century, but not more recently. The publication numbers of inscriptions are not indexed, nor are specific references to ancient sources, although the information that both types of material contain may be; the names of classical authors are included only if they are mentioned in the body of the text. Pottery vessel-forms by number are not indexed, but the different types of pottery (samian, African red slip ware, etc.) are. References to Roman emperors are indexed, but not the time-periods (Claudian, Flavian, Hadrianic, etc.) named after them. References to illustrations are indexed in italics at the end of the relevant entry.